The Egyptian Labor Market: A Focus on Gender and Economic Vulnerability

The Egyptian Labor Market

A Focus on Gender and Economic Vulnerability

Edited by

CAROLINE KRAFFT AND RAGUI ASSAAD

UNIVERSITY PRESS

OXFORD

UNIVERSITY PRESS

Great Clarendon Street, Oxford, OX2 6DP,
United Kingdom

Oxford University Press is a department of the University of Oxford.
It furthers the University's objective of excellence in research, scholarship,
and education by publishing worldwide. Oxford is a registered trade mark of
Oxford University Press in the UK and in certain other countries

Published in the United States of America by Oxford University Press
198 Madison Avenue, New York, NY 10016, United States of America

British Library Cataloguing in Publication Data
Data available

Library of Congress Control Number: 2021952028

ISBN 978-0-19-284791-1

DOI: 10.1093/oso/9780192847911.001.0001

Printed and bound by
CPI Group (UK) Ltd, Croydon, CR0 4YY

Acknowledgments

The success of an endeavor at the scale of the Egypt Labor Market Panel Survey (ELMPS), which underlies this volume, is predicated on the efforts and collaboration of thousands of individuals. Central to this work are the respondents themselves, some of whom have patiently responded to our numerous questions for over 20 years. We are grateful to them as well as to the hundreds of enumerators who had to endure challenging working conditions and long days to complete thousands of multi-hour interviews with a great deal of patience and care. The Economic Research Forum (ERF) would like to express its deep gratitude to its long-standing partner in the implementation of the ELMPS, the Central Agency for Public Mobilization and Statistics (CAPMAS), the main statistical arm of the Egyptian government. In particular, we extend our sincere thanks to General Abou Bakr El-Guindy, former President of CAPMAS, General Khairat Barakat, the current President, and Abdel-Hameed Sharafeldin, director of the Social and Population Statistics Sector at the time of the 2018 wave of the ELMPS, whose leadership and support at all stages of the work not only made this survey possible, but also a distinct success. Other CAPMAS officials whose contributions were critical to the success of the survey include Taher Saleh, Tarek Saadallah, Abdel Wahab Mohamed Ali, Khaled Maher, Hoda Fangary, Ahmed Gamal Ramadan, Ali Hebeish Kamel, Fatma Elashry, Mostafa Younes Youssef, Ahmed Maher Amin, Ahmed Wael Mahmoud, Sabri Morgan, Amr Atef Abdel Salam, Hassan Hammam, Mohamed Alaaeldin Abdelrahman, Iman Elhusseini, Rawya Waguih Abdelmeguid, Abdelsalam Dessouki Abdelsalam, Ali Hassan Mohamed, Magdi Saad, Sara Sayed Mohammed, and Mahmoud Elssadany. Numerous other CAPMAS staff ranging from field supervisors to data coders and logistics managers, too numerous to mention here by name, worked diligently to make this endeavor a success. We are deeply grateful to them all.

ERF would also like to thank Caroline Krafft and her team at St. Catherine University, including Caitlyn Keo, Kapono Asuncion, Taylor Flak, Madeline Harter, Lyndsay Kast, and Catherine McConnell, for their excellent work in programming the questionnaire on ODK-X to enable the use of tablets in data collection. Their work contributed greatly to the very high data quality achieved in the 2018 wave of the ELMPS.

ERF appreciates the support of the World Bank, the International Labour Organization, Agence Française de Développement, UN Women, and the Arab Fund for Economic and Social Development for the Egypt Labor Market Panel Survey 2018. Conference discussants, moderators, and participants vastly enriched this work with their expertise, including H.E. Hala El-Said, H.E. General Khairat Barakat, H.E. Nevine Kabbage, Magued Osman, Tarek Tawfik, Maria Laura Sanchez Puerta, Hana Yoshimoto, Nada Massoud, Heba Nassar, Gielan Elmessiri, Hala Hattab, Hania Sholkamy, Kobrom Abay, Luca Fedi, Hussein Abdel Aziz, Ibrahim Awad, Laurent de Boeck, Magdy Khaled, Ahmed Kamali, Amirah El-Haddad, Alia El Mahdi, Eric Oechslin, Anda David, Abdelhamid Sharafeddine, Laila El-Khawaga, Sevane Ananian, Sherine Al Shawarby, Leonardo Menchini, Maha Rabat, Ayman Zohry, and Samer Atallah.

ERF would also like to acknowledge the members of its own staff who have worked tirelessly on all aspects of the survey and the subsequent dissemination activities, including helping to raise the necessary funds, communicate with and report to multiple donors, provide technical and IT support, manage all aspects of administration and finance for such a complex undertaking, organize research workshops and dissemination conferences, help produce working papers, policy briefs, and blogs, and guide the process that led to the publication of this volume, to name just a few of their roles. We specifically want to acknowledge Ibrahim Elbadawi, Managing Director, Sherine Ghoneim, Director of Communications and Policy Outreach, Yasmine Fahim, Director of Research and Programs, Mohamed Yousri, Director of Administration and Finance, Eman Elhadary, Senior Programs Officer, Christiane Wissa, former Statistics Manager, Aalaa Naguib and Sara Taraman, former Program Officers, Sherif Ossama, Finance Manager, Mohamed Aladdine, Senior Accountant, Anais Hagopian, Administration Manager, Hoda Azmi, Conference Manager, and Marwa Afifi, Executive Assistant to the Managing Director.

The findings, interpretations, and conclusions expressed in this publication are entirely those of the authors and should not be attributed to the Economic Research Forum, its Board of Trustees, or its donors.

Contents

Foreword

With the major upheavals experienced by Egypt's society and economy in the aftermath of the January 25, 2011 revolution, it has become increasingly important to monitor developments in the lives of ordinary people. It is particularly important to ascertain their vulnerability to shocks and the extent to which policies, programs, and institutions provide the necessary protection and security. This volume aims to do just that. With an underlying emphasis on vulnerability and a lens that is sensitive to gender differences and inequities, the contributors to this volume illuminate different aspects of Egyptians' lives, including labor supply behavior, the ability to access good quality and well-paying jobs, food security, vulnerability to shocks and coping mechanisms, health status, and access to health care services.

This is the fourth volume on the Egyptian labor market produced by Economic Research Forum (ERF) researchers over the past twenty years and the second volume on Egypt published by Oxford University Press. It is part of a broader series on Arab labor markets, which also includes two volumes on Jordan and one on Tunisia. This volume draws on the 2018 wave of the Egypt Labor Market Panel Survey (ELMPS). This is the fourth wave of the ELMPS, which builds on preceding waves carried out by ERF in collaboration with the Egyptian Central Agency for Public Mobilization and Statistics in 1998, 2006, and 2012. The ELMPS is designed to track individuals and households across the various waves. The surveys collect rich longitudinal data on essential aspects of their lives, such as their socioeconomic status, employment and livelihoods, educational trajectories, residential mobility and migration experiences, family formation and demographic behavior, gender norm attitudes and women's empowerment measures, and much more. Each wave of the survey adds a refresher sample to maintain the representativeness of the overall sample, as well as to allow a renewed focus on important phenomena. For example, in 2018, the refresher sample, while continuing to be nationally representative, oversampled households in Egypt's 1,000 poorest villages to allow for a more in-depth analysis of this vulnerable population. The four waves of the ELMPS are part of a growing series of similar surveys carried out by ERF in collaboration with national statistical offices, which include two waves in Jordan in 2010 and 2016 and one wave in Tunisia in 2014. The harmonized and integrated microdata from these surveys is made publicly available to researchers through ERF's Open Access Microdata Initiative (www.erfdataportal.com). Over the years, these datasets have proven to be the backbone of research on labor markets and human development issues in the three countries represented so far.

By supporting the continued implementation of these rich panel surveys and expanding their country coverage, ERF demonstrates its commitment to strengthening the research infrastructure in this essential area of study, which allows us to ascertain the effects of broad economic, political, and social developments, and the associated policy and program responses, on the lives and livelihoods of ordinary people. I would like to express my sincere gratitude to the volume editors, Caroline Krafft and Ragui Assaad, for their unflagging efforts and leadership throughout all the steps of this process, from survey design and implementation to data analysis and drafting and review of manuscripts. The authors, reviewers, and technical editors also deserve our thanks and appreciation for their excellent work throughout the production of this volume. ERF also owes a great deal of gratitude to its partners at the Central Agency for Public Mobilization and Statistics, who have contributed to the success of this endeavor in every possible way. Finally, I would like to thank ERF's donors, the Arab Fund for Economic and Social Development, the World Bank, Agence Française de Développement, UN Women, and the International Labour Organization, who made this work possible through their financial contributions and technical advice.

Ibrahim Elbadawi
Managing Director
Economic Research Forum

List of Figures

List of Tables

List of Contributors

Abdelaziz Alsharawy, Virginia Tech and Princeton University

Mona Amer, Independent Consultant

Ragui Assaad, University of Minnesota and the Economic Research Forum

Marian Atallah, Paris School of Economics and University of Paris 1 Panthéon-Sorbonne

Ghada Barsoum, American University in Cairo

Anda David, Agence Française de Développement

Maye Ehab, Bamberg Graduate School of Social Sciences

Nelly Elmallakh, Paris School of Economics, Institut Convergences Migrations, and World Bank

Luca Fedi, International Labour Organization

Rami Galal, World Bank

Dina Abdalla, Department of Economic Development, Government of Dubai

Rasha Hassan, Population Council

Imane Helmy, Independent Consultant

Caitlyn Keo, University of Minnesota

Caroline Krafft, St. Catherine University

Reham Rizk, Universities of Canada

Ali Rashed, Islamic Development Bank

Rania Roushdy, American University in Cairo

Mona Said, American University in Cairo

Colette Salemi, University of Minnesota

Mina Sami, American University in Cairo

Irene Selwaness, Cairo University

Maia Sieverding, American University of Beirut

Jackline Wahba, University of Southampton

Introduction

The Egyptian economy had begun to recover from the challenges that followed the January 25, 2011 revolution when tough but necessary economic reform measures were adopted in 2016 and 2017. In the midst of Egypt's recovery, it was hit by the global COVID-19 pandemic and the widespread disruptions it caused. While Egypt is no stranger to external shocks, the magnitude of these shocks was particularly pronounced. The economic turbulence they caused undoubtedly had major effects on labor market outcomes and on household livelihoods and well-being more generally.

Nevertheless, it is important to note that the weak labor market outcomes and the disappointing trajectory of these outcomes that we document in this book are also partly caused by long-run structural and institutional distortions. These distortions have prevented the necessary transformation from low-productivity, mostly informal employment to higher productivity and more formal employment. Previous economic reforms have managed to reduce the outsize role of the public sector in the economy, and to place the economy onto a more market-oriented trajectory, but they have failed to institute the right incentives and institutional framework for robust, job-creating private sector growth. As we will demonstrate in this volume, the result of this recent economic trajectory has been anemic job creation that has failed to keep up with population growth, and a quality of jobs that has tended toward informality, precariousness, low productivity, and, thus, low remuneration. In this introduction, we provide important context for developments in Egypt's labor market by discussing the cyclical developments of the Egyptian economy since the deep economic crisis precipitated by the January 25, 2011 revolution through 2020. We then move to a discussion of structural impediments that have prevented the economy from reaching its job creation potential.

Fitful Recovery

After reaching a low of 1.8 percent per annum (p.a.) in fiscal year (FY) 2010/11, Egypt's real gross domestic product (GDP) growth increased slightly to 2.2 percent p.a. in the following year and remained roughly at that level through 2012/13 (Ministry of Planning and Economic Development, 2020). In the meantime, most other macroeconomic indicators were deteriorating rapidly. The fiscal deficit

Caroline Krafft and Ragui Assaad, *Introduction* In: *The Egyptian Labor Market: A Focus on Gender and Economic Vulnerability*. Edited by: Caroline Krafft and Ragui Assaad, Oxford University Press. © Economic Research Forum 2022.
DOI: 10.1093/oso/9780192847911.003.0001

increased steadily from 7.8 percent of GDP in FY 2010/11 to 13.7 percent of GDP in FY 2012/13. The current account deficit widened from 2.0 percent of GDP to 3.1 percent of GDP in the same period, while official reserves fell from US$35.2 billon (6.9 months of imports) to a dangerously low US$14.5 billion in FY 2012/13 (2.4 months of imports) (World Bank, 2015).

A slow recovery began in FY 2013/14 with GDP growth climbing to 2.9 percent p.a. in that year and to 4.4 percent p.a. in FY 2014/15, but stalling at roughly that level through FY 2016/17 (Ministry of Planning and Economic Development, 2020). The recovery was initially supported by large aid and investment flows from the Gulf States, but these flows soon subsided, leading to a severe foreign exchange crisis in FY 2015/16. After narrowing to 11.4 percent of GDP in FY 2014/15, the budget deficit widened again to 12.5 percent of GDP in FY 2015/16. The current account deficit shot up from 3.6 percent to 6.0 percent of GDP in the same period and international reserves remained dangerously low at US$17.5 billion or 3.7 months of imports (World Bank, 2019).

Economic Reform

Confronted with these pervasive macroeconomic and external imbalances, the Egyptian government was forced to adopt a stabilization program with the support of the International Monetary Fund. The program's central plank was the flotation of the Egyptian pound in December 2016. This resulted in an overnight devaluation of the official exchange rate in excess of 125 percent. The reform program also aimed at fiscal consolidation through the introduction of a value added tax in place of the existing sales tax, as well as gradual reductions in energy subsidies and the government wage bill. These reforms were accompanied by legislative reforms to improve the business climate and attract private investment (World Bank, 2019).

While these reforms succeeded in narrowing fiscal and external deficits and in rekindling economic growth, their immediate impact was a spike in inflation. The headline consumer price index inflation shot up from an annual rate of 13.6 percent in October 2016 to 30.2 percent in February 2017, and remained at roughly that level through November 2017, only to gradually return to its pre-flotation level by March 2018 and stay at roughly that level through 2018 (Central Bank of Egypt, 2020). Thus, the inflationary episode following the flotation of the pound ended at roughly the time data were being collected for the 2018 wave of the Egypt Labor Market Panel Survey (ELMPS), on which this book is based. Because wages in Egypt tend to be fairly rigid in nominal terms, inflationary episodes such as this one are usually accompanied by significant real wage erosion (Datt and Olmsted, 2004; Cichello, Abou-Ali, and Marotta, 2013).

Despite the erosion in real purchasing power it caused, the reform program adopted in late 2016 and 2017 was successful in stabilizing the macroeconomy and restoring economic growth. By FY 2017/18, the GDP growth rate reached 5.3 percent p.a. and it further increased to 5.6 percent p.a. in FY 2018/19, only to decline to 3.6 percent p.a. in FY 2019/20, which includes a 1.7 percent p.a. COVID-19 related contraction in the fourth quarter of the fiscal year (April to June) (World Bank, 2020). The pre-COVID-19 recovery in economic growth did not, however, generate a strong employment response. As shown in Chapter 2, the employment to population ratio for the population 15+, or the employment rate for short, declined sharply from 2010 to 2011 and has continued to decline steadily since then, going from 47.7 percent in 2010 to 38.9 percent in 2019 (CAPMAS, 2011, 2020a). It had declined further to 35.1 percent by the second quarter of 2020 as a result of the COVID-19 pandemic (CAPMAS, 2020c). The steady decline in the employment rate basically indicates that employment growth did not keep up with the growth of the working age population. Furthermore, as we show in Chapters 2 and 3, job quality has also deteriorated since 2012, with greater informalization and precariousness, and falling real wages. These results suggest that there are more fundamental reasons for the weakness of labor market outcomes in Egypt than simply the various economic shocks that the country has experienced in the past decade, an issue we turn to next.

Economic Policies and Low-Productivity Growth

To understand the weak link between GDP growth and employment growth in Egypt, it is necessary to examine, albeit briefly, the pattern of economic growth over the past few decades and the policies that have led to this pattern. For years following the first and second oil shocks, Egypt's economy was strongly affected by the Dutch Disease phenomenon, resulting from an appreciation of the real exchange rate as a result of windfall revenues from oil and gas and remittances from Egyptian workers working in oil-rich countries (World Bank, 2014). The effect of the Dutch Disease is to promote growth in non-tradable sectors such as construction, real estate, transportation and retail, and wholesale trade, rather than in tradable sectors such as agriculture and manufacturing. These non-tradable sectors, such as real estate, tend to be highly capital intensive (after the initial construction period), and create jobs outside the formal sector, such as jobs in construction, transportation, and retail trade. Other policies associated with being a net oil producer for a long time, such as widespread energy subsidies, tend to encourage energy-intensive industries, which also happen to be capital-intensive.

During the Mubarak presidency, the approach to private sector development favored firms that were closely connected to the regime rather than broad incentives to private sector growth. These firms were able to corner large shares of the bank financing available to the private sector on favorable terms, and thus had higher returns to capital investment, leading them to opt for more capital-intensive sectors and modes of production (Diwan, Keefer, and Schiffbauer, 2014; Chekir and Diwan, 2015). Finally, the poor performance of the financial system in channeling the savings of high-income groups tends to favor investments in high-end real estate, which has been booming in Egypt in recent years. Such investments are highly capital intensive, generating few jobs once the building is built and generating low-quality precarious employment while the building is under construction (Liang and McIntosh, 1998). The bias of private investment toward high-end real estate has been further reinforced by public investments in large capital-intensive infrastructure and urban development projects.

The end result of these policies was a pattern of growth characterized by limited productivity growth, low employment intensity, and low job quality (Assaad et al., 2019; Assaad, Krafft, and Yassin, 2020). The limited productivity growth was both the result of slow productivity growth within sectors as well as limited reallocation of labor to sectors with high and growing productivity. In fact, employment appears to have been reallocated to sectors with slower than average productivity growth, leading to a drag on GDP per worker growth (World Bank, 2020). The sectors that gained in employment share from 2004 to 2018 included construction, wholesale and retail trade, transport, social services, and restaurants and hotels, all of which had relatively low value added per worker growth during that period (World Bank, 2020). Several of these sectors, namely construction and transport, tend to create jobs outside fixed establishments; jobs that are characterized by informality, precariousness, and poor working conditions, as we demonstrate in Chapter 2.

The employment trend in manufacturing is particularly telling in that regard. While the share of private sector employment within establishments has risen somewhat since 1996, the share of manufacturing employment within that segment of employment has been falling steadily from 32 percent in 1996 to 20 percent in 2017 (Assaad et al., 2019). Moreover, productivity in private sector manufacturing has been declining (World Bank, 2020). The trends within manufacturing are also telling. The subsectors within private manufacturing that have increased their employment shares from 2016 to 2018, namely food, beverages, and tobacco, non-metallic minerals and basic metals, and spinning, weaving and garments, tend also to be the sectors that have had the lowest cumulative change in productivity, mirroring the negative relationship between productivity growth and employment growth in the economy as a whole (World Bank, 2020).

A Focus on Gender and Vulnerability

This book updates our understanding of the Egyptian labor market in light of recent developments and long-term structural challenges. The work has a particular focus on gender and vulnerability. Egypt's education gender gap has been closing (Elbadawy, 2015; Krafft, 2015). Since women's labor force participation rises with education, the expectation was that the rising tide of education would increase female labor force participation. Despite the rapid increase in women's educational attainment, female labor force participation had been stagnant or declining through the 2010s (Assaad and Krafft, 2015b; Assaad et al., 2020). A key focus of this book is understanding why female labor force participation has remained so low. Challenges reconciling work and domestic responsibilities, rooted in gendered social norms, challenging working conditions in the private sector, and the decline of the public sector are key factors explored throughout.

Vulnerability, the "prospect of eroding people's capabilities and choices" (UNDP, 2014, p. 1), is a critical concept for understanding not only poor outcomes today but also the risk of deteriorating outcomes in the future. Vulnerability can be evaluated at the individual, household, or society level, and is particularly useful in understanding the risks of poor outcomes in the face of a shock. For example, on a household level, vulnerability might be manifested in the risk of falling into poverty with a bad harvest. On a society-wide level, vulnerability might be manifested in a sparse social safety net for workers who lose their jobs. Particular groups may be structurally vulnerable—such as women, youth, or the poor—owing to persistent social, economic, or legal inequities (UNDP, 2014). Understanding vulnerability and who is structurally vulnerable in the economy and society is critically important to building resilience, so that people are protected in the face of shocks.

Although this work uses data up to and including 2018 and was undertaken before the onset of the COVID-19 pandemic, the focus on gender and vulnerability was prescient. Women, given their key caregiving roles, disproportionately suffered as the pandemic shut down schools and nurseries. While Egypt's schools and nurseries partially reopened in fall 2020, they did not do so full time or at full capacity, creating a further challenge for women trying to reconcile work outside the home with a second shift, indeed increasingly a double shift, of caregiving (Economic Research Forum and UN Women, 2020). Understanding the challenges women faced pre-pandemic will be critically important to efforts to support their return to the labor force during and after the pandemic.

Vulnerable work had been on the rise in Egypt, although in varying forms, through 2018 (Assaad and Krafft, 2015c; Rashad and Sharaf, 2018). Poverty, an important manifestation of vulnerability, rose in Egypt from a 28 percent household poverty rate in 2015 to 33 percent in 2017/2018 (CAPMAS, 2020b). After rising with the devaluation and accompanying inflation, poverty was slightly lower, 30 percent, in 2019/20 as inflation rates fell (Moneim, 2020). How poverty has been affected by COVID-19 remains to be seen.

While much has been made of high youth unemployment rates in Egypt, workers who cannot afford to remain openly unemployed but struggle with underemployment, low wages, and poor working conditions are much more vulnerable to shocks (Krafft and Assaad, 2014). The increasing informalization of work, with fewer workers holding contracts or having social insurance (Chapter 2;

Assaad and Krafft, 2015c), has left informal workers especially vulnerable to shocks. Updating our understanding of the vulnerability of workers is critically important to designing policies and programs to protect them from shocks, including the COVID-19 pandemic.

ELMPS Data

This book uses the 2018 wave of the ELMPS, along with the preceding waves in 2012, 2006, 1998, and the 1988 special round of the Labor Force Survey, to understand the evolution of the labor market, with a special focus on gender and vulnerability. The work builds not only on the existence of these data public goods (Assaad and Barsoum, 2000; Barsoum, 2009; Assaad and Krafft, 2013; Krafft, Assaad, and Rahman, 2021), but also on the rich body of past research tracing the evolution of the labor market after structural adjustment (Assaad, 2002), economic recovery (Assaad, 2009), and the January 25, 2011 uprising (Assaad and Krafft, 2015a).

The initial ELMPS included a nationally representative sample of 4,816 households, with questions comparable to the 1988 special round of the Labor Force Survey (Assaad and Barsoum, 2000). In 2006, the second wave of the ELMPS followed as many of those households as could be located and any households that split off from the base wave households, as well as adding a refresher sample of 2,500 households, yielding 8,351 households in total (Assaad and Roushdy, 2009; Barsoum, 2009). The 2012 wave again followed previous wave households and split households, and added a refresher sample of 2,000 households, to yield 12,060 households in total (Assaad and Krafft, 2013). In 2018, previous wave households, split households, and a refresher sample oversampling the 1,000 poorest villages in Egypt generated a final sample of 15,746 households and 61,231 individuals (Krafft, Assaad, and Rahman, 2021). A total of 86,270 unique individuals were captured across the ELMPS waves, with 49,615 individuals observed in multiple waves, forming a panel that can be studied over time.

In addition to the ELMPS 2018 refresher sample focusing on the thousand poorest villages, the focus on gender and vulnerability was enhanced through additions and improvements to the questionnaire design. For instance, a section on shocks and coping mechanisms was added to the questionnaire. Questions on gender role attitudes were, for the first time, asked of both men and women. Additional questions were added on receipt of important social protection programs, such as food ration cards. These additions allow researchers, for the first time, to assess a number of critical issues in the economy and society as well as their interlinkages.

A particularly valuable feature of the ELMPSs is the ability to analyze the links between demographic, social, and economic issues. On the household level, information on housing and assets, current migrants, transfers and remittances, income sources, shocks and coping, non-farm enterprises, agricultural assets, landholding, livestock, crops, and other agriculture income was collected. On the individual level, information was gathered on residential mobility, mothers' and fathers' characteristics, siblings, health, education, subsistence and domestic work, employment and unemployment, characteristics of main jobs and secondary jobs, a full labor market history, marriage, a birth history, female employment, earnings in the primary and secondary job, return migration, information technology, savings and borrowing, and social and economic attitudes. These rich data are critically important for understanding complex issues such as the link between the labor market and fertility (Krafft, 2020) or how employment shapes marriage timing (Krafft and Assaad, 2020).

The Chapters

The chapters of the book update and expand our understanding of Egypt's labor market, economy, and society. In Chapter 1, Caroline Krafft, Ragui Assaad, and Caitlyn Keo explore the evolution of labor supply, labor force participation, and unemployment from 1998 to 2018, with a particular focus on gender and female labor force participation. While demographic pressures have temporarily abated, the "echo" of the youth bulge generation has placed substantial pressures on the education system, and in a decade will begin entering the labor market, creating renewed labor supply challenges. Compounding the fall in labor supply pressures, labor force participation has decreased among both men and women. While the decline among women is long-standing, the drop among men is a new development. Although standard measures of unemployment remained stable in 2018, discouraged unemployment rose. Limited hopes for good jobs may be reducing labor supply and discouraging potential workers.

Whether Egypt is creating good jobs is explored by Ragui Assaad, Abdelaziz Alsharawy, and Colette Salemi in Chapter 2. Although the economy, in terms of GDP, was growing through 2018, employment growth was weak. The public sector continued to decline, and while the formal private sector grew, its growth did not make up for the public sector's decline, such that informality rose. Informal wage employment outside fixed establishments (e.g. in construction and transportation) grew particularly rapidly. These developments were associated with a deterioration in job quality, increasing precarity and vulnerability, and a rising share of workers becoming vulnerable to shocks. Chapter 3, by Mona Said, Rami Galal, and Mina Sami, examines how wages and inequality have evolved in Egypt. Real wages in Egypt fell between 2012 and 2018, although the degree of deterioration varied across different groups of workers. The working poor and women were particularly vulnerable to lower wages. At the same time, inequality in wages increased, and social mobility remained low and stagnant.

The next chapters focus on specific and important segments of the labor market: the school to work transition and youth (Chapter 4), government employment (Chapter 5), and entrepreneurship (Chapter 6). Chapter 4, by Mona Amer and Marian Atallah, details the difficulties youth face in entering the labor market, including the rising informality and vulnerability of youth employment. The labor market, which was already rigid, has become increasingly so, further limiting exits from vulnerable employment to better jobs. Socioeconomic background is a key driver of initial status in the labor market, and thus youth labor market trajectories and vulnerability. Chapter 5, by Ghada Barsoum and Dina Abdalla, explores employment in government. It highlights a key dynamic behind the decline in female labor force participation and the rising informality of youth employment: the decline of government employment. Government employment, with substantially better benefits and conditions than private sector employment, remains preferred by Egyptian youth, particularly young women. The decline of the sector has reduced employment opportunities for women. The government sector is becoming more educated and is aging, which presents some important opportunities to right-size employment as well as improve service delivery. Chapter 6, by Reham Rizk and Ali Rashed, explores gender and entrepreneurship. Focusing on non-agricultural enterprises, the chapter finds that, while non-farm enterprises play an important role in the economy and in employment, women are less likely to engage in or own such enterprises. Participation in enterprises has been declining for men, but not for women. However, women's enterprises are more likely to be informal, have lower capital, and be home-based, suggesting women may be engaging primarily in survival self-employment, with their potential for creating employment through entrepreneurship remaining untapped.

Chapter 7, by Anda David, Nelly Elmallakh, and Jackline Wahba, explores internal and international migration, which are important responses to economic vulnerability. Internal migration remains low in Egypt, a key explanation for the country's low level of urbanization. International migration remains an important economic strategy; yet few individuals engage in both internal and international migration. It is primarily men who migrate internally (and especially internationally) for work, while women rarely migrate internationally and primarily migrate internally for family reasons. Chapter 8, by Caitlyn Keo, Caroline Krafft, and Luca Fedi, focuses on Egypt's large rural population, specifically rural women, exploring their opportunities and vulnerabilities. Although rural women have lower levels of economic participation by standard measures than men or urban women, this chapter illustrates the important role rural women play in the economy, tending livestock, helping with farming, and supporting non-farm enterprises, as well as engaging in critical domestic work.

The final three chapters take particular advantage of new material in the ELMPS 2018 on social protection (Chapter 9), exposure to shocks and coping (Chapter 10), and health and vulnerability (Chapter 11). Chapter 9, by Irene

Selwaness and Maye Ehab, explores how social insurance coverage through work has evolved over time, demonstrating a decline in social insurance coverage, increasing employment vulnerability, as well as a decline in social protection coverage generally. The chapter also investigates two new important conditional cash transfer programs in Egypt, Takaful and Karama, as well as food ration cards. Lastly, the chapter explores health insurance coverage, noting particularly large gaps among women and especially rural women as well as youth. Chapter 10, by Imane Helmy and Rania Roushdy, investigates households' vulnerability and resilience to shocks. In 2018, almost a quarter of Egyptian households experienced food insecurity, 14 percent experienced economic shocks, and 5 percent health shocks. Households coped with shocks primarily by reducing their consumption (including reducing investments in health and education), as well as borrowing or receiving assistance from neighbors, relatives, and friends. Chapter 11, by Maia Sieverding and Rasha Hassan, explores the links between health and economic vulnerability. The chapter shows a substantial burden of poor health among both working-age and elderly populations, including in terms of disability and low wellbeing. Poor urban women and those in precarious and hazardous employment are particularly vulnerable to poor health.

Although all our data are from 2018, prior to COVID-19, all the chapters discuss the implications of their findings for understanding the potential impact of COVID-19 on Egypt's labor market, economy, and society. Our focus on vulnerability helps us identify those who are at the greatest risk from COVID-19-related shocks. We also provide an epilogue discussing the emerging evidence, at this writing, of the impact of COVID-19, illustrating how vulnerable workers and women have been particularly impacted by the crisis.

This book provides a critically important context for understanding the Egyptian labor market, gender, and vulnerability, but there is much more that can be done by future researchers with the rich data. The panel can be exploited to look at important dynamics and potentially achieve causal identification. The Egyptian data can also be analyzed in conjunction with the 2014 Tunisia Labor Market Panel Survey (Assaad et al., 2016; Assaad and Boughzala, 2018), the 2010 and 2016 waves of the Jordan Labor Market Panel Survey (Assaad, 2014; Krafft and Assaad, 2019, 2021) and data collection planned for future countries and waves. All data are publicly available from the Economic Research Forum's (ERF)'s Open Access Microdata Initiative at www.erfdataportal.com as part of ERF's commitment to supporting economic research and informed policymaking. The research in this book, as well as future analyses of the data, will be particularly important in understanding the labor market and vulnerability prior to the COVID-19 pandemic and in designing effective social and economic policy responses.

Caroline Krafft and Ragui Assaad

July 2021

References

Assaad, R. (ed.) (2002) *The Egyptian Labor Market in an Era of Reform*. Cairo: American University in Cairo Press.

Assaad, R. (ed.) (2009) *The Egyptian Labor Market Revisited*. Cairo: American University in Cairo Press.

Assaad, R. (ed.) (2014) *The Jordanian Labour Market in the New Millennium*. Oxford: Oxford University Press.

Assaad, R. and G. Barsoum (2000) *Egypt Labor Market Survey, 1998: Report on the Data Collection and Preparation*. Cairo, Egypt. Available at: http://www.erfdataportal.com/index.php/catalog/28/download/260.

Assaad, R. and M. Boughzala. (eds) (2018) *The Tunisian Labor Market in an Era of Transition*. Oxford: Oxford University Press.

Assaad, R. and C. Krafft. (2013) "The Egypt Labor Market Panel Survey: Introducing the 2012 Round." *IZA Journal of Labor & Development*, 2 (8): 1–30.

Assaad, R. and C. Krafft. (eds) (2015a) *The Egyptian Labor Market in an Era of Revolution*. Oxford: Oxford University Press.

Assaad, R. and C. Krafft. (2015b) "The Evolution of Labor Supply and Unemployment in The Egyptian Economy: 1988–2012," in *The Egyptian Labor Market in an Era of Revolution*, edited by R. Assaad and C. Krafft, pp. 1–26. Oxford: Oxford University Press,.

Assaad, R. and C. Krafft (2015c) "The Structure and Evolution of Employment in Egypt: 1998–2012," in Assaad, R. and Krafft, C. (eds) *The Egyptian Labor Market in an Era of Revolution*, pp. 27–51. Oxford: Oxford University Press.

Assaad, R., C. Krafft, and S. Yassin (2020) "Job Creation or Labor Absorption? An Analysis of Private Sector Job Growth in Egypt." *Middle East Development Journal*, 12 (2): 177–207. doi: 10.1080/17938120.2020.1753978.

Assaad, R. and R. Roushdy (2009) "Methodological Appendix 3: An Analysis of Sample Attrition in the Egypt Labor Market Panel Survey 2006," in R. Assaad (ed.) *The Egyptian Labor Market Revisited*, pp. 303–16. Cairo: American University in Cairo Press.

Assaad, R. et al. (2016) "Introducing the Tunisia Labor Market Panel Survey 2014." *IZA Journal of Labor & Development*, 5 (15): 1–21.

Assaad, R. et al. (2019) "Job Creation in Egypt: A Sectoral and Geographical Analysis Focusing on Private Establishments, 1996–2017." Economic Research Forum Policy Research Report. Cairo.

Assaad, R. et al. (2020) "Explaining the MENA Paradox: Rising Educational Attainment, Yet Stagnant Female Labor Force Participation." *Demographic Research*, 43 (28): 817–50.

Barsoum, G. (2009) "Methodological Appendix 1: The Egypt Labor Market Panel Survey 2006: Documentation of the Data Collection Process," in R. Assaad (ed.)

The Egyptian Labor Market Revisited, pp. 259–84. Cairo: American University in Cairo Press.

CAPMAS (Central Agency for Public Mobilization and Statistics). (2011) *Annual Bulletin Labor Force Survey 2010*. Cairo: CAPMAS.

CAPMAS (2020a) *Annual Bulletin Labor Force Survey 2019*. Cairo: CAPMAS.

CAPMAS (2020b) "Poverty Indicators from Household Income, Expenditure and Consumption Survey 2017/18." *Egypt Statistics Magazine*, January: 14–15.

CAPMAS (2020c) *Quarterly Bulletin of the Labor Force Survey, Second Quarter, Apr/May/Jun 2020*. Cairo: CAPMAS.

Central Bank of Egypt (2020) *Inflation Historical*. Available at: https://www.cbe.org.eg/en/EconomicResearch/Statistics/Pages/InflationHistorical.aspx (Accessed: November 26, 2020).

Chekir, H. and I. Diwan (2015) "Crony Capitalism in Egypt." *Journal of Globalisation and Development*, 5 (2): 177–211. doi: 10.1515/jgd-2014-0025.

Cichello, P., H. Abou-Ali, and D. Marotta (2013) "What Happened to Real Earnings in Egypt, 2008 to 2009?" *IZA Journal of Labor and Development*, 2 (1): 1–38. doi: 10.1186/2193-9020-2-10.

Datt, G. and J.C. Olmsted (2004) "Induced Wage Effects of Changes in Food Prices in Egypt." *Journal of Development Studies*, 40 (4): 137–66. doi: 10.1080/00220380410001673229.

Diwan, I., P. Keefer, and M. Schiffbauer (2014) *On Top of the Pyramids: Cronyism and Private Sector Growth in Egypt*. Washington, DC: World Bank (Mimeo).

Economic Research Forum and UN Women (2020) *Progress of Women in the Arab States 2020: The Role of the Care Economy in Promoting Gender Equality*. Cairo: UN Women.

Elbadawy, A. (2015) "Education in Egypt: Improvements in Attainment, Problems with Quality and Inequality," in R. Assaad and C. Krafft (eds) *The Egyptian Labor Market in an Era of Revolution*, pp. 127–46. Oxford: Oxford University Press.

Krafft, C. (2015) "Youth's Educational Experiences in Egypt: Who Attends School, Who Succeeds, and Who Struggles," in R. Roushdy and M. Sieverding (eds) *Panel Survey of Young People in Egypt (SYPE) 2014: Generating Evidence for Policy and Programs*, pp. 49–97. New York: Population Council.

Krafft, C. (2020) "Why is Fertility on the Rise in Egypt? The Role of Women's Employment Opportunities." *Journal of Population Economics*, 33 (4): 1173–1218. doi: 10.1007/s00148-020-00770-w.

Krafft, C. and Assaad, R. (2014) "Why the Unemployment Rate is a Misleading Indicator of Labor Market Health in Egypt." Economic Research Forum Policy Perspective 14. Cairo, Egypt.

Krafft, C. and Assaad, R. (2021) "Introducing the Jordan Labor Market Panel Survey 2016." *IZA Journal of Development and Migration* 12:08.

Krafft, C. and R. Assaad (eds) (2019) *The Jordanian Labor Market Between Fragility and Resilience*. Oxford: Oxford University Press.

Krafft, C. and R. Assaad (2020) "Employment's Role in Enabling and Constraining Marriage in the Middle East and North Africa." *Demography* 57: 2297–2325. doi: 10.1007/s13524-020-00932-1.

Krafft, C., R. Assaad, and K.W. Rahman (2021) "Introducing the Egypt Labor Market Panel Survey 2018." *IZA Journal of Development and Migration* (Forthcoming).

Liang, Y. and W. McIntosh (1998) "Employment Growth and Real Estate Return: Are They Linked?" *Journal of Real Estate Portfolio Management*, 4 (2): 125–33. doi: 10.1080/10835547.1998.12089560.

Ministry of Planning and Economic Development (2020) *Gross Domestic Product.* Available at: https://mped.gov.eg/GrossDomestic?lang=en (Accessed: November 26, 2020).

Moneim, D. (2020) "This is the First Time Egypt Sees a Decrease in its Poverty Rate since 1999." *Ahram Online*, December 3. Available at: http://english.ahram.org.eg/NewsContent/3/12/396107/Business/Economy/Egypt's-poverty-rate-declines-to--CAPMAS.aspx (Accessed: December 7, 2020).

Rashad, A.S. and M.F. Sharaf (2018) "Does Precarious Employment Damage Youth Mental Health, Wellbeing, and Marriage? Evidence from Egypt Using Longitudinal Data." Economic Research Forum Working Paper Series No. 1200. Cairo.

UNDP (United Nations Development Programme) (2014) *Human Development Report 2014: Sustaining Human Progress: Reducing Vulnerabilities and Building Resilience.* New York: UNDP.

World Bank (2014) *Arab Republic of Egypt: More Jobs, Better Jobs: A Priority for Egypt.* Washington, DC: World Bank.

World Bank (2015) *Egypt Economic Monitor: Paving the Way to a Sustained Recovery.* Washington, DC: World Bank.

World Bank (2019) *Egypt Economic Monitor: From Floating to Thriving: Taking Egypt's Exports to New Levels.* Washington, DC: World Bank.

World Bank (2020) *Egypt Economic Monitor: From Crisis to Economic Transformation: Unlocking Egypt's Productivity and Job-Creation Potential.* Washington, DC: World Bank.

1

The Evolution of Labor Supply in Egypt, 1988–2018

A Gendered Analysis

Caroline Krafft, Ragui Assaad, and Caitlyn Keo

1.1 Introduction

Egypt's labor market has faced a number of challenges since the turn of the century. In the 1990s, the economy struggled with substantial structural reforms and labor supply pressures related to the youth bulge. While labor market conditions improved in the early 2000s, the global financial crisis and the ensuing global economic slowdown were a challenge for Egypt as well. Soon afterwards, the January 25, 2011 revolution led to a period of substantial political and economic uncertainty. Economic growth has recovered in recent years after the introduction of a series of economic reforms and the stabilization of the political situation, but Egypt continues to face the long-term challenges of creating enough productive employment for its growing and increasingly educated workforce (Assaad, Krafft, and Yassin, 2020; World Bank, 2020).

This chapter investigates Egypt's labor supply, starting with the growth and changing composition of the working age population. Subsequently, we examine the changing patterns of labor force participation by sex, age, and education. These patterns mediate between the demographic trends and the actual patterns of labor supply in the economy. As part of our focus on female labor force participation, we examine changes in the timing of marriage and fertility, as well as their implications for the labor force behavior of women. To understand the evolution of labor supply, the chapter uses data from the four waves of the Egypt Labor Market Panel Survey (ELMPS) conducted in 1998, 2006, 2012, and 2018, as well as, when possible, data from the 1988 special round of the Labor Force Survey (LFS). This breadth of data allows us to study how the demographic structure of the population and labor force behavior have evolved over several decades.[1] This work builds on previous research on the evolution of labor supply

---

[1] For more information on ELMPS 1998, see Assaad and Barsoum (2000). For more information on ELMPS 2006, see Barsoum (2009). For more information on ELMPS 2012, see Assaad and Krafft (2013).

Caroline Krafft, Ragui Assaad, and Caitlyn Keo, *The Evolution of Labor Supply in Egypt, 1988–2018: A Gendered Analysis*
In: *The Egyptian Labor Market: A Focus on Gender and Economic Vulnerability.* Edited by: Caroline Krafft and Ragui Assaad,
Oxford University Press. © Economic Research Forum 2022. DOI: 10.1093/oso/9780192847911.003.0002

in Egypt using the preceding waves of the ELMPS (Assaad, 2002, 2009; Assaad and Krafft, 2015a, 2015b).

The main finding that emerges from our analysis is that labor supply pressures have subsided greatly during the 2012–18 period as the growth of youth and young adult populations abated. The reduced demographic pressure on labor supply was compounded by a decline in labor force participation and employment rates among both men and women. The decline in participation among men is a relatively recent phenomenon and one affecting both younger and older men and men at all education levels. The decline in participation among women has occurred despite the substantial increase in educational attainment among women and the traditionally strong relationship between education and economic participation for women in Egypt. Rates of participation have steadily declined among educated Egyptian women since 1998. The decline is most likely driven by the reduction in employment opportunities in the public sector, without a commensurate increase in suitable opportunities in the private sector (Assaad et al., 2020). This trend especially affects married women. While overall unemployment rates, measured in the standard way, have remained fairly stable since 2006, broad unemployment has increased more, reflecting a rise in discouraged unemployment among both men and women.

In what follows, we characterize the evolution of the working age population, labor force participation, employment, and unemployment from 1988 to 2018 by age, sex, educational attainment, and location. Since marriage, childbearing, and childrearing particularly affect women's labor force participation, we further show important trends in age at marriage and fertility as well as their relationship with labor supply.

1.2 Demographic Change in Egypt

In this section, we focus on key aspects of demographic change in Egypt. We start with population growth for the population as a whole and for various age groups of particular relevance to labor supply. We also examine the evolution of the age and geographic compositions of the population. We end the section by examining marriage and fertility trends as key determinants of both population trends and trends in women's labor force participation.

1.2.1 Population growth and the age composition of the population

Over the 1990s and 2000s, one of the main features of Egypt's demographic transition has been the emergence of a pronounced "youth bulge" resulting from rapidly

---

For more information on ELMPS 2018, see Krafft, Assaad, and Rahman (2021). ELMPS data are publicly available from www.erfdataportal.com.

falling early childhood mortality, especially in the early 1980s, which was not matched by a commensurate decline in fertility (Rashad, 1989; Miller and Hirschhorn, 1995; Robinson and El-Zanaty, 2006; Assaad and Roudi-Fahimi, 2007).

As shown in Figure 1.1, the bulge generation was still in its infancy in 1988 and moved to the 10–14 and 15–19 age groups in 1998. By 2006, the youth bulge was at its peak, with a clear rise in the share of the 15–19 and 20–24 age groups. By 2012, the bulge had shifted to the 25–29 age group, many of whom were already starting to have children, leading to an "echo" among those aged 0–4 (Krafft and Assaad, 2014a). By 2018, the bulge generation had reached the age of 30–34 and the echo generation was centered around school-entry age, namely 5–9. The size of the echo was compounded by a temporary increase in the total fertility rate (TFR) from 3.0 to 3.5 children per woman, an issue we return to below (Ministry of Health and Population, El-Zanaty and Associates, and ICF International, 2015; Krafft, 2020).

The changing age structure of the population had direct implications for the rates at which various age groups of relevance to the labor supply were growing. As shown in Table 1.1, Egypt's overall population has been growing at a fairly stable rate of about 2 percent per annum (p.a.) over the 30-year period from 1988 to 2018. However, this overall rate of population growth masks substantial variations in population growth across age groups. From 1988 to 1998, the most rapidly growing age group was youth aged 15–24, which grew at 3.4 percent p.a., more than one and half times the rate of overall population growth (2.1 percent p.a.), a phenomenon that reflected the peak of the youth bulge. This led to a fairly rapid growth of the working age population at a rate of 3.0 percent p.a. and, accordingly, substantial labor supply pressures.

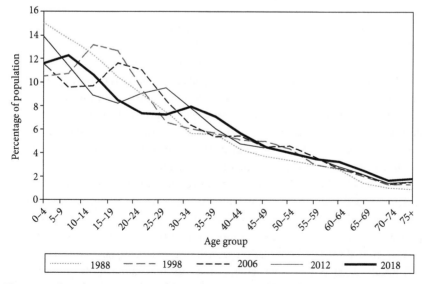

Figure 1.1 Population structure of Egypt (percentage in five-year age group), 1988–2018.
Source: Authors' calculations based on data from LFS 1988 and ELMPS 1998–2018.

Table 1.1 Average annual growth rates (percentages) of the total population and selected age groups, 1988–2018.

	Children	Youth	Young Adults	Working Age	All
Ages:	0–14	15–24	25–29	15–64	
Urban					
1988–98	0.1	2.4	−0.3	2.3	1.7
1998–2006	0.2	1.8	5.4	2.4	1.9
2006–12	4.5	−2.6	2.8	1.1	2.2
2012–18	0.7	−0.8	−3.6	0.3	0.6
Rural					
1988–98	0.4	4.1	1.7	3.6	2.3
1998–2006	0.7	2.4	4.6	2.6	1.9
2006–12	3.4	−2.2	5.3	1.4	2.2
2012–18	2.6	1.0	−2.4	2.2	2.4
Total					
1988–98	0.3	3.4	0.8	3.0	2.1
1998–2006	0.5	2.2	5.0	2.5	1.9
2006–12	3.8	−2.3	4.2	1.2	2.2
2012–18	1.9	0.3	−2.9	1.3	1.7

Source: Authors' calculations based on data from LFS 1988 and ELMPS 1998–2018.

In the 1998–2006 period, the bulge had moved to the young adult population (ages 25–29), which grew at a rate of 5.0 percent p.a., continuing strong labor supply pressures, especially among the relatively educated, who enter the labor market at a later age and tend to spend longer in unemployment upon entry. The growth of the working age population slowed somewhat during this period to 2.5 percent p.a.

In the 2006–12 period, the young adult age group continued to grow fast at 4.2 percent p.a., but the youth group actually contracted at a rate of 2.3 percent p.a. This shift marked the start of a period of reduced labor supply pressures, which dropped the growth of the working age population to only 1.2 percent p.a. The emergence of the echo of the bulge was clearly apparent in the growth of the child population during this period. After having grown at only 0.5 percent p.a. during the previous period, the child population growth accelerated to 3.8 percent p.a., reflecting both the growth in the population of women in their peak child-bearing years as well as the increase in fertility.

In the 2012–18 period, the contraction reached the young adult population, which declined at a rate of 2.9 percent p.a. Together with the slow growth of the youth population (0.3 percent p.a.), this marked a period of reduced labor supply pressure. At the same time, the resumption of fertility decline resulted in a slight deceleration of the child population growth to 1.9 percent p.a.

Thus, the aging of the bulge generation means that labor supply pressures subsided somewhat in the 2010s, but the progression of the echo suggests that these pressures are likely to resume soon. The effects of the echo are now being felt in the primary school system and will reach the labor market within the next ten to fifteen years.[2]

Using the most recent wave of the ELMPS from 2018, Figure 1.2 shows the age structure of the population in urban and rural areas by sex in the form of population pyramids. This figure shows that, in 2018, the bulge was fairly pronounced in both the 30–34 and 35–39 age groups in urban areas and the 30–34 age group in rural areas. The trough that follows the bulge (in 2018, centered on the 20–24 age group) was also more pronounced in urban areas. The echo was apparent in both contexts, but was attenuating faster in urban areas, owing to faster fertility declines there.[3] Additionally, among the youngest cohorts in rural areas (aged 0–9), there were slightly higher percentages of young boys than young girls, likely owing to son preference (Yount, Langsten, and Hill, 2000).

The population structure patterns are clearly reflected in the differential rates of growth of various age groups in urban and rural areas. Returning to Table 1.1,

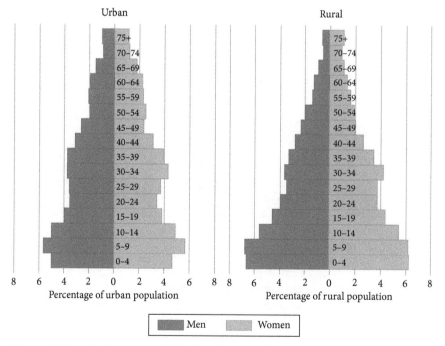

Figure 1.2 Population structure of Egypt (percentage in age group), by location and sex, 2018.

Source: Authors' calculations based on data from ELMPS 2018.

---

[2] See Assaad (2020) for projections of Egypt's population and labor force by age, sex, and educational attainment through 2050.
[3] See Chapter 8 for an exploration of fertility patterns by location.

we can see that higher fertility in rural areas resulted in a higher rate of population growth there relative to urban areas. Rural areas also experienced a higher rate of growth of the youth population in the 1988–98 period and a more pronounced growth of the young adult population in the 2006–12 period. In the 2012–18 period, rural areas were still experiencing fairly high growth in the working age population (2.2 percent p.a.), whereas that growth had slowed down substantially in urban areas to just 0.3 percent p.a.

1.2.2 The regional composition of the population

The ELMPS does not cover the Frontier governorates, so to analyze the geographic distribution of the population over time, we examine six regions: Greater Cairo, Alexandria and the Suez Canal region, Urban Lower Egypt, Urban Upper Egypt, which constitute the four urban regions, and Rural Lower Egypt and Rural Upper Egypt, which constitute the two rural regions.[4] Figure 1.3 shows the

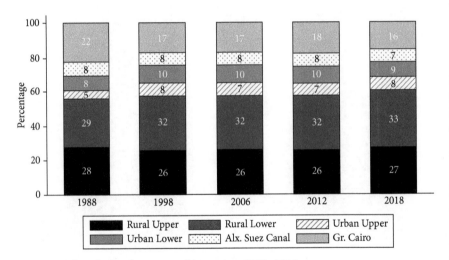

Figure 1.3 Population (percentage) by region, 1988–2018.
Source: Authors' calculations based on data from LFS 1988 and ELMPS 1998–2018.

---

[4] The Frontier governorates include Red Sea, El-Wadi El-Gedid, Matrouh, and North and South Sinai. Together these governorates constituted 1.7 percent of Egypt's population in 2017 (CAPMAS, 2019). Greater Cairo includes Cairo governorate and the cities of Giza in Giza governorate and Shobra El-Kheimah in Kalyubia governorate. The Alexandria and Suez Canal region includes Alexandria, Suez, and Port-Said governorates, which are entirely urban, as well as the urban portions of Ismailia governorate. The remaining locations are allocated to urban and rural Lower and Upper Egypt depending on whether they are urban or rural. In Greater Cairo, less than half a percent (0.3 percent) of people across all five waves of the ELMPS (N=80) reported being in rural areas. Therefore, we discuss Greater Cairo as an exclusively urban region.

distribution of the population by region and survey wave. The share of the population in rural areas has increased between 1988 and 2018 from 56 percent to 60 percent.[5] This rural shift appears to be most directly because of the consistent (but small) increases in Rural Lower Egypt, from 29 percent of the population in 1988 to 33 percent in 2018. Rural Upper Egypt first experienced a decline in its share from 1988 to 1998, stability from 1998 to 2012, and then a slight increase in its share from 2012 to 2018. The region that has experienced the greatest decline in its population share over time was the Greater Cairo region, whose share went from 22 percent in 1988 to 16 percent in 2018. Other urban regions have essentially maintained their share, at least since 1998.

1.2.3 Trends in fertility and marriage patterns

As shown in Figure 1.4, the TFR in Egypt has been on a generally declining trend since 1980, but this trend has slowed appreciably since 1997, with important periods of increasing fertility. The first reversal was in the 1997–2000 period, when fertility increased from 3.3 to 3.5. Fertility resumed its decline from 2000 to 2008 (3.0), albeit at a somewhat slower trend than in the 1980 to 1997 period. More recently, there was a second reversal, from 2008 to 2012, when the TFR increased from 3.0 to 3.5 children per woman and then remained at that level in 2014. The 2018 wave of the ELMPS is the first to confirm that the decline in TFR has resumed since the last round of the Demographic Health Survey (DHS), which was carried out in 2014. At 3.1 children per woman, the TFR in 2018 remains slightly higher than its lowest recorded level of 3.0 children per woman reached in 2006 and 2008.

One important other aspect of fertility change is that contraceptive prevalence rates have increased. Among currently married women aged 15–49, 62.6 percent were taking some steps to prevent pregnancy in ELMPS 2018, compared with only 58.5 percent in the DHS 2014 (Ministry of Health and Population, El-Zanaty and Associates, and ICF International, 2015). The 63 percent rate is the highest contraceptive prevalence rate ever observed in Egypt; rates were around 60 percent in 2003–8. The increased prevalence also includes a slight increase in the use of intrauterine devices (from 51.4 percent in DHS 2014 to 53.3 percent in ELMPS 2018) as well as the pill (from 27.4 percent in DHS 2014 to 34.9 percent in ELMPS) along with a decrease in injectables (from 14.5 percent in DHS 2014 to 10.0 percent in ELMPS 2018). The changes in family planning prevalence and mix may have played an important role in the recent fertility decline.

---

[5] Chapter 7 further discusses internal migration and the lack of urbanization in Egypt and Chapter 8 discusses the higher fertility rates in rural areas.

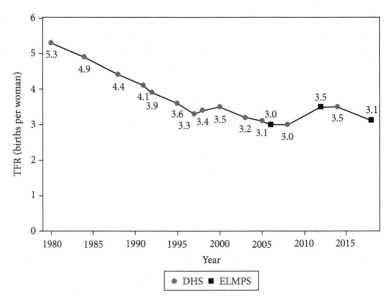

Figure 1.4 Total fertility rate (TFR, births per woman), 1980–2018.

Note: TFRs for 1980, 1984, and 1991 are 12 months preceding the survey. TFRs for 2018, 2012, and 2006 are three years preceding the survey; the remainder are 1–36 months preceding the survey.

Source: TFRs for 1980–2005 and 2008 are from El-Zanaty and Way (2009) and are primarily Demographic and Health Survey statistics. TFR for 2014 is from the 2014 Demographic and Health Survey (Ministry of Health and Population, El-Zanaty and Associates, and ICF International, 2015). TFRs for 2006 and 2012 from Krafft (2020). TFRs for 2018 based on authors' calculations using STATA program tfr2 on the ELMPS 2018.

As suggested by the trends in age-specific fertility rates (ASFRs) shown in Figure 1.5, the observed decrease in TFR between 2012 and 2018 was primarily driven by decreased childbearing for women aged 25–39. There was hardly any change in fertility among those aged 20–24 from 2012 to 2018. As a result, the 20–24 cohort had the highest ASFR (188 births per 1,000 women) by 2018, unlike previous waves where the highest levels were reached at age 25–29. ASFRs at ages 25–29 and 30–34 were lower in 2018 than 2012 and even slightly lower than in 2006 for the 25–34 age group. The reversal in the unusual increase in fertility that was observed between 2006 and 2012 has important implications for Egypt's future labor supply. Egypt's demographic future will depend on whether fertility continues to decline, stabilizes, or reverses again.[6]

Changes in age at marriage are related to both changes in fertility and women's labor force participation. Figure 1.6 examines the proportion of men and women married at various ages, by birth year. The proportion of women married by age

---

[6] See Assaad (2020) for projections based on the UN population division's medium variant assumptions.

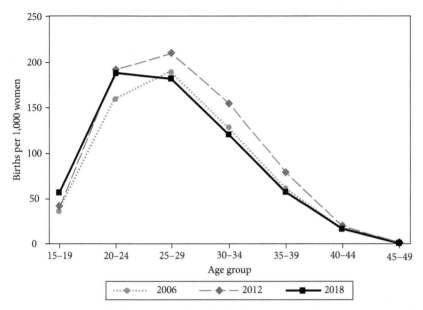

Figure 1.5 Age specific fertility rates (ASFRs, births per 1,000 women), women aged 15–49, 2006–18.

Source: ASFRs for 2006 and 2012 from Krafft (2020). ASFRs for 2018 based on authors' calculations using STATA program tfr2 on the ELMPS 2018.

16 has fallen across cohorts, but the share married by age 18, after falling for cohorts born in 1960 through the early 1980s, has stabilized at around 25 percent. The proportion married by age 20 was just under 50 percent for those born in 1960, fell for cohorts born in the 1960s and 1970s, and then has started to rise again for women born in the 1980s and 1990s, suggesting that the trend in increasingly late marriage has reversed. A similar albeit more pronounced pattern is observed for those married by age 22. As a result, the median age at marriage for women aged 15–59 in 2018 was 21 years old, lower than the previous 22 years old (Assaad, Krafft, and Selwaness, 2017). The increase in the proportion married by these ages may have contributed to the increase in ASFR for 20–24-year-olds between 2006 and 2012, as women in Egypt usually attempt to commence child-bearing promptly after marriage. The shares of women married at older ages (25 and 28) have also risen, suggesting that marriage age has declined across its entire distribution. While the share of men married at each age also rose over time (corroborating the possible effect of more flexible housing laws on allowing both men and women to marry earlier),[7] there is some evidence that this trend

---

[7] See Assaad, Krafft, and Rolando (2021) and Assaad and Ramadan (2008) for a discussion of how changes in housing laws in Egypt have contributed to reducing the age of marriage.

Figure 1.6 Proportion married at various ages, by sex and birth year, 2018.
Note: Lowess running mean smoother with bandwidth two.
Source: Authors' calculations based on data from ELMPS 2018.

may be reversing for the youngest cohort of men. Spousal age gaps and the structure of the youth bulge and echo may have resulted in a temporary decrease in the supply of younger (female) spouses for men. These marriage market dynamics merit further investigation.

1.3 Trends in Educational Attainment

Along with the size and age structure of the population, its education composition is a critical aspect of labor supply. We examine the evolution of educational attainment along six education levels as is typical in Egypt: illiterate, read and write, less than intermediate (equivalent to primary and lower secondary), intermediate (equivalent to upper secondary), above intermediate (two-year postsecondary), and university and higher (four-year post-secondary and higher). We focus on individuals aged 25–64, to capture those who are likely to have completed their educational progression.

Over time, there have been large declines in illiteracy and steady increases in higher levels of education, such as intermediate and university degrees or higher.

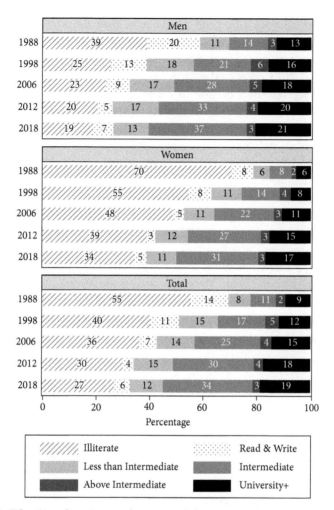

Figure 1.7 Educational attainment (percentage), by sex, ages 25–64, 1988–2018.
Source: Authors' calculations based on data from LFS 1988 and ELMPS 1998–2018.

As shown in Figure 1.7, between 1988 and 2018, the share of the population that was illiterate was halved, falling from 55 percent to 27 percent. Over the same span, there has been a 23 percentage point increase in the share of the adult population with intermediate education (from 11 percent to 34 percent) and a 10 percentage point increase for those with university degrees or higher (from 9 percent to 19 percent). The reductions in illiteracy and the increases in intermediate and university education were even larger for women, who started with a higher level of illiteracy and lower educational attainment. Although women were almost twice as likely as men to be illiterate in 2018 (34 percent versus 19 percent), like men they experienced a 51 percent decline in their illiteracy rates since 1988 (from 70 percent to 34 percent). The proportion of women ending up with intermediate degrees increased from 8 percent to 31 percent over the 30-year period from 1988 to 2018 compared with from 14 percent to 37 percent for men. Similarly, the proportion of women attaining university education or higher increased from 6 percent to 17 percent, compared with from 13 percent to 21 percent for men. The gender gap in higher education has therefore narrowed from 7 percentage points in 1998 to 4 percentage points in 2018.

An examination of educational attainment by cohort of birth shows that large changes in attainment occurred for cohorts born between 1955 and 1975, but that the rate of increase in attainment moderated somewhat for more recent cohorts. Figure 1.8 illustrates the highest level of education completed by year of birth for all individuals between the ages of 25 and 64 in 2018 (i.e. born between 1953 and 1993). The percentage of people who remained illiterate dropped substantially, from nearly 50 percent of those born in the early 1950s to nearly 15 percent of those born in the early 1990s. The share of those who can only read and write or had less than an intermediate education remained fairly stable. As illiteracy decreased, the categories that increased the most were intermediate education and university and above education. The intermediate education category is made up

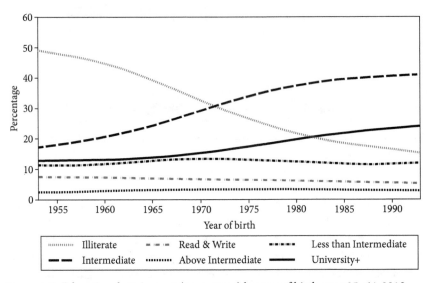

Figure 1.8 Educational attainment (percentage) by year of birth, ages 25–64, 2018.

Note: Lowess smoothed running mean with bandwidth two. Restricted to those cohorts aged at least 25 (birth year in 1993 or earlier) to ensure educational attainment is the final level completed.

Source: Authors' calculations based on data from ELMPS 2018.

mostly of technical secondary degree holders, since those obtaining general secondary degrees tend to go on to higher education (Assaad, 2010). This category increased very rapidly to about 35 percent for those born in 1975, and then its increase slowed somewhat for subsequent cohorts. It reached just over 40 percent for those born in the early 1990s, becoming by far the most common educational attainment in Egypt in recent years. The proportion with university education was slow to increase at first, but started taking off for those born in 1970 only to see its growth slow as well among recent cohorts. By the cohorts born in the 1990s, more than 20 percent had acquired university education or higher.

Commensurate with the increase in levels of education overall, the average years of schooling has continued to rise for both men and women (Figure 1.9). Among those aged 25–64 in 2018, men averaged 9.3 years of school and women 7.6 (the average was 8.4 overall). Despite the narrowing of the education gender gap over time, for those born in 1985 or later the gap between men and women has persisted, with a difference of about one additional year in school on average for men. This gender gap is closing among younger cohorts, not shown; for instance, in both the 2012 and 2018 waves, there was less than a percentage point difference in enrollment between girls and boys aged 6–17. The rising education levels in Egypt and closing of the gender gap have critical implications for the nature of the labor supply and Egypt's potential human resources.

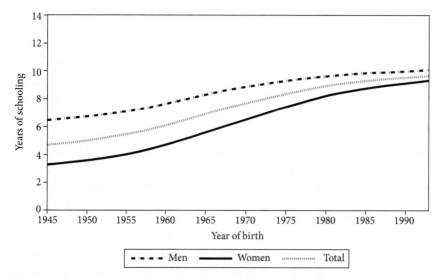

Figure 1.9 Average years of schooling by year of birth and sex, 2018.

Note: Lowess smoothed running mean with bandwidth two. Restricted to those cohorts aged 25+ (birth year in 1993 or earlier) to ensure educational attainment is the final level completed.

Source: Authors' calculations based on data from ELMPS 2018.

1.4 The Evolution of the Labor Force and Labor Force Participation

1.4.1 Trends in the labor force

While the working age population is a measure of potential labor supply, the actual size of the labor force results from how this potential is realized through labor force behavior, namely employment and job-seeking behavior. The economically active population or labor force consists of the employed and unemployed, but there are varying definitions of both these concepts that result in several possible definitions of the labor force. In all the definitions we discuss here, we limit ourselves to the current labor force, which is based on a reference period of the seven days that precede the date of the interview. We also focus our attention on the labor force aged 15–64.

We primarily use a market definition of employment, which is equivalent to the "work for pay or profit" definition of the 19th International Conference of Labor Statisticians (ILO, 2013). The market definition of employment includes all those who were occupied for at least one hour per week in an activity for the purpose of obtaining either pay or profit, as either wage workers, employers, self-employed workers, or unpaid family workers. The extended labor force definition of economic activity further includes those who were involved in the production or processing of primary commodities for own household consumption, sometimes referred to as subsistence work.

We distinguish between two types of unemployment, standard unemployment and broad unemployment. Under both definitions, the unemployed must want to work, to have not worked even one hour in the past seven days according to the definition of work used, and to be available to start work within two weeks. The standard definition of unemployment further adds a search criterion, that an individual actively searched for work within the past three months.[8] The broad definition of unemployment does not require search and therefore includes among the unemployed the discouraged unemployed who are no longer actively searching. With two definitions of employment and two of unemployment, there are four possible definitions of the labor force. The special round of the Labor Force Survey of October 1988 only captured the extended definition of employment.

According to the standard market definition of the labor force (which is the most restricted definition among the four), the labor force in Egypt grew from 17 million in 1998 to 25 million in 2018 (Figure 1.10). This growth at an average annual rate of 1.9 percent p.a. is similar to the 1.8 percent p.a. growth rate of the

---

[8] Owing to an unfortunate translation error, the Arabic questionnaire in 2018 asked about search in the past four weeks rather than past three months, which may lead to a slight underestimation of search.

working age population during that 20-year period (Table 1.2). The similarity of the growth rate of the labor force and that of the working age population over the long run masks substantial variations over time. Over the period 1998–2006, the rate of growth of the standard market labor force substantially exceeded that of the working age population (3.7 percent p.a. versus 2.5 percent p.a.). This was in part because this was a period of rapid growth in the young adult population, as we saw in Table 1.1. This rate slowed substantially in the 2006–12 period, when the standard market labor force grew slower than the working age population

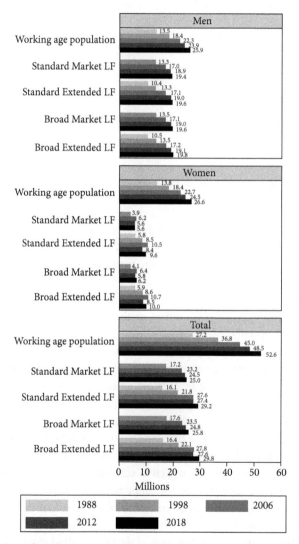

Figure 1.10 Size of working age population and labor force (millions), by definition and sex, ages 15–64, 1988–2018.

Source: Authors' calculations based on data from LFS 1988 and ELMPS 1998–2018.

Table 1.2 Average annual growth rates (percentages) of the working age population and labor force, by definition, 1988–2018.

	Working age pop.	Standard market LF	Standard ext. LF	Broad market LF	Broad ext. LF
Men					
1988–98	3.1		2.0		2.0
1998–2006	2.4	3.0	3.2	2.9	3.1
2006–12	1.2	1.6	1.5	1.6	1.5
2012–18	1.3	0.5	0.6	0.6	0.7
Women					
1988–98	2.9		3.5		3.4
1998–2006	2.7	5.7	2.3	5.6	2.3
2006–12	1.3	−1.7	−4.1	−1.8	−4.1
2012–18	1.4	−0.1	2.8	1.2	3.2
Total					
1988–98	3.0		2.6		2.6
1998–2006	2.5	3.7	2.9	3.6	2.8
2006–12	1.2	0.8	−0.4	0.8	−0.4
2012–18	1.3	0.4	1.3	0.7	1.5

Source: Authors' calculations based on data from LFS 1988 and ELMPS 1998–2018.

(0.8 percent p.a. vs. 1.2 percent p.a.) (Table 1.2). The growth rate of the standard market labor force slowed even further in the 2012–18 period to just 0.4 percent p.a., compared with 1.3 percent p.a. for the working age population. These results imply that the participation rate in the standard market labor force declined substantially at the same time the growth of the potential labor force was slowing.

Using the most expansive definition of the labor force, the broad extended definition, the Egyptian labor force grew from 22 million in 1998 to 30 million in 2018 or at a rate of 1.5 percent p.a., somewhat slower than the growth of the working-age population. Again, there was a great deal of variation over time in the growth of the labor force by this definition. It grew at 2.8 percent p.a. in 1998–2006, contracted by -0.4 percent p.a. from 2006 to 2012, and then grew again by 1.5 percent p.a. from 2012 to 2018. The more rapid growth of the labor force by this definition relative to the standard market definition suggests that the number of discouraged unemployed was growing rapidly, as was the number of individuals (especially women) engaged in subsistence activities at home.

Until 2012, which definition of the labor force one used did not matter too much for men. The male labor force consisted of 13 million in 1998, 17 million in 2006, and 19 million in 2012, regardless of the definition used (Figure 1.10). By 2018, the estimate varied from 19.4 million for the standard market labor force to 19.8 million for the broad extended labor force. However, which definition one uses matters a lot for the estimation of the female labor force. In 1998, the female labor force estimate varied from 3.9 million according to the most restrictive definition (the standard market definition) to more than double, 8.6 million, according to the most expansive definition (the broad extended definition). The difference was almost all owing to the large number of women who engage exclusively in subsistence work. By 2018, the standard market female labor force had grown to 5.6 million, a rate of growth of 1.8 percent p.a. from 1998 to 2018, but the broad extended labor force had grown to 10.0 million, implying a lower growth rate of 0.8 percent p.a. Thus, over time, women in Egypt were somewhat more likely to engage in market work than in subsistence work. The female standard market labor force actually contracted at a rate of 0.1 percent p.a. in the 2012–18 period, in contrast to the female broad extended labor force, which grew at a rate of 3.2 percent p.a. (Table 1.2).

Comparing the standard and broad definitions of the market labor force allows us to ascertain the degree to which discouraged unemployment has grown. The contrast is particularly large for women, for whom the broad market labor force grew at 1.2 percent p.a. as compared to the 0.1 percent p.a. contraction of the standard market labor force over the 2012–18 period. This suggests that discouraged unemployment (which is the difference between the two) grew substantially among women in the 2012–18 period. Although 635,000 women were identified as discouraged unemployed in 2018 (12.4 percent of all active women), 158,000 were identified as such in 2012. These figures imply that the rate of growth of discouraged unemployment between 2012 and 2018 was a dramatic 23 percent p.a. for women, as compared with 11 percent p.a. for men.

1.4.2 Trends in labor force participation

In what follows, we focus on participation using the standard market definition of the labor force. However, Figure 1.11 presents all four labor force definitions. Based on the standard market definition, participation rates have been falling from 2012 to 2018 for both men and women. For the working-age population as a whole, standard market participation rates increased from 47 percent in 1998 to 52 percent in 2006, then fell slightly to 51 percent in 2012, and then fell more sharply to 48 percent in 2018.[9] These totals hide larger differences between men and women. Among men, labor force participation increased from 73 percent in 1998 to 77 percent in 2006 and then to 80 percent in 2012, only to reverse and

---

[9] The standard market labor force participation rate was significantly higher overall for 2006 and 2012 than for 1998, but the 2018 rate was not significantly higher than 1998. Participation was significantly higher for men in 2006–18 than in 1998. It was significantly higher for women in 2006 than in 1998, but not statistically different when comparing 2012 or 2018 with 1998.

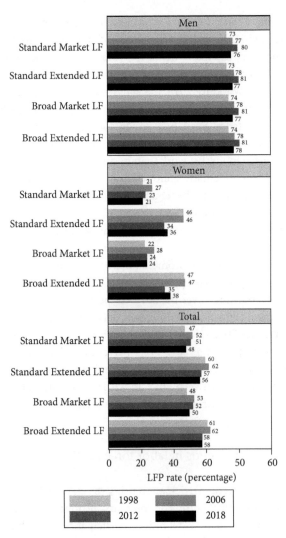

Figure 1.11 Labor force participation rate (percentage), by sex and definition, ages 15–64, 1998–2018.
Source: Authors' calculations based on data from ELMPS 1998–2018.

decrease to 76 percent by 2018. The decline of participation among men is, therefore, a relatively recent phenomenon that requires further investigation.

Women in Egypt have historically had far lower participation rates than men. According to the International Labour Organization (ILO) modelled estimates, female participation rates in Egypt, at 25 percent in 2018 for the 15–64 age group, were the 11th lowest among 189 countries for which the ILO produces estimates (ILO, 2019). These estimates were somewhat higher than the ELMPS 2018 estimate of 21 percent. According to the ELMPS, the female standard market labor force participation rate increased from 21 percent in 1998 to a high of 27 percent in 2006, but declined to 23 percent in 2012 and back to 21 percent in 2018.[10] The declining trends in participation account for the growing divergence we observed between the growth of the working age population (the potential labor supply) and the labor force (the actual labor supply). For men and women in Egypt, the working age population was growing at a rate of 1.3–1.4 percent p.a. from 2012 to 2018 (Table 1.2), but the standard market labor force was only growing at a rate of 0.5 percent p.a. for men and actually contracted at a rate of 0.1 percent p.a. for women in the same period. At least in the case of women, the rapid growth in discouraged unemployment indicates that these trends are not just due to supply side factors but may also be responding to opportunity structures in the economy.

1.4.3 The age profile of labor force participation

As shown in Figure 1.12, labor force participation rates have the usual inverted U-shape by age for both men and women. There were substantial declines in participation from 2012 to 2018 for men at both ends of the age distribution. Men under the age of 35 have experienced sizable declines in participation between 2012 and 2018. There was also a noticeable decline among men above the age of 55. Among women, there was a substantial decline in participation from 2012 to 2018 for all ages through age 40, likely due to diminishing opportunities for young

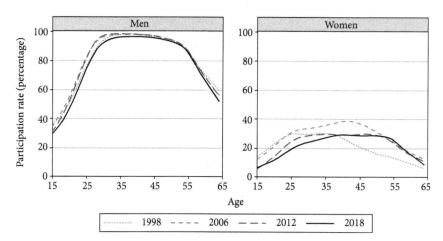

Figure 1.12 Labor force participation rate (percentage), standard market definition, by sex and age, ages 15–64, 1998–2018.

Note: Lowess smoothed running mean with bandwidth 0.4.

Source: Authors' calculations based on data from ELMPS 1998–2018.

---

[10] While standard market female labor force participation rates were similar on average in 1998, 2012, and 2018, there were significant changes in terms of the determinants of participation such as age and education over time.

women to work in the public sector.[11] From age 40 onward, participation rates have remained roughly the same as in 2012.

1.4.4 The education profile of labor force participation

Figure 1.13 shows labor force participation by educational attainment. Labor force participation rates were lowest for men with less than intermediate education (many of whom may still have been in school) and highest among men with little or no education (i.e. illiterate or read and write) and for men with above intermediate education and university or higher. However, participation at these levels for men declined in 2018 across education levels compared with previous waves. Labor force participation among women increased with education. With increasing educational attainment, we would expect higher overall female participation over time. This is not happening, however, because participation rates among educated women have been decreasing substantially over time. For example, at the intermediate level (the most common educational attainment in Egypt) participation has dropped from 42 percent in 1998 to 20 percent in 2018. Similarly, participation among university educated women fell from 73 percent in 1998 to 51 percent in 2018. So, while participation for men fell across all education levels,

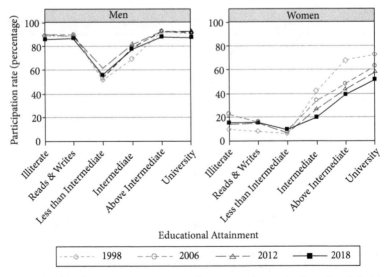

Figure 1.13 Labor force participation rate (percentage), standard market definition, by education and sex, ages 15–64, 1998–2018.
Source: Authors' calculations based on data from ELMPS 1998–2018.

---

[11] For further discussion of employment trends by sector, see Chapter 2.

for women it declined more for the educated, although it remained low for the less educated. The decline in participation among educated women has been attributed to declining employment opportunities in the public sector (Assaad et al., 2020).

1.5 The Evolution of Employment in Egypt

1.5.1 Trends in employment rates

In this section, we examine trends in employment rates (the employment-to-population ratio). Figure 1.14 shows both market and extended employment rates by sex and wave. Aside from a spike in 2006, the extended employment rate has been falling over time. The market employment rate rose from 42 percent in 1998 to 48 percent in 2006, dropped slightly to 47 percent in 2012, and then more precipitously to 44 percent in 2018. Again, for males, there was little difference between the market and extended employment rates. Like labor force participation rates, male employment rates were rising from 1998 to 2012, but then fell from 77 percent in 2012 to 72 percent in 2018.

For women, the market employment rate was almost half the extended rate in 2018, accounting for the large fraction of women engaged in subsistence work. Only 17 percent of Egyptian women aged 15–64 were employed in 2018 according to the market definition, which is now the accepted international definition of

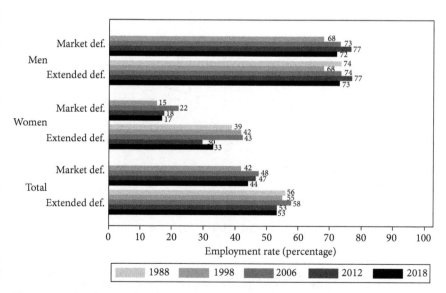

Figure 1.14 Employment rate (percentage), by sex and definition, ages 15–64, 1988–2018.
Note: Employment is based on a seven-day reference period.
Source: Authors' calculations based on data from LFS 1988 and ELMPS 1998–2018.

employment as adopted by the 19th International Conference of Labor Statisticians (ILO, 2013). The decline in female employment rates started earlier than for men. Female market employment rates fell from 22 percent in 2006 to 18 percent in 2012, and declined further to 17 percent from 2012 to 2018.[12]

1.5.2 The age profile of employment rates[13]

The shape of the age profile for men in market employment generally shows rising employment rates through approximately age 30 and then a plateau at over 90 percent from age 30 to 55 (Figure 1.15). Around age 55, male employment rates begin to decline, likely because men begin to retire. However, in 2018, employment rates for young men looked more like 1998 patterns, and the employment rate for prime-age men (ages 30 to 55) was lower than in any previous year. The decline in overall employment rates for men from 2012 to 2018 permeates virtually the entire age distribution.

For women, employment rates appear to rise steadily with age until about age 40, when they flatten out a bit and then decline when women reach their early

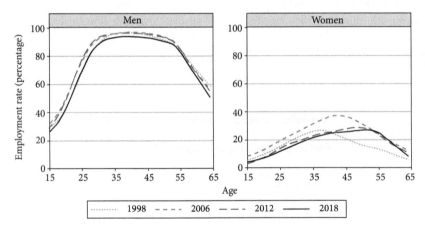

Figure 1.15 Employment rate (percentage), market definition, by sex and age, ages 15–64, 1998–2018.

Note: Employment is based on a seven-day reference period. Lowess smoothed running mean with bandwidth 0.4.

Source: Authors' calculations based on data from ELMPS 1998–2018.

---

[12] While the female market employment rates in 2006 and 2012 were significantly higher than in 1998, the rate in 2018 was not statistically different from 1998. Rates for men and overall were higher in 2006–18 than in 1998.

[13] The subsequent discussion focuses exclusively on the market definition of employment. See Chapter 8 for a more detailed discussion of subsistence employment among rural women in Egypt.

50s. The peak employment rate appears to have steadily shifted to later ages from 1998 to 2006 to 2012. This shift is probably because women who acquired government jobs in the 1970s and 1980s are retaining these jobs until retirement (see Chapter 5 for more on government workers). Although the age profile of employment is similar in 2012 and 2018, we observe a decline in employment rates for women between the ages of 20 and 50.

1.5.3 The education profile of employment rates

As in the case of labor force participation, employment rates decreased from 2012 to 2018 across the education spectrum for men. The pattern of falling participation since 1998 for educated women is reflected in their employment rates. For example, employment rates for women with intermediate education have fallen from 1998 to 2018, going from 22 percent to 15 percent (Figure 1.16). A similar steadily declining trend can be seen for women with above intermediate education and those with university education or above.[14]

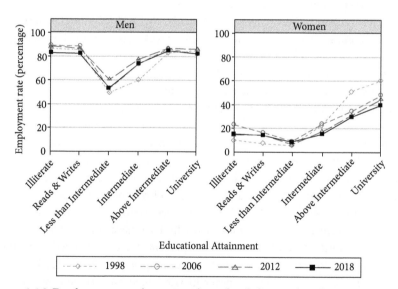

Figure 1.16 Employment rate (percentage), market definition, by education and sex, ages 15–64, 1998–2018.

Note: Employment is based on a seven-day reference period.

Source: Authors' calculations based on data from ELMPS 1998–2018.

---

[14] Changes over time were statistically significant, but educational attainment still had a positive and statistically significant association with market employment even in 2018.

1.5.4   Family formation and employment

After marriage, intra-household dynamics and the changing opportunity cost of time affect married women's decisions to work (Hoodfar, 1997; Hendy, 2015; Assaad, Krafft, and Selwaness, 2017; Selwaness and Krafft, 2021). Since, according to prevalent gender norms in Egypt, women are the primary caregivers, this can substantially shift the opportunity cost of their time and employment decisions. If they engage in market work, women still face an entire "second shift" of domestic responsibilities and care work (Chapter 8; Economic Research Forum and UN Women, 2020). Women's market work is also limited by social norms that prioritize work for men when jobs are scarce, prioritize marriage ahead of career for women, and limit women's work outside the home (Sieverding and Hassan, 2016; El Feki, Heilman, and Barker, 2017). The type of work that is socially acceptable, particularly for married women, also limits women's employment opportunities, with "reservation working conditions" (Dougherty, 2014) that are more easily met in the public than private sector or through home-based self-employment (this point is explored further in Chapter 2). Although some social norms have shifted in favor of greater gender equity in work and society over time, others have remained highly persistent across generations (Sieverding, 2012; El Feki, Heilman, and Barker, 2017; Miyata and Yamada, 2017). Finally, the transformation of the economy away from public sector work has curtailed employment opportunities for married women (See Chapter 2 and Assaad et al., 2020). Public sector work is considered more family-friendly than private wage work, which is less likely to accommodate women's "second shift."

In Figure 1.17, we look at employment rates by sex and marital status for individuals aged 15–64 who were not enrolled in school (as this might bias results for the never married). Overall, rates of employment for ever-married men were much higher than rates for never-married men, since employment is a prerequisite for marriage for men (Assaad, Binzel, and Gadallah, 2010; Krafft and Assaad, 2020). Regardless of marital status, however, employment rates for men decreased substantially between 2012 and 2018; rates decreased seven percentage points (from 73 percent to 66 percent) for men who have never married and by three percentage points (from 92 percent to 89 percent) for ever-married men. These rates were even lower than they were two decades prior in 1998. In 1998, employment rates were 67 percent for never-married men and 91 percent for ever-married men.

In contrast to men, employment rates for never-married women were slightly higher than rates for ever-married women. While employment is a prerequisite to marriage for men, women may work prior to marriage and then exit (Assaad, Krafft, and Selwaness, 2017; Krafft and Assaad, 2020), a trend we will explore further. However, the rate of employment for never-married women has hardly

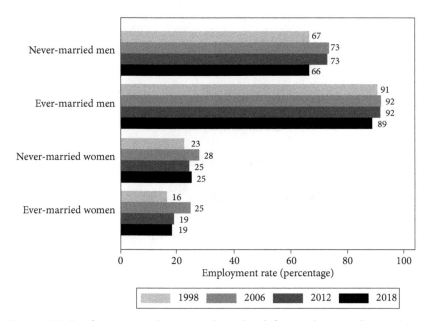

Figure 1.17 Employment rate (percentage), market definition, by sex and marital status, not enrolled in school, ages 15–64, 1998–2018.

Note: Ever-married women includes women who are married, divorced, and widowed. Employment is based on a seven-day reference period.

Source: Authors' calculations based on data from ELMPS 1998–2018.

changed over the past two decades. Most recently, in 2018 the employment rate was 25 percent for never-married women compared with 23 percent in 1998. Similarly, the rate was only 3 percentage points higher for ever-married women in 2018 compared with 1998 (increased from 16 percent to 19 percent) and substantially lower than in 2006 (decreased from 25 percent to 19 percent).

Time and financial constraints related to raising children can influence women's employment decisions. Figure 1.18 examines employment rates for ever-married women aged 20–54 by their youngest child's age—ages 0–2, 3–5, 6–11, and 12–17—compared with ever married women with no children under 18. Analyses start in 2006, the first year with birth history data. Employment rates rise for women as their youngest child gets older. In 2018, the employment rate was 13 percent for ever-married women with a youngest child under two years old, compared with 26 percent for those with a youngest child aged 12–17. However, employment rates have been decreasing over time across all groups. For example, in 2006, the employment rate for women with infants and toddlers (ages 0–2) was 18 percent, and this declined to 13 percent by 2018. Among women with a youngest child aged 12–17, the employment rate was 38 percent in 2006 compared with 26 percent in 2018.

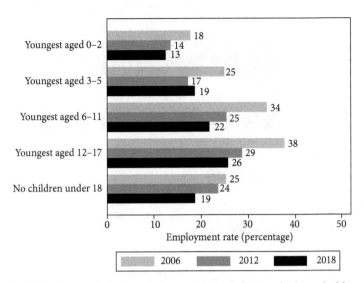

Figure 1.18 Employment rate (percentage), market definition, by household composition, ever-married women aged 20–54, 2006–18.

Note: Ever-married women includes women who are married, divorced, and widowed. Employment is based on a seven-day reference period.

Source: Authors' calculations based on data from ELMPS 2006–18.

Women exit the private sector at marriage, contributing to lower employment rates among married women. Figure 1.19 shows labor market status by years since marriage for men and women for those who married in the 20 years prior to the 2018 wave.[15] Zero represents the year of marriage. Men's employment rises in the run-up to marriage (negative years). Private sector employment for men peaks right at marriage and remains stable for a few years thereafter before falling; this decrease is likely men transitioning into public sector and non-wage jobs. The high rates of employment in the years preceding marriage, for men, allow them to both be promising marital prospects and accumulate the resources necessary to marry (Krafft and Assaad, 2020). Women's participation in private sector employment peaks two years before marriage, drops slightly one year before marriage as women anticipate their change in marital status, and then is cut in half from 4 percent to 2 percent the year of marriage. In contrast, public sector employment continues to rise with time and is hardly affected by the timing of marriage. Non-wage work also rises for women, more so at and after marriage, as new opportunities may open up as well as non-wage work, which is often home-based, being easier to reconcile with marriage (see Chapter 6). These trends strongly underscore the lack of compatibility between

---

[15] Note the difference in the y-axis scale between the two panels.

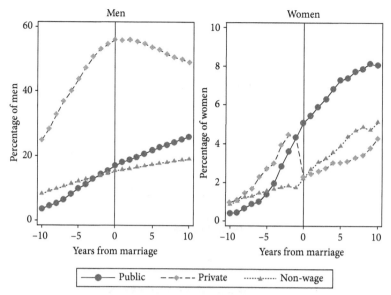

Figure 1.19 Employment status by years since marriage and sex (percentage), individuals married in the 20 years preceding the 2018 wave, aged 15–64, 2018.
Note: The y-axis scale is different across the two panels.
Source: Authors' calculations based on data from ELMPS 2018.

private sector wage work and women's marital responsibilities (Hendy, 2011, 2015; Assaad, Krafft, and Selwaness, 2017).

1.6 The Evolution of Unemployment in Egypt

Unemployment in Egypt is primarily a structural challenge rather than a cyclical phenomenon (Krafft and Assaad, 2014b). The age and education profile of the labor force, as well as the number of educated new entrants, are key drivers of unemployment rates. We begin this section by examining trends in unemployment rates by definition and sex. We follow with age and education profiles of the standard market definition of unemployment by sex.

1.6.1 Trends in unemployment

Since 2006, the standard (search required) market rate of unemployment has been relatively stable, varying between 8.2 percent and 8.7 percent, after having come down from 11.7 percent in 1998 (Figure 1.20). Since differences in trends across the extended and market definitions of employment were similar, we focus

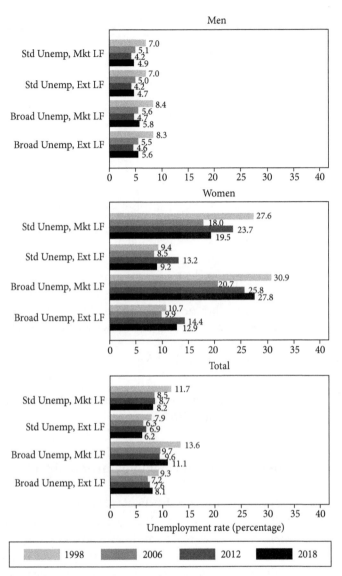

Figure 1.20 Unemployment rate (percentage), by sex and definition, ages 15–64, 1998–2018.

Note: Unemployment uses a seven-day reference period.

Source: Authors' calculations based on data from ELMPS 1998–2018.

here on the market definition. The broad definition of unemployment, which includes the discouraged unemployed, tells a slightly different story. While broad, market unemployment was 9.7 percent in 2006 and 9.6 percent in 2012, it then increased in 2018 to 11.1 percent, an increase of almost two percentage points from 2012, although it was still below the 1998 rate of 13.6 percent.

The overall unemployment rate masks the large differences in unemployment between men and women in Egypt. Men's standard market unemployment rate in 2018, at 4.9 percent, was almost the same as in 2006 (5.1 percent) and slightly above where it was in 2012 (4.2 percent), but well below 1998 (7.0 percent). Broad market unemployment rates were up in 2018 for men, rising from a low of 4.7 percent in 2012 to 5.8 percent in 2018. Women's unemployment rates were four times those of men (19.5 percent using the standard market definition in 2018). Although women's standard market unemployment rate fell from 2012 (23.7 percent) to 2018 (19.5 percent), the broad market unemployment rate rose from 2006 to 25.8 percent in 2012 and 27.8 percent in 2018. The rise in broad unemployment, wherein individuals want to work but were not actively searching, suggests that an increasing share of individuals in the labor force were discouraged about their job opportunities.

1.6.2 The age profile of unemployment

Unemployment is primarily a new entrant phenomenon in Egypt. As shown in Figure 1.21, unemployment rates for men peaked at earlier ages, in the late teens, in 2018, and were higher for the youngest men in 2018 than in 2006 or 2012. In those years, the peak unemployment rate for men was closer to ages 22–25. As we shall see, these patterns were closely linked to changes in unemployment by education. Unemployment in the 35 years and older range, for men, was notably

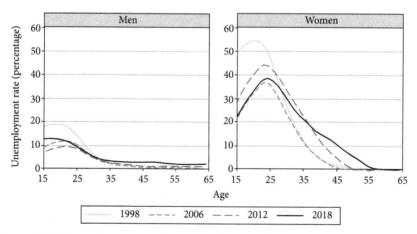

Figure 1.21 Unemployment rate (percentage), standard market definition, by sex and age, ages 15–64, 1998–2018.

Note: Unemployment is based on a seven-day reference period. Lowess smoothed running mean with bandwidth 0.4.

Source: Authors' calculations based on data from ELMPS 1998–2018.

higher in 2018 than in previous waves, albeit still much lower than at young ages. In 2018, unemployment peaked at almost 40 percent for women aged 25 and remained over 20 percent through age 35. Although the peak around age 25 was similar to 2006 and 2012, rates were higher at older ages (35 and above) than in previous rounds. Unemployment for women was extending into older ages, the counterpoint to falling employment rates at these ages.

1.6.3 The education profile of unemployment

In 2018, the male unemployment rate had increased for the less educated but remained similar to 2012 for those with intermediate and higher education (Figure 1.22). The rise in less-educated unemployment was linked with the rise in late teen unemployment, as less educated young men enter the labor market early. While historically unemployment was a young, educated new entrant phenomenon, for men at least, the unemployment-education relationship has weakened considerably over time. The female unemployment rate in 2018 had also increased for the less educated, but unemployment rates remained highest among those with intermediate and higher education, around 25 percent. This rate has prevailed for the university educated since 2006. Notably, the unemployment rate for those with intermediate education fell substantially between 2012 and 2018. Since

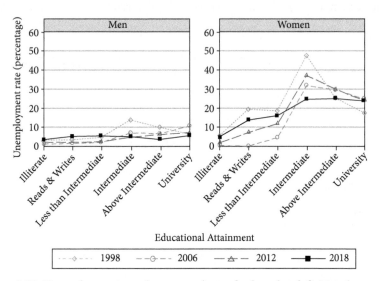

Figure 1.22 Unemployment rate (percentage), standard market definition, by education and sex, ages 15–64, 1998–2018.

Note: Unemployment is based on a seven-day reference period.

Source: Authors' calculations based on data from ELMPS 1998–2018.

these women have not increased their employment, they are particularly likely to have been withdrawing from participation.

1.7 Conclusions

Since the 1980s, Egypt has experienced demographic developments that have strongly shaped the size and composition of labor supply. The most notable among them is the emergence of the youth bulge phenomenon in the late 1980s and 1990s. The bulge is now well past peak labor market insertion ages. The aging of the bulge has led to very slow growth or even contraction of the youth and young adult populations in recent years and therefore attenuated labor supply pressures. Nevertheless, these pressures will soon start building again as the large echo generation, the children of the youth bulge generation, reach labor market entry age in the next ten to fifteen years. The size of this generation was made even bigger by a temporary but substantial increase in fertility that started between 2008 and 2012. This generation, centered around school entry age, has placed enormous pressures on the schooling system and this pressure will soon be transmitted to labor markets. Policymakers need to prepare for these forth-coming challenges. Education levels continue to rise in Egypt, albeit less rapidly than before, as secondary education has become more prevalent and university enrollments have reached higher levels.

The attenuation of demographic pressures on labor supply has been compounded by decreasing participation (and employment) rates among both men and women. The decline in participation among women has been ongoing since 2006, despite the closing of the gender gap in education and the historically strong relationship between participation and education for Egyptian women. In fact, falling participation rates among educated women have more than made up for the shifting composition toward groups with higher education levels, leading to an overall drop in women's participation. The decline in participation among educated women can in turn be explained by declining employment opportunities in the public sector at a time when the private sector continues to be inhospitable to women, particularly married women (Assaad et al., 2020). Gender norms about care work and women's market work limit whether and what work outside the home is acceptable. These norms have changed little over time (Sieverding, 2012; Dougherty, 2014; Sieverding and Hassan, 2016; El Feki, Heilman, and Barker, 2017; Miyata and Yamada, 2017; Economic Research Forum and UN Women, 2020). Weak labor demand overall, and even more so in sectors that employ women (Assaad et al., 2019) further con-strains women's employment opportunities.

The decline in participation among men is a more recent phenomenon that is less well understood. The falling participation spanned a variety of ages well beyond the ages of schooling, suggesting that it was not just a delay due to rising levels of education. Some of it was at the older end of the age distribution, suggesting earlier retirements. The decline involved men at all education levels and not just those who might have been pursuing more schooling. Coupled with evidence about rising rates of discouraged unemployment, it suggests that the declining trend in participation may be due, at least in part, to deteriorating opportunity structures and weak labor demand (Assaad et al., 2019; Assaad, Krafft, and Yassin, 2020), but this is clearly a trend in need of further investigation.

As of 2018, unemployment, by the standard definition, had remained very stable, but broad unemployment, which does not require active job search, had increased, implying higher levels of discouragement. The increase in discouragement was much higher among women than among men, further suggesting that declining participation was due to a less hospitable labor market. There were signs that unemployment had decreased for educated men but risen for the less educated as well as those in their teens and prime aged; this constitutes an important shift in the nature of male unemployment away from educated new entrants. For women, unemployment remained predominantly an educated, new entrant phenomenon, although now persisting into even later ages. Continuing to track and further research these developments will be critically important for understanding the future of Egypt's labor market and economy.

The COVID-19 pandemic and ensuing economic challenges, which began after our data were collected, have the potential to radically reshape labor supply and particularly female labor force participation in Egypt. Unemployment, which had declined a little from 2018 to early 2020, increased to 9.6 percent overall in the second quarter of 2020, up from 7.7 percent in the first quarter (CAPMAS, 2020a, 2020b). Employment rates for both men and women fell (particularly vulnerable groups are discussed in Chapter 2). Men's unemployment rates rose substantially from 4.5 percent in the first quarter of 2020 to 8.5 percent in the second quarter, while women's unemployment rates fell from 22 percent to 16 percent. Women were more likely to withdraw from the labor force altogether. Women's labor force participation rates went from 16 percent in the first quarter of 2020 to 12 percent in the second quarter of 2020 (CAPMAS, 2020a, 2020b). Women's disproportionate caregiving responsibilities, while schools and nurseries were shut and subsequently remained less available (CARE, 2020; OECD, 2020), may preclude those who were working from returning to work and those who might seek work from doing so. Norms that already strongly emphasized prioritizing jobs for men in times of scarcity (Chapter 8; El Feki, Heilman, and Barker, 2017), may lead to further reductions in women's labor force participation as the economic challenges continue. Understanding both Egypt's pre-existing labor supply challenges and the impact of COVID-19 will be a critical area for future research.

Acknowledgments

We acknowledge the general support of the World Bank, the International Labour Organization, Agence Française de Développement, UN Women, and the Arab Fund for Economic and Social Development for the Egypt Labor Market Panel Survey 2018, on which this chapter is based. The authors appreciate the research assistance of Barbara Salinas. We appreciate the comments of participants in the 2019 "The Egyptian Labor Market: A Focus on Gender and Economic Vulnerability" workshop, especially those of our discussant Magued Osman.

References

Assaad, R. (ed.). (2002) *The Egyptian Labor Market in an Era of Reform*. Cairo: American University in Cairo Press.

Assaad, R. (ed.). (2009) *The Egyptian Labor Market Revisited*. Cairo: American University in Cairo Press.

Assaad, R. (2010) Equality for All? Egypt's Free Public Higher Education Policy Breeds Inequality of Opportunity, Economic Research Forum Policy Perspective. 2. Cairo.

Assaad, R. (2020) "Prospects for Egypt's Population and Labor Force: 2000 to 2050." Economic Research Forum Working Paper Series No. 1398. Cairo.

Assaad, R. and G. Barsoum (2000) Egypt Labor Market Survey, 1998: Report on the Data Collection and Preparation. Cairo, Egypt. Available at: http://www.erfdataportal.com/index.php/catalog/28/download/260 (Accessed online July 8, 2021).

Assaad, R., C. Binzel, and M. Gadallah (2010) "Transitions to Employment and Marriage among Young Men in Egypt." *Middle East Development Journal*, 2 (1): 39–88.

Assaad, R. and C. Krafft (2013) "The Egypt Labor Market Panel Survey: Introducing the 2012 Round." *IZA Journal of Labor & Development*, 2 (8): 1–30.

Assaad, R. and C. Krafft (eds). (2015a) *The Egyptian Labor Market in an Era of Revolution*. Oxford: Oxford University Press.

Assaad, R. and C. Krafft (2015b) "The Evolution of Labor Supply and Unemployment in The Egyptian Economy: 1988–2012," in R. Assaad and C. Krafft (eds) *The Egyptian Labor Market in an Era of Revolution*, pp. 1–26. Oxford: Oxford University Press.

Assaad, R., C. Krafft, and D.J. Rolando (2021) "Evaluating the Impact of Housing Market Liberalization on the Timing of Marriage: Evidence from Egypt" *Population Studies*, DOI: 10.1080/00324728.2021.1914853.

Assaad, R., C. Krafft, and I. Selwaness (2017) "The Impact of Marriage on Women's Employment in the Middle East and North Africa." Economic Research Forum Working Paper Series No. 1086. Cairo.

Assaad, R., C. Krafft, and S. Yassin (2020). "Job Creation or Labor Absorption? An Analysis of Private Sector Job Growth in Egypt." *Middle East Development Journal*, 12 (2): 177–207. doi: 10.1080/17938120.2020.1753978.

Assaad, R. and M. Ramadan (2008) "Did Housing Policy Reforms Curb the Delay in Marriage Among Young Men in Egypt?" Middle East Youth Initiative Policy Outlook, 1. Washington, DC.

Assaad, R. and F. Roudi-Fahimi (2007) "Youth in the Middle East and North Africa: Demographic Opportunity or Challenge?" Population Reference Bureau Policy Brief. Washington, DC.

Assaad, R. et al. (2019) "Job Creation in Egypt: A Sectoral and Geographical Analysis Focusing on Private Establishments, 1996–2017." Economic Research Forum Policy Research Report. Cairo.

Assaad, R. et al. (2020) "Explaining the MENA Paradox: Rising Educational Attainment, Yet Stagnant Female Labor Force Participation." *Demographic Research*, 43 (28): 817–50.

Barsoum, G. (2009) "Methodological Appendix 1: The Egypt Labor Market Panel Survey 2006: Documentation of the Data Collection Process," in R. Assaad. (ed.) *The Egyptian Labor Market Revisited*, pp. 259–84. Cairo: American University in Cairo Press.

CAPMAS (Central Agency for Public Mobilization and Statistics). (2019) *Egypt in Figures 2019*. Cairo: CAPMAS.

CAPMAS (2020a) Quarterly Bulletin of the Labor Force Survey, First Quarter, Jan/Feb/Mar 2020. Cairo: CAPMAS.

CAPMAS (2020b) Quarterly Bulletin of the Labor Force Survey, Second Quarter, Apr/May/Jun 2020. Cairo: CAPMAS.

CARE (2020) CARE MENA COVID-19 Response: Rapid Gender Analysis – COVID-19 Middle East and North Africa Region. CARE.

Dougherty, C. (2014) "The Labour Market for Youth in Egypt: Evidence from the 2012 School to Work Transition Survey." Silatech, Working Paper 14–2. Doha.

Economic Research Forum and UN Women (2020) Progress of Women in the Arab States 2020: The Role of the Care Economy in Promoting Gender Equality. Cairo: UN Women.

El Feki, S., B. Heilman, and G. Barker (eds) (2017) Understanding Masculinities: Results from the International Men and Gender Equality Survey (IMAGES)—Middle East and North Africa. UN Women and Promundo-US.

El-Zanaty, F. and A. Way (2009) *Egypt Demographic and Health Survey 2008*. Cairo: Ministry of Health, El-Zanaty and Associates, and Macro International.

Hendy, R. (2011) Marriage and Labor Market Transitions: A Structural Dynamic Model. Mimeo.

Hendy, R. (2015) "Women's Participation in the Egyptian Labor Market: 1998–2012," in R. Assaad and C. Krafft (eds) *The Egyptian Labor Market in an Era of Revolution*, pp. 147–61. Oxford: Oxford University Press.

Hoodfar, H. (1997) Between Marriage and the Market: Intimate Politics and Survival in Cairo. Berkeley: University of California Press.

ILO (International Labour Organization) (2013) Resolution Concerning Statistics of Work, Employment, and Labour Underutilization Adopted by the Nineteenth International Conference of Labour Statisticians (October 2013).

ILO. (2019) Labour Force Participation Rate by Sex and Age—ILO Modelled Estimates, July 2018 (%). Available at: www.ilo.org/ilostat (Accessed: August 21, 2019).

Krafft, C. (2020) "Why is Fertility on the Rise in Egypt? The Role of Women's Employment Opportunities." *Journal of Population Economics*, 33 (4): 1173–1218. doi: 10.1007/s00148-020-00770-w.

Krafft, C. and R. Assaad (2014a) "Beware of the Echo: The Impending Return of Demographic Pressures in Egypt." Economic Research Forum Policy Perspective, 12. Cairo.

Krafft, C. and R. Assaad (2014b) "Why the Unemployment Rate is a Misleading Indicator of Labor Market Health in Egypt." Economic Research Forum Policy Perspective, 14. Cairo.

Krafft, C. and R. Assaad (2020) "Employment's Role in Enabling and Constraining Marriage in the Middle East and North Africa." *Demography*, 57: 2297–2325. doi: 10.1007/s13524-020-00932-1.

Krafft, C., R. Assaad, and K.W. Rahman (2021) "Introducing the Egypt Labor Market Panel Survey 2018." *IZA Journal of Development and Migration* (Forthcoming).

Miller, P. and N. Hirschhorn (1995) "The Effect of a National Control of Diarrheal Diseases Program on Mortality: The Case of Egypt." *Social Science & Medicine*, 40 (10): S1–S30.

Ministry of Health and Population, El-Zanaty and Associates, and ICF International (2015) *Egypt Demographic and Health Survey*. Cairo: Ministry of Health and Population and ICF International.

Miyata, S. and H. Yamada (2017) "Do Female Gender Role Attitudes Affect Labour Market Participation in Egypt?" *The Journal of Development Studies*, 52 (6): 876–94. doi: 10.1080/00220388.2015.1113262.

OECD (Organisation for Economic Co-Operation and Development). (2020) COVID-19 Crisis in the MENA Region: Impact on Gender Equality and Policy Responses, Tackling Coronavirus (COVID-19): Contributing to a Global Effort. Paris: OECD.

Rashad, H. (1989) "Oral Rehydration Therapy and its Effect on Child Mortality in Egypt." *Journal of Biosocial Science*, 21 (S10): 105–13. doi: 10.1017/S0021932000025311.

Robinson, W. and F. El-Zanaty (2006) *The Demographic Revolution in Modern Egypt*. Lanham, MD: Lexington Books.

Selwaness, I. and C. Krafft (2021) "The Dynamics of Family Formation and Women's Work: What Facilitates and Hinders Female Employment in the Middle East and North Africa?" *Population Research and Policy Review*, 40: 533–87.

Sieverding, M. (2012) *Gender and Generational Change in Egypt*. PhD thesis. Berkeley: University of California.

Sieverding, M. and R. Hassan (2016) "Her Future is Marriage": Young People's Attitudes towards Gender Roles and the Gender Gap in Egypt. Cairo: Population Council.

World Bank (2020) Egypt Economic Monitor: From Crisis to Economic Transformation: Unlocking Egypt's Productivity and Job-Creation Potential. Washington, DC: World Bank.

Yount, K. M., R. Langsten, and K. Hill (2000) "The Effect of Gender Preference on Contraceptive Use and Fertility in Rural Egypt." *Studies in Family Planning*, 31 (4): 290–300. doi: 10.2307/172237.

2

Is the Egyptian Economy Creating Good Jobs? Job Creation and Economic Vulnerability, 1998–2018

Ragui Assaad, Abdelaziz Alsharawy, and Colette Salemi

2.1 Introduction

The global financial crisis of 2008–9 and the January 25, 2011 revolution led to a period of economic crisis and instability in Egypt. Gross domestic product (GDP) growth slowed substantially in 2011 and remained below population growth through 2013. After 2013, assistance from Gulf countries helped to narrow the widening external and fiscal balance and shore up rapidly depleting foreign exchange reserves, leading to a modest recovery in GDP growth (World Bank, 2015). This assistance soon dried up, resulting in a severe foreign exchange crisis in 2015/16. Eventually, this crisis forced the Egyptian government to adopt a multi-year stabilization program sponsored by the International Monetary Fund (IMF) in late 2016. The centerpiece of the program was a flotation of the Egyptian pound in November 2016, leading to a substantial devaluation of the currency. But the program also included fiscal consolidation through a new value added tax and a reduction in pervasive energy subsidies (World Bank, 2019). The devaluation of the pound caused a spike in inflation that lasted nearly a year, through the end of 2017 (World Bank, 2019). The stabilization program appears to have been successful in curbing the large balance of payments and fiscal deficits and in restoring economic growth, which had reached 5.3 percent in the financial year 2017/18.[1] But the impacts of the crisis and the subsequent stabilization program on both the quantity and quality of employment in the Egyptian economy have not yet been ascertained.

The 2018 wave of the Egypt Labor Market Panel Survey (ELMPS) offers a valuable opportunity to examine changes in employment that correspond to these economic developments. Building on the 2012 wave, which took place during the

[1] See the Introduction for more details about the macroeconomic and policy environment preceding the 2018 wave of the ELMPS, on which this chapter is based.

Ragui Assaad, Abdelaziz Alsharawy, and Colette Salemi, *Is the Egyptian Economy Creating Good Jobs? Job Creation and Economic Vulnerability, 1998–2018* In: *The Egyptian Labor Market: A Focus on Gender and Economic Vulnerability.* Edited by: Caroline Krafft and Ragui Assaad, Oxford University Press. © Economic Research Forum 2022. DOI: 10.1093/oso/9780192847911.003.0003

depths of the post-revolution crisis, the 2018 wave allows us to ascertain whether there was substantial recovery in the employment situation both in terms of quantity and quality of jobs.

One of the primary ways in which the post-revolution crisis affected the Egyptian labor market was to exacerbate the precariousness of employment, especially among informal workers in the private sector (Krafft and Assaad, 2014). Although there were some increases in open unemployment, the major effects of the crisis were seen in the increase of irregularity in employment and in the rates of involuntary part-time work among informally employed workers (Assaad and Krafft, 2015).[2]

In addition to these cyclical factors, there have been long-run structural factors affecting the Egyptian economy, including the gradual decline of employment in agriculture, the ongoing process of de-industrialization, the boom in high-end real estate and construction sectors, and the downsizing of government and public enterprise employment (Assaad and Barsoum, 2009; Assaad et al., 2019; Ayed Mouelhi and Ghazali, 2020; World Bank, 2020). These trends have been ongoing since the early 1980s and have had profound effects on the labor market.

Accordingly, our objective in this chapter is to determine the quantity and quality of the jobs being created in the Egyptian economy over the 20-year period from 1998 to 2018. By focusing on job quality, we can examine the prevalence and distribution of vulnerable work in Egypt over time. Following from the discussion in the Introduction of this book, we argue that certain types of work exacerbate household-level vulnerabilities to shocks. For example, a household may face an economic crisis if the primary earners are working informally (without health insurance) and those workers become too sick to earn a wage. Vulnerable work not only erodes resiliency to shocks, but can also increase household exposure to shocks. For example, if the worker is more exposed to workplace hazards and faces a higher likelihood of workplace injuries, then an unanticipated shock (illness or injury) may first manifest on the job site. Throughout this paper, we are particularly attentive to signs of worker vulnerability such as informality, irregularity, lack of benefits, working outside fixed establishments, and exposure to workplace hazards.

We complement our evaluation of work quality and worker vulnerability with an examination of worker satisfaction. To do so, we examine variations in worker self-reported satisfaction with their jobs. We also examine the degree of underemployment in terms of both involuntary part-time work and the match between educational qualifications and the requirements of one's job.

---

[2] Open unemployment is defined as not working a single hour during the reference week, desiring to work, and being available for it, whereas involuntary part-time work (or visible underemployment) is defined as working fewer than 35 hours per week because of not finding work for the remainder of the time.

Our findings indicate that the economic recovery of 2013–18 was essentially a jobless recovery. Although employment to population ratios (EPRs) were pro-cyclical in the past with some lag, in this recovery EPRs have continued to fall, suggesting that employment was not keeping up with population growth despite the recovery in GDP growth rates. This relatively negative picture on the growth of overall employment is counteracted by the fact that a smaller proportion of informal workers described their work as irregular, and a smaller proportion of workers were in involuntary part-time employment in 2018 than in 2012.

With regard to the evolution of the quality of employment over time, we find that, with the continued contraction of the public sector and the slow growth of formal private wage employment, the informalization of employment continued apace. Informal wage employment, in particular, continued to increase as a share of total employment, going from 24 percent in 2006 to 31 percent in 2012 to 39 percent in 2018. Informal wage employment outside a fixed establishment— which as we will show, was one of the most vulnerable forms of employment in Egypt—nearly doubled its share in overall employment from 12 percent in 2006 to 23 percent in 2018, a reflection of the rapid growth of the construction and transport sectors in the Egyptian economy. Although informal wage work outside establishments was more likely to be irregular than other forms of employment, the extent of irregularity within it had declined since 2012, leading to an overall decline in employment irregularity. Nonetheless, the high and growing percent-age of workers undertaking informal wage work outside establishments under-scores the vulnerability of these workers to economic downturns, such as the one caused by the COVID-19 crisis. Workers employed within private establishments were increasingly more likely to be in small, as opposed to micro-establishments. This should bode well for job quality, as small establishments were more likely than micro-establishments to provide formal jobs and more likely to provide paid and sick leave and health insurance. However, the positive development in terms of the distribution of employment by establishment size was counteracted by the increased informalization of employment within small and even medium and large establishments, resulting in higher rates of informality overall.

Our findings on the decline of formality in the Egyptian labor market have important distributional implications. Poor workers (as measured by the lowest quintile of an asset index) never had much access to formal employment, and that access continued to decline marginally. On the other hand, workers in the top quintile continued to have good access to formal jobs as they increasingly transi-tioned to formal private sector jobs as public sector employment contracted. It was workers in the middle of the wealth distribution whose access to formal employment was substantially reduced as the increase in formal private employ-ment failed to compensate for the decline in public employment. With non-wage employment also declining for these groups, they became increasingly reliant on informal wage employment, and in particular on this kind of employment outside fixed establishments, which we have identified as the most vulnerable form of employment in Egypt. This finding is in line with other writings that have documented the hollowing out of the middle class in Egypt as public sector employment declines (Assaad et al., 2018; Devarajan and Ianchovichina, 2018; Diwan, 2013).

Women in Egypt were much less likely than men to engage in informal wage employment outside establishments owing to the widespread perception that such employment exposes them to unacceptable risks of harassment and insecurity (Barsoum, 2019). They responded to the decline in public sector employment and the anemic growth of formal private employment in part by staying out of the workforce as documented in Chapter 1, and in part by increasing their participation in both informal wage and non-wage work inside establishments. Poor women in particular had large declines in the share of employment in non-wage work outside establishments, most of which was home-based work, and increased shares of non-wage work in establishments and informal wage work.

Besides suffering from high levels of employment irregularity, informal wage and non-wage workers outside fixed establishments had the highest levels of workplace hazards, relatively high rates of workplace injuries, and, together with other informal workers, high degrees of overqualification for their jobs.

Finally, in analyzing the results on overall job satisfaction and different aspects of jobs' satisfaction, we found that levels of satisfaction closely reflected actual job conditions. As expected, the lowest levels of job satisfaction were expressed by informal wage workers outside establishments, followed by their counterparts employed inside establishments. Non-wage workers generally had higher levels of job satisfaction and formally employed wage workers had the highest levels. But we also found that levels of job satisfaction rose the most between 2012 and 2018 for the workers who were the least satisfied in 2018, suggesting that differences in favor of formally employed workers were even larger in 2012. The greater improvement in satisfaction among the most vulnerable workers was ostensibly a reflection of the relative improvement in job security they had experienced as the economy recovered.

2.2 Employment and GDP Growth

An examination of the relationship between employment and GDP growth in Egypt reveals that employment is quite responsive to growth, but with a one- to two-year lag. As shown in Figure 2.1, GDP growth in Egypt has varied substantially over time since the early 2000s. After a period of sharp deceleration in the early 2000s, GDP growth recovered gradually in the mid-2000s to reach 7 percent per annum (p.a.) in 2007–8. It decelerated again during, and shortly after, the Global Financial Crisis in 2009 and 2010 before virtually collapsing after

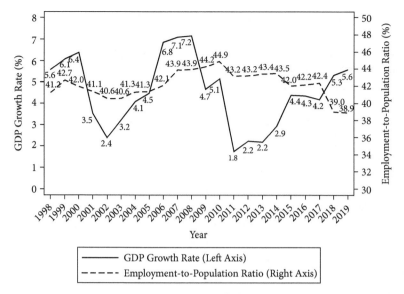

Figure 2.1 Annual GDP growth rate and employment-to-population ratio (EPR) (percentage), aged 15+, 1998–2019.

Source: GDP growth rates are from World Bank World Development Indicators, except for 2018 and 2019, which are from IMF (2020). Employment to population ratios are from the Annual Bulletins of the Labor Force Survey (CAPMAS, n.d.).

the outbreak of the January 25, 2011 revolution, when it fell to 1.8 percent p.a., a rate substantially lower than the average rate of population growth in the 2006–17 period (2.5 percent p.a.) (CAPMAS, 2019). It remained close to that depressed level until 2013. GDP growth began to recover in 2014 and 2015, and stalled in 2016 and 2017 prior to and soon after the adoption of the IMF-supported stabilization program toward the end of 2016. Growth recovered again in 2018, reaching 5.3 percent p.a., and accelerated further to 5.6 percent p.a. in 2019 (IMF, 2020). Despite a contraction at an annual rate of 1.7 percent p.a. at the height of the COVID-19 lockdown in the April to June quarter of 2020, World Bank estimates place the annual growth rate for 2020 at 3.6 percent p.a. (World Bank, 2021).

As shown in Figure 2.1, employment rates, as measured by the employment to population ratio (EPR) for the population aged 15 and older, responded positively to growth in the mid-2000s, but with a lag. In conjunction with the acceleration of growth in this period, the EPR rose from around 41 percent in 2002 to 44 percent in 2008. It continued to rise to about 45 percent by 2010 despite the deceleration in growth in 2009. However, since 2011, the EPR has been on a continuous downward trend despite the resumption of GDP growth in 2014. Most notably, the recent acceleration of growth from 2017 to 2018 was not accompanied by a reversal in the decline of the EPR. By 2018, the EPR had declined to 39 percent, an even lower level than in 2001 and 2002, when GDP growth was at its lowest levels.[3] Thus, the most recent recovery in GDP growth has not (yet) generated the sort of employment growth that raises the EPR as recoveries have done in the past.

Using data on aggregate employment and GDP from 2000 to 2017 and a simple ordinary least squares regression method, we estimate an employment elasticity with respect to GDP in Egypt of 0.90, which is quite high by international standards, but in line with previous estimates for the Middle East region.[4] This figure suggests that a 1 percent change in GDP spurs an almost analogous percentage change in employment of 0.9. Kapsos (2006) provides estimates for the elasticity of total employment with respect to GDP for a wide range of countries and world regions. According to these estimates, the average elasticity for the world in the 1999–2003 period was 0.30, but the average for the Middle East was 0.91, for North Africa 0.51, for Sub-Saharan Africa 0.53, and for Southeast Asia 0.82. These estimates and the data shown in Figure 2.1 suggest that employment at the extensive margin (i.e. as measured by the number of people employed for at least one hour in the reference week) did respond to economic growth in the past, albeit with some delay. Later, we also examine the intensive margin of employment, as measured by the number of hours of work per week and the extent of visible underemployment as measured by involuntary part-time work. However, the recent apparent de-linking between economic growth and changes in the EPR that we can observe since 2014 in Egypt indicates that, at least at the extensive margin, the employment response to the recent expansion of economic activity has not kept up with the growth of the working age population.

2.3 The Changing Composition of Employment

In this section, we start by examining the structure of employment over time along a typology that we create from various job characteristics, namely the sector of ownership, formality, work inside or outside fixed establishments, and employment status. We refer to this job taxonomy as the type of employment. We then move to analyze employment by industry to examine the evolving structure of the economy over time.

The ELMPS measures employment according to two definitions, namely the market and extended definitions, and for two reference periods, a short period of one week prior to the interview and a long one of three months prior to the

---

[3] The ELMPS estimates employment rates for the population 15–64 to have declined from 47 percent in 2012 to 44 percent in 2018, essentially following the same trend as the Labor Force Survey (see Chapter 1).
[4] Using data from the World Bank World Development Indicators for GDP and the Labor Force Survey for employment, we regressed the natural log of employment on the national log of GDP from 2000 to 2017 using OLS. We obtained a coefficient of 0.896 with a standard error of 0.191. The R^2 for the regression was 0.58.

interview. The market definition corresponds to the definition of employment recommended by the 19th International Conference of Labor Statisticians (ICLS) (ILO, 2013), which restricts the definition of employment to work for pay or profit. The extended definition adds to employment based on the market definition subsistence work, or work for the purpose of producing or processing primary commodities even if these activities are exclusively for the purpose of the household's own consumption. In Egypt, the use of the extended versus the market definition typically makes little difference for male employment but has a large effect on female employment rates, owing to widespread involvement of women in animal husbandry and related activities for their household's consumption (see Chapter 1; Langsten and Salem, 2008). In what follows, we use the market definition of employment unless otherwise stated. We also use employment in the short reference period of one week, which is referred to as "current" employment, as opposed to "usual" employment when the longer reference period is used.[5]

2.3.1 Structure of employment by type of employment

The taxonomy of type of employment that we have created consists of six mutually exclusive categories:

1) Public sector employment, which includes government and public enterprise employment. The category is almost entirely made up of formal wage work, so we do not break it down further along formality and employment status.
2) Formal private wage work, which requires that a worker be hired for a wage in the private sector and have either a legal contract (of definite or indefinite duration) or social insurance coverage. This category consists almost entirely of workers working within fixed establishments, so we do not break it down further along this dimension.
3) Informal private wage work inside fixed establishments, which requires that workers be hired for a wage by a private sector employer without the benefit of either a legal contract or social insurance and be working inside a fixed establishment, such as a shop, office building, factory, or workshop.
4) Informal private wage workers outside fixed establishments, which requires that workers be hired as wage workers by a private sector employer without the benefit of either a legal contract or social insurance and be working

---

[5] The ELMPS collects detailed information on job characteristics for the longest duration main job in the three-month reference period. However, this essentially corresponds to the main job in the one-week reference period, as only 3 percent of employed individuals had changed their main jobs between the three-month and one-week reference periods.

outside a fixed establishment, such as in a private home, a field, a construction site, or on a moving vehicle.

5) Non-wage work inside establishments, which includes employers, self-employed individuals, and unpaid family workers working inside fixed establishments.

6) Non-wage work outside establishments, which includes employers, self-employed individuals, and unpaid family workers working outside fixed establishments.

Figure 2.2 shows the structure of employment by type for men and women of working age in Egypt according to the market and extended definitions of employment. As expected, there was little difference in the composition of employment according to the two definitions for men, but there was a substantial difference for women.

Starting with an analysis of the structure of employment according to the market definition, we note that the share of the public sector in overall employment resumed its decreasing trend after stalling from 2006 to 2012, reaching 26 percent in 2018. The share of formal private wage employment increased marginally from

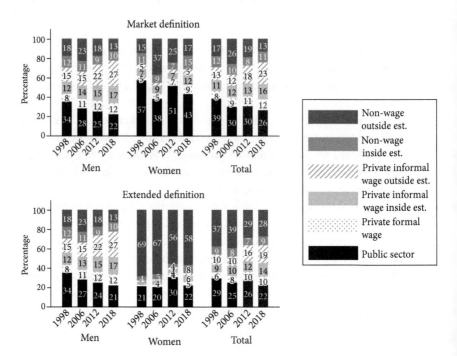

Figure 2.2 The structure of employment by job type and sex (percentage), employed individuals (market and extended definitions) aged 15–64, 1998–2018.

Source: Authors' calculations based on data from ELMPS 1998–2018.

11 percent in 2012 to 12 percent in 2018, continuing the slowly rising trend since 1998. The slight increase in this category's share was not nearly enough to counteract the long-term decline in the public sector share. As a result, the share of formal wage employment in the economy continued its long-run declining trend from 47 percent in 1998 to 41 percent in 2012 and 38 percent in 2018, confirming the long-term structural trend of informalization of the Egyptian labor market as the public sector contracts. Even within private sector wage work, the share of formal jobs had declined from 27 percent in 2006 to 23 percent in 2018 as informal jobs in the private sector grew more rapidly than formal jobs.

The share of private informal wage employment within establishments increased somewhat more rapidly in the 2012 to 2018 period, going from 13 percent to 16 percent, compared with the 2006–12 period, where it only increased from 12 percent to 13 percent. Similarly, the share of private informal employment outside establishments increased from 18 percent to 23 percent, to continue on its steeply increasing trend since 2006. The sharp increase in private informal employment outside establishments is most likely a reflection of the rapid growth of the construction and transport industries in recent years, an issue that we return to. Private informal employment as a whole increased its share from 24 percent in both 1998 and 2006 to 31 percent in 2012 and to 39 percent in 2018, a 63 percent relative increase in 12 years.

The share of employment in non-wage work inside establishments first declined from 12 percent in 1998 to 8 percent in 2012, and then increased to 11 percent in 2018. In contrast, the share of non-wage work outside establishments, about a third of which was in agriculture, declined steeply from 26 percent in 2006 to 19 percent in 2012, and then to 13 percent in 2018.

For employed women, the highest share of employment was in public sector employment, but the share of such employment among employed women fell appreciably from 51 percent in 2012 to 43 percent in 2018. The proportion of women in formal private wage work increased from 7 percent to 9 percent, but, again, not enough to counteract the fall in the share of public sector employment. Instead, the share of informal private sector wage employment increased substantially from 10 percent to 17 percent, with most of the increase being for employment within establishments. Female non-wage employment inside establishments more than doubled its share from 2012 to 2018, going from 7 percent to 15 percent, while female non-wage employment outside establishments saw a substantial decline. As a result, the overall proportion of non-wage workers among employed women remained stable at 32 percent.

The picture for women looks quite different when we consider the extended employment definition. In this case, non-wage work outside establishments made up a considerably larger fraction of employment since all subsistence workers are classified in this category. After declining from 67 percent in 2006 to 56 percent in 2012, the share of female non-wage workers outside establishments went back up to 58 percent in 2018. Together with the 8 percent of female workers who were non-wage workers inside establishments, nearly two-thirds of female workers, who were considered working according to the extended definition of employment, were non-wage workers in 2018.[6] From this point onward, we restrict our attention to the market definition of employment that is work for the purpose of pay or profit.

In Figure 2.3 (for men) and Figure 2.4 (for women), we examine the structure of employment by type and over time as a function of household wealth to assess how employment structure changed by socioeconomic status.[7] As shown in Figure 2.3, the share of public sector work among employed men increases steadily with wealth. This share declined over time in all wealth quintiles, with the decline being largest in the second and third wealth quintiles and smallest in the top quintile. While the share of public sector work fell by 44 percent in the second quintile and 48 percent in the third quintile from 1998 to 2018, it fell by only 26 percent in the top quintile. Thus, the persistent decline in public sector employment has had a greater impact on the lower and middle classes when compared with the upper income groups.

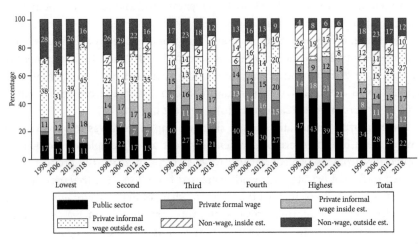

Figure 2.3 The structure of employment by job type and wealth quintile (percentage), employed men (market definition) aged 15–64, 1998–2018.

Source: Authors' calculations based on data from ELMPS 1998–2018.

[6] See Chapter 8 for a more detailed discussion of women's involvement in subsistence work in Egypt and Chapter 6 for a discussion of women's entrepreneurship (non-wage work).
[7] Wealth quintiles are based on a wealth index estimated by factor analysis using information about household ownership of durable goods and housing conditions. The construction of the index uses a methodology proposed by Filmer and Pritchett (2001) and Montgomery et al. (2000). We also examine employment status as a function of the individual's own educational attainment as another measure of socioeconomic status. The patterns are quite similar as those by wealth, so we relegate these figures to an appendix. See Figure A2.1 and Figure A2.2.

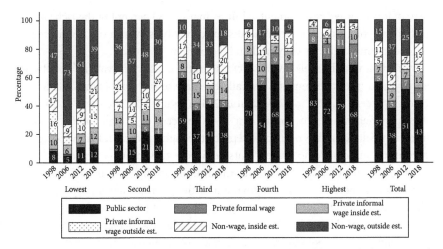

Figure 2.4 The structure of employment by job type and wealth quintile (percentage), employed women (market definition) aged 15–64, 1998–2018.

Source: Authors' calculations based on data from ELMPS 1998–2018.

There was an even greater gradient by wealth in the share of private formal wage employment, which went from only 6 percent for the poorest group in 2018 to 21 percent for the wealthiest. Again, the gradient has increased over time, suggesting that access to private formal wage employment became increasingly limited to individuals from wealthier backgrounds over time; this somewhat alarming finding is consistent with the results of Assaad and Krafft (2020).

Adding up public sector employment and private formal wage employment, we can trace how access to formal wage employment changed from 1998 to 2018 by wealth status. Although access to formal wage employment declined for all wealth groups, it declined the least for the richest (by only 8 percent in relative terms) and the most for the second and third wealth quintiles (by 31 percent for both). The poorest, who had very limited access to formality to start with, saw an 11 percent decline in access to formal jobs over the 20-year period.

Figure 2.4 shows that the wealth gradient was even steeper in terms of public sector employment and formality in general in the case of women. In 2018, the share of public sector employment among employed women increased from 12 percent for those in the lowest quintile to 68 percent for those in the highest one, a factor of 5.7. Again, it was women in the middle of the wealth distribution (third quintile) who had the greatest decline in public sector work from 1998 to 2018. They experienced a relative decline of 36 percent compared with 18 percent for the richest group.

At only 1 percent, formal private sector wage work was almost non-existent for the poorest employed women. It was nearly 15 times higher (15 percent) for the richest two quintiles. Overall, only 13 percent of the poorest employed women were in formal wage employment, while as many as 83 percent of the richest were in that category, suggesting that access to formality is even more predicated on socioeconomic status for women than it is for men.

Men at all wealth levels saw an increase in the share of private informal wage employment in establishments. Overall, the share of such employment increased from 12 percent in 1998 to 17 percent in 2018 (Figure 2.3). The share of this kind of employment was fairly constant at 17–20 percent of overall employment for different wealth quintiles of men, except for the highest where it fell to 15 percent. In contrast, informal employment outside fixed establishments, one of the more precarious forms of employment, was much more strongly predicated on wealth. It made up 45 percent of the employment of the poorest men; a proportion that fell steadily by wealth quintile, reaching only 8 percent for the richest. Again, men in the middle of the wealth distribution saw the largest increases in the proportion of this type of employment, an indication of an increase in employment precarity for the middle class in Egypt.

The pattern of informal wage employment among women was less regular. The poorest women tended to be concentrated in non-wage employment rather than wage work. Women in the second and third quintiles had a higher rate of informal wage work both inside and outside establishments and women in the top two quintiles were more likely to be employed in formal public or private wage work. In general, women appeared to try to avoid informal wage work outside establishments owing to its potential exposure to harassment and reputational risks (Barsoum, 2019), but the share of such work among the poorest women had increased substantially from 6 percent in 2006 to 10 percent in 2012, then further to 15 percent in 2018 (Figure 2.6).[8] Overall, this kind of work constituted only 5 percent of women's employment in 2018, compared with 27 percent for men.

As we have noted, the share of non-wage work, especially that occurring outside establishments, has substantially declined in recent years for men. Figure 2.3 shows that the decline was most substantial among the poorest men, who are strongly concentrated in this kind of work. The share of non-wage work outside establishments went down from 35 percent of employment in 2006 to 16 percent for the poorest men, probably a reflection of declining access to land in the agricultural sector. The decline in non-wage work was more modest for men in the third, fourth, and fifth quintiles, as these men were more likely to be non-wage workers within establishments.

The share of non-wage work in poor women's employment was high but declining over time. Among poor, employed women, 60 percent were in non-wage

---

[8] Domestic work for hire falls in this category of work, but it is clear that because of the stigma attached to such work, it is severely underreported in surveys. Anecdotal evidence indicates that many women who work as domestic workers do not even tell their neighbors or their non-immediate family members that they are doing this kind of work.

employment in 2018 (inside or outside an establishment), down from 70 percent in 2012 and 82 percent in 2006 (Figure 2.4). As in the case for poor men, non-wage employment among poor women was highly concentrated outside fixed establishments in 2018, but, again like their male counterparts, this share had declined substantially since 2006. In contrast, the share of poor women employed as non-wage workers within establishments increased substantially from 9 percent in 2012 to 21 percent in 2018.

The proportion of employed women in non-wage work declined strongly with wealth, especially after the second wealth quintile. By the fifth wealth quintile, the proportion of women in non-wage work was down to 7 percent. Thus, socioeconomic status strongly shaped what kind of work women were willing to engage in. Women in the upper socioeconomic statuses were highly concentrated in public sector work and to a lesser extent in private formal wage work, whereas women in the lower socioeconomic strata were highly concentrated in non-wage work. This stark segmentation of employment by socioeconomic status (SES) would be further exacerbated if the extended definition of employment (which includes subsistence work) was used. Since it was mostly women from the lower social strata who engaged in subsistence work, mostly as unpaid family workers, it would make the pattern of employment across SES even more prominent.

Women with lower socioeconomic status may find non-wage employment more attractive over, for instance, informal wage employment outside establishments (which is prevalent among men of similar background), owing to their ability to conduct such employment from home. Figure 2.5 shows the prevalence of working from home for non-wage workers by type for both men and women. While the vast majority of men engaged in non-wage employment worked outside their homes, a substantial proportion of women who were non-wage workers worked from home, but this proportion declined from 39 percent in 2012 to 29 percent in 2018, mostly owing to a steep drop among unpaid family workers. The proportion working from home was highest for female self-employed workers and lowest for female employers, but even among employers, nearly one in five (19 percent) worked from home in 2018.

2.3.2 The structure of employment by industry

We analyze in this section the changing structure of employment in Egypt by industry across the four waves of the ELMPS. To reduce the number of industry sectors and avoid too many very small categories, we lump together some of the one-digit level industry sectors into larger categories. The final ten categories we use are: A: Agriculture, Forestry and Fishing, BCDE: Mining, Manufacturing and Utilities, F: Construction, G: Wholesale and Retail Trade, H: Transportation and Storage, I: Accommodation and Food Service, JKLMN: Professional, Information,

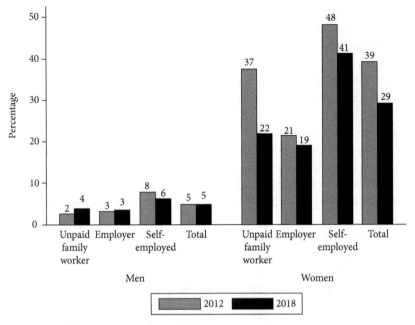

Figure 2.5 Working from home by employment status and sex (percentage), employed individuals in non-wage employment aged 15–64, 2012, 2018.
Source: Authors' calculations based on data from ELMPS 2012 and 2018.

Financial, Real Estate, Administrative and Support Services, P: Education, Q: Health and Social Work, ORSTU: Other Services, which includes public administration, arts and entertainment, other service activities, activities of households as employers, and activities of extra-territorial organizations.

The results of the ELMPS confirm that over the past 20 years, the Egyptian economy has continued to experience a structural transformation from tradable sectors such as agriculture and manufacturing to non-tradeable sectors such as construction, trade, and distribution, as discussed in the Introduction to this volume. As we saw earlier, it has also experienced a transformation away from the public sector toward a more private sector-oriented economy, which is reflected here in the decline of the employment shares of the education, health and social work, and other services categories. These structural shifts have complex causes, which include the long-term effects of the over-valuation of the real exchange rate in response to oil and oil-related revenues, such as remittances (the Dutch Disease phenomenon), as well as long-standing industrial policies that favored capital and energy-intensive industries and led to early de-industrialization (World Bank, 2014; Ayed Mouelhi and Ghazali, 2020).

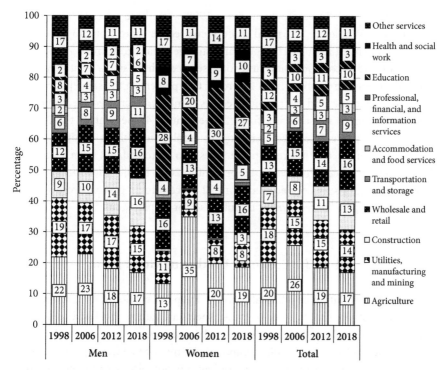

Figure 2.6 The structure of employment by activity and sex (percentage), employed individuals (market definition) aged 15–64, 1998–2018.

Note: Data labels of less than two percent are not shown.

Source: Authors' calculations based on data from ELMPS 1998–2018.

As shown in Figure 2.6, the share of agriculture in overall employment fell from 20 percent in 1998 to 17 percent in 2018.[9] The share of mining, manufacturing and utilities fell from 18 percent in 1998 to 14 percent in 2018, indicating substantial de-industrialization.[10] In contrast, the share of the construction sector in total employment has nearly doubled from 7 percent in 1998 to 13 percent in 2018. The fact that the share of employment in construction alone became almost as large as that in mining, manufacturing, and utilities combined attests to the importance of the real estate boom as one of the main drivers of growth in the Egyptian economy in recent years. The other sectors that have experienced

---

[9] The jump in agricultural employment in 2006 is due to a large increase in female employment in agriculture in that year, which is probably a measurement artifact.

[10] Recent analyses of employment within private establishments have come to similar conclusions about the extent of de-industrialization in Egypt since 1996 and the decline in the role of manufacturing in job creation (Assaad, Krafft, and Yassin, 2018; Assaad et al., 2019).

substantial growth in employment since 1998 were those related to trade and distribution. Wholesale and retail trade increased its share from 13 percent in 1998 to 16 percent in 2018, transport and storage's share grew from 5 percent to 9 percent and accommodation and food service's share saw a relatively more modest increase in its share from 2 percent to 3 percent in the same period. The construction, trade, and distribution sectors combined increased their shares in total employment substantially from 28 percent to 40 percent in the 20-year period, a 46 percent relative change. The employment share of professional, financial, business, and information services also increased, but from a very low base, from 2.8 percent in 1998 to 4.5 percent in 2018. Finally, the share of social, public, and other services declined from 32 percent to 24 percent from 1998 to 2018, reflecting the retrenchment of public sector employment.

2.4 Is the Economy Producing Good Jobs?

To assess the evolution of job quality in the Egyptian economy, we examine several aspects of job quality. Some of these aspects are rather broad and apply to all types of jobs, such as hours of work and involuntary part-time work. Other aspects, such as formality, regularity, and employment benefits, are primarily relevant for private wage workers. While we have already discussed the evolution of formality and work in and out of establishments in previous sections, we now examine these aspects in more detail, as well as some other job characteristics such as regularity of employment, access to paid and sick leaves, health insurance receipt, hours of work, involuntary part-time work, exposure to workplace hazards, and work injuries. We follow this by a discussion of self-reported measures of job satisfaction for different kinds of workers over time.

2.4.1 Characteristics of private wage employment: formality, regularity, benefits, and working conditions

As we have pointed out, wage work outside fixed establishments, which occurs in fields, streets, homes, construction sites, or vehicles, is almost always informal and strongly associated with poverty. In the coming sections, we show that such work is associated with employment irregularity, poor working conditions, and involuntary part-time work.

As shown in Figure 2.7, the share of employment outside fixed establishments in private wage work was on a slight upward trend, going from 45 percent in 1998 to 48 percent in 2018. This increase was related to the expansion of the construction and the transportation and storage sectors over the past two decades. Although the relative share of agriculture—where jobs are, for the most part, outside fixed establishments—is contracting, this contraction was more than made up for by the expansion of construction and transportation, leading to the slightly increasing share of employment outside establishments. In Figure 2.7, we see that men were much more likely to work outside establishments, and the trend among men was driving the overall trend. As mentioned earlier, women in Egypt try to avoid such work owing to its high level of exposure to possible harassment or the perception of such exposure (Barsoum, 2019).

Within establishments, the most notable trend is the increasing share of employment in small establishments (5–24 workers), mostly at the expense of employment in micro-establishments. The share of employment in micro-establishments (1–4 workers) had been falling steadily since 2006, whereas that of small establishments (5–9 and 10–24 workers) rose substantially, especially from 2012 to 2018, as shown in Figure 2.8. The share of medium establishments (25–49 and 50–99 workers) in wage employment in private establishments actually declined slightly from 2012 to 2018. The share of employment in large establishments increased substantially from 2006 to 2012, but then stabilized at around 28–29 percent.

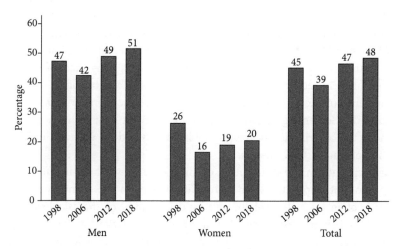

Figure 2.7 Incidence of work outside a fixed establishment by sex (percentage), private wage workers aged 15–64, 1998–2018.

Source: Authors' calculations based on data from ELMPS 1998–2018.

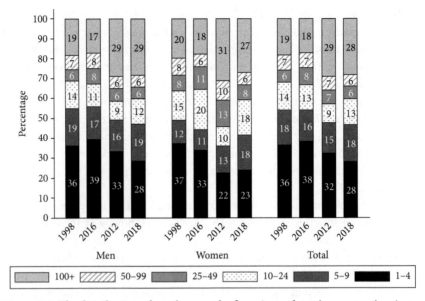

Figure 2.8 The distribution of employment by firm size and sex (percentage), private wage workers in fixed establishments, aged 15–64, 1998–2018.

Source: Authors' calculations based on data from ELMPS 1998–2018.

These results are in partial concordance with a recent study that analyzed establishment census data from 1996, 2006, and 2017. According to the findings of Assaad et al. (2019), the share of micro- and large establishments increased from 1996 to 2006 but shrank from 2006 to 2017 as small and medium establishments both increased their share substantially. The increasing share of small and medium firms in recent years has been termed by the authors of that study the re-emergence of the missing middle in the Egyptian economy. We can confirm this important emerging pattern using ELMPS data, at least with respect to the decline in the contribution of micro-establishments and the increase in the contribution of small establishments.

These changes in the distribution of employment by establishment size can have important implications for the quality of jobs in the economy, since job quality is often a function of the size (and formality) of the establishment in which the job is located. Figure 2.9 displays the evolution of the distribution of private wage employment by regularity and formality for work outside establishments and, by establishment size, for work within establishments. Overall, the proportion of irregular jobs, which consists of intermittent and seasonal jobs, declined substantially from 40 percent in 2012 to 30 percent in 2018, after having risen from 2006 to 2012. The regularity of employment is strongly affected by

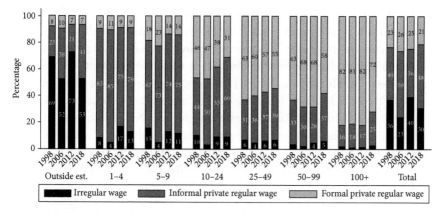

Figure 2.9 The distribution of employment by formality and regularity and by firm size (percentage), private wage workers aged 15–64, 1998–2018

Source: Authors' calculations based on data from ELMPS 1998–2018.

macroeconomic cycles, and the decline in irregularity from 2012 to 2018 is a clear sign of economic recovery and an increase in employment on the intensive margin. Since the jobs that are most vulnerable to employment irregularity are informal jobs, the decline in irregularity was compensated by an increase in informal but regular jobs from 36 percent in 2012 to 48 percent in 2018. The proportion of formal jobs within private wage employment had actually declined from 25 percent in 2012 to 21 percent in 2018, continuing an informalization trend that started in 2006. The increase in informality is thus accompanied by an increase in vulnerability among private wage workers; a vulnerability that is manifested as an increase in irregularity during economic downturns.

It is clear from Figure 2.9 that irregularity was most common in jobs located outside establishments and to a much lesser extent in micro- and small firms. Thus, the declining incidence of irregularity was the result of its decline for those working outside fixed establishments, whose jobs are almost all informal, but can oscillate between irregularity and regularity depending on the state of the economy. There was also a noticeable drop in irregularity among those working in micro-establishments. The declining incidence of irregularity is good news since irregularity is one of the most obvious manifestations of vulnerability in the Egyptian labor market. However, as the proportion of workers working outside fixed establishments continues to increase, these workers continue to be vulnerable to employment irregularity with any economic slowdown. Accordingly, these are the workers whose employment and livelihoods would have been most adversely affected by the crisis accompanying the COVID-19 pandemic.

The shift of private sector employment within establishment away from micro-establishments and toward small establishments portends well for potential improvements in job quality. As shown in Figure 2.9, small establishments tended to have a higher share of formal jobs than micro-establishments. However, at least among establishments of 10–24 workers, this share dropped substantially from 2012 to 2018. Similar drops in the share of formal jobs can be seen for medium and large establishments. This suggests that the heightened informalization of the labor market can be reversed if authorities can maintain a constant level of employment formality among small, medium, and large establishments, most of which are presumably formal themselves. If that can be achieved, the gradual shift of private wage employment to the middle of the firm size distribution could result in increased formalization of employment overall. However, inconsistent application of labor and social insurance laws in recent years has actually resulted in falling rates of formalization of employment among presumably formal firms.

We next examine the quality of private sector jobs in terms of the availability of paid and sick leave benefits. As shown in Figure 2.10, the vast majority of private sector wage workers (82 percent) did not get either paid or sick leave, but the proportion that did get such leave increased from 2006 to 2012 before declining slightly from 2012 to 2018. As expected, the proportion of workers getting paid or sick leaves among those working outside fixed establishments and those in micro-establishments was negligible. It then tended to increase steadily with establishment size. A notable finding, however, is that the proportion getting paid or sick

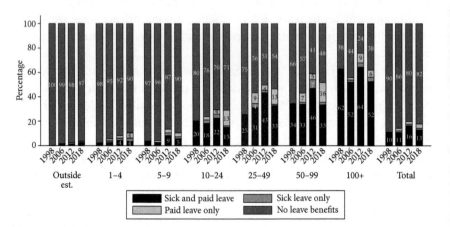

Figure 2.10 Leave benefits by firm size (percentage), private wage workers aged 15–64, 1998–2018.

Note: In 1998, the question about leave did not allow us to distinguish the type of leave obtained.

Source: Authors' calculations based on data from ELMPS 1998–2018.

leave declined appreciably from 2012 to 2018 among workers in establishments of 50–99 and 100+ workers, a reflection of the informalization of employment among those larger firms discussed earlier. This explains the stability of the overall proportion of workers getting paid or sick leave despite the shift in the distribution of workers toward more mid-sized establishments.

Another job characteristic that we examine is the likelihood of receiving job-related health insurance coverage. As shown in Figure 2.11, the proportion of private sector wage workers receiving health insurance increased from 2006 to 2012 from 11 percent to 17 percent, but then fell to 14 percent in 2018. Again, health insurance coverage was almost negligible among those working outside establishments and in micro-establishments. It steadily increased among workers in small establishments of 5–9 workers but then declined since 2006 among those in establishments of 10–24 workers. The pattern was more mixed among workers in larger establishments. There was a large increase in the share getting health insurance in establishments of 50–99 and 100+ workers from 2006 to 2012, but this trend stalled, if not reversed, from 2012 to 2018. Thus, the overall stall in the proportion of workers getting health insurance was due primarily to the stall in these larger establishments as well as in the 10–24 worker category.

Based on the results relating to job formality, receipt of leave, and health insurance coverage, we can see that the quality of jobs in larger, presumably formal, private establishments deteriorated in the 2012–18 period, reversing some of the gains made in the 2006–12 period.

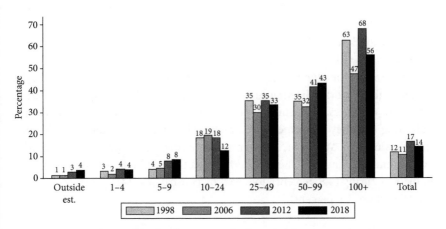

Figure 2.11 Incidence of medical insurance by firm size (percentage), private wage workers aged 15–64, 1998–2018.

Source: Authors' calculations based on data from ELMPS 1998–2018.

2.4.2 Exposure to occupational hazards and work injuries

We move next to exposure to workplace hazards and workplace injuries for all workers, including public sector and non-wage workers. Again, we disaggregate by type of employment (classified by sector, formality, employment status, and work in/out of establishments). The questions about workplace hazards and workplace injuries were added to the ELMPS in the 2018 wave, which means we are unable to ascertain change over time in these outcomes. The list of workplace hazards that we investigate comes from the International Labor Organization (ILO) definition of hazardous work used in the measurement of child labor (ILO, 2018). These questions were then adapted to measure work hazards for all workers.

As shown in Figure 2.12, the most common workplace hazards in Egypt were extreme heat or cold, dust or smoke, loud noises and vibrations, prolonged bending, and a lack of toilet facilities. For all of these hazards (except for noise and vibrations), workers outside establishments, whether engaged in wage or non-wage work, were the most exposed. The only one among these more common hazards that formal wage workers reported some regular exposure to was loud noises and vibration. Formal wage workers were also more likely to be exposed to less common hazards, such as exposure to high-risk equipment and to fire or fuel. Informal wage workers in establishments also had relatively high exposure to dust and smoke, fire or fuel, loud noises and vibrations, and prolonged bending.

The ELMPS 2018 also measured the extent to which workers experienced a workplace-related injury over the previous 12 months. As shown in Figure 2.12, about 3 percent of all workers had some kind of workplace injury in the previous year. Again, as expected, the highest rates of injury were among private informal wage workers outside establishments, with a rate of about 4.5 percent. Surprisingly, the next highest group was formal private workers, followed by non-wage workers outside establishments. Public sector workers were, by far, the least likely group to be exposed to workplace injuries.

When we examine the rate of workplace injury by occupation, we find that the highest rates of work-related industries were for blue collar occupations such as craft work, operators, and elementary occupations, with 4–5 percent of respondents indicating that they had experienced a workplace injury in the past 12 months (not shown here). Moreover, an examination of the rate of work-related injuries by economic activity (not shown here) reveals that the highest injury rates were in manufacturing (4.8 percent), followed by construction (4.2 percent) and then transportation (3.6 percent).

2.4.3 Weekly hours of work and involuntary part-time work

A shorter work week (in terms of hours of work) would typically be considered a sign of better employment conditions, as long as the low number of hours is not

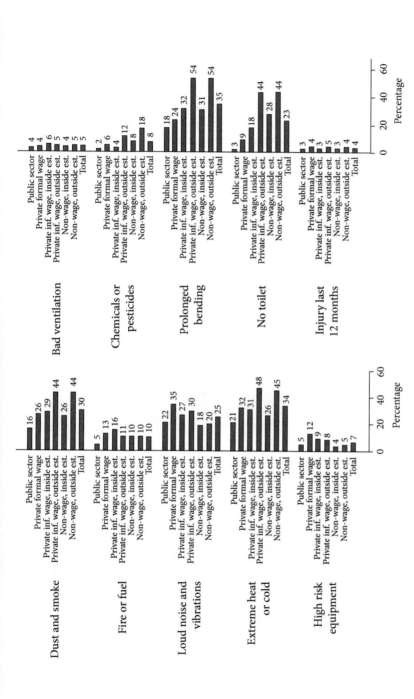

Figure 2.12 Exposure to occupational hazards and incidence of workplace injury by job type (percentage), employed individuals aged 15–64, 2018.

Note: "Inf." is an abbreviation for "informal."

Source: Authors' calculations based on data from ELMPS 2018.

due to an inability to find sufficient work, as in the case of involuntary part-time workers. We therefore examine the trend in weekly hours of work by type of employment before moving to an examination of the extent of involuntary part-time work as a measure of underemployment. As we will see, involuntary part-time work was primarily an issue for wage and non-wage workers who were working outside fixed establishments.

As seen in Figure 2.13, overall, the average number of hours per week had been on a general declining trend since 2006, averaging 46 hours per week in 2018. As expected, the longest work hours reported were those of private sector informal

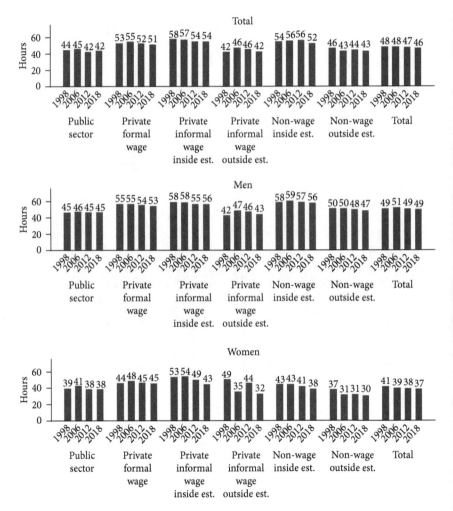

Figure 2.13 Average hours per week by job type and sex, employed individuals aged 15–64, 1998–2018.

Source: Authors' calculations based on data from ELMPS 1998, 2006, 2012 and 2018.

wage workers inside establishments. However, these workers had experienced steady reductions in their weekly work hours from 59 hours per week in 1998 to 54 hours per week in 2018. Their formal counterparts had slightly shorter work weeks of 52 hours and also experienced a reduction in average weekly hours, at least since 2006. As is well known, public sector workers have much shorter hours and these hours reduced as the public sector work week decreased from six to five days per week in 2006 (Bakr, 2006).

Non-wage workers inside establishments reported working as many hours as formal private wage workers. Those working outside fixed establishments typically worked fewer hours whether they were wage or non-wage workers. But this may be because they were unable to find enough employment when their work was intermittent, an issue we will explore.

Women typically worked shorter hours than men in all types of employment. Whereas employed men worked on average 48 hours per week in 2018, employed women worked only 38 hours per week. The largest gender gaps were for private sector workers within establishments. Women working as private wage workers in informal establishments worked 13 fewer hours per week than their male counterparts, whereas those working as non-wage workers in establishments worked 18 fewer hours per week. The smallest gender difference in work hours was that of public sector workers, where women worked seven fewer hours per week than their male counterparts in 2018.

We next examine the extent of underemployment as indicated by the proportion of workers in involuntary part-time work, defined as being employed fewer than 35 hours per week while desiring to work more hours. Involuntary part-time work is a strong indicator of the precariousness of employment and thus vulnerability to economic shocks. Since the overall pattern strongly resembles the pattern for men, we start by discussing the male pattern and then move to that of women. As shown in Figure 2.14, involuntary part-time employment was substantial only among private informal workers outside fixed establishments who made up about 27 percent of all male workers in 2018 (see Figure 2.2). It was prevalent to a lesser extent among non-wage workers and informal wage workers working in fixed establishments. In fact, for the last three categories of workers, it spiked in 2012, a time of substantial economic slowdown, and then returned to its previously low levels in 2018. A positive indicator of more plentiful employment opportunities for informal workers outside establishments was the decline in involuntary part-time work from 18 percent in 2012 to 15 percent 2018, an indication of a pickup in economic activity. Overall, it had declined from 7 percent to 5 percent of male workers over the same period.

For women, involuntary part time work was concentrated among the same group—private informal wage workers outside establishments—but there were a lot fewer of these workers in the female labor force, only 5 percent in 2018 (see Figure 2.2). As shown in Figure 2.14, this category of female workers experienced

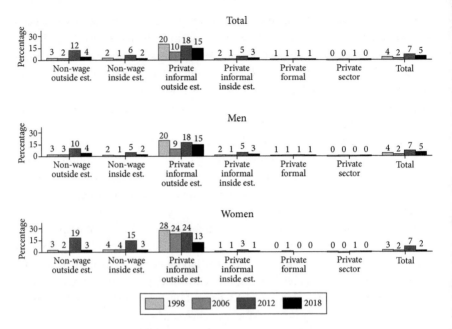

Figure 2.14 Rate of involuntary part-time work by job type and sex (percentage), employed individuals aged 15–64, 1998–2018.

Note: Involuntary part-time work is defined as the proportion of workers working fewer than 35 hours per week involuntarily among all workers in the relevant category.

Source: Authors' calculations based on data from ELMPS 1998–2018.

high rates of involuntary part-time work in previous waves of the survey, even higher than those of their male counterparts. Yet these rates dropped substantially in 2018. As a result, overall rates of involuntary part-time work among female workers dropped from 7 percent in 2012 to just 2 percent in 2018.

Another measure of underemployment is the degree to which one's job matches one's educational attainment. Respondents in the 2012 and 2018 waves were asked about the educational level required for their job, which we compared with their own educational attainment to determine whether they were under-qualified, just qualified or overqualified for their job. As shown in Figure 2.15, very few people reported being underqualified for their job across all job types. However, the proportion who reported being overqualified was substantial and varied a great deal by employment type. Overall, the proportion that reported being overqualified for their jobs increased from 44 percent in 2012 to 47 percent in 2018. The proportion was relatively low in formal employment, especially in the public sector, but rose dramatically for different forms of wage and non-wage informal employment. The extent of overqualification was highest among private informal wage workers outside establishments (66 percent) and only slightly

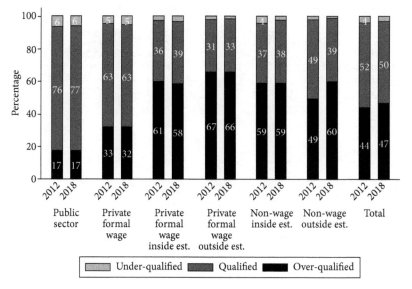

Figure 2.15 Match of job education requirements to educational attainment by job type (percentage), employed individuals aged 15–64, 2012 and 2018.
Source: Authors' calculations based on data from ELMPS 2012 and 2018.

lower among informal wage and non-wage workers in fixed establishments (58–60 percent). The only group among which the overqualified proportion increased from 2012 to 2018 was that of non-wage workers outside establishments, who constituted only 13 percent of workers as shown in Figure 2.2. The proportion overqualified in this group went from 49 percent in 2012 to 60 percent by 2018. The rising overall share of overqualified workers was due to the changing composition of employment toward informal wage employment, both inside and outside establishments, which has high shares of overqualified workers.

In the 2018 wave of the ELMPS, workers were also asked about the type of skill that their job required, with skills classified as basic literacy, mathematics/statistics, physical fitness, computer skills, management skills, customer service skills, and foreign language skills. Figure 2.16 represents a heat map that indicates the proportion who reported the need for each of these skills by job type. A darker color indicates a higher proportion of jobs requiring that particular skill. It is clear from the overall shading patterns that the highest skill requirements were for formal private and public sector jobs, with an emphasis on literacy and numeracy skills. These jobs also had the highest requirements for customer service and foreign language skills. The lowest skill requirements, at least among the skills listed, were reported by workers who worked outside fixed establishments, both as wage and non-wage workers. Lastly, the extent to which physical fitness was required was more or less uniform across all job types.

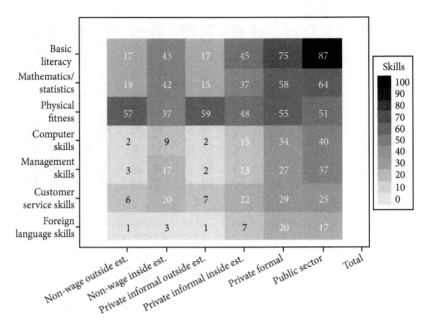

Figure 2.16 Skill requirements by job type (percentage), employed individuals aged 15–64, 2018.
Source: Authors' calculations based on data from ELMPS 2018.

2.4.4 Employment satisfaction by employment type and education over time

In this section, we examine levels of satisfaction with various aspects of one's job for workers in different types of employment and by education, and how these satisfaction levels changed over time for the same worker from 2012 to 2018. Starting with the 2012 wave, the ELMPS began assessing job satisfaction using a five-point Likert scale, with one being the least satisfied and five being the most satisfied. For our analysis, we collapse this Likert scale into two categories: "satisfied" workers who reported a four or higher on the scale (meaning they are at least "rather satisfied" or "very satisfied"); and "not satisfied" workers who reported a score of three or lower (which includes workers who are "neither satisfied nor dissatisfied", workers who are "rather dissatisfied" and workers who are "very dissatisfied"). The questions on job satisfaction covered overall job satisfaction and satisfaction with aspects such as job security, earnings, type of work, work hours, work schedule, working conditions, distance to job, and match between work and qualifications. We present the percentage of workers who were "satisfied" using a heat map with darker colors indicating a higher proportion of satisfied workers.

Along with the share of satisfied workers in 2018, we evaluate the change in the share of satisfied workers from 2012 to 2018 using the repeated measures from the same workers over time. We estimate this change by subtracting the percent of satisfied workers in 2012 from the percent of satisfied workers in 2018. Consequently, a negative number indicates that satisfaction has fallen since 2012, while a positive estimate suggests an increase in the share of those satisfied. Since we are following the same workers over time, we use the status of the worker in 2012 to classify workers. Hence, for statuses that can change over time, such as type of employment, the interpretation of the statistic is the change in satisfaction among people who held that type of job in 2012.

As shown in Figure 2.17, private informal wage workers working outside fixed establishments tended to be the least satisfied with their jobs, and, in particular, with their job security and earnings. The second least satisfied group of workers was the informal wage workers inside establishments, and, again, job security and earnings emerge as the two aspects they were least satisfied with. It is clear that public sector workers were the most satisfied with their employment conditions, with 97 percent expressing overall satisfaction and 90 percent or more satisfied with each job aspect (with the exception of earnings). However, even for earnings, the proportion satisfied among public sector workers (78 percent) was higher than for any other category of workers, including private formal workers (72 percent). The second highest proportion of satisfied workers was among private formal wage workers, 90 percent of whom were satisfied with their jobs. Again, earnings was the aspect they were least satisfied with, followed by distance to work and job security. Non-wage workers occupy an intermediate position in terms of job satisfaction between formally employed workers in the public and private sectors, on one side, and informally employed wage workers on the other. Non-wage workers inside a fixed establishment actually reported overall satisfaction levels that were comparable to those of private formal wage workers. As in the case of private informal wage workers, those non-wage workers outside an establishment reported lower job satisfaction than those inside a fixed establishment. It is actually quite striking how subjective assessments of employment conditions correspond to our objective assessments of these conditions, with informal and non-wage workers working outside establishments having the worst work conditions and public sector workers and employers having the best work conditions.

When we examine the change in the level of satisfaction between 2012 and 2018 by job type, we find that workers, on average, were more satisfied with their jobs in 2018 than they were in 2012. The proportion satisfied with their job overall rose by 14 percentage points (p.p.) for the average worker from 2012 to 2018. The increase in overall satisfaction was largest (30 p.p.) among the least satisfied category, informal wage workers working outside fixed establishments. We observe similar increases (22 p.p.) for their counterparts working inside fixed

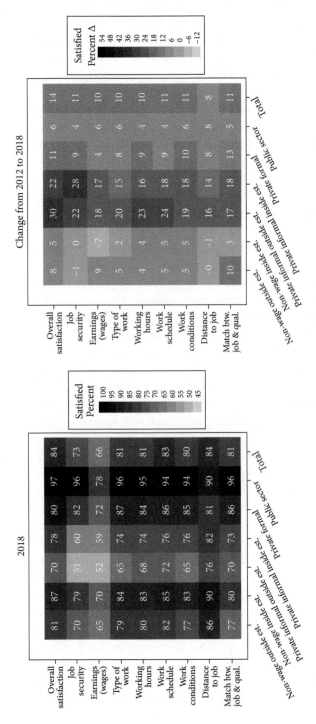

Figure 2.17 Job satisfaction by job type in 2018 and change in job satisfaction from 2012 to 2018 by job type (percentage), employed individuals aged 15–64, 2012 and 2018.

Source: Authors' calculations based on data from ELMPS 2012 and 2018.

establishments. Although these informal wage workers continued to have the lowest satisfaction levels in 2018, they experienced by far the largest improvements between 2012 and 2018. Among the various job aspects, the increase in satisfaction level for these workers was highest for job security both for those working inside and outside establishments. It was also quite high for work hours and work schedule for those working outside establishments. We note that this increase in satisfaction levels corresponded to the sharp reduction in the irregularity of employment from 2012 to 2018, which we observed earlier among this category of workers (see Figure 2.9). This suggests that the economic recovery and the greater regularity of employment it brings for this vulnerable group of workers resulted in a substantive improvement in these workers' wellbeing.

The percentage of workers satisfied with their jobs increased the least among public sector workers, who were already quite satisfied to start with, and among non-wage workers working inside and outside establishments. In fact, it is among this group that we observe the only declines in satisfaction levels in specific aspects of jobs, such as job security, earnings, and distance to work.

Figure 2.18 shows the levels of job satisfaction by the education level of the jobholders. The general trend is rising satisfaction levels with increasing levels of education, with a particularly large jump in the proportion satisfied as we go from secondary to post-secondary education. Nevertheless, the proportion satisfied among workers with basic education was slightly less than it was for those with less than basic education, and the proportion satisfied among university graduates was slightly less than those with post-secondary (two-year) degrees. Satisfaction with almost every aspect of employment appeared to decline between those with less than basic to those with basic education. This is probably because although expectations rise with education, job characteristics do not improve all that much just with the acquisition of basic education. Satisfaction with all job aspects increased as we move from basic to post-secondary education, some quite substantially, as in the case of job security and earnings. But the increases in satisfaction stalled between post-secondary and university, particularly with regard to job security, earnings, and match between jobs and qualifications. Again, this appears to be an instance where expectations were rising faster than actual improvements in employment conditions.

With regard to changing levels of satisfaction by educational attainment, there was somewhat greater improvement in the levels of satisfaction between 2012 and 2018 among those with basic and secondary education than among those at other educational levels. This was particularly true with respect to improvements in satisfaction with job security. In fact, secondary school graduates in particular saw higher improvements in satisfaction than other education groups with all aspects of their jobs, with the possible exception of distance to work. Note that these small increases for more educated individuals might have been due to ceiling effects, where the satisfaction levels were high a priori.

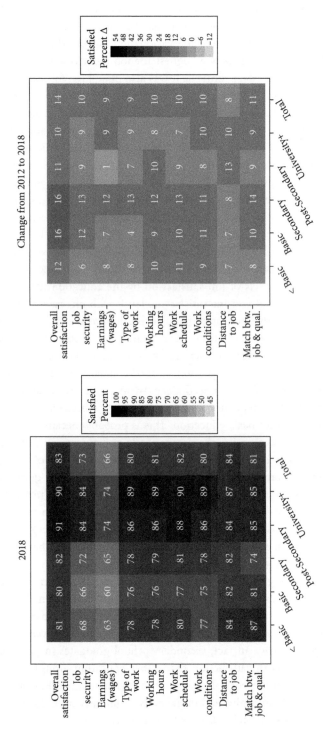

Figure 2.18 Job satisfaction by education in 2018 and change in job satisfaction from 2012 to 2018 by education (percentage), employed individuals aged 15–64, 2012 and 2018.

Source: Authors' calculations based on data from ELMPS 2012 and 2018.

We examine next satisfaction and changes in satisfaction over time by occupation in Figure 2.19. It appears that overall satisfaction follows the skill hierarchy, with professionals and managers being the most satisfied and workers in elementary occupations being the least satisfied. Operators tended to have higher satisfaction rates than either craft or agricultural workers. This overall pattern held for satisfaction with job security, earnings, type of work, and match between qualifications and job. There were slight deviations from this pattern for working hours, work schedule, work conditions, and distance to job. These patterns, once again, suggest that people's subjective assessments of their jobs corresponded fairly closely to their objective employment conditions.

Turning to change in satisfaction levels over time, we find that craft workers in 2012 exhibited the largest increase in satisfaction, with an 18 p.p. jump in the share being satisfied with their working hours and schedule, and a 15 p.p. increase in contentment with job security and work conditions. Agricultural workers in 2012 exhibited a 15 p.p. increase in their satisfaction with wages and earnings. Clerical and service workers from 2012 also exhibited a sizable increase (16 p.p.) in their satisfaction with job security. Meanwhile, the satisfaction levels among professionals and managers in 2012 remained stable over time, exhibiting small increases between 2012 and 2018. Note that these small increases might again have been due to ceiling effects, where managers and professionals were indeed the group with the highest satisfaction levels a priori.

Finally, we look at job satisfaction broken down by gender as shown in Figure 2.20.[11] Across all satisfaction categories, our evidence suggests that women were more satisfied than men. This result is unsurprising, as women in Egypt are more likely to choose unemployment or non-participation over an undesirable job than their male counterparts. Moreover, a large share of Egyptian women worked in the public sector, where satisfaction rates tend to be higher (Figure 2.21).

2.5 Conclusion

This chapter examined the pattern of employment growth in Egypt from 1998 to 2018 and the degree to which the Egyptian economy generated good jobs over that period. With regard to aggregate employment growth, our findings indicate that employment to population ratios have traditionally responded positively to economic growth, albeit with a certain lag. However, this does not seem to be the case in the most recent recovery. Despite substantial increases in GDP growth rates since their low in 2011, employment to population ratios continued to decline since 2010. The absolute number of jobs created has increased somewhat since 2011, but at a slower rate than the working age population.

---

[11] We omit the heat map of change in reported job satisfaction by sex because of a lack of variation in the results. All changes were between 6 and 14 p.p., with changes among women smaller (6–9 p.p.) than among men (8–14 p.p.).

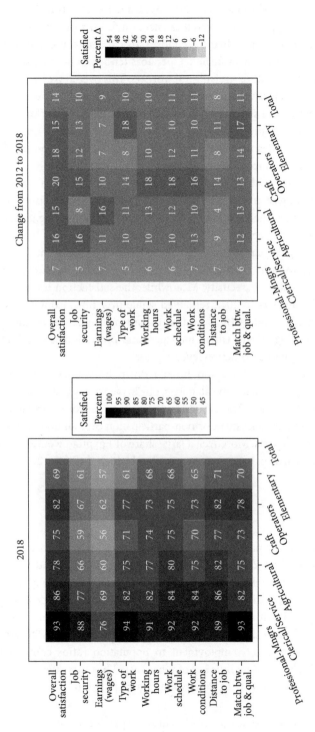

Figure 2.19 Job satisfaction by occupation in 2018 and change in job satisfaction from 2012 to 2018 by occupation (percentage), employed individuals aged 15–64, 2012 and 2018.

Source: Authors' calculations based on data from ELMPS 2012 and 2018.

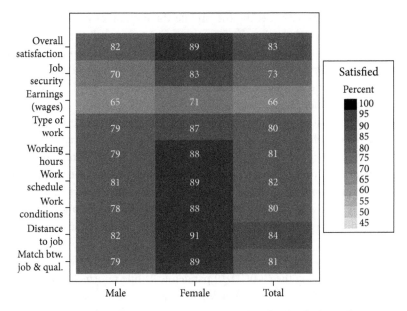

Figure 2.20 Job satisfaction by sex (percentage), employed individuals aged 15–64, 2018.
Source: Authors' calculations based on data from ELMPS 2018.

In terms of composition, the contribution of the public sector, broadly defined, to employment has continued to decline. Concurrently, the share of the formal private sector increased marginally, but not sufficiently to make up for the decline in the public sector, leading to an informalization of overall employment. Within informal employment, the share of wage employment was increasing substantially at the expense of non-wage employment. Non-wage employment outside fixed establishments has dropped substantially since 2006, a reflection of the declining share of agriculture in total employment. The most rapidly growing segment of the labor market was informal wage employment outside fixed establishments, a reflection of the rapid growth of the construction and transportation sectors.

Besides the decline in the share of agriculture and the increase in the share of construction and transportation in overall employment, there was also an increasing share of trade and distribution and a declining share of mining, manufacturing and utilities. This trend reflects a continuing structural shift, at least in terms of employment, toward non-tradeable sectors. The share of professional, financial, business, and information services also increased, although it still constituted a fairly small share of overall employment. The retreat of the public sector resulted in a falling share of education, health, and other services.

The decline in the share of formal employment (in both its public and private forms) has had important distributional consequences. The poorest group of workers had limited access to formal employment to start with and was therefore only marginally affected by its decline. The richest group made up for falling public sector employment with greater private formal employment. It was therefore the middle class (as identified by the middle three quintiles of a wealth index) that saw the greatest decline in formal employment, and thus experienced increased employment vulnerability. This confirms the hollowing out of the middle class in Egypt since the late 1980s, an issue that has been discussed in connection with the root causes of the 2011 uprisings (Diwan, 2013; Assaad et al., 2018; Devarajan and Ianchovichina, 2018; Pellicer et al., 2020).

The informalization of employment and the growing share of it that is located outside fixed establishments is strongly associated with a deterioration in overall job quality and increased vulnerability. Besides not benefiting from any kind of social protection, informal wage workers outside fixed establishments had higher levels of employment irregularity, higher rates of involuntary part-time employment, higher exposure to workplace hazards and rates of injury, and virtually no access to paid leave and health insurance. It is true that the irregularity of employment among these workers declined from 2012 to 2018 as economic conditions improved, but they remain highly vulnerable to any economic downturn, such as the one accompanying the COVID-19 pandemic. While informal workers inside establishments had somewhat better levels of job security and somewhat safer conditions at work, they suffered from long work weeks, high levels of overqualification, and equally low access to paid leaves and health insurance.

A striking result of this chapter is how subjective assessments of job quality correspond closely to the objective job quality measures that we examined. The workers who were least satisfied with their jobs were the informal wage workers outside establishments, followed by their counterparts working in establishments. Non-wage workers inside and outside establishments occupied an intermediate position, and the most satisfied workers were formally employed workers in the public sector, followed by their counterparts in the private sector. Despite the conventional wisdom that the most educated workers were the least satisfied with their jobs, we found that job satisfaction rises steadily with education, as post-secondary and university graduates expressed the highest levels of job satisfaction.

Finally, we found that the overall levels of job satisfaction had increased from 2012 to 2018, reflecting the improvement in economic conditions. This increase was greatest among workers with the lowest levels of job satisfaction, suggesting a narrowing of the differences in satisfaction levels. This is not entirely surprising, since the least satisfied in both years were justifiably the informal wage workers outside establishments who experienced the greatest improvements in employment regularity from 2012 to 2018.

While our data precede the disruptions caused by the COVID-19 pandemic, results from 2018 help us make some predictions as to which workers are most vulnerable in these circumstances. Clearly, the workers who are the least vulnerable to the disruptions caused by the pandemic are public sector workers. Public sector employees remained on the payroll even if they could not actually report to work and even received a pay rise as part of the 100 billion Egyptian Pound (EGP) government response program to the pandemic (Ministry of Planning and

Economic Development, 2020). Formal private sector workers were also protected from layoffs, for the most part, although their hours and pay may have been curtailed in some instances. With a reduction in economic activity and overall mobility, employers and self-employed workers and their families could have also experienced disruptions in their livelihoods, but the magnitude of these disruptions clearly depends on what industries they work in and the extent to which these industries were affected. Together with formally employed wage workers, they benefited from an increase in the annual income exempted from income tax, which was raised from EGP 15,000 to EGP 22,000 per year (Ministry of Planning and Economic Development, 2020).

There is little doubt, however, that informal wage workers, especially those working outside establishments, were the most vulnerable. These workers are generally hired by the day, so their employment is highly susceptible to fluctuations in economic activity, as indicated by their rates of employment irregularity and involuntary part-time work. Recognizing this, the Egyptian government instituted a special exceptional cash transfer program of EGP 500 per month to be paid to irregularly employed workers who registered for assistance with the Ministry of Labor (Ministry of Planning and Economic Development, 2020). The Ministry of Labor established a special website to facilitate the registration of irregular workers. The cash transfer was initially approved for a period of three months and then extended to the end of 2020. So far, it is reported that 1.6 million workers have benefited from this program (Hamdy, 2021). Even if we limit the potential pool of eligible workers to informal wage workers working outside establishments, the group we determined to be most vulnerable, our estimates indicate that these workers constitute 23 percent of overall employment in Egypt, or approximately 6.1 million workers based on the size of total employment in the fourth quarter of 2019.[12] Other categories of workers may be eligible as well, such as some of the informal wage workers inside establishments, and possible some of the non-wage workers as well. Thus, it appears that the current benefits are reaching less than 25 percent of potentially eligible workers.

Further research is clearly needed to ascertain the actual effects of the COVID-19 pandemic on workers and livelihoods in Egypt and the extent to which government measures to mitigate these effects are reaching the most seriously affected groups. To this end, the Economic Research Forum in collaboration with the International Labor Organization is conducting a series of rapid phone surveys to monitor the impact of COVID-19 on households and firms in several North African countries including Egypt. The data from these surveys will go a long way in supporting the kinds of analyses that are necessary to assess the impact of the crisis on the Egyptian labor market.

---

[12] According to CAPMAS, total employment in the fourth quarter of 2019 was estimated at 26.6 million workers (CAPMAS, 2020).

Acknowledgments

The authors acknowledge the general support of the World Bank, the International Labour Organization, Agence Française de Développement, UN Women, and the Arab Fund for Economic and Social Development for funding the ELMPS 2018, on which this chapter is based.

Appendix 2.1

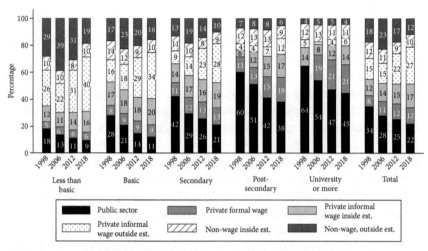

Figure A2.1 The structure of employment by type and education (percentage), employed men (market definition) aged 15–64, 1998–2018.

Source: Authors' calculations based on data from ELMPS 1998–2018.

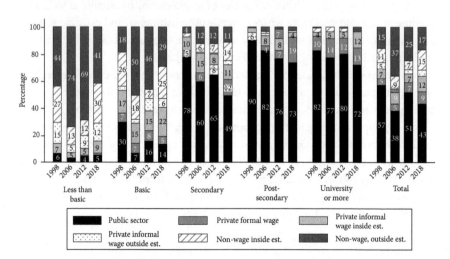

Figure A2.2 The structure of employment by type and education (percentage), employed women (market definition), aged 15–64, 1998–2018.

Source: Authors' calculations based on data from ELMPS 1998–2018.

References

Assaad, R., et al. (2019) Job Creation in Egypt: A Sectoral and Geographical Analysis Focusing on Private Establishments, 1996–2017. Economic Research Forum Policy Paper, Economic Research Forum, Cairo, Egypt.

Assaad, R. and G. Barsoum (2009) "Rising Expectations and Diminishing Opportunities for Egypt's Young," in N. Dhillon and T. Yousef (eds) *Generation in Waiting: The Unfulfilled Promise of Young People in the Middle East*, pp. 67–94. Washington, DC: Brookings Institution Press.

Assaad, R. and C. Krafft (2015) "The Structure and Evolution of Employment in Egypt: 1998–2012," in R. Assaad and C. Krafft (eds) *The Egyptian Labor Market in an Era of Revolution*, pp. 27–51. Oxford: Oxford University Press.

Assaad, R. and C. Krafft (2020) "Excluded Generation: The Growing Challenges of Labor Market Insertion for Egyptian Youth," *Journal of Youth Studies.* 24(2): 186–212. doi: 10.1080/13676261.2020.1714565.

Assaad, R., C. Krafft, and S. Yassin (2018) "Job Creation or Labor Absorption? An Analysis of Private Sector Employment Growth by Industry in Egypt." *Middle East Development Journal*, 12(2), 177–207. doi: 10.1080/17938120.2020.1753978.

Assaad, R. et al. (2018) "Inequality of Opportunity in Wages and Consumption in Egypt," *Review of Income and Wealth*, 64 (S1): S26–S54. doi: 10.1111/roiw.12289.

Ayed Mouelhi, R. Ben and M. Ghazali (2020) "Structural Transformation in Egypt, Morocco and Tunisia: Patterns, Drivers and Constraints," *Economics of Transition and Institutional Change*, 29(1): 35–61. doi: 10.1111/ecot.12258.

Bakr, A. (2006) "In Depth – Gov't Revises Work Week." *Business Monthly*, American Chamber of Commerce in Egypt (February 2006).

Barsoum, G. (2019) "Women, Work, and Family: Education Women's Employment Decisions and Social Policies in Egypt," *Gender, Work, and Organization*, 26 (7): 895–914.

CAPMAS (Central Agency for Public Mobilization and Statistics) (2019) *Egypt in Figures 2019.* Cairo: CAPMAS.

CAPMAS (n.d.) *Labor Force Survey.* Cairo: CAPMAS.

Devarajan, S. and E. Ianchovichina (2018) "A Broken Social Contract, Not High Inequality, Led to the Arab Spring," *Review of Income and Wealth*, 64 (S1): S5–S25. doi: 10.1111/roiw.12288.

Diwan, I. (2013) "Understanding Revolution in the Middle East: The Central Role of the Middle Class," *Middle East Development Journal*, 5 (1): 1–30. doi: 10.1142/S1793812013500041.

Filmer, D. and L. Pritchett (2001) "Estimating Wealth Effects without Expenditure Data—or Tears: An Application to Educational Enrollments in States of India," *Demography*, 38 (1): 115–32.

Hamdy, Osama. 2021. "After Disbursing the Last Installments of the Grant, What Did the State Offer Irregular Workers?" Akhbar El-Yom (March 21).

ILO (International Labour Organization) (2013) Resolution Concerning Statistics of Work, Employment and Labour Underutilization Adopted by the Nineteenth International Conference of Labor Statisticians (October 2013). Available at: https://www.ilo.org/global/statistics-and-databases/meetings-and-events/international-conference-of-labour-statisticians/19/WCMS_230304/lang--en/index.htm (Accessed: March 10, 2018).

ILO (2018) "Resolution to Amend the 18th ICLS Resolution concerning Statistics of Child Labour," in *20th International Conference of Labour Statisticians*. Geneva. Available at: https://www.ilo.org/wcmsp5/groups/public/---dgreports/---stat/documents/meetingdocument/wcms_648624.pdf. [Accessed July 1st, 2021]

IMF (2020) Real GDP Growth: Annual Percent Change. Washington, DC: International Monetary Fund.

Krafft, C. and R. Assaad (2014) Why the Unemployment Rate is a Misleading Indicator of Labor Market Health in Egypt. Economic Research Forum Policy Perspective No. 14. Cairo: Economic Research Forum.

Langsten, R. and R. Salem (2008) "Two Approaches to Measuring Women's Work in Developing Countries : A Comparison of Survey Data from Egypt," *Population and Development Review*, 34 (2): 283–305.

Ministry of Planning and Economic Development (2020) *Measures Undertaken by the Egyptian State to Address the Crisis*. Cairo: Ministry of Planning and Economic Development.

Montgomery, M.R. et al. (2000) "Measuring Living Standards with Proxy Variables," *Demography*, 37 (2): 155–74. doi: 10.2307/2648118.

Pellicer, M. et al. (2020) "Grievances or Skills? The Effect of Education on Youth Political Participation in Egypt and Tunisia," *International Political Science Review*, . doi: 10.1177/0192512120927115.

World Bank (2014) *Arab Republic of Egypt: More Jobs , Better Jobs: A Priority for Egypt*. Washington, DC: World Bank. doi: 10.1016/S0360-3016(01)01519-X.

World Bank (2015) Egypt Economic Monitor: Paving the Way to a Sustained Recovery. Washington DC: World Bank.

World Bank (2019) Egypt Economic Monitor: From Floating to Thriving: Taking Egypt's Exports to New Levels. Washington, DC: World Bank.

World Bank (2020) Egypt Economic Monitor: From Crisis to Economic Transformation: Unlocking Egypt's Productivity and Job-Creation Potential. Washington, DC: World Bank.

World Bank (2021). "Egypt's Economic Update April 2021." Washington D.C.: The World Bank.

3

Evolution of Wages, Inequality, and Social Mobility in Egypt

Mona Said, Rami Galal, and Mina Sami

3.1 Introduction

This chapter explores trends in wages, income inequality, and economic mobility in Egypt over the period 1988–2018. It asks three main questions. First, what are the main features of the Egyptian wage and income structure? Second, how have the circumstances that people were born into shaped their wage outcomes? Third, how have gender- and sector-based wage differentials and returns to education contributed to these changes?

To answer these questions, the chapter makes use of a comprehensive series of datasets collected in Egypt over the period from 1988 to 2018. The Egypt Labor Market Panel Survey (ELMPS) spans four waves in 1998, 2006, 2012, and 2018, and is comparable to the 1988 special round of the Labor Force Survey.[1] These data enable us to provide a descriptive analysis of the levels of wages and income and their distributions over time for a number of key population subgroups. Building on this, and keeping with the equality of opportunity paradigm, the chapter explores the extent to which characteristics at birth influence wage distributions. To further examine mobility within income distribution, the panel aspect of the data allows us to examine the characteristics of those individuals who saw the largest gains or losses in their distributional ranks over time. Finally, to provide a sense of why these changes have taken place, we estimate gender- and sector-based wage differentials and estimate returns to education.

Since 2016, the Egyptian economy has gone through a number of substantial macroeconomic changes associated with important policy reforms, particularly in the areas of exchange rate devaluation and subsidy removals. In the context of an International Monetary Fund package, the government narrowed the fiscal deficit, cut subsidies, and floated the Egyptian pound in November 2016. This resulted in a devaluation of more than 50 percent, leading to inflation in 2016–17

---

[1] The data are publicly available from the Economic Research Forum Open Access Microdata Initiative: www.erfdataportal.com. See Krafft, Assaad, and Rahman (2021) for more information on the ELMPS.

Mona Said, Rami Galal, and Mina Sami, *Evolution of Wages, Inequality, and Social Mobility in Egypt* In: *The Egyptian Labor Market: A Focus on Gender and Economic Vulnerability*. Edited by: Caroline Krafft and Ragui Assaad, Oxford University Press.

of 23.3 percent and in 2017–18 of 21.6 percent (El-Haddad and Gadallah, 2018). These policies have left their mark on labor income. In particular, average real wages have been declining overall, and inequality has been rising, especially among those with lower levels of education and those in the private sector. The share of income accruing to the top 10 percent has expanded at the expense of the low share held by the bottom 50 percent. The share of individuals below the low earnings line has also risen. Contributing to wage inequality, individuals' background characteristics continue to play a role in their wages, though this appears to be quite stable over time.

Although rapid inflation diminished after the period 2017–18, increasing prices for food maintained pressure on the purchasing power and real wages of workers (Tellioglu and Konandreas, 2017). Nominal wages adjust slowly in Egypt, so real wages are substantially influenced by inflation (Datt and Olmsted, 2006; Cichello, Abou-Ali, and Marotta, 2013). As a result, the former upward trend in real wages between 1998 and 2012 has turned to stagnation or declining real wages across most population subgroups.

This chapter is structured as follows. Section 3.2 looks at wage and income levels, and distributions over time. Section 3.3 considers mobility within the wage distribution in two ways. It explores the role of circumstances in determining wage outcomes and the characteristics of those individuals who moved up and down in quintile rank across survey waves. Section 3.4 looks at the role of gender- and sector-based wage differentials and returns to education in influencing wage outcomes. Section 3.5 concludes.

3.2 Wage distributions over time

We review the evolution of the distribution of wages, paying attention to sex, sector of employment, occupation, industry, geographic location, level of education, and job formality. In all calculations, we excluded the top percentile of observations owing to the presence of outliers that greatly skewed the results. The variable used for wages was real monthly wages in 2018 prices. We restricted our sample to wage-workers aged 15–64 with positive wages.

3.2.1 Trends in real wages 1988–2018

Figure 3.1 displays box and whisker plots for wage distributions for the full sample, by sex, with a breakdown by sector and formality. The rectangle in the plot displays observations between the 25th and 75th percentiles (the interquartile range or IQR) with an inner line denoting the median value. The closer this value is to

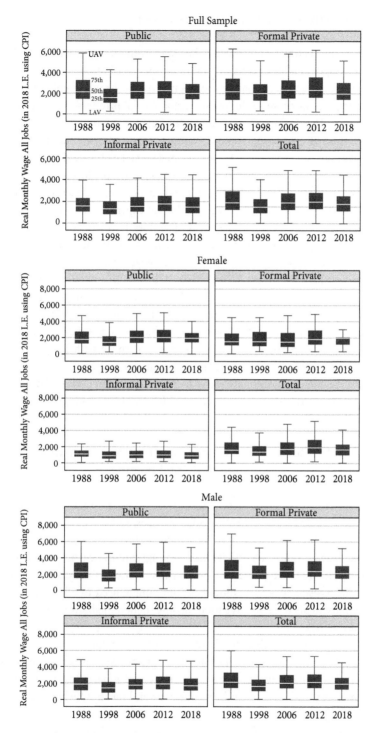

Figure 3.1 Real monthly wage distributions by sector and sex, 2018 Egyptian pounds, ages 15–64, 1988–2018.

Note: Upper Adjacent Value (UAV) = Q3+1.5*IQR; Lower Adjacent Value (LAV) = Q1-1.5*IQR.

Source: Authors' calculations using ELMPS 1988–2018.

one end of the rectangle, the greater the skew in the distribution. The whiskers lead to the upper and lower adjacent values of the distribution.[2]

There was a decline in median real wages in 2018 for the full sample, as well as for the subcategories of those in the public sector, formal private sector, and informal private sector. The distinction of formality in Egypt is important to draw as those working informally, meaning without contracts or social insurance, face relatively adverse working environments relative to formal workers.[3] The median wages for the full sample of workers were, in 2018, close to 1998 levels, the lowest point across all waves of the ELMPS. Formal private sector and public sector workers enjoyed higher median real wages than informal workers, but all experienced declines since 2012. Breaking down wages by sex displays a similar story for men. For women, median real wages in the private sector increased slightly, but this might have been driven by women who faced low wages selecting out of employment.

As can be seen from Figure 3.2 (median), Table A3.2.1 (mean) in Appendix 3.2, median real monthly wages rose at a much lower rate (percentage per annum) in 2006–12 in Egypt, after a rapid increase in the preceding period, 1998–2006 (see Said, Galal, and Sami, 2019). Between 2012 and 2018, median wages declined for all groups and particularly in urban areas, for those with higher education (post-secondary and above) or high and medium occupations, and in the private sector. Overall, mean real monthly wages in 2018 Egyptian pounds fell by 17 percent compared with 2012, whereas median wages fell by 11 percent.

3.2.2   Beyond Wages: Trends in Transfers, Non-wage Income, and Total Income

Regarding individuals' main income sources, in addition to wages, individuals in Egypt derive income from a host of other sources. In the following calculations, we incorporated transfers and non-wage income. Pre-transfer income is the sum of four categories: wages, enterprise earnings, agricultural earnings (harvest, sale of equipment, etc.), and rent and other expenses. Transfers are the sum of pensions, social assistance, and remittances. The sample used in all calculations are all those individuals with positive total income (hence, medians for some types of income are zero).

In Figure 3.3, we note that the share of transfers in total income increased for every single group. As such, the share of pre-transfer income substantially decreased. Transfers as a share of income increased especially rapidly for those with elementary and post-secondary education and for those who worked in the

---

[2] Upper Adjacent Value (UAV) = Q3+1.5*IQR; Lower Adjacent Value (LAV) = Q1-1.5*IQR
[3] Chapter 2 documents and discusses in detail the implications of the decline in formality in the Egyptian labor market over this period.

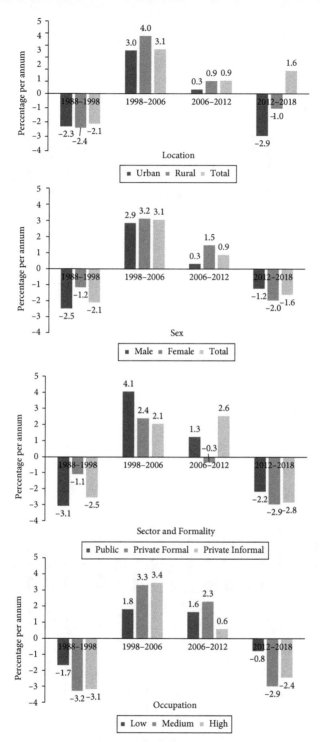

Figure 3.2 Median real monthly wage growth rates (percentage per annum) by location, education, sex, sector, occupation, and formality, 2018 Egyptian pounds, full sample, ages 15–64, 1988–2018.

Note: Occupations have been arranged as follows. High: managers, technicians, and associate professionals; Medium: clerical support, service and sales, and craft and trade workers; Low: agricultural, plant and machinery, and other elementary occupations.

Source: Authors' calculations using ELMPS 1988–2018.

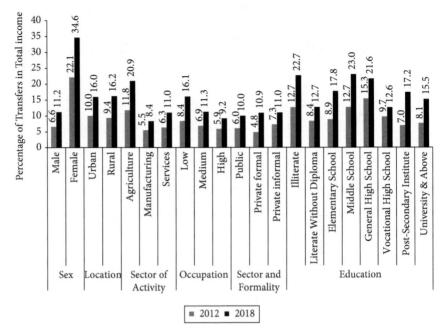

Figure 3.3 Percentage of transfers in total income by individual characteristics, 2018 Egyptian pounds, ages 15–64, 2012–18.

Source: Authors' calculations using ELMPS 2012–18.

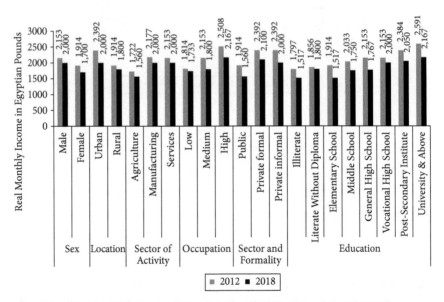

Figure 3.4 Median monthly total income by individual characteristics, 2018 Egyptian pounds, ages 15–64, 2012–18.

Source: Authors' calculations using ELMPS 2012–18.

private formal sector. Transfers increased across the board, but these increases were not sufficient to cover the loss in pre-transfer income, which resulted in there being an overall decrease in total income.

The median income declined for all groups (Figure 3.4). These declines especially affected the public sector workers, as well as those with elementary or high school levels of education. The workers in the public sector experienced a decline in incomes of 18 percent, while those with elementary or high school education saw declines of 21 and 18 percent respectively over the period 2012–18.

3.2.3 Trends in Inequality

Turning to measures of inequality, the share of wages accruing to the top 10 percent was fairly stable, around 26–27 percent, from 1988 to 2012. There was then a very slight increase from 26 percent in 2012 to 28 percent in 2018 at the expense of the middle 40 percent and the bottom 50 percent, which was further squeezed out in 2018. Gini coefficients for real monthly wages, presented in Figure 3.5, show that inequality (as measured by those coefficients), which was consistently 0.34 in previous waves, rose to 0.37 in 2018. Gini coefficients recorded rises for all subgroups, with the sharpest rises among workers in the private sector and those

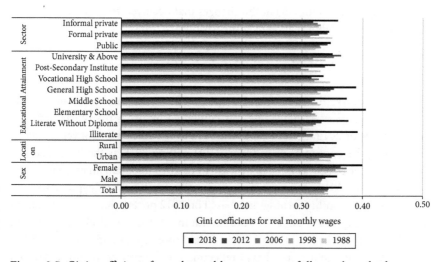

Figure 3.5 Gini coefficients for real monthly wages across full sample and subgroups, ages 15–64, 1988–2018.

Source: Authors' calculations using ELMPS 1988–2018.

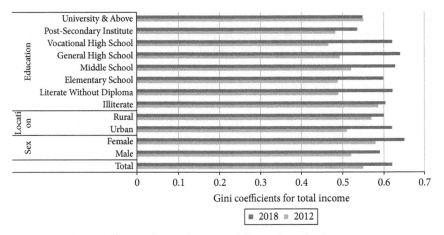

Figure 3.6 Gini coefficients for total income, full sample and subgroups, ages 15–64, 2012–2018.

Source: Authors' calculations using ELMPS 2012–2018.

with no education.[4] Chapter 4 in this book further explores inequality specifically among youth.

Figure 3.6 presents Gini coefficients for total income by subgroups. It confirms that the increase in wage inequality between 2012 and 2018 as measured by the Gini coefficient was observed using all inequality indices, and for both wages and total income, with the largest inequality increases observed among women, the less educated, and those in urban areas. This result calls attention to the importance of studying in more detail the changes that occurred for those classified as low earners in the labor market over the period.

3.2.4 Trends in the share of low earners

In order to analyze the evolution of wages for those who can be classified as the working poor, a low earnings line was computed by using the official national poverty lines for 2012 listed in Table 3.1. The poverty lines were converted to real terms using the consumer price index (CPI), setting 2018 as the base year. The poverty line for 2012 was inflated by the CPI of 2018 to obtain an estimate of the poverty line in 2018. This was done separately for the five Egyptian regions. Hence, the low monthly earnings line based on 2012 poverty lines increased from around 900 Egyptian pounds (LE) per month in 2012 LE to 2,150 LE per month in 2018 LE. It was lowest at 2,002 LE in rural Lower Egypt and highest at 2,350 LE per month in rural Upper Egypt reflecting the differences in family size and dependency ratios. Chapter 8 provides trends in fertility by location.

---

[4] For Generalized Entropy inequality indices see Said, Galal, and Sami, 2019.

Table 3.1 Per capita region-specific low earnings line in 2012 and 2018 Egyptian pounds (based on 2011 poverty line).

Region	in 2012 LE	in 2018 LE
Metropolitan	926	2,215
Lower Egypt urban	845	2,021
Lower Egypt rural	837	2,002
Upper Egypt urban	878	2,100
Upper Egypt rural	983	2,351
Total Egypt	899	2,150

Note: CPI in 2012 is 0.418 (2018=1).
Source: Authors' calculations using ELMPS 1988–2018.

Table 3.2 presents the share of wage earners that can be classified as low earners (i.e. below the low earnings line), by sex, age group, region, educational attainment, industry, and sector. This proportion increased from 51 percent in 2012 to 57 percent in 2018. The increase was greatest for women compared with men, for whom the proportion in 2018 was 68 percent, and for older workers (50–64 years old). Youth remained the group with the highest incidence of working poor, at around 72 percent. The highest proportions of low earners were still in rural Upper Egypt (69 percent) and in the agricultural sector (67 percent). The situation also worsened for educated wage earners, with post-secondary and above education, whereby the share of low earners went up from 37 percent in 2012 to 47 percent in 2018, and for government workers for whom it went up from 45 percent in 2012 to 55 percent in 2018.

3.3 The Influence of Circumstances on Wages and Mobility within the Distribution

This section considers mobility within the wage distribution in two ways. First, in line with the equality of opportunity paradigm (Roemer, 1998), it explores the role of circumstances in determining wage outcomes. Second, it examines the characteristics of those individuals who moved up and down in quintile rank across survey waves. These approaches are complementary in that one is closely related to the literature on intergenerational mobility as it looks at wage distributions based on parental characteristics, while the other focuses on individuals' own movements in the distribution across different waves.

For equality of opportunity to prevail in a society, circumstances should not provide individuals with better outcomes. If equality of opportunity prevailed, then there would not be differences in wage distributions based on circumstance characteristics. One way to assess the presence of inequality of opportunity is to

Table 3.2 Percentage below low earning line and percentage change in share below low earning line, using real monthly wages across total sample and subgroups, ages 15–64, 2012–18.

	2012	2018	Percentage change 2012–18
Total	51	57	13
Sex			
Male	49	55	13
Female	57	68	18
Age Group			
15–24	72	72	1
25–34	55	59	8
35–49	44	55	25
50–64	34	46	36
Region			
Metropolitan	42	50	18
Urban Lower Egypt	47	51	10
Rural Lower Egypt	51	60	18
Urban Upper Egypt	56	57	1
Rural Upper Egypt	62	69	12
Educational Attainment			
None	65	66	1
Basic and secondary	52	59	12
Post–secondary and above	37	47	25
Industry			
Agriculture	71	67	–6
Industry	47	53	15
Services	49	56	14
Sector			
Government	45	55	23
Public enterprise	31	35	12
Private	61	60	0

Source: Authors' calculations using ELMPS 1988–2018.

plot box and whisker distributions for wages by different circumstance characteristics. If inequality of opportunity exists, these distributions will be distinct.

The circumstances that individuals are born into continue to play a determinant role in individuals' wages. Looking at wage outcomes by father's education, there was a consistent ordinal ranking across each wave where the higher the father's level of education, the higher the typical wages of the individual (Figure 3.7). However, compared with 1988, a father with basic or secondary education has seemed to make less of a difference over time, where in 2018, only individuals whose father had a post-secondary or above education seemed to have substantially higher wages, which is consistent with Assaad et al. (2018) and El Enbaby and Galal (2015).[5]

---

[5] In the 1998 ELMPS, father's education was recorded only for those fathers not in the household, unlike in following waves where it was recorded for all fathers.

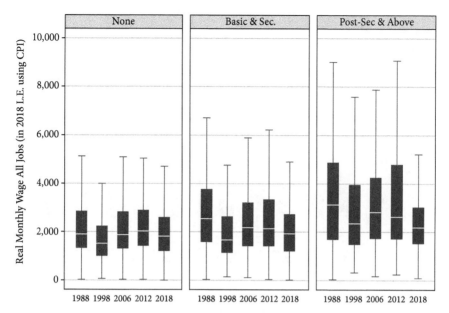

Figure 3.7 Distribution of real monthly wages by father's level of education, full sample, ages 15–64, 2018 Egyptian pounds, 1988–2018.

Source: Authors' calculations using ELMPS 1988–2018.

Observing individuals' wage distributions by their mother's level of education presents a similar ranking, where the greater one's mother's education, the greater one's wages. Comparing wages according to whether an individual was born in a rural or urban area displayed a consistent ordering, where urban-born individuals had higher wages than rural-born ones (Figure 3.8). However, the differences narrowed between 2012 and 2018.

Turning to wage mobility within the earnings distribution, the panel aspect of the data allows us to explore how individuals shifted in rank from one wave of the data to the next. Figure 3.9 presents the percentage of individuals who either moved upwards or downwards, or remained within the same wage quintile rank across pairs of waves. The columns in each graph show individual ranks, and each column includes the share of individuals by their quintile rank in the following wave. The sample consisted of those individuals with positive wages and aged 15–64 in both waves of a pair, thus representing the better off in the population. New entrants were not included, and workers who remained in the labor force would be expected to move up the distribution over time based on experience. Additionally, individuals earning low wages might have left wage work or employment altogether. Despite this, the data can provide some useful information about who performed relatively well compared with others. The overall level of mobility since has remained mostly unchanged. Figure 3.9 shows that in both 2012 and 2018, downward mobility increased for those who started in the top wage quintile;

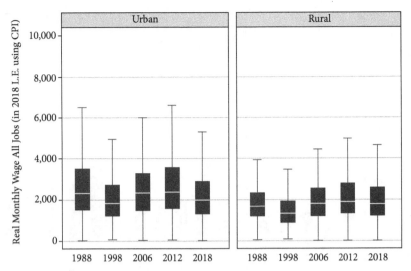

Figure 3.8. Distribution of real monthly wages by location of birth, ages 15–64, 2018 Egyptian pounds, 1988–2018.

Source: Authors' calculations using ELMPS 1988–2018.

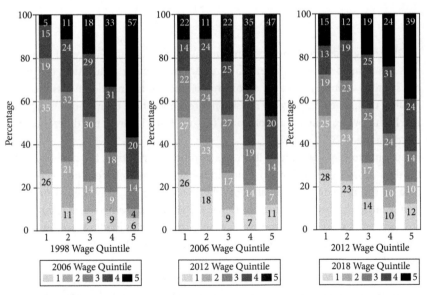

Figure 3.9. Wage quintile rank by previous wave wage quintile rank (percentage), ages 15–64, wage workers in both waves, 1998–2018.

Source: Authors' calculations using ELMPS Panel 1998–2018.

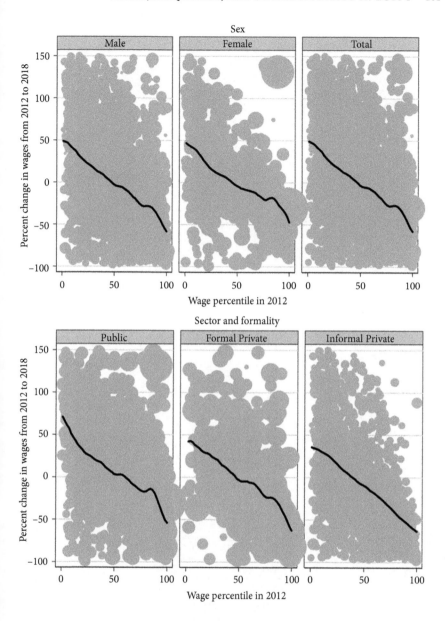

Figure 3.10. Wage growth, percent change in wages 2012–18 by wage percentile in 2012, by sex, sector, education, and occupation, ages 15–64.

Note: Occupations have been arranged as follows. High: managers, technicians, and associate professionals; Medium: clerical support, service and sales, and craft and trade workers; Low: agricultural, plant and machinery, and other elementary occupations.

Source: Authors' calculations using ELMPS 2012–18.

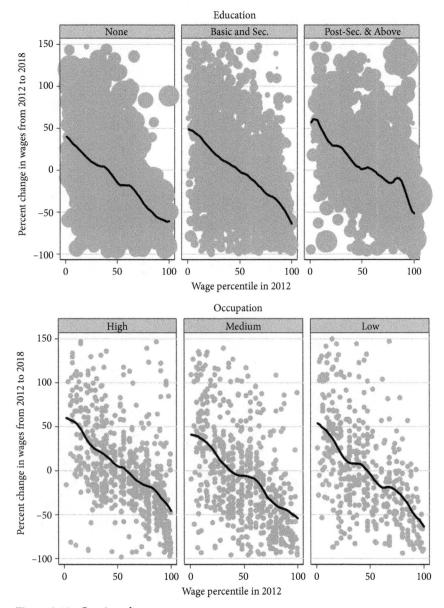

Figure 3.10. Continued

about 39 percent of individuals in the top quintile remained there from the previous wave in 2018, 47 percent in 2012, and 57 percent in 2018. At the lower end of the distribution, just over 70 percent of individuals from the first quintile improved their rank in the following wave, and this indeed was the pattern between 1998 and 2018, indicating that not much changed in this respect.

Figure 3.10 displays a scatter plot with a kernel-weighted local polynomial regression for the relationship between wage growth from 2012 to 2018 and wage percentile in 2012. The lower an individuals' wage percentile rank in 2012, the higher their wage growth to 2018. Conversely, the higher an individual's wage percentile rank in 2012, the greater their chance of experiencing a decline in real wages. This change was highly consistent across all subgroups, by sex, sector, and formality, level of education, and occupation.

3.4 Estimating Returns to Education and Wage Differentials by Sector and Sex

To explore some possible explanations for the evolution of wages and inequality that we have recorded, in this section we measure gender- and sector-based wage differentials, and incremental returns to education from Mincerian wage equation estimates that correct for individuals' differences in characteristics and returns to those characteristics. The Mincerian method offers two main advantages: First, it estimates a linear relationship between logarithm of wage and schooling (Card, 1999). Second, it takes into account the distinction between schooling and work experience variables. However, the method has its limitations, as it does not overcome the endogeneity problem that arises from omitted variables, such as parental connections and motivation (Assaad et al., 2018).

We follow a methodology similar to Said (2015), using an ordinary least squares regression to estimate wages in the public (p), and private (r) sectors as follows:

$$Ln(w_{is}) = X_{is}\beta_s + u_s \qquad (s = p, r)$$

where $Ln(w_{is})$ is log hourly wages of individual i in sector s and X is the set of individual and job-related characteristics known to be of relevance in determining wages. This is estimated for males (m) and females (f), resulting in four equations. See Appendix 3.1. for the methodology to calculate corrected public–private and male–female wage differentials.

We can see the uncorrected (crude) gender (male/female) mean wage ratio in 2018 remained at 1.13 for the total sample, which was similar to the level in 2006 and the ratio based on 2012 ELMPS data reported in the International Labour Organization (ILO) global wage report 2018–19 for hourly wages: 1.14 (ILO, 2018). This ratio, upon correction, turned out to be negative, indicating greater women's hourly earnings when compared with men. However, this result has been attributed to the clustering of women in highly paid jobs and the lack of their representation at the lower end of the spectrum (ILO, 2018).

Table 3.3 presents crude sector and gender wage gaps, expressed as differentials (as opposed to ratios), as well as corrected differentials for 2012 and 2018 based

Table 3.3 Corrected sector and gender wage differentials, 2012–18.

	2012		2018	
	Crude	Corrected	Crude	Corrected
Sector Wage Differentials				
Male public–private	0.00	0.22	−0.09	0.12
Female public–private	0.49	0.65	0.69	0.62
Gender Wage Differentials (Female–Male)				
Public sector	0.08	0.08	0.22	−0.07
Private sector	−0.40	−0.27	−0.56	−0.60

Source: Authors' calculations using ELMPS 2012–18.

on the method outlined. Crude sector and gender wage differentials are simply differences in the means of log hourly wages and thus can be interpreted as percentage differences. Compared with 2012, crude sector wage premiums slightly declined for males but increased for females in 2018. The crude gender gap in favor of men increased in both the private and public sectors.

Corrected sector wage differentials are generated on the basis of ordinary least square estimates of log hourly wage equations for the full sample, as well as for males and females separately in the public and private sectors, for 2012 and 2018. The regression estimates are shown in Tables A3.2.3 and A3.2.4. The wage differentials are calculated as the difference between predicted log hourly wages for public sector employees using the public sector wage equation and their predicted log hourly wages using the private sector equation (expressed as a proportion of the former). Similarly, corrected gender wage differentials are the difference between predicted female wages using the female equation and their predicted wages using the male equation.

Traditionally the corrected gender wage gap has been very compressed or even positive (i.e. indicating higher wages for women) in the public sector (Said, 2015). But, as seen in Table 3.3, between 2012 and 2018, the gender gap turned from 8 percent in favor of women in the public sector to 7 percent in favor of men. In the private sector, the deterioration of the gender wage gap was even more notable, from 27 percent in 2012 to around 60 percent in favor of men. In terms of public sector wage differentials, it decreased from around 22 percent to 12 percent for men, and slightly from 65 percent to 62 percent for women. The latter is a large differential and shows that the continued attractiveness of public sector employment for women in Egypt is based on both wage and non-wage (job security) reasons (see Chapter 5 in this book on the continued preference for public sector employment).

Based on the regression results in Tables A3.2.3 and A3.2.4, it is also possible to calculate incremental rates of return to education. These are the annualized percentage increase in wages for one more year of school within a level, displayed in Table A3.2.5. Middle school is compared with elementary school, vocational and general high school are compared with middle school, and post-secondary institute and university are compared with general high school. The results indicate that returns to education were still much higher in the public than private sector, except for female university graduates, who were rewarded better for their credentials in the private sector. This might be a positive selection story, in which only the best educated and most skilled women were able to participate in the labor market and could find jobs in the private sector, or educated women would only accept private sector jobs when highly paid.

Rising returns for women between 2012 and 2018 in the private sector were observed for middle school and post-secondary institute, and university levels were consistent with rising inequality among them, but the premium they received in the public sector seemed to be for secondary levels. For men, returns declined, especially for general and vocational high school and higher levels. The "vocational track" remains the most inferior route for men (Krafft, 2018).[6]

3.5 Conclusion

Using data from several waves of the ELMPS, this chapter has explored trends in inequality and mobility in Egyptian wage structures. The analysis points to declining real wages and incomes and a rise in inequality between 2012 and 2018. These findings were robust to using different measures of inequality that were sensitive to variations in different parts of the distribution, and to definitions of income that included transfers and non-wage income.

As a result of the above trends, the share of those below the low wage line (working poor) increased, including for older workers, workers with higher education, and government workers, and not just for youth and those in informal employment. Inequality of opportunity was persistent, but did not vary much over time.

Focusing on the panel data (those with wages in multiple waves of the survey) reveals a consistent and sizable degree of mobility within the wage distribution. Those who tended to fare better from 2012 to 2018 were males, those in the public sector, and those with higher education and occupations, but the differences across subgroups were not large. There was a high degree of inequality among women and by sex in the main sample, with a large corrected gender wage gap (broadly indicative of gender-based discrimination), especially in the private sector, that reached 60 percent in 2018 (compared with only 27 percent in 2012).

---

[6] To compare trends in expansion in education and in relation to these low and falling returns to different levels of education, and for more information on education trends over time, see Chapter 1.

Overall, there is evidence that vulnerable groups (including those who had high representation among the working poor) and women fared worse in terms of wage and income developments over the period 2012–18 in Egypt. In particular, the results indicate that recent real wage/income erosion and dispersion in Egypt were consistent with widening gender segmentation. Returns to education, which increased for women with qualifications lower than university education, and for female university graduates in the private sector, were consistent with rising inequality and public sector pay premia observed for them. But this was not the case for men, for whom returns at almost all levels declined in both sectors, as did returns to experience. Thus, the latest increasing inequality trends do not seem to be associated with the standard human capital explanations.

The findings of the chapter call attention to policies and interventions to help generate higher paying and decent jobs for new entrants and especially women in the labor market. These policy actions are becoming particularly crucial following the labor market repercussions of the recent pandemic crisis in 2020, which is likely to have put further pressure on both purchasing power and wages of workers. According to the Central Agency for Public Mobilization and Statistics (CAPMAS) report of 2020, income levels in Egypt have been adversely affected since the pandemic crisis. In particular, 73 percent of Egyptians claimed that their income decreased, especially among those aged 15–34. Taking a closer look at the gender dimension, the pandemic crisis is also expected to disproportionately and adversely affect women, especially given that the share of women who reported becoming unemployed was 30 percent, compared with 26 percent for men (CAPMAS, 2020).

Previous studies showed that investing in the social service sector, the care economy, and knowledge intensive services was particularly attractive to women, and was associated with higher wages and productivity for those workers (see Schricke, 2013; Said et al., 2018). Policies that address different types of gender-based discrimination and the inferior treatment of women in the workplace are very necessary, given the current level of wage inequality between men and women in the Egyptian private sector. These can include gender diversity incentive schemes and sharing the burden of female protective legislation with society (such as paying maternity leave out of social security funds), to incentivize the hiring, retraining, and promotion of women across different occupations.

Acknowledgments

The authors acknowledge the support of Agence Française de Développement (AFD). We also acknowledge the general support of the World Bank, the International Labour Organization, AFD, UN Women, and the Arab Fund for Economic and Social Development for the Egypt Labor Market Panel Survey 2018, on which this chapter is based. We appreciate the invaluable comments from Ragui Assaad, Caroline Krafft, Sevane Ananian, and the participants in the Workshop on The Egyptian Labor Market: A Focus on Gender and Economic Vulnerability, July 2019. All errors are the authors'.

Appendix 3.1. Methodology for calculating public–private and gender wage differentials

Given the parameter estimates in Tables A3.2.3 and A3.2.4 in Appendix 3.2 , public–private wage differentials can be measured at the mean of the sample, using the following decomposition formula:

$$D_p = \ln(\overline{w}_p) - \ln(\overline{w}_r) = \frac{(\beta_p + \beta_r)(\overline{X}_p - \overline{X}_r)}{2} + \frac{(\beta_p - \beta_r)(\overline{X}_p + \overline{X}_r)}{2}.$$

D_p refers to the wage differential between the public and the private sector. $Ln(\overline{w})$ refers to the mean of log wages. This decomposes the wage differential into two main components. The first term, which is "explained," is the part of the differential attributable to differences in observed characteristics of workers. The second term, which is "unexplained," is the part of the differential resulting from differences in the pay structure, or in returns to the characteristics. The unexplained component also includes the differential in base wage (the constant term) that can be interpreted as a premium or pure rent from attachment to a particular sector. Similarly the same formula can be used to decompose the male–female wage gap as follows:

$$D_f = \ln(\overline{w}_m) - \ln(\overline{w}_f) = \frac{(\beta_m + \beta_f)(\overline{X}_m - \overline{X}_f)}{2} + \frac{(\beta_m - \beta_f)(\overline{X}_m + \overline{X}_f)}{2}$$

Here the unexplained component (second term on the right-hand side) is taken to refer to a rough estimate of gender-based discrimination.

Appendix 3.2. Detailed Tables of Findings

Table A3.2.1 Mean real monthly wages in 2018 Egyptian pounds for full sample and subgroups, ages 15–64, 1988–2018.

	Mean					N					Change (in percent)			
	1988	1998	2006	2012	2018	1988	1998	2006	2012	2018	88–98	98–06	06–12	12–18
Total	2,435	1,880	2,442	2,549	2,278	4,205	4,702	7,464	10,160	10,570	−23	30	4	−11
Sex														
Male	2,569	1,927	2,529	2,606	2,324	3,305	3,683	5,917	8,370	8,979	−25	31	3	−11
Female	1,927	1,682	2,099	2,293	2,056	900	1,019	1,547	1,790	1,591	−13	25	9	−10
Age Group														
15–24	1,746	1,338	1,670	1,884	1,741	982	878	1,415	1,598	1,483	−23	25	13	−8
25–34	2,262	1,744	2,277	2,397	2,197	1,412	1,333	2,537	3,992	3,883	−23	31	5	−8
35–49	2,917	2,047	2,698	2,737	2,406	1,296	1,778	2,475	3,144	3,655	−30	32	1	−12
50–64	3,017	2,485	3,254	3,178	2,589	515	713	1,037	1,426	1,549	−18	31	−2	−19
Region														
Urban	2,762	2,207	2,795	2,879	2,503	2,810	3,294	4,503	5,000	4,050	−20	27	3	−13
Rural	1,979	1,543	2,078	2,247	2,119	1,395	1,408	2,961	5,160	6,520	−22	35	8	−6
Industry														
Agriculture	1,678	1,323	1,653	1,851	1,988	534	364	617	1,066	1,551	−21	25	12	7
Manufacturing	2,832	2,100	2,509	2,669	2,298	1,117	1,241	1,983	2,937	3,078	−26	19	6	−14
Services	2,541	1,900	2,540	2,614	2,360	2,245	2,957	4,773	6,027	5,354	−25	34	3	−10
Occupation														
Low	1,936	1,662	2,047	2,115	2,086	875	776	1,426	3,015	3,148	−14	23	3	−1
Medium	2,362	1,715	2,169	2,341	2,175	1,998	2,182	3,128	3,589	4,843	−27	26	8	−7
High	3,012	2,245	2,983	3,114	2,684	1,266	1,744	2,908	3,556	2,463	−25	33	4	−14

	Mean					N					Change (in percent)			
	1988	1998	2006	2012	2018	1988	1998	2006	2012	2018	88–98	98–06	06–12	12–18
Sector and Formality														
Public	1,986	1,639	2,023	2,164	1,946	1,409	1,569	2,914	4,881	6,293	−17	23	7	−10
Private formal	2,645	1,948	2,690	2,839	2,676	2,300	2,656	3,564	4,058	3,144	−26	38	6	−6
Private informal	2,791	2,450	2,860	3,014	2,720	496	477	986	1,221	1,133	−12	17	5	−10
Education														
Illiterate	1,916	1,438	1,966	2,003	1,935	1,077	709	997	1,394	1,542	−25	37	2	−3
Literate without diploma	2,455	1,712	2,255	2,245	2,146	616	411	434	382	633	−30	32	0	−4
Elementary school	2,394	1,818	2,119	2,213	1,974	313	506	738	991	820	−24	17	4	−11
Middle school	2,125	1,899	2,407	2,236	2,057	294	283	353	586	717	−11	27	−7	−8
General high school	3,104	2,287	2,661	2,460	2,182	103	78	59	258	323	−26	16	−8	−11
Vocational high school	2,272	1,710	2,238	2,425	2,237	882	1,272	2,625	3,619	3,965	−25	31	8	−8
Post-secondary institute	2,425	1,872	2,638	2,789	2,562	262	431	492	439	367	−23	41	6	−8
University & above	3,614	2,666	3,236	3,260	2,752	658	1,007	1,765	2,481	2,201	−26	21	1	−16

Source: Authors' calculations using ELMPS 1988–2018.

Table A3.2.2 Mean real hourly wages in 2018 Egyptian pounds for full sample and subgroups, ages 15–64, 1998–2018.

	Male				Female				Total			
	1998	2006	2012	2018	1998	2006	2012	2018	1998	2006	2012	2018
Total	9.9	11.7	13.5	11.2	9.8	11.6	14.3	11.4	9.9	11.7	13.6	11.3
Age group												
15–24	7.0	8.4	10.1	8.9	5.3	5.4	9.4	8.0	6.7	7.8	10.0	8.8
25–34	9.2	10.8	12.4	10.4	8.1	9.6	11.9	10.1	9.0	10.6	12.3	10.4
35–49	10.7	13.0	14.9	11.9	11.2	13.3	14.6	11.1	10.8	13.1	14.8	11.8
50–64	13.2	15.7	17.0	13.5	17.1	18.5	20.4	14.9	13.7	16.2	17.7	13.9
Location												
Urban	11.5	13.6	15.0	12.2	11.2	13.1	15.4	12.3	11.4	13.4	15.1	12.2
Rural	8.5	10.1	12.2	10.6	6.9	8.7	12.2	10.2	8.3	9.9	12.2	10.6
Industry												
Agriculture	8.2	8.9	10.2	10.4	5.3	8.0	10.2	9.0	7.9	8.8	10.2	10.3
Manufacturing	10.3	12.0	13.7	11.4	10.0	9.2	14.1	9.4	10.2	11.7	13.7	11.2
Services	10.1	12.1	14.0	11.4	10.2	12.3	14.4	12.2	10.2	12.2	14.1	11.6
Occupation												
Low	8.8	9.6	11.1	10.4	5.4	5.8	8.9	8.1	8.6	9.2	10.9	10.2
Medium	8.6	10.1	11.8	10.3	8.2	8.6	11.7	10.6	8.6	9.9	11.8	10.3
High	13.2	16.1	18.9	15.2	11.2	13.6	15.5	12.8	12.5	15.2	17.6	14.3
Sector and Formality												
Public	10.7	13.7	16.4	13.7	10.6	13.4	15.8	13.9	10.7	13.6	16.2	13.8
Private formal	11.2	12.9	14.6	12.4	10.7	11.7	12.3	9.0	11.2	12.7	14.4	11.7
Private informal	8.5	9.2	11.1	9.9	5.7	5.8	7.8	7.6	8.3	8.8	10.9	9.8

Education	Male				Female				Total			
	1998	2006	2012	2018	1998	2006	2012	2018	1998	2006	2012	2018
Illiterate	8.2	9.5	11.0	10.1	5.5	6.9	8.2	7.6	7.9	9.3	10.8	9.8
Reads & writes	8.8	10.2	12.0	10.8	4.4	4.6	8.2	6.2	8.7	9.9	11.7	10.5
Primary	8.8	9.7	11.2	9.8	6.7	5.0	9.6	9.8	8.7	9.5	11.1	9.8
Preparatory	8.8	10.6	11.4	9.8	10.5	9.0	10.7	8.4	8.9	10.5	11.4	9.7
General high school	11.6	12.6	12.9	10.7	14.3	11.3	13.3	10.4	12.0	12.3	13.0	10.6
Vocational high school	9.0	11.0	12.6	10.7	8.3	10.5	13.3	10.9	8.8	10.9	12.8	10.7
Post-secondary institute	11.1	12.9	15.2	12.8	10.0	12.1	14.0	10.6	10.7	12.7	14.9	12.2
University & above	15.2	17.0	18.9	14.7	13.2	14.8	16.4	13.6	14.6	16.3	18.1	14.4

Source: Authors' calculations using ELMPS 1988–2018.

Table A3.2.3. Ordinary Least Square estimates of log hourly wage equations, 2012.

	(1)	(2)	(3)	(4)	(5)
	Total	Male Private	Male Public	Female Private	Female Public
Experience	0.029***	0.025***	0.024***	0.040***	0.032***
	(0.001)	(0.003)	(0.004)	(0.011)	(0.005)
Experience squared	−0.000***	−0.000***	−0.000*	−0.001**	−0.000**
	(0.000)	(0.000)	(0.000)	(0.000)	(0.000)
Education (omitted category illiterate)					
Literate without diploma	0.044	0.119**	0.170***	0.063	0.246
	(0.029)	(0.053)	(0.066)	(0.208)	(0.191)
Elementary school	0.082***	0.110***	0.137**	0.111	0.979***
	(0.021)	(0.038)	(0.059)	(0.134)	(0.331)
Middle school	0.123***	0.125***	0.333***	0.201	0.282
	(0.025)	(0.048)	(0.064)	(0.168)	(0.173)
General high school	0.275***	0.307***	0.580***	0.483***	0.485***
	(0.035)	(0.067)	(0.080)	(0.181)	(0.164)
Vocational high school	0.231***	0.199***	0.582***	0.142	0.510***
	(0.017)	(0.034)	(0.048)	(0.098)	(0.136)
Post–secondary institute	0.329***	0.386***	0.644***	0.329**	0.556***
	(0.028)	(0.057)	(0.063)	(0.154)	(0.144)
University & above	0.538***	0.562***	0.927***	0.631***	0.781***
	(0.018)	(0.038)	(0.049)	(0.095)	(0.136)
Constant	1.154***	1.142***	0.809***	0.858***	0.777***
	(0.020)	(0.041)	(0.059)	(0.097)	(0.138)
Observations	10,061	3,052	5,226	349	1,434
R–squared	0.165	0.103	0.224	0.222	0.231

Note: Standard errors in parentheses: ***p <0.01, ** p<0.05, *p<0.1.
Source: Authors' calculations using ELMPS 2012.

Table A3.2.4 Ordinary Least Square estimates of log hourly wage equations, 2018.

	(1)	(2)	(3)	(4)	(5)
	Total	Male Private	Male Public	Female Private	Female Public
Experience	0.025***	0.023***	0.022***	0.014	0.013**
	(0.002)	(0.003)	(0.004)	(0.009)	(0.006)
Experience squared	−0.000***	−0.000***	−0.000***	−0.000	0.000
	(0.000)	(0.000)	(0.000)	(0.000)	(0.000)
Education (omitted category illiterate)					
Literate without diploma	0.108***	0.129**	0.326***	−0.038	−0.084
	(0.032)	(0.054)	(0.082)	(0.170)	(0.302)
Elementary school	0.081***	0.088*	0.147*	−0.003	0.796***
	(0.029)	(0.047)	(0.089)	(0.161)	(0.187)
Middle school	0.160***	0.170***	0.325***	0.237	0.314
	(0.030)	(0.050)	(0.080)	(0.155)	(0.196)
General high school	0.188***	0.081	0.502***	−0.204	0.935***
	(0.040)	(0.067)	(0.096)	(0.183)	(0.168)
Vocational high school	0.173***	0.150***	0.468***	−0.060	0.714***
	(0.021)	(0.036)	(0.061)	(0.110)	(0.115)

	(1)	(2)	(3)	(4)	(5)
	Total	Male Private	Male Public	Female Private	Female Public
Post–secondary institute	0.213***	0.208***	0.624***	0.253	0.569***
	(0.037)	(0.070)	(0.083)	(0.182)	(0.128)
University & above	0.404***	0.319***	0.789***	0.248**	1.004***
	(0.022)	(0.041)	(0.062)	(0.102)	(0.116)
Constant	1.943***	2.004***	1.612***	1.831***	1.353***
	(0.024)	(0.041)	(0.077)	(0.103)	(0.116)
Observations	9,726	3,607	4,642	384	1,093
R–squared	0.084	0.037	0.144	0.068	0.216

Note: Standard errors in parentheses: ***p <0.01, ** p<0.05, *p<0.1.
Source: Authors' calculations using ELMPS 2018.

Table A3.2.5. Annualized incremental returns to education in Egypt (percentage), 2012–18.

		2012	2018	2012-18 percentage points of increase/decrease
Male Public				
	Middle school	6.5	5.9	−0.6
	General high school	8.2	5.9	−2.3
	Vocational high school	8.3	4.8	−3.5
	Post–secondary institute	2.1	4.1	1.9
	University & above	8.7	7.2	−1.5
Male Private				
	Middle school	0.5	2.7	2.2
	General high school	6.1	−3.0	−9.0
	Vocational high school	2.5	−0.7	−3.1
	Post–secondary institute	2.6	4.2	1.6
	University & above	6.4	6.0	−0.4
Female Public				
	Middle school	−23.2	−16.1	7.2
	General high school	6.8	20.7	13.9
	Vocational high school	7.6	13.3	5.7
	Post–secondary institute	2.4	−12.2	−14.6
	University & above	7.4	1.7	−5.7
Female Private				
	Middle school	3.0	8.0	5.0
	General high school	9.4	−14.7	−24.1
	Vocational high school	−2.0	−9.9	−7.9
	Post–secondary institute	−5.1	15.2	20.4
	University & above	3.7	11.3	7.6
Total				
	Middle school	4.1	5.3	1.2
	General high school	5.1	0.9	−4.1
	Vocational high school	3.6	0.4	−3.2
	Post–secondary institute	1.8	0.8	−1.0
	University & above	6.6	5.4	−1.2

Source: Authors' calculations using ELMPS 2012–18.

References

Assaad, Ragui, Caroline Krafft, John E. Roemer, and Djavad Salehi-Isfahani (2018) "Inequality of Opportunity in Wages and Consumption in Egypt," *Review of Income and Wealth*, 64: S26–S54.

CAPMAS (Central Agency for Public Mobilization and Statistics), 2020. *The Effect of Coronavirus on the Egyptian families*, (in Arabic).

Card, David, 1999. "The causal effect of education on earnings," Handbook of Labor Economics, in: O. Ashenfelter & D. Card (ed.), Handbook of Labor Economics, edition 1, volume 3, chapter 30, pages 1801-1863.

Cichello, Paul, Hala Abou-Ali, and Daniela Marotta (2013) "What Happened to Real Earnings in Egypt, 2008 to 2009?" *Journal of Labor & Development*, 10: 27–33.

Datt, Gaurav and Jennifer Olmsted (2006) "Induced Wage Effects of Changes in Food Prices in Egypt," *The Journal of Development Studies*, 40 (4): 137–66.

El Enbaby, Hodo and Rami Galal (2015) "Inequality of Opportunity in Individuals' Wages and Households' Assets in Egypt." Economic Research Forum Working Paper Series No. 942. Cairo.

El-Haddad, Amirah and May Gadallah (2018) "The Informalization of the Egyptian Economy (1982–2012): A Factor in Growing Wage Inequality?" Economic Research Forum Working Paper Series No. 1210.

ILO (International Labour Organization) (2018) *Global Wage Report 2018/19: What Lies Behind Gender Pay Gaps*. Geneva: International Labour Organization.

Krafft, Caroline (2018) "Is School the Best Route to Skills? Returns to Vocational School and Vocational Skills in Egypt," *The Journal of Development Studies*, 54 (7): 1100–20.

Krafft, Caroline, Ragui Assaad and Khandker Wahedur Rahman (2021) 'Introducing the Egypt Labor Market Panel Survey 2018', *IZA Journal of Development and Migration* (Forthcoming).

Roemer, John (1998) Equality of Opportunity. Cambridge, MA: Harvard University Press

Said, Mona (2015) "Wages and Inequality in the Egyptian Labor Market in an Era of Financial Crisis and Revolution," in Ragui Assaad and Caroline Krafft (eds) *The Egyptian Labor Market in an Era of Revolution*, pp. 52–69. Oxford: Oxford University Press.

Said, Mona, Rami Galal, Susan Joekes, and Mina Sami (2018) "Gender Diversity, Productivity, and Wages in Egyptian Firms." Economic Research Forum Working Paper Series No. 1207. Cairo.

Said, Mona, Rami Galal, and Mina Sami (2019) "Inequality and Income Mobility in Egypt." Economic Research Forum Working Paper Series No. 1368. Cairo.

Schricke, Esther (2013) "Occurrence of Cluster Structures in Knowledge-Intensive Services." Fraunhofer ISI, Working Papers Firms and Region Nr. R1/2013). Karlsruhe.

Tellioglu, Isin and Panos Konandreas (2017) "Agricultural Policies, Trade and Sustainable Development in Egypt." Geneva: International Centre for Trade and Sustainable Development, and Rome: United Nations Food and Agriculture Organization.

4

The School to Work Transition and Youth Economic Vulnerability in Egypt

Mona Amer and Marian Atallah

4.1 Introduction

This chapter examines the school to work transition patterns of young people (aged 15–34) in Egypt over the last two decades (1998–2018).[1] In particular, it seeks to update the findings on labor market insertion trajectories using data from the most recent Egyptian Labor Market Panel Survey (ELMPS) fielded in 2018 compared with its previous waves in 1998, 2006, and 2012. We use the labor market history module in the 2018 survey to elicit information on early labor market outcomes, such as the time taken to find the first job and the type of job found after finishing school. Moreover, we set out to define youth economic vulnerability in the work setting and investigate its symptoms in the Egyptian labor market (informality, irregular work, unpaid work, and self-employment). We conclude by shedding light on some of the potential factors behind this vulnerability, including family background and socioeconomic status.

The chapter proceeds as follows. Section 4.2 presents the socioeconomic characteristics of Egyptian youth by depicting trends in demographics, educational attainment, and labor market outcomes (labor force participation, unemployment, and the share of youth neither in education nor in employment) by sex and education level. Section 4.3 focuses on labor market entry by analyzing trends in first labor market status, unemployment duration, and time to first job by sex, educational attainment, and school exit cohort. Specifically, we compare two cohorts of school leavers: those who left school between 2006 and 2010, and those who graduated between 2011 and 2014. This distinction helps us capture the potential changes in the Egyptian labor market following the January 25 uprising in 2011, along with the economic and political shifts that followed.[2] In addition to insertion patterns, labor market dynamics are also explored by examining the

---

[1] Where comparable data are available, we extend the analysis back to 1988 using the 1988 Labor Force Survey.
[2] We do not include those who graduated after 2014 to be able to observe the labor market transitions up to four years following school exit for the younger cohort.

Mona Amer and Marian Atallah, *The School to Work Transition and Youth Economic Vulnerability in Egypt* In: *The Egyptian Labor Market: A Focus on Gender and Economic Vulnerability*. Edited by: Caroline Krafft and Ragui Assaad, Oxford University Press. © Economic Research Forum 2022. DOI: 10.1093/oso/9780192847911.003.0005

early career paths in the first few years after leaving school by sex and school exit cohort. Section 4.4 looks at precarious and vulnerable youth employment trends, taking into account informality, irregularity, unpaid work, and self-employment by sex and education level. Finally, Section 4.5 investigates family background (mother's education and father's occupation) as a potential channel for inequality of opportunity in the labor market by sex and school exit cohort. We conclude and discuss the implications of our findings in Section 4.6.

4.2 Socioeconomic Characteristics of Youth

4.2.1 Demographics of youth

In 2018, Egypt had 27.6 million people aged 15–34, representing around a third of the total population (Figures 4.1 and 4.2). The share of young people had been increasing from 1988, reaching a peak in 2006, then started to decline in 2012 and 2018. Looking at the age subgroups in Figure 4.2, the decline appears to have been driven by the drop in the shares of the intermediate age groups (20–24 and 25–29), whereas the shares of the youngest and oldest groups (15–19 and 30–34) showed a slight increase. The decline in the shares of youth in their twenties is consistent with the aging of the youth bulge previously documented in the Egyptian labor market; see, for example, Amer (2015) and Assaad and Krafft (2015).[3]

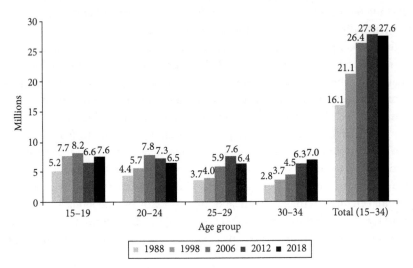

Figure 4.1   Youth population size (in millions) by age group, ages 15–34, 1988–2018.
Source: Authors' calculations based on LFS 1988, ELMPS 1998–2018.

---

[3] See Chapter 1 for more details on the evolution of the population structure in Egypt between 1988 and 2018.

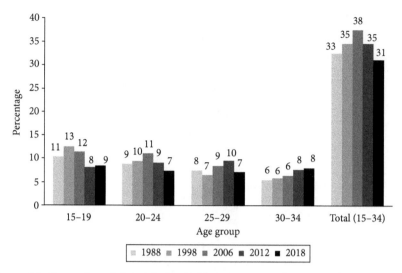

Figure 4.2 Share of youth in total population by age group (percentage), ages 15–34, 1988–2018.

Source: Authors' calculations based on LFS 1988, ELMPS 1998–2018.

4.2.2 Educational attainment

Figure 4.3 examines the education profiles of young people between 1988 and 2018. In 2018, secondary education was the most common level of educational attainment, with 39 percent of those aged 15–34 being secondary-degree holders. On the contrary, less than 15 percent were holders of university or post-graduate degrees, with a slightly higher representation of women. Going back in time, it can be observed that the share of those with no formal schooling (illiterate/read and write) fell substantially for both sexes between 1988 and 1998, reflecting improved access to schooling over this period. The reduction was more pronounced for women, with the share of uneducated women going down from more than a half to only a third of the young female population. However, between 2012 and 2018, the education distribution did not exhibit much change, especially for men. For women, a small increase in basic education resulted in a continued decline in illiteracy rates.

4.2.3 Labor market outcomes and youth not in education, employment or training (NEET)

This section focuses on youth labor market outcomes, including labor force participation, unemployment rates, unemployment duration as well as the share and characteristics of NEET youth. In terms of labor force participation, strong gender

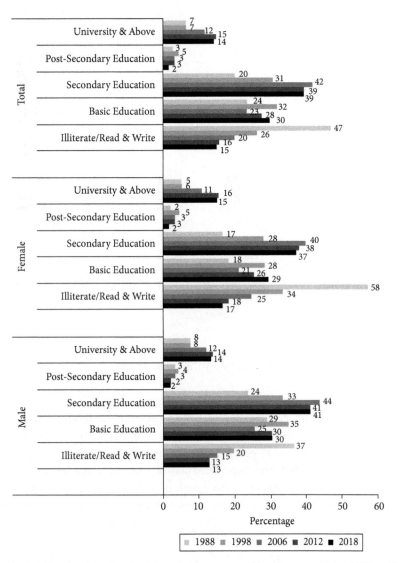

Figure 4.3 Youth educational attainment (percentage) by sex, ages 15–34, 1988–2018.
Source: Authors' calculations based on LFS 1988, ELMPS 1998–2018.

differences appear in Figure 4.4. While around 64 percent of men aged 15–34 participated in the labor market in 2018, the participation rate was only 17 percent for women. It is also worth noting that labor force participation rates decreased from 2012 to 2018 by around 7 percentage points for men and 4 percentage points for women. The decline was most severe for those aged 20–24, suggesting delayed labor market entry. The only age/sex subgroup that had higher labor force participation rates in 2018 than in 2012 was that of women aged 15–19, whose participation went up by around 3 percentage points between the two waves.

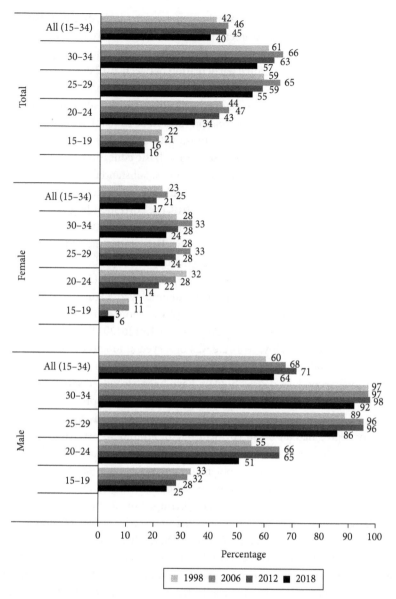

Figure 4.4 Labor force participation rate (percentage), by sex and age group, ages 15–34, 1998–2018.

Note: Standard (search required) market labor force definition, seven-day reference period.

Source: Authors' calculations based on ELMPS 1998–2018.

Figure 4.5 plots labor force participation rates by level of education. When considering both men and women, those with a university education had the highest participation rates across all rounds. As for the change in participation over time, the drop in labor force participation between 2012 and 2018 previously documented in Figure 4.4 was most pronounced among men with post-secondary education and women with secondary education. Finally, although men in all education groups had lower participation rates in 2018 relative to 2012, women's labor force participation declined for those with secondary education or above, but rose slightly for women in the illiterate and basic education groups.

In addition to labor force participation rates, substantial differences exist in unemployment rates by sex (Figure 4.6). While the unemployment rate stood at around 8 percent for men aged 15–34 in 2018, the corresponding rate for women was four times higher (at 32 percent).[4] As for the change between 2012 and 2018, the unemployment rate went up for men, particularly among the youngest age group (15–19) who witnessed a doubling of unemployment rates, but fell noticeably for women especially among the youngest (15–19) and the oldest (30–34) age groups.

Regarding the educational status of the unemployed, Figure 4.7 suggests that unemployment among young people in Egypt was more concentrated among the highly educated, as pointed out by Assaad and Krafft (2014). In both 2012 and 2018, the highest unemployment rate was observed among those with university education (around 22 percent). Meanwhile, the unemployment rates for secondary and post-secondary degree-holders have been steadily declining over time. Focusing on differences by sex, educated women had disproportionately high unemployment rates relative to their male counterparts. For instance, women with a university degree had an unemployment rate of around 38 percent in 2018, more than triple the unemployment rate of men with the same educational attainment.

Besides the incidence of unemployment, unemployment duration serves as an important indicator for the health of the labor market and the ease of finding a job. Figure 4.8 reports median current unemployment duration by education level. Broader education categories are used to ensure a sufficient sample size in each category. For those unemployed in 2018, median unemployment duration was highest among those with a secondary education (47 months). Over time, the largest increase in median unemployment duration occurred among women with below-secondary education, with a spike from 57 months in 2012 to 101 months in 2018, the highest value observed across all groups and survey rounds. On the contrary, median unemployment duration fell for the least educated men from 21 months in 2012 to only eight months in 2018.

We now turn to examine the profile of NEET individuals among youth aged 15–29 years. As the datasets do not identify individuals currently in training,

---

[4] These rates were higher than the unemployment rates in the general population (aged 15–64) reported in Chapter 1, which stood at around 5 percent for men and 20 percent for women.

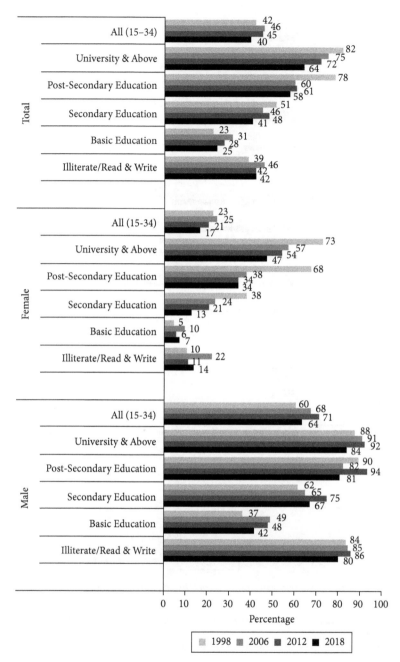

Figure 4.5 Labor force participation rate (percentage), by sex and educational attainment, ages 15–34, 1998–2018.

Note: Standard (search required) market labor force definition, seven-day reference period.

Source: Authors' calculations based on ELMPS 1998–2018.

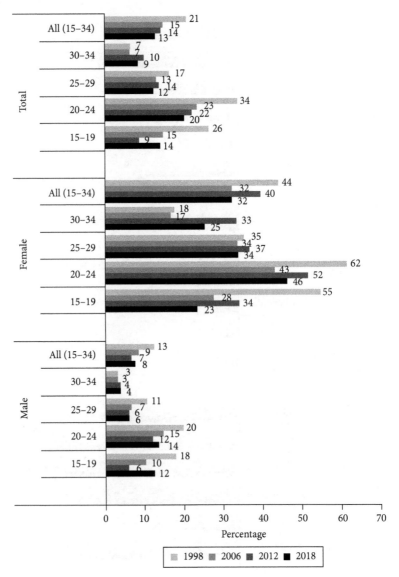

Figure 4.6 Unemployment rate (percentage), by sex and age group, ages 15–34, 1998–2018.

Note: Standard (search required) unemployment definition and market employment definition, seven-day reference period.

Source: Authors' calculations based on ELMPS 1998–2018.

NEET is defined as those who are not in education or employment using the market definition of economic activity and excluding men serving in the military.[5] In 2018, the share of women who were NEET was substantially higher than the share

---

[5] This is done by excluding male respondents who report "other" as the reason for being out of the labor force, a category that mostly captures service in the military for young men.

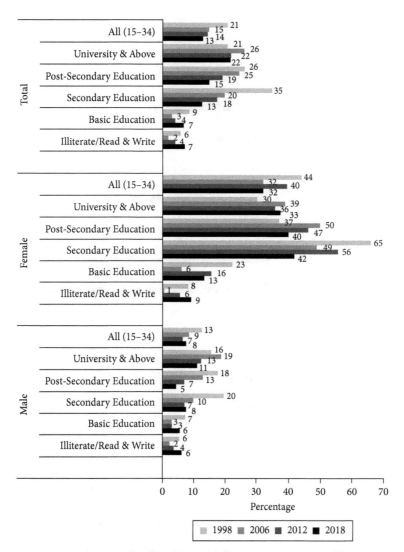

Figure 4.7 Unemployment rate (percentage), by sex and educational level, ages 15–34, 1998–2018.

Note: Standard (search required) unemployment definition and market employment definition, seven-day reference period.

Source: Authors' calculations based on ELMPS 1998–2018.

of men who were NEET (Figure 4.9). This is unsurprising and reflects both lower labor force participation (Figure 4.4) and higher unemployment (Figure 4.6) among women. However, between 2012 and 2018, the share of NEET youth increased for men but fell for women, with an overall reduction of around 3 percentage points for both sexes combined. In terms of age, the highest NEET rate in 2018 was observed among those aged 25–29 for women (82 percent), and those aged 20–24 for men (11 percent).

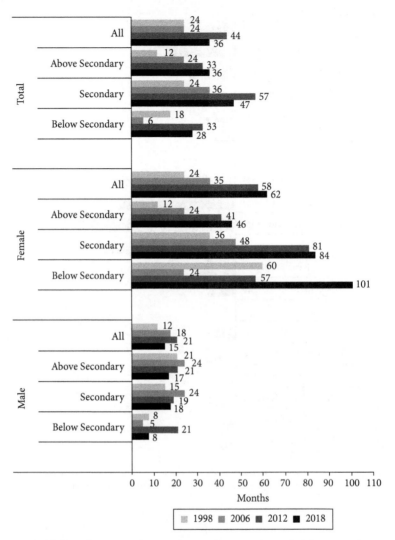

Figure 4.8 Median duration of current unemployment (months), by sex and educational attainment, ages 15–34, 1998–2018.

Note: Standard (search required) unemployment definition and market employment definition, seven-day reference period.

Source: Authors' calculations based on ELMPS 1998–2018.

Figure 4.10 sheds light on the exact labor market status of NEET individuals. Here again, clear differences emerge along gender lines. While around 86 percent of NEET women were out of the labor force in 2018, 55 percent of NEET men were unemployed men actively searching for a job. The share of discouraged unemployment (those available for work but not searching) was lower for women

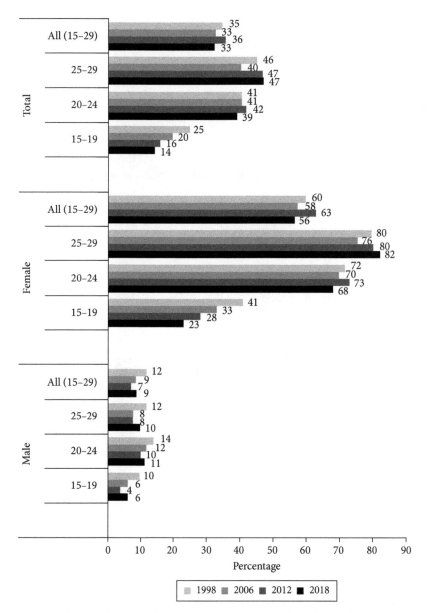

Figure 4.9 NEET rate (percentage), by sex and age, ages 15–29, 1998–2018.

Note: Market employment definition, seven-day reference period.

Source: Authors' calculations based on ELMPS 1998–2018.

than for men but increased between 2012 and 2018 by 3–4 percentage points for both sexes.

Turning to the geographical dimension, Figure 4.11 plots the NEET rate by sex and location (urban versus rural areas). In general, a larger percentage of women

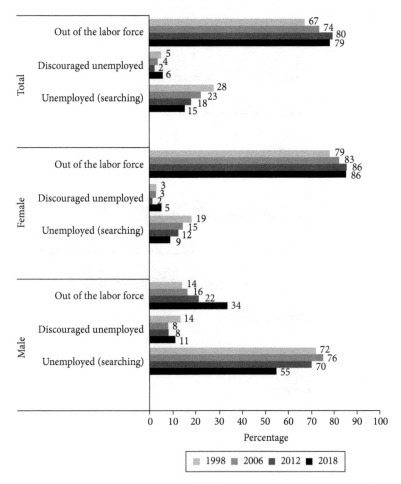

Figure 4.10 Labor market status among NEET (percentage), by sex, ages 15–29, 1998–2018.

Note: Market employment definition, seven-day reference period.

Source: Authors' calculations based on ELMPS 1998–2018.

who were NEET resided in rural areas than in urban locations in recent years, but the opposite was true for men. Different trends by sex were also observed when examining the change between 2012 and 2018, with the percent of NEET falling in both rural and urban areas for women but rising for men especially in rural areas.

4.3   Labor Market Entry and the School to Work Transition

This section presents the dynamics of insertion into the labor market by examining the trends in first labor market status after school, in the duration to the first job (in months of unemployment and in years spent either in unemployment or

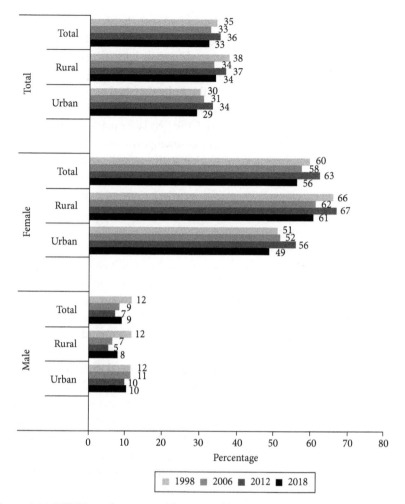

Figure 4.11 NEET rate (percentage) by sex and location, ages 15–29, market labor force definition, 1998–2018.

Note: Market employment definition, seven-day reference period.

Source: Authors' calculations based on ELMPS 1998–2018.

inactivity), in the age at first job by sex and educational attainment, and the pathways over two and four years from initial labor market status after school.

4.3.1 Distribution of first labor market statuses

The first labor market status was retrieved from the labor market history module of ELMPS 2018.[6] This module retraces retrospectively the history of employment,

---

[6] Given the limited administrative capacity and the high rates of labor market informality in many developing countries, Assaad, Krafft, and Yassin (2018) argue that retrospective modules can be a

unemployment, and inactivity of the individual since he/she left school.[7] It provides information, for those who ever worked, on the date of the end of school, the start and end dates of the first and subsequent jobs (that lasted at least six months), the characteristics of each job (economic sector, employment stability, contract, social security), and whether the individual had an unemployment or inactivity spell (that lasted at least six months) between the date of school exit and the first job. For those who never worked, the first labor market status is defined by their current status, which can be either unemployment or inactivity. We distinguish between the following labor market statuses: public employment, private formal employment (with a contract or social security), private informal employment (with neither a contract nor social security), non-wage employment (comprising employers and the self-employed), unpaid family work, unemployment, and inactivity.

To get a more precise picture of labor market insertion patterns, Figure 4.12 examines the first labor market status for men by education, distinguishing between two cohorts of school exit (those who graduated in the years 2006–10 versus 2011–14). The choice of these two school exit cohorts allows distinguishing individuals who have completed their studies before and after the major political turbulences that started in 2011 and the sharp economic downturn that followed.

As displayed in Figure 4.12, the majority of men worked when they left school. But between the two cohorts, this proportion fell from around 62 percent to 57 percent owing to a considerable increase in the share of inactive men, which went up from 8 percent to 12 percent.[8] This result confirms the decline in male labor force participation documented in Section 4.2. The increasing share of male inactivity has been at the expense of all types of employment whose shares have fallen, especially non-wage work, formal (public and private) employment and unpaid family work. The share of informal employment has remained more or less stable across school exit cohorts.

As depicted in Figure 4.13, the overwhelming majority of women were inactive or unemployed after leaving the education system or at age 15 across school exit cohorts. Among those who completed their studies more recently, 78 percent

practical and realistic way to study labor market dynamics in these contexts, despite being subject to potential measurement issues such as recall bias.

[7] In the labor market history module, unemployment and inactivity spells after school and before the first job are reported only for those who have been to school. For those who never went to school or left school before the age of 15, the "school exit year" is set as the year when the individual turned 15 years old.

[8] In Egypt, military service is compulsory for men and its duration varies between one and three years depending on their education level. Military service is therefore not an individual choice. In order to avoid any bias that might occur, men who reported being out of the labor force owing to their military service were excluded from the inactive population. Nevertheless, the proportion of inactive men increased substantially between the two cohorts.

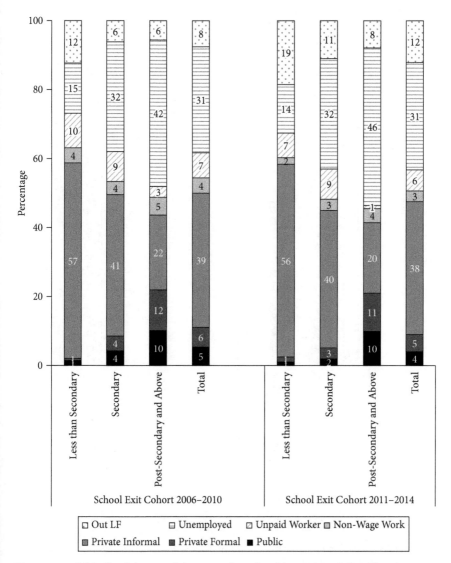

Figure 4.12 Male first labor market status after school (percentage), by education level and school exit cohort.

Note: Standard market labor force definition.

Source: Authors' calculations based on ELMPS 2018.

were inactive and 12 percent were unemployed; only 10 percent were employed (mainly in the public sector or as informal private wage workers). Non-wage work and unpaid family work were negligible. Overall, there has been little change between the two cohorts except for a minor decrease in the share of unemployed women, offset by a slight increase in the share of formal private wage work and non-wage work as well as the proportion of inactive women.

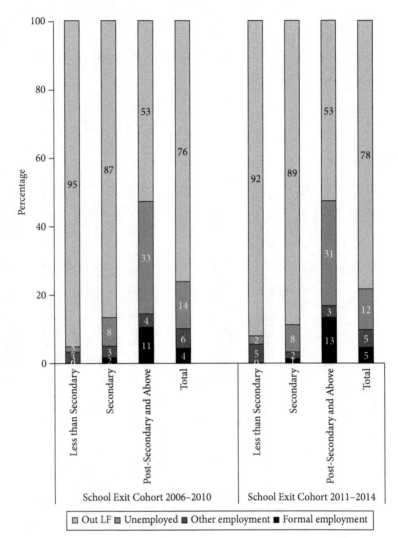

Figure 4.13   Female first labor market status after school (percentage), by education level and school exit cohort.

Note: Standard market labor force definition.

Source: Authors' calculations based on ELMPS 2018.

Education plays a role in the initial sorting of individuals across employment sectors. As reported in Figure 4.12 for both male cohorts of school exit, there is a clear negative correlation between educational attainment and informal employment, but a positive correlation between education and unemployment, confirming the pattern described in Figure 4.7 for current unemployment rates. Indeed, it appears that the more educated and better-off individuals were the ones who could afford to stay unemployed while searching for a formal job, while the more vulnerable group with lower education tended to be pushed (by necessity) into the informal sector. The increase in male inactivity at school exit could be seen at all levels of education, but particularly among secondary and lower than secondary school graduates. Among the most educated, all forms of private employment decreased in the recent cohort whereas unemployment was on the rise.

As presented in Figure 4.13, an overwhelming majority of women with below-secondary education stayed out of the labor force. Additionally, in both school exit cohorts, formal employment and in particular public sector jobs were more likely to be held by women with post-secondary education. First-time unemployment was particularly high for the most educated women, but slightly declined from 33 percent in the older cohort to 31 percent among more recent graduates.

4.3.2   Unemployment duration to first job

In the labor economics literature, it is commonly known that a longer unemployment duration adversely affects the probability of finding a job in the future, a phenomenon known as "negative duration dependence."[9] In the MENA region, Assaad and Krafft (2016b) documented higher long-term unemployment rates in Egypt in 2012 (measured by the share of those who had been unemployed for more than two years) than in Jordan and Tunisia. They also showed that in all three countries, the long-term unemployed were mostly new labor market entrants with no prior work experience, suggesting that unemployment was largely a labor market insertion problem.

For those who have worked before, unemployment duration is estimated using the labor market history module,[10] which records any unemployment spell that lasted at least six months prior to the first job (that also lasted at least six months). For individuals who never worked and are currently unemployed, the unemployment duration corresponds to the current (right-censored) unemployment duration.

Figure 4.14 shows the proportion of individuals finding a (first) job among those initially unemployed by months of unemployment on the horizontal axis. As expected, women tend to stay longer in unemployment than men. And whereas after 180 months spent in unemployment all men eventually found a job,

---

[9] Using experimental evidence, Kroft, Lange, and Notowidigdo (2013) found that the probability of receiving a callback for a job interview significantly decreased with the length of a candidate's unemployment spell, with the majority of the decline occurring during the first eight months. Likewise, Van Belle et al. (2018) showed that potential employers perceive longer unemployment as a signal of lower motivation.

[10] Only for individuals who went to school. For those who have never been to school, the unemployment duration corresponds only to the censored current unemployment duration.

only around 54 percent of women ended up finding a job. The concavity of the curves (especially for men) implies that the job-finding rate among the unemployed decreased by time spent in unemployment (particularly in the range of 0–100 months), after which the rate of exit from unemployment started to slightly pick up.

Figure 4.14 also shows that educational attainment makes it easier to exit unemployment for men. However, virtually all men, regardless of their education level, eventually found a job. Job-finding rates were generally higher for unemployed men with post-secondary education and above, followed by secondary-degree holders whose job-finding probability was in turn higher than those with basic education (up to 140 months of unemployment duration). For example, after 100 months in unemployment, 70 percent of men with below-secondary education level found employment, compared with 78 percent of men graduating from secondary school and 87 percent of men with a post-secondary or university degree. While the less educated men were less likely to be initially unemployed, they stayed longer in unemployment.

Women, whatever their education level, took longer to exit unemployment and find a job than men. The job-finding rates of female post-secondary degree holders clearly exceeded that of secondary-degree holders, who in turn had higher

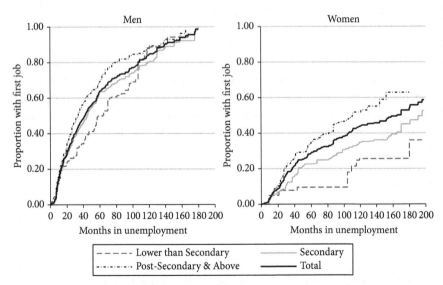

Figure 4.14 Proportion obtaining a first job by unemployment duration to first job (months), sex and educational attainment, ever or never worked, ages 15–34, 2018.
Note: Kaplan-Meier failure estimates. Standard market labor force definition.
Source: Authors' calculations based on ELMPS 2018.

job-finding rates than women with lower-than-secondary education.[11] For example, after 100 months in unemployment, only 8 percent of the least educated women found a job, compared with 39 percent of women with a secondary school diploma and 57 percent of the most educated women.

4.3.3 Time to first job

This section investigates the trends in time to first job by sex and educational attainment. Time to first job is the time (estimated in years) between the date of school exit,[12] and the start date of the first job, which could either be spent in unemployment or in inactivity. Figure 4.15 shows that male job-finding rates increased at a decreasing rate with years since school exit as reflected by the concavity of the curves in the left panel. Job finding follows a similar pattern across exit cohorts but with a slight deterioration among more recent graduates. For example, four years after leaving school, 55 percent of the men from the older school cohort were employed compared with 51 percent of the men who graduated more recently. As presented in Figure 4.16, female job-finding rates increased almost linearly over the years from school exit but at much lower rates than male job-finding rates. Indeed, four years after leaving school only 9 percent of women had landed a job. A very slight improvement in the job-finding rate can be observed for women who exited school more recently.

Figure 4.15 dissects the time to first job by level of education and school exit cohort for men, suggesting that job-finding rates increase with education. Among those who exited school in 2006–10, four years after leaving school around 58 percent of secondary-degree holders and 65 percent of post-secondary and university graduates had found a job, compared with only 25 percent of below-secondary graduates.

The most noticeable finding is that secondary-school graduates who exited school after 2010 seem to have been doing worse than their counterparts who graduated between 2006 and 2010. For instance, four years after leaving school, 55 percent of recent secondary graduates were employed as opposed to 67 percent of older secondary graduates. The job-finding rates of the below-secondary and post-secondary and above graduates did not change much across school exit cohorts.

Figure 4.16 repeats the exercise for women, also revealing a larger gap in job-finding rates between women with below- versus above-secondary education. Among the 2006–10 school exit cohort, four years after graduation nearly

---

[11] The job-finding curve for women in the below-secondary category is imprecisely estimated owing to the small sample size of less educated women who experienced unemployment.

[12] Or age 15 if the individual never went to school or dropped out from school before turning 15.

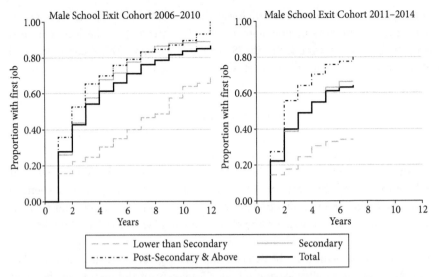

Figure 4.15 Male proportion obtaining a first job by time to first job (years), school exit cohort and educational attainment, ever or never worked.

Note: Kaplan-Meier failure estimates. Standard market labor force definition.

Source: Authors' calculations based on ELMPS 2018.

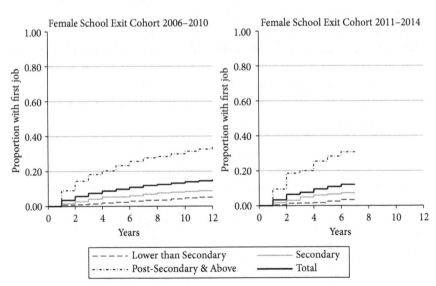

Figure 4.16 Female proportion obtaining a first job by time to first job (years), school exit cohort and educational attainment, ever or never worked.

Note: Kaplan-Meier failure estimates. Standard market labor force definition.

Source: Authors' calculations based on ELMPS 2018.

25 percent of women with a post-secondary diploma or above obtained a job compared with only 5 percent of women with a secondary degree and 2 percent of women with below-secondary education. Women with a post-secondary degree or above who completed their education between 2011 and 2014 spent less time getting a job. The patterns of job-finding rates were similar for women with secondary and below secondary education across school exit cohorts.

4.3.4 Age at first job

Figures 4.17 and 4.18 depict the proportion obtaining a first job by age, educational attainment, and school exit cohort for men and women. They show that women tended to obtain their first job at an older age than men. By the age of 30, more than 90 percent of men had obtained a job, regardless of their school exit cohort, whereas at the same age less than 30 percent of women were employed.[13] The comparison of the two male and female cohorts shows no major difference.

As illustrated in Figure 4.17 the more educated men were, the older they were when first employed as a result of pursuing longer studies. However, from the age of 18, the curves for men with secondary and with lower secondary education converged for the older cohort. The patterns of insertion into the labor market by age and education level differed only slightly by school exit cohort.

Figure 4.18 shows relatively different patterns for women. Until the age of 20–22 more educated women were less likely to have worked owing to longer studies. From the age of 22, the age at which university graduates typically complete their education, women with a post-secondary or university degree continued to find first jobs, while the proportion of less educated women getting a job increased very slightly or even stagnated. The patterns were similar across cohorts.

4.3.5 Nature of first job and mobility prospects

Building on labor market insertion patterns, this section focuses on labor market dynamics and job mobility by looking at changes in labor market status two and four years after school exit by sex and initial labor market status. Owing to a relatively small number of observations when breaking down transition rates by first labor market status, Figure 4.19a presents only male persistency rates (the percentage remaining in the same status) for those who were employed or

---

[13] For women, the figure presents the proportion obtaining a first job for ages 0–29, as beyond age 30 the number of observations is too small.

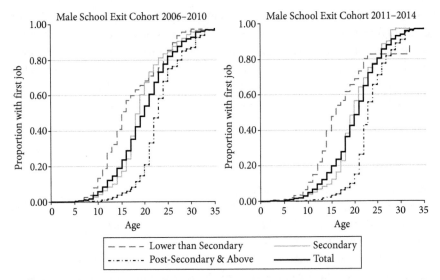

Figure 4.17 Male proportion obtaining a first job by age, educational attainment and school exit cohort, ever or never worked.

Note: Kaplan-Meier failure estimates. Standard market labor force definition.

Source: Authors' calculations based on ELMPS 2018.

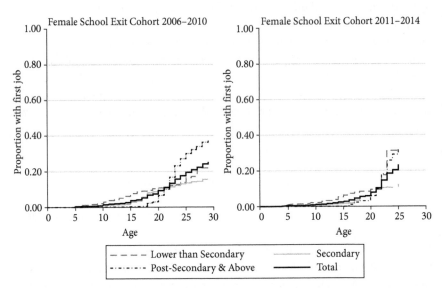

Figure 4.18 Female proportion obtaining a first job by age, educational attainment, and school exit cohort, ever or never worked.

Note: Kaplan-Meier failure estimates. Standard market labor force definition.

Source: Authors' calculations based on ELMPS 2018.

inactive right after leaving school. Figure 4.19b presents male pathways from unemployment.

Figure 4.19a reveals a high degree of persistency in different labor market states. Even four years after school exit, over 84 percent of young men who started out as public, private formal or informal employees and as non-wage workers remained in the same type of employment for both school exit cohorts. Albeit with smaller persistency rates (ranging between 60 and 80 percent), unpaid family work and inactivity were also quite stable.[14] Overall, these results paint a very rigid picture of the Egyptian labor market, where individuals who began their career in one form of employment were unlikely to transition to another status, resulting in very low mobility rates.[15]

Unemployment was the least persistent initial labor market status and therefore transitions from unemployment are illustrated in Figure 4.19b. Although more than one-third of men who were initially unemployed remained unemployed four years later, another third eventually found an informal private job, and almost 20 percent found a formal (public or private) job among those who graduated between 2011 and 2014. Compared with the older cohort, more recent male graduates tended to find less formal employment and more informal employment and non-wage employment. For instance, transitions from unemployment to informal work increased from 34 percent to 36 percent, transitions from unemployment to non-wage employment increased from 3 percent to 6 percent, and those to formal employment fell from 23 percent to 19 percent.

Likewise, the labor market for women was very rigid (Figure 4.20a). This was especially true for women who were initially employed or out of the labor force.[16] For women who started out in the public sector, Figure 4.20a shows a higher persistence of public sector employment over time for the 2011–14 school exit cohort, with 100 percent of women staying in public employment after four years (compared with 90 percent in the 2006–10 cohort). Higher persistence rates for formal private employment were also observed for the recent cohort, although the small sample size of women employed in this sector suggests that one should interpret these trends with caution. The persistency rate for women in private informal employment was lower than in formal employment (68 percent after

---

[14] Among the most persistent statuses, only the transitions from inactivity to another employment status have enough observations to be commented on. When initially inactive men changed status, it was to work as a private informal worker: 22 percent among the older school cohort and 17 percent among the more recent one.

[15] These results confirm the findings of Yassin (2016) and Yassine (2015), which relied on the historical labor market status module of ELMPS 2012 and concluded that the Egyptian labor market was rigid and that, as expected, public employment was very stable compared with private wage work and non-wage work. However, Yassin (2016) showed that job-to-job transitions were more common among young people (men and women) than among older people.

[16] Persistency rates for women who were initially non-wage workers are not displayed owing to too few observations (fewer than 25).

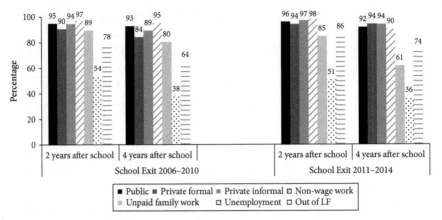

Figure 4.19a Male persistency rates (percentage) over two and four years from school exit by initial labor market status and year of exit from school.

Note: Standard labor market employment definition.

Source: Authors' calculations based on ELMPS 2018.

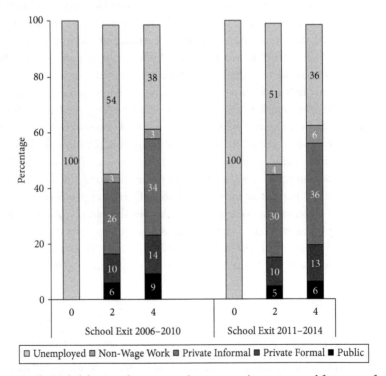

Figure 4.19b Male labor market statuses (percentages) over two and four years from school exit by year of exit from school, first status unemployment.

Note: Standard labor market employment definition.

Source: Authors' calculations based on ELMPS 2018.

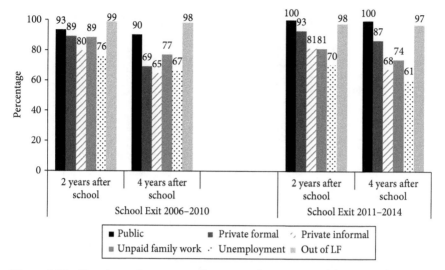

Figure 4.20a Female persistency rates (percentage) over two and four years from school exit by initial labor market status and year of exit from school.
Note: Standard labor market employment definition.
Source: Authors' calculations based on ELMPS 2018.

four years among the recent cohort) and remained stable across school exit cohorts. Similar to their male counterparts, female unemployment was the least persistent labor market status among the recent cohort.

Figure 4.20b presents the transition patterns from unemployment for women, showing more transitions to the informal private sector in the 2011–14 cohort relative to those who completed their education between 2006 and 2010. While only 3 percent of initially unemployed women from the older cohort ended up in informal private employment four years later, the corresponding rate for the younger cohort was 14 percent, reflecting a huge growth in informality and a fall in formal public and private employment among recent female graduates.

Alternatively, Figure 4.21 shows the first job status as well as job status four and eight years later by year of entry into the first job among employed men who started their jobs between 2000 and 2010. In the top left panel, the share of non-wage work either as a first status or as a job status four and eight years from job entry is more or less stable. In the top right panel, a decreasing trend appears in public sector employment especially among men who began their careers in more recent years. Trends in private formal jobs are depicted in the bottom left panel, revealing very little variation in the share of first jobs within the formal private sector by year of job start. The three curves depicting initial job status and job status four and eight years into the future almost coincide, revealing little variation in the incidence of private formal employment at different points of young people's careers. Finally, the bottom right panel shows the trends for informal

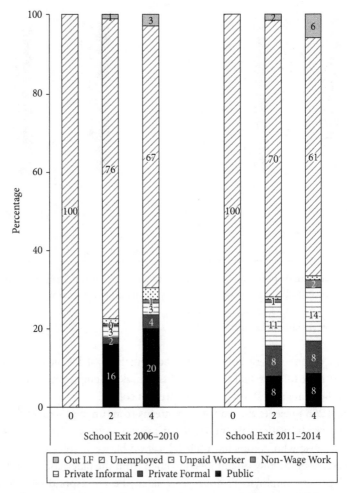

Figure 4.20b Female labor market statuses (percentages) over two and four years from exit from school by year of exit from school, first status unemployment.
Note: Standard labor market employment definition.
Source: Authors' calculations based on ELMPS 2018.

private work. First, compared with other forms of employment, informal private jobs accounted for the majority of men's employment, exceeding 60 percent for new job-holders in recent years. Even among those who had already been working, informality was on the rise. Interestingly, the curves depicting trends in this job status closely mirror those for public sector employment in the top right panel but move in the opposite direction, reflecting an inverse correlation between employment patterns across the two sectors.

Relative to the changes in job status over time for men, the trends observed for women were more volatile, as evident in Figure 4.22. The top left panel shows an

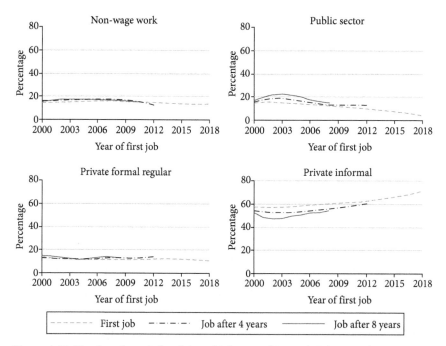

Figure 4.21   Employed men's first job and job status four and eight years later (percentage) by start year of first job.
Note: Market employment definition.
Source: Authors' calculations based on ELMPS 2018.

increase in non-wage work for women who started their jobs after 2003, which was true both for the newly employed (first status) and those already working (four and eight years later). This rise in non-wage work among women could potentially be a response to the decline in public sector employment that started around the same time (top right panel). Compared with men, it is worth noting that a larger percentage of women were hired in the public sector. This sector is traditionally preferred by women owing to its stability and benefits, but is becoming less stable, as reflected by the sharply declining share of public sector jobs. Moving to the bottom left panel, formal private employment shows a stagnating share for different cohorts of job entry, as was the case for men. Lastly, the bottom right panel plots the share of informal private employment among working women. Again, the increasing trend in informality closely matches the decreasing trend in public sector employment. The large decline in the share of public sector jobs documented in the top right panel is coupled with a substantial increase in informal private employment for the same cohorts of job entrants. This suggests that the informal sector acts as the alternative form of employment for women who would have liked to work in the public sector but were unable to land a public sector job owing to the decline in public sector hiring in recent

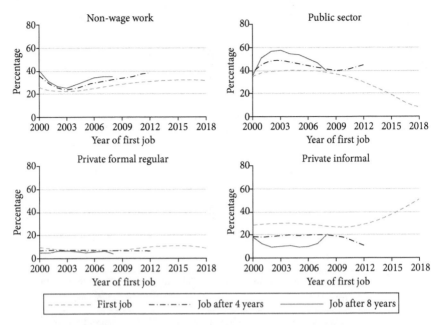

Figure 4.22 Employed women's first job and job status four and eight years later (percentage) by start year of first job.

Note: Market employment definition.

Source: Authors' calculations based on ELMPS 2018.

years.[17] Assaad, Krafft, and Salemi (2019) argued that the shrinking of the public sector and the rigidity of the formal private sector resulted in a limited supply of good jobs and that these jobs are increasingly allocated by socioeconomic status, an issue we discuss further in Section 4.5.

4.4 Jobs and Youth Economic Vulnerability

4.4.1 Informality and irregular employment

This section presents trends in precarious employment among youth. Precarious employment is a proxy of vulnerable employment situations such as the absence of a work contract or social security or the prevalence of work irregularity and

---

[17] El-Haddad (2020) shed light on the historical transformation of the social contract in Egypt from one based on job provision by the public sector (in the 1950s and 1960s) to an "unsocial" social contract that favored liberalization at the expense of rising inequality and informality. Although the latter was one of the main reasons behind the January 25 uprising, it had become entrenched and harder to change over time, leaving a legacy of dualism in social and economic institutions, including in the labor market.

unpaid work. We consider four forms of precarious work: private regular informal work, which refers to permanent or temporary wage work without a written
contract or social security coverage; private irregular wage work, which concerns
casual or seasonal work;[18] self-employment,[19] and unpaid family work.

Figures 4.23a and 4.23b show that precarious employment has become the
norm for Egyptian youth. In 2018, it represented more than two-thirds and three-
quarters of total young male jobs in urban and rural locations respectively, more
than two-thirds of young female jobs in rural locations, and 44 percent of young
women's employment in urban areas.

Private regular informal employment was the most common form of precarious employment for men in both urban and rural locations and for young women
in urban areas. It reached 43 percent of total young male employment in urban
areas and 35 percent in rural locations, 29 percent of total young female employment in urban areas, and 16 percent in rural areas. Given its agricultural nature
and because of social norms, unpaid family work was particularly present in rural
areas and among young employed women. Irregular wage work was also important
among young employed men, reaching 15 percent of total male employment in
urban areas and 28 percent in rural areas. In 2018, self-employment was relatively
marginal, accounting for 6–8 percent of young men's work in urban and rural
locations and for 5 percent of young female employment in urban areas, as
opposed to 14 percent of young female work in rural areas.

Precarious employment as a percentage of youth employment has greatly
increased over the last two decades for both men and women and in both urban
and rural areas.[20] It has risen more sharply for women and in urban areas. The
shares of most forms of precarious work in youth employment have increased
between 2012 and 2018 for men, except for unpaid family work, self-employment
in urban areas, and irregular work (even though it had increased sharply between
2006 and 2012). For women, the only form of precarious employment whose
share declined was that of unpaid work in rural areas (from 33 percent in 2012 to
30 percent in 2018).

Figure 4.24a presents the percentage of precarious employment in the total
employment of young men by education level between 1998 and 2018. Higher

---

[18] In more than 97 percent of the cases, irregular wage work was also informal (without a written
contract or social security coverage)

[19] Although self-employment is a heterogeneous category, in most cases it represents a type of precarious employment. For instance, based on the ELMPS 2012, Krafft and Rizk (2021) demonstrated
that the self-employed were relatively older, less educated, and from a disadvantaged socioeconomic
background. They also had lower earnings and rarely benefited from health insurance or social security. Relying on the household enterprise modules, Chapter 6 shows that although women were rarely
entrepreneurs (either employers or self-employed), female entrepreneurs were even more vulnerable
than male entrepreneurs. They were less educated, with lower current capital and more informal
activities.

[20] Sobhy (2021) highlights the rise in informality and precarity in recent years (particularly among
the poor) as undesirable features of the changing social contract in Egypt.

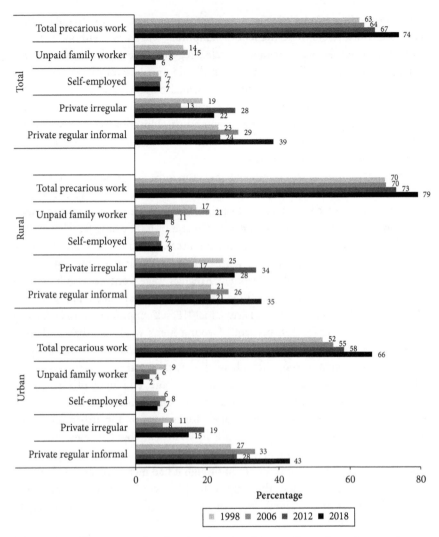

Figure 4.23a Percentage of male precarious employment in total employment by location (urban/rural), ages 15–34, 1998–2018.

Note: Market employment definition.

Source: Authors' calculations based on ELMPS 1998–2018.

levels of education were associated with lower shares of precarious employment. However, in 2018, although precarious employment was less important for the most highly educated young men relative to lower education groups, it represented almost the majority of their employment. In 2018, the percentage of precarious work was 90 percent among the least educated, 76 percent among secondary-school graduates, and 44 percent among university graduates. Informal employment represented the major bulk of precarious employment, regardless of

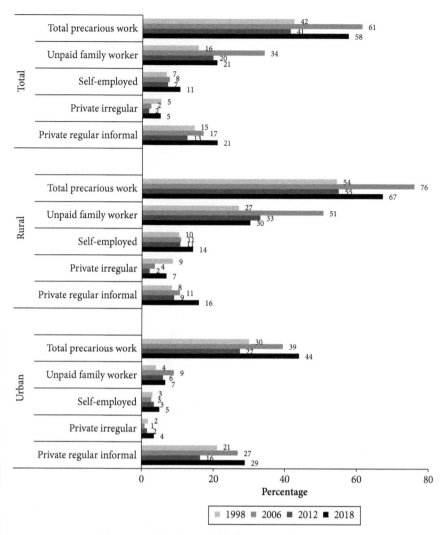

Figure 4.23b Percentage of female precarious employment in total employment by location (urban/rural), ages 15–34, 1998–2018.

Note: Market employment definition.

Source: Authors' calculations based on ELMPS 1998–2018.

education level. It accounted for 40 percent of jobs for young men with an education level of less than or equal to secondary and nearly one-third of male jobs among university graduates.

The relative weight of different types of precarious work varied by education level, and in particular according to whether young male workers had a degree lower or higher than secondary. In 2018, more than two-thirds of working young men with a secondary education or less were either in informal employment (40 percent) or in irregular employment (between one-fourth and one-third). Self-employment and unpaid jobs accounted each for less than 10 percent of jobs for

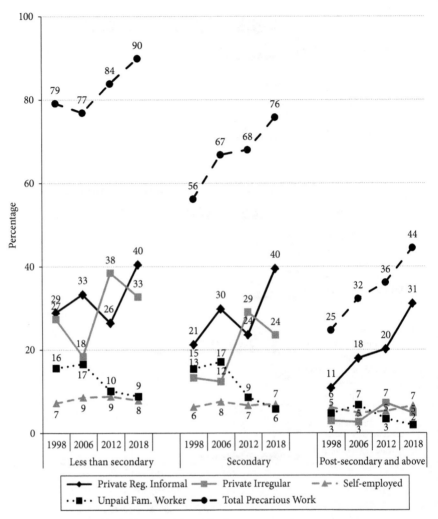

Figure 4.24a Percentage of male precarious employment in total employment by education level, ages 15–34, 1998–2018.

Note: Market employment definition.

Source: Authors' calculations based on ELMPS 1998–2018.

these young men. In 2018, among university graduates precarious employment constituted mainly informal jobs (31 percent), while the other forms of precarious employment (including irregular work) were relatively marginal.

Over the past two decades, the share of precarious employment in total young male employment has risen for all education levels. But it has progressed much faster among university graduates. Indeed, it increased by 14 percent for young men with less than secondary education, by 35 percent among

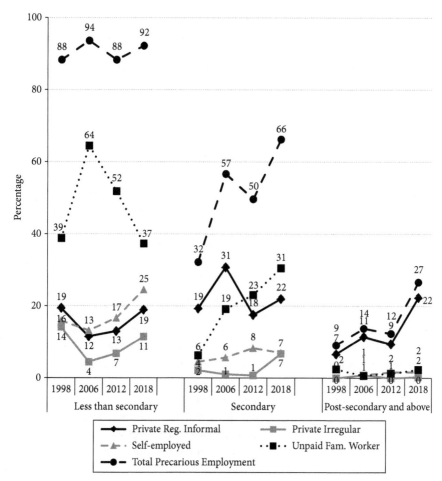

Figure 4.24b Percentage of female precarious employment in total employment by education level, ages 15–34, 1998–2018.

Note: Market employment definition.

Source: Authors' calculations based on ELMPS 1998–2018.

secondary-education graduates, and by 80 percent among university graduates. Between 1998 and 2018, all types of precarious employment increased with the exception of unpaid family work. The percentage of unpaid family work fell sharply for young men across all education levels. On the contrary, private informal, irregular work, and self-employment have increased. Notably, between 1998 and 2018, the percentage of informal (regular) employment has tripled among university graduates.

Figure 4.24b reports the trend in the percentage of female precarious employment by educational attainment from 1998 to 2018. This graph shows that in 2018 the share of precarious employment in the total employment of young women correlated negatively with education level, as was the case for men. Precarious employment accounted for 92 percent of female employment among below-secondary graduates, 66 percent among secondary graduates, and 27 percent among university graduates. Not only was precarious employment less prevalent among young employed women with post-secondary education, but its composition also differed compared with their less educated counterparts. The less educated women were, the more confined they were to the most precarious forms of employment (unpaid family work and irregular work). In 2018, young employed women with less than secondary education were mainly unpaid family workers (37 percent) or self-employed (25 percent). Unpaid family work represented almost one-third of young women's employment among those with a secondary education. Although irregular employment was quite minor across education levels, it was more prevalent among young working women with less than secondary (11 percent) or secondary education (7 percent) compared with those with post-secondary or university education. In 2018, the precarious employment of young women with a tertiary degree consisted almost exclusively of informal employment.

The percentage of precarious employment progressed at different growth rates between 1998 and 2018 according to the level of education. In particular, more educated women faced a more rapid increase in precarious employment as a percentage of total employment over time. While the percentage of precarious employment increased by 5 percent among the least educated young female workers, it doubled among young working women with secondary education and almost tripled among the most educated young female workers. Most of this growth occurred between 2012 and 2018. Whereas the share of both informal and irregular employment rose sharply among young employed women with secondary education or less, only the share of informal employment increased rapidly among women with tertiary education.

4.5   Risk Factors: Family Background and Socioeconomic Status

Previous research on Egyptian youth has shown that key transitions to adulthood including education, employment, and marriage are highly dependent on social class and family background or privilege.[21] Based on ELMPS 2012, Assaad and Krafft (2020) illustrated the fact that socioeconomic background played a central role in transitions to adulthood and in particular the employment transition. For instance, secondary and above-secondary educated young people whose fathers also had secondary or higher education were more likely to get a first formal job, especially in the private sector. Gebel and Heyne (2014) explored young women's

---

[21] Chapter 3 also shows that circumstances such as parental background and area of birth played an important role in determining wages.

pathways to education, work, and family formation focusing on unequal access to education and how family background can shape these important and interrelated life outcomes.

To investigate the potential channels behind weak labor market opportunities and high economic vulnerability, we use two proxies for the social and economic background of the natal household in which the individual was raised: (1) mother's educational attainment (defined in three categories: below secondary, secondary, and above secondary) and (2) father's occupation (blue collar versus white collar) when the individual was 15 years old. We explore the correlation between these indicators and the person's own initial labor market outcomes. These variables are preferred to wealth status since they are predetermined and therefore less likely to be endogenous to employment and earnings during the individual's working life.

4.5.1 First labor market status by mother's education

Figure 4.25 reveals a positive correlation between mother's education and formal (public and private) employment as a first status, with the highest share of formal jobs observed among individuals with the most educated mothers, highlighting the role of family background in labor market insertion. Looking at differences by sex and school exit cohort, it seems that men with the most educated mothers in the recent cohort were more likely to access the public sector than their counterparts in the older cohort (14 percent versus 9 percent), while the opposite was true for women.[22] Another striking finding is the jump in inactivity rates among men with above-secondary educated mothers, from only 3 percent in the older cohort to 13 percent in the younger cohort.

On the other hand, there appears to be a negative relationship between mother's education and male informal employment, with this status being the dominant labor market state (43 percent) for both older and younger men with the least educated mothers. Remarkably, the share of informal private employment declines considerably among men with secondary-educated mothers and is lowest among men with the most educated mothers. For women, however, lower mother's education strongly predicts inactivity, with more than 80 percent of women with the least educated mothers being out of the labor force after finishing school. This share consistently drops as the mother's education increases. Contrasting the two cohorts of women, one can observe a substantial increase in informality among recent female graduates with the most educated mothers, with the percentage of informal employment rising from only 4 percent in the older

---

[22] Other than this change in the sex composition of public sector jobs, the overall share of public employment as a first labor market status remained more or less stable across cohorts.

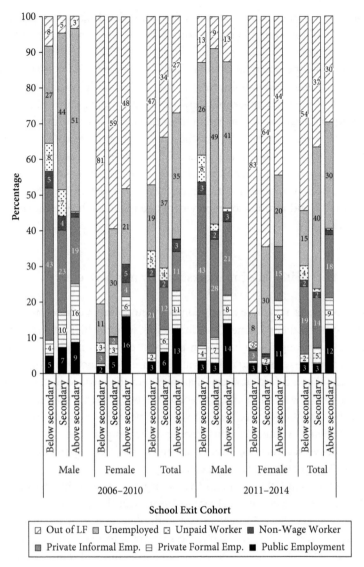

Figure 4.25 First labor market status by mother's education, sex, and school exit cohort (percentage), ages 15–34.

Note: Standard market labor force definition.

Source: Authors' calculations based on ELMPS 2018.

cohort to 15 percent in the more recent cohort. This suggests that more women with higher socioeconomic status were accepting informal jobs after 2011, a finding that is consistent with public sector jobs becoming scarcer and more difficult to access over time, especially for women. In the more recent cohort, only 11 percent of women with the highest-educated mothers landed a first job in the public sector, compared with 16 percent in the older cohort.

4.5.2 First labor market status by father's occupation

Moving to first labor market status by father's occupation,[23] Figure 4.26 shows that having a father with a white-collar job when the individual was 15 was

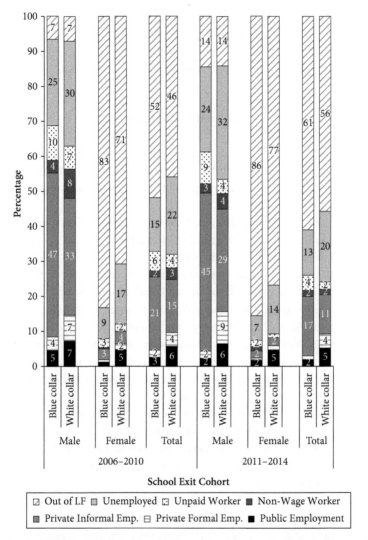

Figure 4.26   First labor market status by father's occupation (percentage), sex and school exit cohort, ages 15–34.

Note: Standard market labor force definition.

Source: Authors' calculations based on ELMPS 2018.

[23] White-collar occupations include managers, professionals, technicians and associate professionals, clerical support workers, and service and sales workers, while blue-collar occupations include agricultural, forestry and fishery workers, crafts and related trades workers, plant and machine operators, and assemblers and elementary occupations.

positively correlated with initial public sector employment Similarly, having a white-collar father was associated with lower male informal employment. On the other hand, unemployment as a first status was higher among men and women with fathers in white-collar occupations relative to blue-collar jobs, corroborating the argument that unemployment tends be more common among the better-off in Egypt (those who can afford to wait for better jobs). Finally, although male labor force participation showed no difference by father's occupation in both cohorts, women with white-collar fathers were more likely to participate in the labor market than those with blue-collar fathers.

4.5 Discussion and Conclusion

Despite its decreasing share in the total population, the Egyptian youth population continued to represent a substantial demographic group that placed pressure on the labor market. This chapter highlights the difficulties young people faced when entering the labor market.

First, the decline in labor force participation continued for young men and women, with a sharper drop between 2012 and 2018 for the 20–24-year-olds and among the most educated, especially women.

Second, the male youth unemployment rate has increased (especially among the less educated) and although the overall female youth unemployment rate has declined, it has increased for female university graduates. Moreover, the duration of current unemployment has increased for women at all levels of education.

Third, the analysis of first labor market status shows an increase in inactivity particularly among young men and a slight decrease in employment. However, the share of first informal jobs in total first employment went up for both men and women. This rise in unprotected and vulnerable employment was particularly pronounced for the most educated women. And although the time taken to obtain a first job has shrunk, it has led more and more to unprotected jobs. These indicators point to a spike in precarious employment, particularly in the form of informal jobs (without social security coverage or a work contract), especially among the most educated.

The section on labor market mobility over two and four years has shown that the Egyptian labor market is very rigid and has become increasingly so. All forms of employment were more persistent. And while unemployment has been less persistent, unemployment outflows are increasingly towards informal employment and less and less towards public employment or formal private employment, which were the main alternative exit destinations from unemployment.

Finally, in addition to the individual's education level, socioeconomic background shows a strong positive association with better labor market outcomes.

This could work via the individual's own human capital since more affluent parents tend to invest more in the education of their children, giving them better opportunities later in life, but additional mechanisms could be at work such as the direct influence of social status and networking.[24] Eventually, the higher the family's socioeconomic background, the better the initial placement in the labor market, with fewer informal jobs and more public or formal private employment. In terms of policy relevance, this suggests the need for early interventions to bridge the gap between impoverished and better-off children early on, as there is evidence that these differences in initial conditions translate into magnified gaps in labor markets outcomes, which persist well into the future.

With the additional challenges of the COVID-19 pandemic, precarious youth employment is likely to increase further. A recent report by the Central Agency for Public Mobilization and Statistics (CAPMAS, 2020) revealed that young people were disproportionately affected by the pandemic, with more than 65 percent of individuals aged 15–34 reporting a change in their work status and more than 85 percent reporting a drop in their earnings following the outbreak. These percentages were lower for older individuals, suggesting that youth bore a heavier burden of the negative labor market effects induced by the COVID-19 pandemic.

We do not yet have data that would allow us to determine the impact of the COVID-19 health crisis on labor market dynamics. However, the rate of involuntary job losses (mainly private formal and informal jobs) is expected to increase, as was the case in 2009–11 following the financial crisis and the January 25 uprising, as shown by Yassine (2015). This is confirmed by preliminary evidence from CAPMAS (2020) which reported a decline in working hours/days and an increase in irregularity and job loss after the pandemic. As more data become available, these effects should be quantified by future research to provide evidence-based recommendations for decision-makers to better navigate the uncertainty and to minimize social and economic losses.

Acknowledgments

The authors would like to thank Caroline Krafft, Ragui Assaad, and Colette Salemi for their valuable comments and suggestions. We acknowledge the support of the International Labour Organization and the Economic Research Forum for this chapter, under the project "The Egyptian Labor Market: A Focus on Gender and Economic Vulnerability."

---

[24] See Assaad and Krafft (2016a) for more on inequality of opportunity in MENA education systems and labor markets, which results from individuals being rewarded for their circumstances or social class rather than their level of skills or effort.

References

Amer, Mona (2015) "Patterns of Labor Market Insertion in Egypt: 1998–2012." In Ragui Assaad and Caroline Krafft (eds), *The Egyptian Labor Market in an Era of Revolution*. Oxford: Oxford University Press, pp. 70–89.

Assaad, Ragui and Caroline Krafft (2014) "Why the Unemployment Rate is a Misleading Indicator of Labor Market Health in Egypt." Economic Research Forum Policy Perspective No. 14. Cairo.

Assaad, Ragui and Caroline Krafft (2020) "Excluded Generation: The Growing Challenges of Labor Market Insertion for Egyptian Youth," *Journal of Youth Studies*, 24 (2): 186–212.

Assaad, Ragui and Caroline Krafft (2016a) "Inequality of Opportunity in the Labor Market for Higher Education Graduates in Egypt and Jordan," in I. Diwan and A. Galal (eds) *The Middle East Economies in Times of Transition*. International Economic Association Series. London: Palgrave Macmillan. pp. 159–185.

Assaad, Ragui and Caroline Krafft (2016b) "Labor Market Dynamics and Youth Unemployment in the Middle East and North Africa: Evidence from Egypt, Jordan and Tunisia." Economic Research Forum Working Paper Series No. 993. Cairo.

Assaad, Ragui and Caroline Krafft (2015) "The Evolution of Labor Supply and Unemployment in the Egyptian Economy: 1988–2012." In Ragui Assaad and Caroline Krafft (eds), *The Egyptian Labor Market in an Era of Revolution*. Oxford: Oxford University Press, pp. 70–89.

Assaad, Ragui, Caroline Krafft, and Colette Salemi (2019) "Socioeconomic Status and the Changing Nature of School-to-Work Transitions in Egypt, Jordan and Tunisia." Economic Research Forum Working Paper Series No. 1287. Cairo.

Assaad, Ragui, Caroline Krafft, and Shaimaa Yassin (2018) "Comparing Retrospective and Panel Data Collection Methods to Assess Labor Market Dynamics," *IZA Journal of Development and Migration*, 8 (17): 1–34.

CAPMAS (Central Agency for Public Mobilization and Statistics) (2020) "Impact of COVID-19 on the Egyptian Households." Central Agency for Public Mobilization and Statistics. (in Arabic).

El-Haddad, Amirah (2020) "Redefining the Social Contract in the Wake of the Arab Spring: The Experiences of Egypt, Morocco and Tunisia," *World Development*, 127 (104774): 1–22.

Gebel, Michael and Stefanie Heyne (2014) *Transitions to Adulthood in the Middle East and North Africa: Young Women's Rising?* New York: Palgrave Macmillan.

Krafft, Caroline and Reham Rizk (2021) "The Promise and Peril of Youth Entrepreneurship in MENA". *International Journal of Manpower*. DOI: 10.1108/ IJM-05-2020-0200.

Kroft, Kory, Fabian Lange, and Matthew J. Notowidigdo (2013) "Duration Dependence and Labor Market Conditions: Evidence from a Field Experiment," *The Quarterly Journal of Economics*, 128 (3): 1123–67.

Sobhy, Hania (2021) "The Lived Social Contract in Schools: From Protection to the Production of Hegemony," *World Development* 137 (104986): 1–15.

Van Belle, Eva et al. (2018) "Why Are Employers Put Off by Long Spells of Unemployment?", *European Sociological Review*, 34 (6): 694–710.

Yassin, Shaimaa (2016) "Constructing Labor Market Transitions Recall Weights in Retrospective Data: An Application to Egypt and Jordan." Institute of Economic Research, IRENE Working Paper No. 16-07. University of Neuchâtel, Neuchâtel.

Yassine, Chaimaa (2015) "Job Accession, Separation, and Mobility," in Ragui Assaad and Caroline Krafft (eds) *The Egyptian Labor Market in an Era of Revolution.* Oxford: Oxford University Press, pp. 218–240.

5

Still the Employer of Choice

Evolution of Public Sector Employment in Egypt

Ghada Barsoum and Dina Abdalla

5.1 Introduction

The public sector has been described as the employer of choice among youth in Egypt (Barsoum, 2016). Conditions of shorter working hours, job security, a stable income, and access to paid leave all contribute to this preference, particularly in comparison to the predominantly informal private sector. Public sector hiring has been, historically, a part of the social contract in Egypt (Desai, Olofsgard, and Yousef, 2009; Assaad, 2014; Assaad and Barsoum, 2019). The educated (operationalized in this chapter as those with secondary education and above) have been offered guaranteed employment by legal stipulations dating back to 1962. This has created a situation of labor market dualism, with better quality jobs with benefits reserved for the politically volatile group of the educated, as Assaad (2014) argues. However, this labor market dualism has long created incentives to queue for public sector jobs among the educated and the misallocation of human capital to queue for government jobs (Assaad, 1997). Fiscal pressures and a bloated public service led to retrenchment in public sector hiring (World Bank, 2016). The evolution of public sector employment in Egypt reflects tensions between a continued preference for public sector jobs on the labor supply side and fiscal pressures pushing for right-sizing the sector on the state side.

The sizeable public sector is not unique to Egypt. The Middle East and North Africa (MENA) region continues to have large public sectors relative to those in comparable countries (Assaad and Barsoum, 2019). However, similar to other countries in the region, the sector's hiring has been slowing and the share of the sector in the labor market has been declining, partly owing to the increased number of new entrants to the labor market and partly owing to fiscal pressures (Assaad and Barsoum, 2019). These policy changes have impacted the composition of the public sector in the region in a number of ways. These include a growing feminization reflecting women's increased access to education; the aging of the workforce in the public sector reflecting the slowed hiring; and the increased

Ghada Barsoum and Dina Abdalla, *Still the Employer of Choice: Evolution of Public Sector Employment in Egypt* In: *The Egyptian Labor Market: A Focus on Gender and Economic Vulnerability*. Edited by: Caroline Krafft and Ragui Assaad, Oxford University Press. © Economic Research Forum 2022. DOI: 10.1093/oso/9780192847911.003.0006

level of education among workers in the sector reflecting increased education levels in the population (Assaad and Barsoum, 2019).

This chapter investigates the evolution of public sector employment in Egypt using the Egypt Labor Market Panel Survey (ELMPS) data. We limit the analysis of public sector to government (civil service) employees, owing to the specificity and small share of employees in state-owned enterprises in Egypt (see Chapter 2). The chapter starts by exploring the continued preference for the public sector by looking at job preferences among the unemployed. The analysis shows that public sector jobs are highly favored. Differences in employment conditions between the government and private sectors are investigated as part of this discussion in an attempt to explain this continued preference. In the second section of the chapter, we look at the evolution of the share of government employment in Egypt, comparing data from different waves of the ELMPS. In the third section, we take a look inside the government and compare the characteristics of government workers over time.

The analysis in this chapter shows that the public sector continues to be a preferred sector of employment. The share of the government sector in employment has declined since 1998, yet it has stabilized when comparing 2012 and 2018. Inside the government, we show that the sector is becoming more educated as it consistently hires more workers with university and post-graduate education. Despite the growing share of working women in the government, women have not yet reached gender parity within the government. The government workforce is also getting slightly more feminized, with the share of women in the sector slowly increasing over time. The share of government employment among employed women is much higher than among employed men. However, the share of government employment remains very small among all women, reflecting the low rate of female labor force participation in the country (Chapter 1). Yet, despite the increasing presence of women in the government and the growing feminization within its workforce, the sector's share of hiring men is consistently double that of hiring women across all age groups. This is particularly the case among the youngest age group, which could signify a reversal, or at least a stalling, of the feminization process in the sector in coming decades. The government workforce in Egypt, however, is also aging, with one-third of its employees in the age category of 48–60 as of 2018. There are many policy implications from these patterns of change in the government workforce, including potential for right-sizing and improving the efficiency and effectiveness of the sector.

5.2 The Public Sector as the Employer of Choice in Egypt

Unemployed respondents in the ELMPS were asked about the minimum acceptable wage (reservation wage) by sector of employment: public sector, formal private (with a contract or social insurance), and informal private (with neither a contract nor social insurance). Consistently, those who were unemployed had lower reservation wages for being hired in the public sector than in either the formal and informal private sector. Figure 5.1 shows the distribution of reservation wages by sector of employment and sex in 2018. The figure shows that the minimum acceptable wage in the public sector is consistently lower than the private sector for both unemployed men and women.

Among unemployed men, the reported median reservation wage was EGP 2,000 in the public sector and EGP 3,000 in the formal and informal private sector. Corresponding with earlier trends (Barsoum, 2016) the reservation wage was lower for women. Among unemployed women, the median reservation wage was EGP 1,700 in the public sector; EGP 2,500 in the formal private sector, and EGP 2,000 for the informal private sector.[1]

Similarly, when asked about preferred occupations, 83 percent of the unemployed reported that they would accept a job as an employee in the public sector. More women (89 percent) reported this preference than men (77 percent), signifying the continued preference for this sector among women (Barsoum, 2019). This

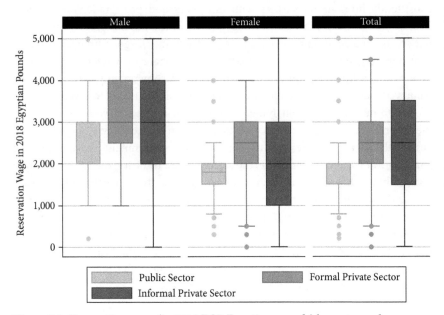

Figure 5.1 Reservation wage (in 2018 EGP, Egyptian pounds) by sector and sex among the unemployed (aged 15–64), 2018.
Source: Authors' calculations based on ELMPS 2018.

---

[1] Outliers were removed, restricting to reservation wages less than 5,000.

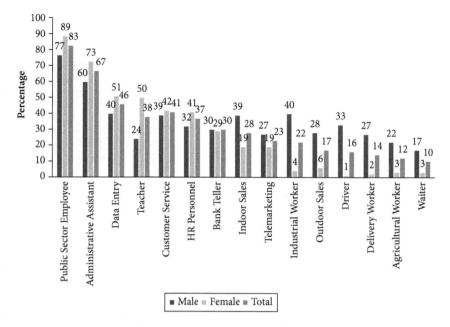

Figure 5.2 Percentage of the unemployed (aged 15–64) who would accept different jobs, by sex, 2018.

Source: Authors' calculations based on ELMPS 2018.

was the highest rate among all the jobs asked about in the survey, as illustrated in Figure 5.2. The figure also captures the desirability of certain occupations, namely administrative jobs, among the unemployed. Jobs in hospitality (waiter) showed the lowest level of desirability among the unemployed. This pattern was also stronger among women than men.

The preference for public sector employment can be explained by the difference in job quality between the public sector and the private sector. We limit the analysis in Table 5.1 to those with secondary education and above to make sure that we are comparing workers in the public and private sectors with similar educational characteristics. We also distinguish between work inside establishments (fixed places of work) and outside establishments in the private sector. As the table shows, the government offered favorable conditions in terms of paid leave, social insurance, health insurance, and the average number of working hours per day. Moreover, workers in the government were more likely to report being satisfied (rather or fully) about their work and their wages than workers in the private sector.

Table 5.1 shows that while access to work benefits was almost universal among government workers, private sector employment inside establishments provided social insurance to only 38 percent of its workers and less than half of its workers had paid leave (40 percent). Those in the private sector outside establishments,

Table 5.1 Job characteristics among the employed (aged 15–64) with secondary education and above, by sector, 2018.

Benefit	Government	Private inside est.	Private outside est.	Total
Social insurance (%)	84	38	13	59
Health insurance (%)	96	36	11	69
Paid sick leave (%)	95	40	11	70
Paid leaves (%)	95	48	11	72
Average number of working hours/week	39	52	46	45
Level of satisfaction (rather or fully satisfied) about wage level (%)	79	70	58	74
Reported being satisfied (rather or fully satisfied) about their work (%)	98	88	67	74
N	1,786	1,314	434	3,534

Source: Authors' calculations based on ELMPS 2018.

who are primarily in the informal economy, had much worse working conditions, despite their level of education. Paid leaves were only accessible to 11 percent of workers outside establishments, and only 13 percent had social insurance. Workers in the government also worked shorter work weeks, averaging 39 hours. This figure increased to 52 hours for those working in the private sector inside establishments, and to 46 hours for those working outside establishments. All these conditions explain the level of reported work satisfaction, where workers in the government were more likely to report being rather or fully satisfied about their wages (79 percent) and their work in general (98 percent) than those working outside establishments (reporting 58 percent for work and 67 percent for wages).

5.3 Is the Government Still Employing Fresh Graduates?

If the public sector is still the employer of choice among the unemployed, particularly the youth, does it offer them the jobs they aspire to? Figure 5.3 shows the share of government employment comparing the different waves of the ELMPS. The figure shows that there has been a decline in the share of government work in employment for all working men and women from 33 percent in 1998 to 26 percent in 2018.

This decline, however, has not been steady. The 2012 data shows a stabilization in the share of government employment. This was in response to the mass demonstrations in 2011, when the government in Egypt responded to populist demands to increase hiring in the public sector (Beschel and Yousef, 2016). This shows the political significance of public sector hiring as a tool to gain the

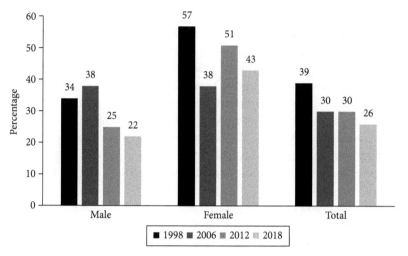

Figure 5.3 Percentage of the employed (aged 15–64) working in government by sex and wave, 1998–2018.
Source: Authors' calculations based on ELMPS 1998–2018.

support of the educated as a politically volatile group (Amin et al., 2012). The pattern of hiring youth into the public sector in response to political unrest has been observed elsewhere in the Arab region (Beschel and Yousef, 2016).

The government employed a higher proportion of working women than working men. This does not mean that the majority of workers in the sector were women, since so few women work. This simply shows that when women worked in Egypt, they were more likely to work in the government. The decline in employment in the government has particularly affected women (Chapter 2). The role of the government in employing women declined from a high of 57 percent of working women in 1998 to 43 percent among working women in 2018. This signified a serious decline in the role of this sector in employing women in Egypt, which resonates with the results of Assaad at al. (2020) in discussing the MENA paradox of rising educational attainment, yet stagnant female labor force participation.

5.4 Inside the Government: Worker Characteristics

In this section, we look at the characteristics of workers in the government and compare data on workers in the sector in the four waves of 1998, 2006, 2012, and 2018. We also compare workers in the sector in the three age groups of 18–35, 36–47, and 48–60 in 2018. The choice of these age categories and age range is deliberate. Hiring in the public sector has a minimum legal age that was set at 16 in Law 47 (issued in 1978). The same law stipulates that during hiring, preference is given to older age applicants among of those meeting the job requirements, which de facto increased the minimum age. The minimum legal age for hiring in the public sector was increased to 18 years in Law 81 (issued in 2016). Given the delay in hiring graduates, we start at 18 as the most realistic lowest age for hiring in the government. The obligatory retirement age for workers in the public sector is set at 60 years old in both regulations, which sets the range for the maximum age covered in this section.[2] In this section, we examine the education, education specializations, sex composition, and economic activities of workers within the sector. We also look at how these workers found their jobs and the type of work contracts they have.

A key observation is that the government workforce is getting more educated. Figure 5.4 compares the educational attainment level of government employees by the three age groups, in 2018. The figure shows that the share of those with university education among government workers aged 18–35 is 50 percent. This is to be compared with 42 percent among those aged 36–47, and with 32 percent among those aged 48–60. There is also a higher proportion of those with post-graduate education among the youngest age group (6 percent) compared with the oldest group (2 percent). These differences among the youngest age group came at the expense of the lowered share of those with vocational secondary and below. For example, the share of those with vocational secondary education dropped to 25 percent among the youngest age group, compared with 38 percent among the oldest age group. Similarly, the share of illiterate workers dropped to 2 percent in the youngest age category, compared with 8 percent in the oldest group.

While Figure 5.4 shows the difference between the three age groups, it is important to see whether the growth of the share of the educated is faster for the government than for the population as a whole. To investigate this, we look at the percentage of the employed in the government by education (focusing on those with primary and above) and sex in the four waves. Consistent with results in the previous section, Figure 5.5 shows that the share of government employment has declined for all education levels. However, the figure shows that the share of government employment among men with primary education declined from 18 percent in 1998 to 7 percent in 2018 (a 61 percent decline), while it declined from 56 percent to 38 percent (only a 32 percent decline) for men with university and above.

This decline in share of employment of the least educated in favor of the most educated is more pronounced among women. The share of government employment among women with primary education declined from 11 percent in 1998 to 8 percent in 2018 (a 27 percent decline), while it declined from 78 percent to

---

[2] In exceptional cases, the law allows the extension of contracts beyond this retirement age for experts in specific fields.

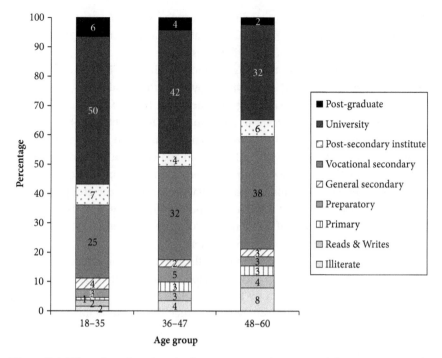

Figure 5.4 Education of workers in the government (percentage), by age group, aged 18–60, 2018.

Source: Authors' calculations based on ELMPS 2018.

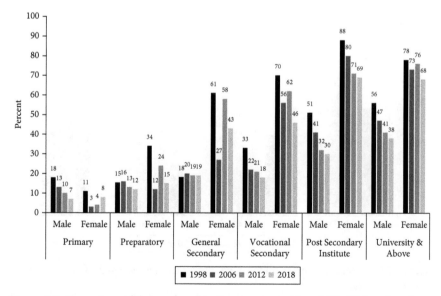

Figure 5.5 Percentage of the employed in the government (aged 18–60) by education level and sex, 1998–2018.

Source: Authors' calculations based on ELMPS 1998–2018.

68 percent (only a 13 percent decline) for women with university and above. These results are consistent with the data about the gender disaggregation of workers in the government that we will discuss.

The government is also getting slightly more feminized. Figure 5.6 shows the composition of government employment by age group and sex across waves. Overall, the share of women in the government rose from 31 percent in 1998 to 34 percent in 2006, to 36 percent in 2012, and then fell slightly to 35 percent in 2018. The share of women in the government has increased from 1998 to 2018 among the youngest age category (18–35) from 40 percent in 1998 to 43 percent in 2018. It is still the case, however, that women have not reached gender parity in the government. Figure 5.6 also illustrates that for the oldest age group, the share of women increased from 19 percent to 35 percent from 1998 to 2018. However, for ages 36–47, the share of women was 30 percent in both 1998 and 2018, although it rose and then fell again in the interim.

As Figure 5.7 shows, in 2018, women in the government were predominantly in the field of education (53 percent). The second largest group was public administration (17 percent), followed by human health and social work (16 percent). Men worked in more varied economic activities. Similar to women, the three

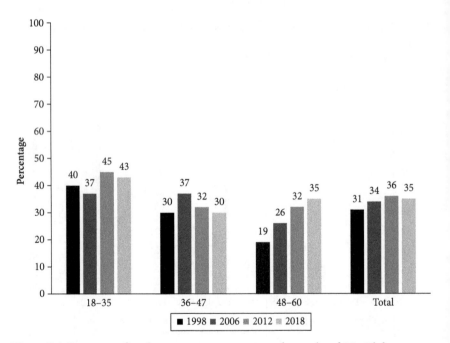

Figure 5.6 Percentage female among government employees (aged 18–60), by age group and wave, 1998–2018.

Source: Authors' calculations based on ELMPS 2006–2018.

economic activities of education, health, and public administration were the main economic activities for men. However, men also had much higher presence in manufacturing, construction, and transportation.

These limited economic activities for women in the government reflect their education specializations. As Figure 5.8 shows for 2018, the largest education specialization among women in the government was education (20 percent), followed by the share of other university degrees (16 percent). Men in the government showed a more diverse education background, with vocational secondary industrial education being the highest attained education for 17 percent of men, followed by commerce and law (12 percent) at the university level.

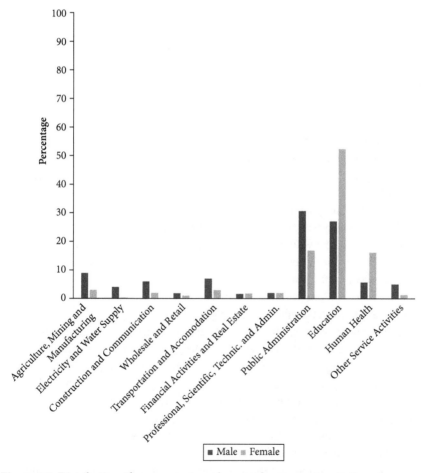

Figure 5.7 Distribution of government employment by economic activity and sex (ages 18–60), in 2018 (percentage).

Source: Authors' calculations based on ELMPS 2018.

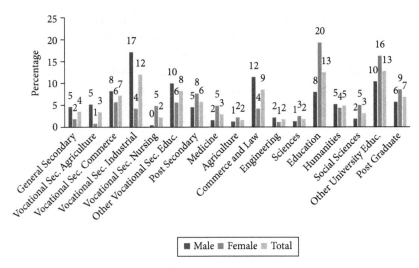

Male ■ Female ▨ Total

Figure 5.8 Education specialization (percentage) among government employees with secondary and above education (aged 18–60), by sex, 2018.
Source: Authors' calculations based on ELMPS 2018.

The government workforce in Egypt is also aging. We compare the age structure of government workers along the different waves of 1998, 2006, 2012, and 2018 in Figure 5.9. The figure shows that 39 percent of workers in the government were in the oldest age category of 48–60 years in 2018. This figure has consistently increased. It went up from 24 percent in 1998 to 29 percent in 2006 to 33 percent in 2012, to reach a peak in 2018 of 39 percent. Conversely, the share of government workers in the youngest age category 18–35 was down from 36 percent in 1998 to 31 percent in 2006. It slightly increased to 32 percent in 2012 owing to reasons related to the political unrest, as discussed earlier, but declined sharply to 23 percent in 2018. Assaad and Barsoum (2019) showed a similar pattern when analyzing data from the labor force sample survey.

To investigate whether this age structure is driven by reduced employment, we examine the share of employment in the government by age group and sex among the employed. Figure 5.10 shows that the share of government employment is much lower among the youngest age categories than in the oldest age categories. This difference is most pronounced when comparing 1998 and 2018. The government hired 53 percent of working women in the age category of 18–35 in 1998. This share dropped to 30 percent in 2018. The government has a much higher retention rate of working women than the private sector in Egypt (Chapter 1). This is reflected in the higher share of working women among the older age categories. Women exit the private sector upon marriage (Chapter 1), but this pattern does not hold for the government. This result helps to explain the higher share of government employment among older working women than

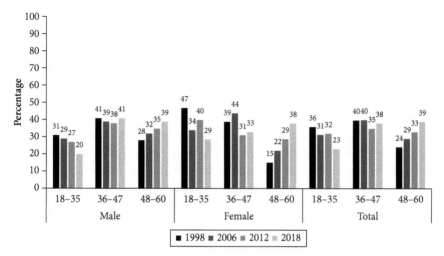

Figure 5.9 Age structure (percentage) of those in the government (aged 18–60), by wave and sex, 1998–2018.
Source: Authors' calculations based on ELMPS 1998–2018.

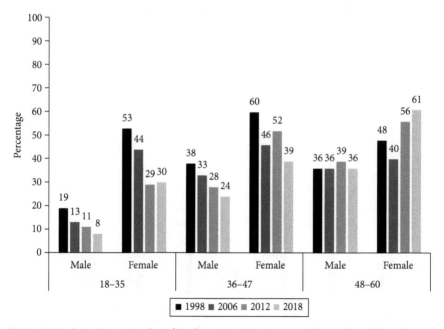

Figure 5.10 Percentage employed in the government among the employed (aged 18–60), by age group and sex, 1998–2018.
Source: Authors' calculations based on ELMPS 1998–2018.

among younger working women. The sector hired 60 percent of working women (36–47) in 1998. This share went down to 46 percent in 2006, up to 52 percent in 2012, and down again to 39 percent in 2018.

We also examined the share of government employment among all those aged 18–60. Figure 5.11 shows that despite the fact that the government employed a high proportion of working women, its share among all women (of all labor market statuses, including not employed) remained very small. The government only employed 10 percent of all women in the age category 36–47 years and 4 percent of women in the age category 18–35. Despite the increasing presence of women in the government and the growing feminization within its workforce, the sector's rate of employing men was consistently double that of employing women across all age groups. This was particularly the case among the youngest age group, which could signify a reversal, or at least a stalling, of the feminization process in the sector in coming decades.

We also compare how workers in the government obtained their job across the different survey waves. We aim to investigate if hiring in the government is getting more meritocratic. We operationalize meritocracy as relying on competition as opposed to friends and relatives. Figure 5.12 shows that women were more likely to get government jobs through government offices and job competitions than men. We also find that working men in the government were more likely to

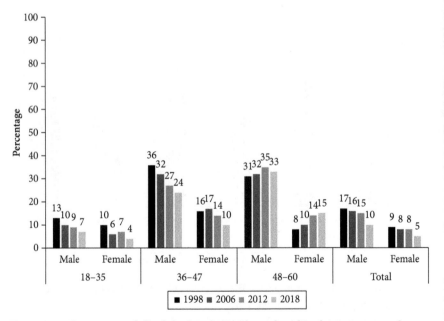

Figure 5.11 Percentage of all adults (aged 18–60) employed in the government, by age group and sex, 1998–2018.

Source: Authors' calculations based on ELMPS 1998–2018.

rely on friends and relatives to find a government job. Comparing data across the four waves, we see a steady decline in the role of government offices from 1998 to 2018 for both men and women; an increase in the role of competitions; and an increase in the role of friends and relatives in finding jobs in the government.

Finally, we look at the nature of work contracts among those in the government. Figure 5.13 shows that there was a higher share of those without a work contract among the youngest age groups when comparing the two points of 2012 and 2018. The share increased from 6 percent in 2012 to 9 percent in 2018. The share of those with fixed-term (definite duration) contracts in the same age cohort was down from 17 percent in 2012 to 6 percent in 2018. It is likely that those in the age group 48–60 misreported the status of their contractual agreement in the government. This can be explained by the fact that the hiring process in the government, particularly for this older cohort, did not involve an actual signing of a contract. This is consistent with data discussed by Barsoum (2016) about government hiring in Egypt.

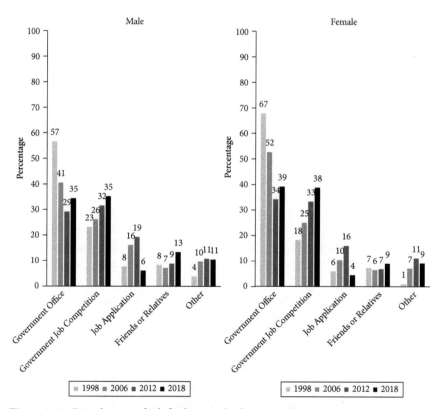

Figure 5.12   Distribution of job finding methods among those employed in the government (aged 18–60), by wave (percentage), 1998–2018.

Source: Authors' calculations based on ELMPS 1998–2018.

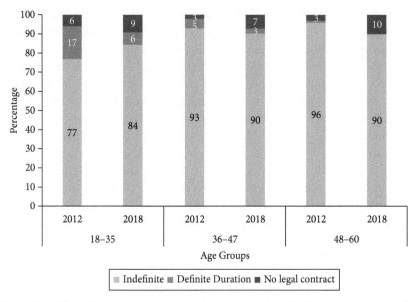

Figure 5.13 Type of contracts (percentage) among workers in the government (aged 18–60), by age group and wave, 2012–18.

Source: Authors' calculations based on ELMPS 2018.

5.5 Discussion and Conclusion

The government in Egypt remains the preferred sector of employment. It offers much better working conditions than the private sector, with those in the private sector outside establishments facing the worst conditions. In fact, the government remains a haven of job stability and benefits within a national context of rising job informality (Chapter 2). However, the rate of government employment among new entrants to the labor market has been declining. This is a timely policy approach that aims to right-size the sector. Public sector hiring has served for decades as a political tool to get the support of politically volatile groups of educated new entrants to the labor market (Assaad and Barsoum, 2019). Separating public sector hiring from politics is a step in the right direction. It is also a step towards making hiring in the sector based on talent and needs in order to increase its meritocracy and efficiency.

These hiring policy changes, however, have had an effect on the age composition of the workforce in government, with the upcoming retirement of many workers. The staff body in the government sector is witnessing a demographic transition, with the analysis showing that 39 percent of workers were in the oldest age category of 48–60 in 2018. This is an opportunity for restructuring, the recruitment of talent, and the build-up of a more educated workforce. Specifically, the analysis of the different characteristics of workers in the government shows a number of emerging patterns. The sector is clearly more educated. It is slightly more feminized, but not yet at gender parity. It is also an aging sector, with more than one third of its employees in the age category 48–60. There is, therefore, a potential opportunity for reforming the sector, creating innovation in government and increased efficiency as these aging employees retire.

For this highly sought-after employment sector, hiring based on merit can potentially improve the quality of public services. However, the analysis in this chapter shows that the use of these informal channels to finding jobs in the sector has increased when data from different waves are compared. Women in the government were more likely to get their jobs through competitions and application to institutions, as opposed to getting their jobs through contacts, than men.

Women's share in government hiring has not reached gender parity, despite increasing access to higher education. Women still do not constitute half the workers in the government, despite a trend of feminization. Women were still in what can be described as "gender-appropriate" activities in the government, with education institutions hiring the largest share. Perhaps the limited working hours in this field attract more women, who have competing tasks for their time as mothers (Barsoum, 2019).

More policy focus needs to be placed on improving job quality in the private sector. Low job quality may limit the preference for employment in the private sector. This requires an urgent debate on policies that aim to offer more inclusive and universal social and health insurance systems to those working in the private sector. As the data provided in this chapter show, access to such systems remains a privilege to those in the government sector and a small proportion of those in the private sector. De Gobbi and Nesporova (2005) argued for the implementation of "flexicurity" policies in Egypt. These policies would allow for balancing the need for labor market flexibility and employment security through well-functioning labor market institutions, active labor market policies, and social insurance policies (De Gobbi and Nesporova, 2005). This approach was pioneered in Denmark in the 1960s (Madsen, 2014). Such policies give employers the flexibility to control the size of their workforce while allowing for unemployment benefits for those who might lose their jobs, along with effective training and active labor market policies (Ploug, 2014). While the implementation of active labor market policies has had many challenges in the region (Barsoum, 2018), there is a need for concerted efforts to balance the preference for public sector jobs.

It is reasonable to speculate that the preference for public sector hiring will increase with the COVID-19 pandemic. During the lockdown, workers in the public sector were among those who received full pay while staying at home; and it was indeed mostly a situation of "staying at home" as opposed to "working from home" owing to the limited use of technology in many agencies. A recent survey by Egypt's Central Agency for Public Mobilization and Statistics (CAPMAS) showed that as of May 2020, as a result of the pandemic, 73 percent of respondents reported a drop in income (CAPMAS, 2020: 6). While the survey does not disaggregate results by sector of employment, it is most likely that those who lost income were not government employees. Pay is fixed for government employees and is set by law. It might be that some workers would lose benefits such as overtime pay, but the basic salary would not be affected. More importantly, none of the permanent workers in the government experienced job loss owing to the pandemic. The CAPMAS report shows that about one-quarter of those who reported a change of their employment status (65 percent) have become unemployed (CAPMAS, 2020: 4–6). The pandemic has created more reasons for the continued preference for public sector employment.

References

Amin, Magdi, et al. (2012) *After the Spring: Economic Transitions in the Arab World.* Oxford: Oxford University Press.

Assaad, Ragui (2014) "Making Sense of Arab Labor Markets: The Enduring Legacy of Dualism." *IZA Journal of Labor & Development,* 3 (6): 1–25.

Assaad, Ragui (1997) "The Effects of Public Sector Hiring and Compensation Policies on the Egyptian Labor Market." *World Bank Economic Review,* 11 (1): 85–118.

Assaad, Ragui and Ghada Barsoum (2019) "Public Employment in the Middle East and North Africa." IZA World of Labor 2019: 463. doi: 10.15185/izawol.463.

Assaad, R. et al. (2020) "Explaining the MENA Paradox: Rising Educational Attainment, Yet Stagnant Female Labor Force Participation." *Demographic Research,* 43 (28): 817–50.

Barsoum, Ghada (2016) "The Public Sector as the Employer of Choice Among Youth in Egypt: The Relevance of Public Service Motivation Theory," *International Journal of Public Administration,* 39 (3): 205–15.

Barsoum, Ghada (2018) "Can Youth Activation Policies Be Central to Social Policies in MENA Countries?" *International Social Security Review,* 71 (2): 39–56. https://onlinelibrary.wiley.com/doi/full/10.1111/issr.12165.

Barsoum, Ghada (2019) "Women, Work and Family: Educated Women's Employment Decisions and Social Policies in Egypt," *Gender Work and Organization,* 26 (7): 895–914.

Beschel Jr., Robert P. and Tarik M. Yousef (2016) "Public Sector Reform," in Ishac Diwan and Ahmed (eds) *The Middle East Economies in Times of Transition.* International Economic Association Series, pp. 259–75. London: Palgrave Macmillan.

CAPMAS (Central Agency for Public Mobilization and Statistics) (2020) *The Impact of the Corona Virus on Egyptian Families until May 2020.* Cairo: CAPMAS.

De Gobbi, S. and Nesporova, A. 2005. *Towards a New Balance between Labour Market. Flexibility and Employment Security for Egypt.* International Labor Organization. Employment Policies Unit Employment Strategy Department. International Labor Organization.

Desai, Raj M., Anders Olofsgard, and Tarik Yousef (2009) "The Logic of Authoritarian Bargains," *Economics & Politics*, 21 (1): 93–125.

Madsen, P. K. (2004). The Danish model of 'flexicurity': experiences and lessons. *Transfer: European Review of Labour and Research*, 10(2), 187–207.

Ploug, Niels (2014) "Investing in People to Promote Activation and Empowerment: The Case of Denmark and Lessons for Other Countries," *International Social Security Review*, 67 (3–4): 61–74.

World Bank (2016) "Middle East and North Africa Public Employment and Governance in MENA." Report No: ACS18501. Washington, DC: World Bank.

6

Trends and Patterns of Women's Entrepreneurship in Egypt

Reham Rizk and Ali Rashed

6.1 Introduction

Women entrepreneurs are considered an untapped source of economic growth and job creation (Minniti and Naude, 2010; Berger and Kuckertz, 2016). Despite the rise of women entrepreneurs globally, women lag behind men in entrepreneurship, particularly in the Middle East and North Africa region. In the region, women's participation in entrepreneurship is less than half the rate of men, with the exception of Qatar (GEM, 2018).

Egypt has a consistent gender gap in entrepreneurship. While 1.8 percent of women owned a business, 10.3 percent of men did so (Ismail, Tolba, and Barakat, 2016). Additionally, 8 percent of women compared with 21 percent of men were involved in early stage entrepreneurship, setting up a business or with a business that was younger than three and a half years old. These patterns indicate the systematic challenges facing women who are starting and continuing their own enterprise (Ismail, Tolba, and Barakat, 2016). On the other hand, women may participate in survival self-employment owing to their constrained labor market opportunities (see Chapter 2 this volume). Women are more likely to leave private sector wage work after marriage owing to the domestic work burden within marriage, but may continue or even increase their participation in non-wage work, including entrepreneurship (Assaad, Krafft, and Selwaness, 2017; Selwaness and Krafft, 2020; Chapter 2).

In the global context, there is growing literature that elaborates the challenges facing women's entrepreneurship. Enterprises owned by women face additional barriers to finance (Marlow and Patton, 2005; El Mahdi and Rashed, 2007; Rashed and Sieverding, 2015), and this could be the reason fewer women engage in enterprise work than men (Devine, 1994; Kevane and Wydick, 2001; Georgellis and Wall, 2005; Kim, 2007). Female-led enterprises are more likely to continue being small in size or exit owing to limited financial resources (Rajan and Petersen,

Reham Rizk and Ali Rashed, *Trends and Patterns of Women's Entrepreneurship in Egypt* In: *The Egyptian Labor Market: A Focus on Gender and Economic Vulnerability*. Edited by: Caroline Krafft and Ragui Assaad, Oxford University Press.
© Economic Research Forum 2022. DOI: 10.1093/oso/9780192847911.003.0007

1994; Carter and Allen, 1997). Moreover, women receive discriminatory treatment when dealing with financial institutions (Brush, 1992; Verheul and Thurik, 2001; Kara, 2010) which drives them to depend on their own personal resources or borrow from family members (Rajan and Petersen, 1994).

The decision of women to engage in entrepreneurial work is strongly associated with family, where women do not view their business as a separate economic entity but an attempt to improve their family's future (Brush, 1992). Motherhood, childcare, and spouse's type of work impact the likelihood women pursue entrepreneurial activities (Tonoyan, Budig, and Strohmeyer, 2010; Klyver, Nielsen, and Evald, 2013). Entrepreneurship for women could lead to more respect in their marital relationship, in addition to provision of more food, clothing, and schooling for children (Parasuraman and Simmers, 2001; DeMartino and Barbato, 2003). However, in many cases women struggle to achieve work and family balance (Ufuk and Özgen, 2001; Winn, 2004; Shelton, 2006). Among the difficulties, time allocated to home chores and family-related tasks were more for female than male entrepreneurs (Cliff, 1998; Jurik, 1998). Women also faced difficulties securing their husband's support and approval (McGowan et al., 2012). Entrepreneurship for women is more likely to be out of necessity rather than opportunity (Du-Rietz and Henrekson, 2000; Luke and Munshi, 2011). Women may have no other option for viable employment opportunities owing to their lower levels of education, lack of experience, and limited financial resources (Kelley, et al. 2011).

The chapter addresses the following questions about women's entrepreneurship, for the case of Egypt: (1) What share of households have non-agricultural enterprises and how has this varied across female- and male-headed households and over time? (2) What share of men and women own enterprises and how does this differ by their characteristics? (3) What are the characteristics of female-owned enterprises vis-à-vis male-owned enterprises? (4) What are the gendered patterns of participation in enterprises?

The findings of the chapter show a persistent gender gap in entrepreneurship. The percentage of households with non-agricultural enterprises has been declining since 2006. Female-headed households with enterprises also continued to be fewer, older, poorer, and more rural than male-headed households. Female-owned enterprises were more likely to be informal. There were growing shares of female-owned enterprises engaged in wholesale and retail activities and operating at home or in a fixed establishment. As well as being less likely to own enterprises, women were less likely to participate in enterprise work than men.

The chapter is organized as follows. Section 6.2 describes the data and methods. Section 6.3 presents the descriptive analysis. Section 6.4 provides the discussion and conclusion.

6.2 Data and Methods

Our analysis uses the Egypt Labor Market Panel Survey (ELMPS) waves of 1998, 2006, 2012, and 2018 (Krafft, Assaad, and Rahman, 2021).[1] ELMPS is a nationally representative panel survey that has detailed modules with data on agricultural and non-agricultural enterprises. This chapter focuses solely on non-agricultural enterprises. All households are asked the non-agricultural enterprise module, and responding to the agricultural or non-agricultural module is required if any household member has a work status of employer (hires other workers), self-employed, or unpaid family worker. Data are collected on all household non-agricultural enterprises, potentially more than one. The module has rich information on different topics such as formality, access to finance, economic activity, location, number of workers, capital, and ownership.

For the purpose of this chapter, women's participation in a household enterprise is defined as being one of the three people who worked the most on at least one enterprise (only three were collected per enterprise). We define an enterprise owner as the individual who worked the most on the enterprise (see Chapter 8 this volume for a comparison of different measures of engagement and ownership). Female- versus male-headed households are identified based on who was reported as the household head in the roster. The formality definition used in our analysis is based on whether the enterprise is registered, or whether there are accounting books kept for the enterprise, or whether the owner has a business license. The enterprise is defined as formal if it meets any of these criteria.

6.3 Results

The results are presented as follows; first, we examine the share of households that have non-agricultural enterprises and how has this varied across female- and male-headed households and over time. Second, we investigate the share of men and women who own enterprises and how this differs by their characteristics. Third, we investigate the characteristics of female-owned enterprises vis-à-vis male-owned enterprises with respect to capital, location, employment, formality, and access to finance. Finally, we show the patterns and trends of women's participation in enterprise work compared with those of men.

---

[1] The data are publicly available at www.erfdataportal.com.

6.3.1 Households with enterprises

Figure 6.1 shows the percentage of households with non-agricultural enterprises in Egypt and how this has evolved over time and by head's sex. The share of households with enterprises slightly increased over the period 1998–2006, from 20 percent in 1998 to 22 percent in 2012 and then declined sharply over the period 2012–18 from 19 percent to 14 percent. The reduction started after the 2011 uprising and the subsequent economic turmoil, which led to a deterioration in labor market conditions (see Chapter 2 this volume), evidenced by lower employment rates and economic opportunities (Assaad and Krafft, 2015; Krafft, Assaad and Rahman, 2021). Post-uprising there were decreases in sales and increases in costs to those who were employers or self-employed. Additionally, there was an increased likelihood that household non-agricultural enterprises would close (Krafft, 2016).

Female-headed households were less likely to have enterprises. While in 2018, 16 percent of male-headed households had non-agricultural enterprises, just 6 percent of female-headed households had enterprises. The declining trend of enterprises affected both male- and female-headed households.

Figure 6.2 shows the percentage of households with enterprises by head's sex, head's age group, and wave. Households with prime-aged heads (30–49 years of age) were more likely to have enterprises. In 2018, 17 percent of households with prime-aged male heads had enterprises. Just 6 percent of prime-age female-headed households had an enterprise. For female-headed households, enterprises

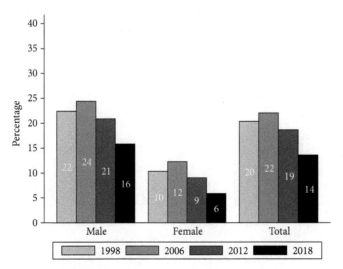

Figure 6.1 Percentage of households with non-agricultural enterprises by head's sex and wave, 1998–2018.
Source: Authors' calculations based on ELMPS 1998–2018.

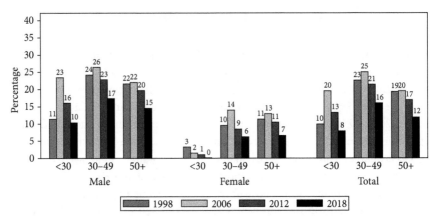

Figure 6.2 Percentage of households with non-agricultural enterprises by head's sex, head's age group, and wave, 1998–2018.

Source: Authors' calculations based on ELMPS 1998–2018.

tended to be more common at ages 50 and older than ages 30–49, but the opposite was true for male-headed households. Households with young (age less than 30) heads had the lowest rates of enterprises.

As shown in Figure 6.3, the share of households with non-agriculture enterprises in 2018 was higher in urban Lower Egypt (19 percent) and urban Upper Egypt (17 percent), while the share declined substantially over time in Greater Cairo and Alexandria and Suez Canal, and was 11 percent for both in 2018. Male-headed households followed the overall pattern. The pattern was reversed for female-headed households, with higher rates of enterprises in rural Lower Egypt (8 percent) and urban Lower Egypt (7 percent), followed by 6 percent in Alexandria and Suez Canal, 5 percent in rural Upper Egypt, and just 3 percent in Greater Cairo.

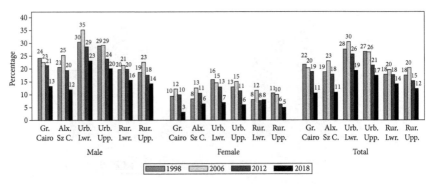

Figure 6.3 Percentage of households with non-agricultural enterprises by head's sex, region, and wave, 1998–2019.

Source: Authors' calculations based on ELMPS 1998–2018.

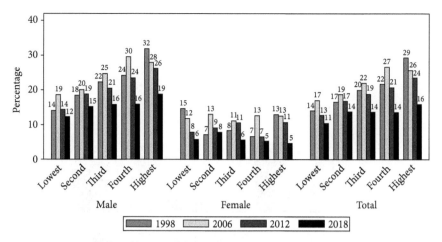

Figure 6.4 Percentage of households with non-agricultural enterprises by head's sex, wealth quintile, and wave, 1998–2018.
Source: Authors' calculations based on ELMPS 1998–2018.

Figure 6.4 shows the share of households with enterprises by head's sex and wealth quintile. Non-agricultural enterprises were disproportionally owned by wealthier households; while 11 percent of the poorest households had enterprises in 2018, 16 percent of those in the richest quintile had enterprises. The overall pattern holds for male-headed households. The pattern is reversed for households headed by females, where 6–8 percent of female-headed households in the poorest through third quintile in 2018 had enterprises compared with just 5 percent of households in the fourth and top wealth quintiles.

6.3.2 Non-agricultural enterprise owners

Looking across the four waves of the ELMPS also showed some changes in the rate of non-agricultural enterprise ownership over time, as shown in Figure 6.5. The rate of enterprise ownership was stable over the period 1998–2012 and started to decline over the period 2012–18, from 7.2 percent of individuals aged 15–64 owning enterprises in 2012 to 5.6 percent in 2018. Women were less likely to be enterprise owners than men, but there was a slight increase in the rates of women owning enterprises from 1.9 percent in 2012 to 2.2 percent in 2018.

In 2018, there were few differences in owning enterprises by individuals' education overall (5–6 percent across education levels). However, there were substantial differences when disaggregated by sex. Less educated women were more likely to own enterprises than more educated women; 4 percent of illiterate women owned enterprises in 2018 compared with 1–2 percent of women with other education levels. Conversely, more educated men were more likely to own enterprises

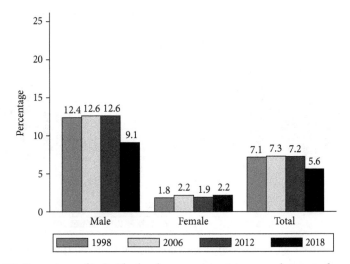

Figure 6.5 Percentage of individuals who are enterprise owners by sex and wave, ages 15–64, 1998–2018.

Source: Authors' calculations based on ELMPS 1998–2018.

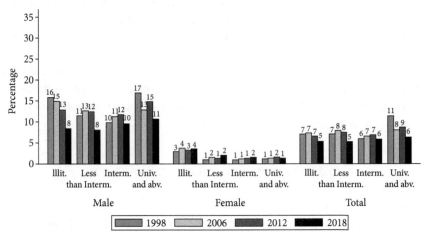

Figure 6.6 Percentage of individuals who are enterprise owners by education, sex, and wave, ages 15–64, 1998–2018.

Source: Authors' calculations based on ELMPS 1998–2018.

than less educated men; 10 percent for those with intermediate degrees and 11 percent for those with university degrees compared with 8 percent for lower education levels in 2018.

Figure 6.7 shows enterprise ownership by age group, sex, and wave. Those aged 30–49 or 50 and older were more likely to be enterprise owners than those less than 30. This pattern relates to the fact that entrepreneurship is predominantly undertaken by older adults with greater work experience and capital acquisition

(Krafft and Rizk, 2021). While patterns were similar over time for women, for men it used to be that enterprise ownership was slightly more common at ages 30–49, but that was no longer the case in 2018.

Father's education, as a signal of the socioeconomic status of individuals, is shown in Figure 6.8. The percentage of men who were enterprise owners was higher among those with less educated fathers, and the same was true for women. For example, in 2018, 7 percent of those with illiterate fathers owned an enterprise compared with 3 percent of those with university educated fathers.

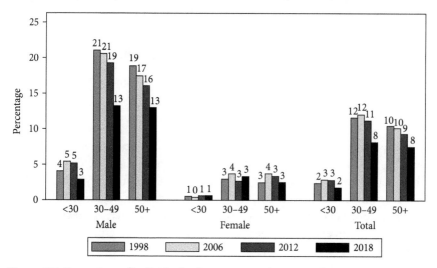

Figure 6.7 Percentage of individuals who are enterprise owners by age group, sex, and wave, ages 15–64, 1998–2018.

Source: Authors' calculations based on ELMPS 1998–2018.

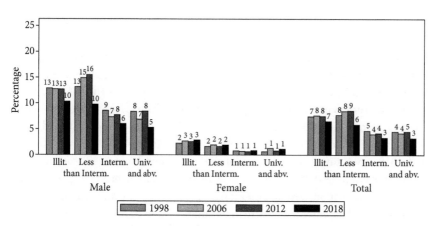

Figure 6.8 Percentage of individuals who are enterprise owners by father's education, sex, and wave, ages 15–64, 1998–2018.

Source: Authors' calculations based on ELMPS 1998–2018.

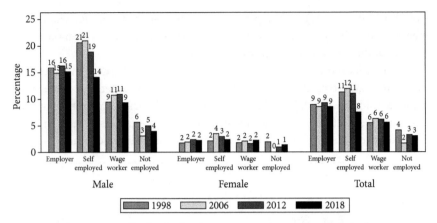

Figure 6.9 Percentage of individuals who are enterprise owners by father's employment, sex, and wave, ages 15–64, 1998–2018.

Source: Authors' calculations based on ELMPS 1998–2018.

Enterprise ownership may be linked to a family business (Figure 6.9). Social, physical, and human capital could be passed through families. Overall, those whose fathers were employers or self-employed were more likely to themselves own enterprises (8–9 percent in 2018 versus 6 percent for wage worker fathers). Father's employment was, however, primarily related to enterprise ownership for men; women with employer fathers had the same rates of enterprise ownership as women with wage worker fathers.

6.3.3 Characteristics of enterprises

We now turn to the characteristics of non-agricultural household enterprises. Figure 6.10 shows the economic activity of non-agricultural household enterprises by wave and owner sex. The share of enterprises owned by women engaged in manufacturing and related trades was 17–18 percent in 1998 to 2006, then started to decline to 15 percent in 2012 and to 11 percent in 2018. The share of male-owned enterprises in manufacturing and related trades has largely fallen over time from 17 percent in 1998 to 12 percent in 2018. The share of female-owned enterprises in wholesale and retail rose from 72 percent in 1998 to 74 percent in 2012 and 2018. Over time, the share of enterprises owned by men in transport rose from 9 percent in 1998 to 16 percent in 2018. For female-owned enterprises, transport and construction were uncommon. For both men and women, only a small percentage of their enterprises were in accommodation or food service.

Figure 6.11 demonstrates the location of enterprises by owner sex. The most common locations for female-owned enterprises were home (44 percent in 2018), followed by having a shop (24 percent). Having an office/flat/building/rooms

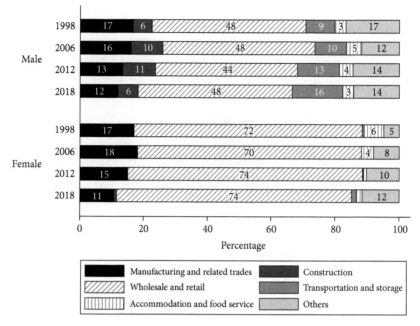

Figure 6.10 Economic activity of non-agricultural household enterprises by wave and owner sex (percentage of enterprises), 1998–2018.

Note: Labels suppressed for values less than 3 percent.

Source: Authors' calculations based on ELMPS 1998–2018.

showed an increase from 11 percent in 1998 to 15 percent in 2018. Being a mobile worker (6 percent) or work in a shop/factory and transport-based were less common for women-owned enterprises. The percentage of women-owned enterprises that were street vendors declined from 20 percent in 1998 to 9 percent in 2018. The most common locations of enterprises owned by men were shops (38 percent) followed by mobile workers (20 percent), street vendors (9 percent), own home (9 percent), office/flat/building/rooms (9 percent), and lastly workshop/factory and transport-based (8 percent each).

Another very important aspect of household enterprises is their current capital,[2] as shown in Figure 6.12. Compared to male-owned enterprises, the share of enterprises owned by women with high capital was low. For example, in 2018, 11 percent of female-owned enterprises had no capital compared to 6 percent of male-owned enterprises. Male-owned enterprises commonly had EGP 5,000–9,999 of capital in 2018, 45 percent, compared with 12 percent for women-owned enterprises. Additionally, 25 percent of male-owned enterprises had EGP 10,000 or more of capital, compared to 7 percent for female-owned enterprises.

---

[2] The current capital was reported in nominal prices and in categories.

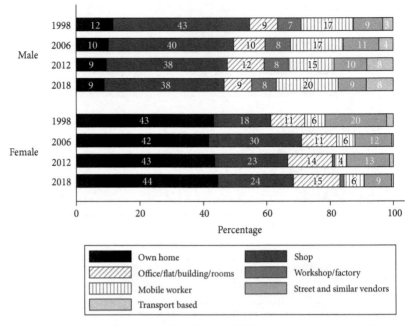

Figure 6.11 Location of non-agricultural household enterprises by wave and owner sex (percentage of enterprises), 1998–2018.

Note: Labels suppressed for values less than 3 percent.

Source: Authors' calculations based on ELMPS 1998–2018.

Figure 6.13 shows the share of household enterprises held in partnership by owner sex and wave. Sole proprietorship was still dominant among household enterprises with a partnership share of around 9–11 percent over the period 1998–2018. Male-owned businesses were more likely to be in partnership (11 percent in 2018) than female-owned businesses (6 percent in 2018, albeit an increase from the previous 1–3 percent).

Figure 6.14 shows the formality status of enterprises by owner sex and wave. Formality is defined as having either a license, registration, or accounting books. Overall, the share of non-agricultural enterprises that were formal declined from 55 percent in 1998 to 45 percent in 2012, but in 2018 there was an increase in enterprises that were formal by 2 percentage points (to 47 percent). The share of enterprises owned by women that were formal increased from 21 percent in 2012 to 25 percent in 2018. For male owners, the rate increased from 48 percent in 2012 to 51 percent in 2018.

Figure 6.15 shows the percentage of household enterprises that received formal loans by owner sex and wave. One of the important factors that limits the capacity of enterprises to continue and grow is the availability of finance. The ELMPS data identified several sources where enterprise owners could receive formal loans or

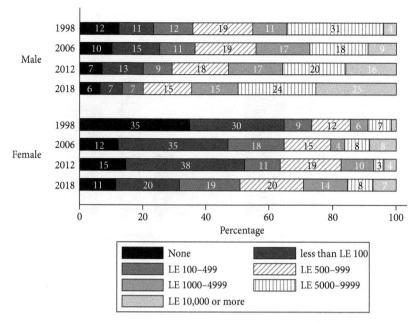

Figure 6.12 Nominal capital of non-agricultural household enterprises by wave and owner sex (percentage), 1998–2018.

Note: Labels suppressed for values less than 3 percent.

Source: Authors' calculations based on ELMPS 1998–2018.

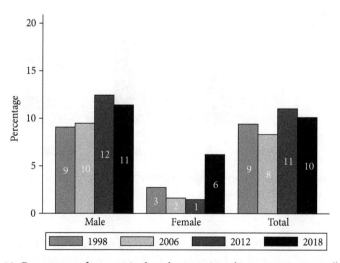

Figure 6.13 Percentage of non-agricultural enterprises that were in partnership by wave and owner sex, 1998–2018.

Source: Authors' calculations based on ELMPS 1998–2018.

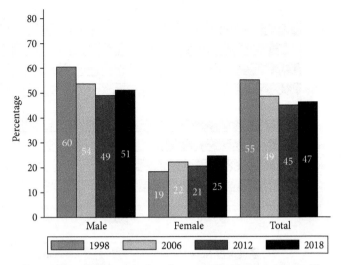

Figure 6.14 Percentage of non-agricultural enterprises that were formal by wave and owner sex, 1998–2018.
Source: Authors' calculations based on ELMPS 1998–2018.

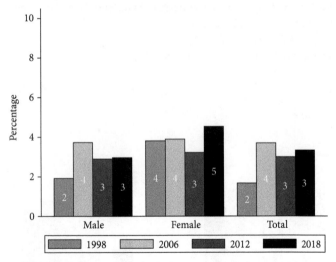

Figure 6.15 Percentage of non-agricultural enterprises that received formal loans by wave and owner sex, 1998–2018.
Source: Authors' calculations based on ELMPS 1998–2018.

any other financial support such as the Nasser Development Bank, the Micro Small Medium Enterprise Development Agency, public and private banks, non-governmental organizations (NGOs), and religious institutions. Overall, the percentage of enterprises that received formal loans was stable at 3 percent over the period 2012–18. The percentage of male-owned enterprises followed the overall time trend, while the percentage of enterprises owned by women had a small increase in receiving loans, from 3 percent in 2012 to 5 percent in 2018.

Turning to the contribution of household enterprises to employment, Table 6.1 shows the distribution of changes in the number of employees in household enterprises by head's sex and wave. Overall, the share of household enterprises with outside (non-household member) workers declined from 31 percent in 2012 to 24 percent in 2018. Female-headed households were less likely to employ outside workers, 11 percent in 2018 compared with 25 percent for men.

The share of enterprises that added workers in the previous year fell from 16 percent in 1998 to 10 percent in 2012, then increased to 13 percent in 2018. Male and female rates of adding workers were similar to the total in 2018. At the same time, enterprises were unlikely to lose workers in the past year (12 percent) in 2012 and 2018. Female-headed households with enterprises were less likely to lose workers in 2018 (2 percent) than male-headed households with enterprises (13 percent).

In the questions that tracked the changes in the number of workers over the past three years, there was an increase in the percentage reporting an increase in number of workers, from 5 percent in 2012 to 8 percent in 2018. There was also a decline in the percentage reporting a decrease in the number of workers, from 18 percent in 2012 to 11 percent in 2018. Female-headed households were more likely to have no change than male-headed households.

Table 6.2 examines the amount of employment in enterprises. Overall, around 5.6 million workers in 1998 were engaged in household enterprises, 7.4 million in 2006, 6.4 million as of 2012, and finally 5.4 million in 2018. Female- and male-headed households with enterprises followed the overall trend. Almost 412,000 workers engaged in enterprise work in female-headed households compared with 5 million workers engaged in male-headed households. The vast majority of employment in female-headed households was household member employment, with only 32,000 outside workers employed in 2018, compared with 1.4 million outside workers employed in enterprises in male-headed households.

To gain more insights into the dynamics behind these levels, we looked to the number of workers that were added and lost in the past year. While 238,000 workers were added and 289,000 were lost in 2012, just 204,000 workers were added and 179,000 were lost in 2018. For female-headed households with enterprises, 16,000 were added in 2012 and 6,000 in 2018, while 13,000 were lost in 2012, declining to 1,000 in 2018.

6.3.4 Household members participating in non-agricultural enterprises

We turn now to the percentage of household members engaged in non-agricultural enterprises (potentially multiple members per household, up to three

Table 6.1 Non-agricultural enterprises and outside employment, by head sex and wave (percentage), 1998–2018.

	Male				Female				Total			
	1998	2006	2012	2018	1998	2006	2012	2018	1998	2006	2012	2018
Employ outside workers												
No	70	68	68	75	81	81	78	89	71	70	69	76
Yes	30	32	32	25	20	19	22	11	29	31	31	24
Add workers in the past year												
No	84	80	91	87	84	87	80	89	84	80	90	87
Yes	16	20	9	13	16	13	20	11	16	20	10	13
Lose workers in the past year												
No	87	85	88	88	97	93	83	99	88	85	88	88
Yes	13	16	12	13	3	7	17	2	12	15	12	12
Change in number of workers in past three years												
Increase	6	13	5	8	13	5	6	7	6	13	5	8
Decrease	6	8	19	12	0	10	7	6	6	8	18	11
No change	81	76	72	76	77	83	83	82	81	77	73	76
Enterprise < 3 years	7	3	5	5	10	2	5	5	7	3	5	5
Total	100	100	100	100	100	100	100	100	100	100	100	100
N	1041	1842	2113	2031	100	202	202	220	1141	2044	2315	2251

Source: Authors' calculations based on ELMPS 1998–2018.

Table 6.2 Employment and employment dynamics in enterprises by head sex and wave (in thousands), 1998–2018.

Wave	Male Total employment	Household member employment	Out of household employment	Workers added in the past year	Workers lost in the past year
	Male				
1998	5317	3139	2178	465	401
2006	6926	3821	3105	563	343
2012	5969	3903	2066	222	275
2018	5021	3558	1463	198	178
	Female				
1998	287	255	33	13	3
2006	562	438	124	9	5
2012	513	401	113	16	13
2018	412	380	32	6	1
	Total				
1998	5604	3394	2210	478	404
2006	7488	4259	3229	573	348
2012	6482	4304	2178	238	289
2018	5434	3938	1495	204	179

Source: Authors' calculations based on ELMPS 1998–2018.

per enterprise). Figure 6.16 shows how the percentage of individuals aged 15–64 engaged in enterprises evolved over time. There were relatively few individuals engaged in non-agricultural enterprises over time, 8 percent over the period 1998 to 2012 and 7 percent in 2018. Among women, the percentage engaged in enterprises was generally stable at 3 percent with a slight decline in 2012 to 2 percent, before recovering to 3 percent in 2018. Among men, the percentage engaged was large compared with women: the rate increased from 13 percent in 1998 to 14 percent between 2006 and 2012, then fell to 11 percent in 2018.

Figure 6.17 shows the participation of household members in non-agricultural household enterprises by education, sex, and wave. In 2018, a similar share (7 percent) of individuals engaged in enterprises across education levels. There

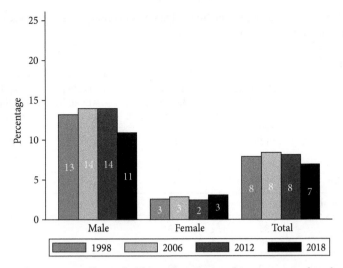

Figure 6.16 Percentage of household members engaged in non-agricultural enterprises by sex and wave, ages 15–64, 1998–2018.
Source: Authors' calculations based on ELMPS 1998–2018.

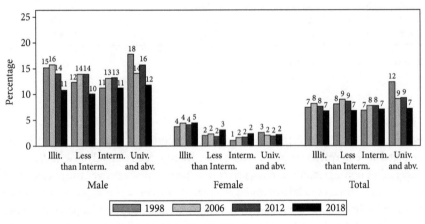

Figure 6.17 Percentage of household members engaged in non-agricultural enterprises by education, sex and wave, ages 15–64, 1998–2018.
Source: Authors' calculations based on ELMPS 1998–2018.

was modest fluctuation over time at most education levels. However, the percentage of individuals with university degrees engaged in enterprises fell from 12 percent in 1998 to 9 percent in 2006 and 2012, then 7 percent in 2018. As with ownership, among women, illiterates were more likely to participate. For men, in 2018, there were limited differences in participation by education (10–12 percent).

Figure 6.18 demonstrates the percentage of individuals engaged in enterprises by sex, age group, and wave. Overall, the percentage of individuals engaged in

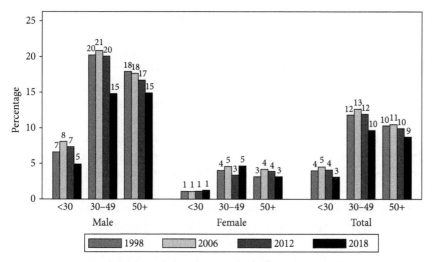

Figure 6.18 Percentage of household members engaged in non-agricultural enterprises by age group, sex, and wave, ages 15–64, 1998–2018.
Source: Authors' calculations based on ELMPS 1998–2018.

enterprises was highest for the 30–49-year-olds and lowest for those who were below the age of 30. In 2018, 1 percent of women below 30 participated, 5 percent aged 30–49, and 3 percent above 50. Likewise, 5 percent of men below 30 participated and 15 percent for both the 30–49 age group and above 50.

6.4 Discussions and Conclusions

The chapter offers a comprehensive investigation of the patterns and trends of women's role in enterprises in Egypt from 1998 to 2018. The findings of the chapter suggest a number of important gendered patterns of headship, ownership, and engagement with enterprise work on different levels.

First, the percentage of households with enterprises has been declining since 2006. Female-headed households with enterprises continued to be fewer, older, poorer, and more rural than male-headed households. Women were also less likely to engage in enterprise work than men. Women engaged in enterprise work were more likely to be less educated, older, and in rural locations. Although entrepreneurship remains male-dominated, the share of women among entrepreneurs is rising. Feminization in entrepreneurship is a global trend, where countries with high levels of entrepreneurial activity are associated with more women entrepreneurs (Verheul, van Stel and Thurik, 2004). This pattern is attributed to not only cultural and social norms, but also to the difficulty of balancing work and family responsibilities, particularly for married women (Carter and Allen, 1997; DeTienne and Justo, 2008). Thus, for women who need to work at home, entrepreneurship is a practical solution that provides financial support for their family while allowing them to handle their domestic responsibilities (Georgellis and Wall, 2005; Bertaux and Crable, 2007; Sarfaraz, Faghih and Majd, 2014).

Turning to the characteristics of enterprise owners, the percentage of women owning an enterprise was much lower than men. There was still an education gap between men and women owners, with illiterate individuals more likely to be owners among women and university educated individuals among men. Entrepreneurship was undertaken by older adults, who possessed capital and had work experience. With respect to enterprise characteristics, there was a growing share of female-owned enterprises engaged in wholesale and retail activities, but this was stable for male-owned enterprises. There were high rates of female-owned enterprises operating at home or in a fixed establishment such as an office/flat/building/rooms. However, women were less likely to have formal enterprises.

After analyzing the financial profile of household enterprises, female-owned enterprises reported lower current capital than those owned by men. As has been noted in the global literature, provision of access to finance is a fundamental driver to enterprise development in Egypt. Since 2012, Egypt has implemented different public sector initiatives aiming to increase access to loans. Among the prominent initiatives are Mastoura, adopted by the Ministry of Social Solidarity and funded by Tahya-Misr Fund, which aims to provide women with loans to start up their own business, at a total cost of EGP 250 million. The program was associated with 15,000 new projects (Ministry of Social Solidarity, 2018). There is also Fekratak Sherketak (Ministry of Investment and International Cooperation, 2018), which is a program designed by the Ministry to support and empower youth entrepreneurs by offering funding, mentorship, and training to develop and grow their business.

In the food and beverages sector, there are two initiatives, namely Sharea 306 (306 Street) and Sharea Misr (Egypt Street), the former funded by Tahya-Misr Fund and the latter by Cairo governorate (Ministry of Investment and International Cooperation, 2018); both allocate locations for youth entrepreneurs to sell their products. Additionally, public banks, such as Misr Bank (Banque Misr, 2014), in addition to civil society and NGO programs, worked on improving access to finance (Sawiris Foundation for Social Development, 2015).

There has been a decrease in the overall number of workers in household enterprises since 2012. These changes were driven by a decrease in the use of both outside and household workers. At the same time, there was a slight increase in hiring in the previous year. Female-headed households were much less likely to employ outside workers and employed far fewer workers.

Although our data predate the COVID-19 pandemic, they have important implications for its impact. The impact of COVID-19 on household income was enormous. Almost 33 percent of households reported that their income could not satisfy their needs during the pandemic outbreak as of May 2020 (CAPMAS, 2020). The reduction in income was mainly driven by the service sector—where, as we demonstrated, women entrepreneurs were concentrated—owing to lockdown. COVID-19 and its economic impact may push more women to engage in entrepreneurship out of necessity, so they can support their family needs (Breisinger et al., 2020). The government should consider how best to support women's entrepreneurship to offset losses in poor household earnings owing to the pandemic.

Overall, the gender gap in entrepreneurship persists. There are a growing number of initiatives and resources designed to close the gender gap in entrepreneurship ranging from entrepreneurial skill training to the provision of credit and investment funding. However, more needs to be done to ensure women have economic opportunities through entrepreneurship.

Acknowledgments

The authors acknowledge the support of Agence Française de Développement (AFD). We also acknowledge the general support of the World Bank, the International Labour Organization, AFD, UN Women, and the Arab Fund for Economic and Social Development for the Egypt Labor Market Panel Survey 2018, on which this chapter is based. The authors would like to thank Caroline Krafft and Ragui Assaad for their valuable comments and suggestions.

References

Assaad, R. and Krafft, C. (2015) 'The Evolution of Labor Supply and Unemployment in the Egyptian Economy: 1988-2012', *The Egyptian Labor Market in an Era of Revolution*, pp. 1–26.

Assaad, R., Krafft, C. and Selwaness, I. (2017) *The Impact of Marriage on Women's Employment in the Middle East and North Africa*, Economic Research Forum Working Paper Series. 1086. Cairo, Egypt.

Banque Misr (2014). *Mashrouaay intiative for funding SMEs, Central Bank supervision, Central Bank of Egypt*. Cairo: Egypt.

Berger, E. S. C. and Kuckertz, A. (2016) 'Female entrepreneurship in startup ecosystems worldwide', *Journal of Business Research*, 69(11), pp. 5163–5168. doi: 10.1016/j.jbusres.2016.04.098.

Bertaux, N. and Crable, E. (2007) 'Learning About Women. Economic Development, Entrepreneurship and the Environment in India: a Case Study', *Journal of Developmental Entrepreneurship*, 12(04), pp. 467–478. doi: 10.1142/s1084946707000757.

Breisinger, C. et al. (2020) 'Impact of COVID-19 on the Egyptian economy: Economic sectors, jobs, and households', *International Food Policy Research Institute*, (June). doi: 10.2499/p15738coll2.133764.

Brush, C. G. (1992) 'Research on Women Business Owners: Past Trends, a New Perspective and Future Directions', *Entrepreneurship Theory and Practice*, 16(4), pp. 5–30. doi: 10.1177/104225879201600401.

CAPMAS. (2020) 'Impact of COVID-19 on Egyptian househholds', *Central Agency for Public Mobilization and Statistics*, (May).

Carter, N. and Allen, K. (1997) 'Size determinants of women-owned businesses: Choice or barriers to resources?', *Entrepreneurship and Regional Development*, 9(3), pp. 211–220. doi: 10.1080/08985629700000012.

Cliff, J. E. (1998) 'Does one size fit all? Exploring the relationship between attitudes towards growth, gender, and business size', *Journal of Business Venturing*, 13(6), pp. 523–542. doi: 10.1016/S0883-9026(97)00071-2.

DeMartino, R. and Barbato, R. (2003) 'Differences between women and men MBA entrepreneurs: Exploring family flexibility and wealth creation as career motivators', *Journal of Business Venturing*, 18(6), pp. 815–832. doi: 10.1016/S0883-9026(03)00003-X.

DeTienne, D. R. and Justo, R. (2008) 'Family situation and the exit event: an extension of threshold theory', *Frontiers of Entrepreneurship Research*, 28(14), pp. 1–13. Available at: http://fusionmx.babson.edu/entrep/fer/2008FER/chapter_14/paperfr_xiv_2.html.

Devine, T. (1994) 'Changes in Wage-and-Salary Returns to Skill and the Recent Rise in Female Self-Employment', *The American Economic Review*, 84(2), pp. 108–113.

Du-Rietz, A. and Henrekson, M. (2000) 'Testing the Female Underperformance Hypothesis', *Small Business Economics*, 14(1), pp. 1–10.

GEM (2018) *Global Entrepreneurship Monitor Global Report 2017/18*, *Global Entrepreneurship Monitor*. Global Entrepreneurship Research Association.

Georgellis, Y. and Wall, H. J. (2005) 'Gender differences in self-employment', *International Review of Applied Economics*, 19(3), pp. 321–342. doi: 10.1080/02692170500119854.

Ismail, A., Tolba, A. and Barakat, S. (2016) *GEM Egypt National Report 2016/17*. American University in Cairo.

Jurik, N. (1998) 'Getting away and getting by: The experiences of self-employed homeworkers', *Work and Occupations*, 25(1), pp. 7–35.

Kara, O. (2010) 'Comparing two approaches to the rate of return to investment in education', *Education Economics*, 18(2), pp. 153–165. doi: 10.1080/09645290802416486.

Kevane, M. and Wydick, B. (2001) 'Microenterprise lending to female entrepreneurs: sacrificing economic growth for poverty alleviation?', *World Development*, 29(7), pp. 1225–1236.

Kelley, Brush, G. & Litovsky, (2011). *The Global Entrepreneurship Monitor: 2010 Women's Report*. Wellesley : MA: Babson College & GERA.

Kim, G. S. (2007) 'The analysis of self-employment levels over the life-cycle', *Quarterly Review of Economics and Finance*, 47, pp. 397–410. doi: 10.1016/j.qref.2006.06.004.

Klyver, K., Nielsen, S. L. and Evald, M. R. (2013) 'Women's self-employment: An act of institutional (dis)integration? A multilevel, cross-country study', *Journal of Business Venturing*, 28(4), pp. 474–488. doi: 10.1016/j.jbusvent.2012.07.002.

Krafft, C. (2016) 'Understanding the Dynamics of Household Enterprises in Egypt: Birth, Death, Growth, and Transformation', *Economic Research Forum Working Paper Series*, 983. Cairo, Egypt.

Krafft, C., Assaad, R. and Rahman, K. W. (2019) 'Introducing the Egypt Labor Market Panel Survey 2018', *IZA Journal of Development and Migration* (Forthcoming).

Krafft, C. and Rizk, R. (2021) 'The promise and peril of youth enterpreneurship in MENA', *International Journal of Manpower*, doi: 10.1108/IJM-05-2020-0200.

Luke, N. and Munshi, K. (2011) 'Women as agents of change: Female income and mobility in India', *Journal of Development Economics*, 94(1), pp. 1–17. doi: 10.1016/j.jdeveco.2010.01.002.

El Mahdi, A. and Rashed, A. (2007) 'The Changing Economic Environment and the Development of the Micro and Small Enterprises in Egypt 2006', *Economic Research Forum Working Paper Series*, No. 0706.

Marlow, S. and Patton, D. (2005) 'All credit to men? Entrepreneurship, finance, and gender', *Entrepreneurship theory and practice*, 29(6), pp. 717–735.

McGowan, P. *et al.* (2012) 'Female entrepreneurship and the management of business and domestic roles: Motivations, expectations and realities', *Entrepreneurship and Regional Development*, 24(1–2), pp. 53–72. doi: 10.1080/08985626.2012.637351.

Minniti, M. and Naude, W. (2010) 'What Do We Know about the Patterns and Determinants of Female Entrepreneurship across Countries ?', *European Journal of Development Research*, 22, pp. 227–293. doi: 10.1057/ejdr.2010.17.

Ministry of Investment and International Cooperation (2018). *Fekratek Sherkatak Intiative for youth start-ups*. Cairo: Egypt.

Ministry of Social Solidarity (2018) *Mastoura Intiative for lending women enterpreneurs*. Cairo: Egypt.

Parasuraman, S. and Simmers (2001) 'Type of Employment, Work-Family Conflict and Well-Being: A Comparative Study', *Journal of Organizational Behavior*, 22(5), pp. 551–568. doi: 10.1002/job.

Rajan, R. G. and Petersen, M. A. (1994) 'The Benefits of Lending Relationships: Evidence from Small Business Data', *The Journal of Finance*, 49(1), pp. 3–37. doi: 10.1093/bjc/azp031.

Rashed, A. and Sieverding, M. (2015) 'Micro and small household enterprises in Egypt: Potential for growth and employment generation', *The Egyptian Labor Market in an Era of Revolution*, pp. 182–197.

Sarfaraz, L., Faghih, N. and Majd, A. (2014) 'The relationship between women entrepreneurship and gender equality', *Journal of Global Entrepreneurship Research*, 4(1), pp. 1–11. doi: 10.1186/2251-7316-2-6.

Sawiris Foundation for Social Development (2015). *Women empowerment and labor market competition*. Cairo: Egypt.

Selwaness, I. and Krafft, C. (2020) 'The Dynamics of Family Formation and Women's Work: What Facilitates and Hinders Female Employment in the Middle East and North Africa', *Population Research and Policy Review*. doi: 10.1007/s11113-020-09596-6.

Shelton, L. (2006) 'Female entrepreneurs, work-family conflict, and venture performance: new insights into the work-family interface', *Journal of Small Business Management*, 44(2), pp. 285-297.

Tonoyan, V., Budig, M. and Strohmeyer, R. (2010) 'Exploring the heterogeneity of women's entrepreneurship: The impact of family structure and family policies in Europe and the US', *Women Entrepreneurs and the Global Environment for Growth: A Research Perspective*, (January 2014), pp. 137–160. doi: 10.4337/9781849806633.00013.

Ufuk, H. and Özgen, Ö. (2001) 'Interaction between the business and family lives of women entrepreneurs in Turkey', *Journal of Business Ethics*, 31(2), pp. 95–106. doi: 10.1023/A:1010712023858.

Verheul, I., van Stel, J. and Thurik, R. (2004) 'Explaining female and male entrepreneurship across 29 countries', *The Papers on Entrepreneurship, Growth and Public Policy, Max Planck Institute for Reserach into Economic Systems Group Enterpreneurship*, No. 0804.

Verheul, I. and Thurik, R. (2001) 'Start-up capital: "Does gender matter?"', *Small Business Economics*, 16(4), pp. 329–345.

Winn, J. (2004) 'Entrepreneurship: not an easy path to top management for women', *Women in Management Review*, 19(3), pp. 143–153. doi: 10.1108/09649420410529852.

7

Internal versus International Migration in Egypt

Together or Far Apart

Anda David, Nelly Elmallakh, and Jackline Wahba

7.1 Introduction

For many developing countries, urbanization is an inevitable consequence of economic development—while over-urbanization is a challenge. Egypt is a country with a population of almost 100 million, with a quarter of the population living in the capital city, Cairo. This high population concentration provides opportunities, but also serious negative externalities. Hence, there has been a strong drive to build new cities and towns on the outskirts of Greater Cairo, as well as building a new capital.

In this context, an important issue is the extent to which internal migration has been responsible for urbanization in Egypt, as opposed to natural population growth, which, as indicated in Chapter 1, is only 2 percent per annum. Previous studies document very low internal migration rates in Egypt (e.g. Wahba, 2009; Herrera and Badr, 2012). The first half of the twentieth century witnessed a large flow of the rural population moving into urban areas, but this urbanization has since halted. The current share of the rural population is virtually at the same level as it was 50 years ago (57 percent), according to the United Nations Development Programme (UNDP, 2019) and until recently the average annual growth rates were similar in urban and rural areas (see Chapter 1). At the same time, Egypt remains the largest migrant sending country in the Middle East and North Africa (MENA) region and the one with the largest population. Thus, it is important to understand how the demographic flows shape Egyptian society.

This chapter studies the recent patterns and trends of internal migration in Egypt. It also examines the relationship between internal and international migration, given the importance of international migration since the 1970s. Egypt has been an important labor sending country to neighboring Arab countries. At the peak, almost 10 percent of the labor force was return migrants. The most tangible consequence of international migration in Egypt is remittances, which have been an important source of its foreign currency. Remittances from Egyptians

Anda David, Nelly Elmallakh, and Jackline Wahba, *Internal versus International Migration in Egypt: Together or Far Apart*
In: *The Egyptian Labor Market: A Focus on Gender and Economic Vulnerability*. Edited by: Caroline Krafft and Ragui Assaad,
Oxford University Press. © Economic Research Forum 2022. DOI: 10.1093/oso/9780192847911.003.0008

working abroad reached USD 29 billion in 2018, making Egypt the world's fifth top recipient of remittances that year according to the World Bank (2019) and reflecting the significance of international migration.

This chapter also investigates whether internal and international migration substitute or complement each other. More precisely, it studies the different patterns of internal migration, their evolution over the last decade, and the profile of internal migrants. It also examines the patterns and trends of international migration and return migration, and whether these patterns have changed since the Arab Spring. Furthermore, it studies the extent to which internal migration rates have changed relative to changes in international migration rates, and measures whether both types of migration have increased over the last few decades or moved in opposite directions. We finally investigate whether there is any evidence that individuals engage in both types of migration, internal and international. It is worth highlighting that migration could be a coping strategy for dealing with economic shocks and vulnerability.[1] For some, migration, in particular internal mobility, is a strategy to diversify risk (*ex ante*) before shocks to smooth income (see Stark, 1991), while for others migration can be an (*ex post*) aftershock reaction to survive. However, it is well documented that given the high costs of migration, especially international migration, credit constraints prevent the poorest and the most vulnerable from migrating (Grogger and Hanson, 2011). Hence, studying trends and patterns of migration is important.

While our analysis is based on 2018 data, we have to acknowledge that the 2020 COVID-19 pandemic is likely to change some of the current patterns of migration observed in this chapter. We briefly reflect on this at the end of Section 7.3.2, highlighting that while the impact of migration on Egyptian society seems to have decreased over the period 2012–18, the pandemic might increase the relevance of migration, as returns are significantly increasing and remittances are forecasted to decrease, both being consequences of the global pandemic.

7.2 Data and Methodology

In this chapter, we use data from the Egypt Labor Market Panel Survey (ELMPS). The ELMPS is a nationally representative panel survey carried out by the Economic Research Forum in cooperation with Egypt's Central Agency for Public Mobilization and Statistics. The ELMPS is a wide-ranging panel survey that covers topics such as employment, unemployment, job dynamics, and earnings, and also provides very rich information on residential mobility, international and return migration experiences, education, and socioeconomic characteristics.

---

[1] Chapter 10 examines household vulnerability and resilience to shocks, but does not study migration as a coping strategy.

The ELMPS has been administered to nationally representative samples since 1998. The 2018 ELMPS follows three survey waves that were conducted in 1998, 2006, and 2012.[2] The 2018 round surveyed 61,231 individuals who belonged to 15,746 households. It tracks households and individuals that were previously interviewed in 2012, some of which were also interviewed in 1998 and 2006. Others belong to a refresher sample of households added in 2018.

Using the ELMPS 2018, we examine the evolution of internal migration since the 1980s, relying on retrospective information on individuals' mobility. Individuals were asked if they had changed their location of residence from their place of birth, whether the move was inside Egypt or abroad, the year of the move, the governorate, city, or town (*qism* or *markaz*) and village (*shyakha*) relating to the move. Individuals could report as many moves as occurred, with the maximum number reported in the ELMPS 2018 being equal to 20 geographical moves. Based on this retrospective information, we were able to track individuals' mobility over various decades, starting from the 1980s. Therefore, the analysis considers internal mobility in the 1980s, 1990s, 2000s, and 2010s, though it is important to note that while for most decades we consider ten years (e.g. for the 1980s, we consider 1980–89), for the 2010s we only observe nine years (2010–18), and the last year is partial, as the survey was fielded starting in April 2018.

For internal migration, first, we studied internal migration patterns for mobility between regions,[3] governorates, cities/towns, and villages by decade of migration. For each decade we only considered individuals who were aged between 15 and 64 years old in that decade. We examine the evolution of internal migration rates during these periods and define an internal migrant as an individual who changed his or her location of residence in the years under consideration compared with his or her previous location of residence.[4] For instance, in the 1980s, when considering mobility between villages, we define an internal migrant as an individual who changed his village of residence in the years between 1980 and 1989, compared with his previous village of residence. Similarly, when considering mobility between cities/towns, or between governorates or between regions, we define an internal migrant as an individual who changed his or her city/town, governorate, or region of residence compared with his or her previous city/town, governorate, or region of residence. For internal migration, we also examined internal mobility between urban and rural areas.

---

[2] See Krafft, Assaad, and Rahman (2021) for further details on ELMPS 2018. Data is publicly available through the Open Access Microdata Initiative, www.erfdataportal.com.
[3] Greater Cairo, Alexandria and the Suez Canal cities, Urban Lower Egypt, Urban Upper Egypt, Rural Lower Egypt, and Rural Upper Egypt.
[4] For the 1980s we consider the years between 1980 and 1989 inclusive. For the 1990s we consider the years between 1990 and 1999 inclusive. For the 2000s we consider the years between 2000 and 2009 inclusive. For the 2010s we consider the years between 2010 and 2018 inclusive.

Finally, we examined internal migration based on place of birth. We compare an individual's residence at birth with current residence at the time of the survey using the four waves of ELMPS. Here we rely on an alternative definition of internal migration. According to this definition, an internal migrant is an individual who changed his or her governorate of residence compared with the governorate of birth or an individual who was living in an urban area at birth and moved to a rural area (and vice versa).

For the analysis of recent trends in international and return migration, we relied on two survey waves of the ELMPS: 2012 and 2018. The return migration module surveyed individuals aged between 15 and 59 years old. It asked surveyed individuals whether they had worked abroad for six months or more and features return migrants' characteristics before, during, and after migration, frequency of migration, reasons for migration, reasons for return, year and country of first migration episode, year of final return, whether the individual travelled alone or with other family members, and whether the individual planned on traveling temporarily or permanently, as well as other relevant information about remittances and savings abroad, among other information.

Household members were also asked if they had household members living or working overseas. Information on the characteristics of these current migrants and their migration experience was collected including age, sex, education, reason for migration, year of migration, country of destination, labor market status, employment status, and sector of employment before migration. In this chapter, we examine the recent trends in international and return migration, focusing on individuals aged between 15 and 59 years old. First, we examine the share of international migrants and return migrants by year of migration. We also examine the distribution of international and return migrants across destination countries. Moreover, we examine international migration and return migration rates by levels of education and by sex. We also analyze the employment characteristics of international migrants before migration in terms of work and employment statuses. For return migrants we investigate the reasons for migration and the reasons for return. Relying on individual and household level data, we compute international and return migration rates by sex, as well as the incidence of any overseas migration (international and return) at the individual and household levels. Moreover, we also examine migration intentions by sex and education, as well as the incidence of remittance recipiency in male- and female-headed households.

We attempt to capture complementarity versus substitution between internal, international, and return migration by examining these migration rates in 2012 and 2018, the two most recent ELMPS rounds. In order to capture complementarity versus substitution, we investigated the relationship between international and internal migration by analyzing the internal migration rates among returnees and non-returnees, as well as the return migration rates among internal migrants and non-internal migrants.

7.3 Migration in Egypt

7.3.1 Trends and characteristics of internal migration

Egypt is known to have one of the lowest internal migration rates in the world, with Herrera and Badr (2012) having estimated it at around 8 percent, compared with a world average of around 15 percent. Using the ELMPS 2018, we find a similar figure: 9 percent of individuals had moved from their place of birth (the percentage reaches 12 percent if we restrict the sample to those aged 15 or older). However, this internal migration rate captures all moves from an individual's birthplace, including those that were short distance moves within the same city.

In order to have a dynamic view of internal migration we computed, for different administrative divisions, internal migration rates by decade. In Figure 7.1, we plot the evolution of internal migration rates between regions, and we see that mobility was low. The highest regional migration rates were in the 1980s and the lowest in 2010s. Overall, regional migration rates were around 2–3 percent over those four decades. Similar trends were observed for migration rates between governorates in Figure 7.2.[5] Higher rates of inter-governorate migration occurred in the 1980s, while the 2010s had the lowest rates. Although inter-village migration (Figure A7.1) and inter-town/city migration rates (Figure A7.2) were slightly higher, the patterns and trends were very similar to the regional migration rates.

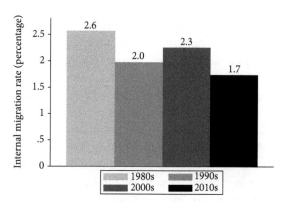

Figure 7.1 Internal migration rates (percentage) by decade of migration, mobility between regions, 1980–2018.

Note: Mobility between regions corresponds to any type of move that involves a change in the region of residence in the years under consideration compared with the previous region, unless reversed at the end of the decade.

Source: Authors' calculations based on ELMPS 2018.

---

[5] The intergovernorate internal migration rates are sometimes larger than the inter-region internal migration rates as regions in Egypt are not groups of governorates, but their definition combines both groups of governorates and urban/rural location.

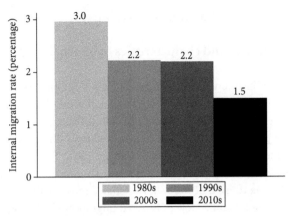

Figure 7.2 Internal migration rates (percentage) by decade of migration, mobility between governorates, 1980–2018.

Note: Mobility between governorates corresponds to any type of move that involves a change in the governorate of residence in the years under consideration compared with the previous governorate, unless reversed at the end of the decade.

Source: Authors' calculations based on ELMPS 2018.

Interestingly, if we only analyze migration across urban to rural settings, we see a clear decrease in rural to urban migration rates between the 1980s and 1990s, but an almost stable trend in the 1990s and 2000s, before a sharp drop in the 2010s (Figure 7.3).

In order to capture internal migration irrespective of the decade, we compared the place of birth with the current place of residence at different waves of the panel. We also looked at urban to rural migration in addition to rural to urban migration. Table 7.1 shows similar rural to urban migration patterns to those in Figure 7.3, a downward trend in rural to urban when comparing 2012 and 2018. There was a steep decrease in mobility from 5.4 percent for rural to urban migration in 2012 (4.7 percent for urban to rural migration) to 3.9 percent in 2018 (3.1 percent for urban to rural migration). Similarly, if we use the panel structure of ELMPS we can compute mobility across urban and rural settings by analyzing changes in locations in different waves of the survey (Table 7.1).

Focusing on the four waves since 1998, we see a decrease in mobility across each of the periods covered by the survey. Rural to urban migration was dominant, although the difference with urban to rural migration was very small. If we focus on changes in location between survey waves, we observe a gradual decline in rural to urban migration from 2.6 percent in the period 1998–2006 to 1.2 percent in 2012–18. Urban to rural migration likewise declined from 2.4 percent to 0.9 percent. It is important to note that comparing 2012 with 2018 is useful in highlighting the impact of the Egyptian revolution in 2011. This has led to a period of political and economic instability and resulted almost in stagnation, or even a fall in internal mobility rates.

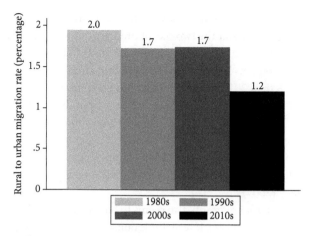

Figure 7.3 Rural to urban migration rates (percentage) by decade of migration, 1980–2018.

Note: For each decade, we computed the rural to urban migration rate as the share of individuals who moved to an urban area while previously residing in a rural area, unless reversed at the end of the decade.

Source: Authors' calculations based on ELMPS 2018.

Table 7.1 Rural to urban and urban to rural migration rates, 1998–2018 (percentage).

	Rural to Urban	Urban to Rural
1998–2006	2.6	2.4
2006–12	1.7	1.3
2012–18	1.2	0.9
Birthplace–2012	5.4	4.7
Birthplace–2018	3.9	3.1

Note: First three rows are based on ELMPS panel. The analysis is restricted to individuals aged at least 15 in 1998 and less than 65 in 2006 (first row), to individuals aged at least 15 in 2006 and less than 65 in 2012 (second row), and to individuals aged at least 15 in 2012 and less than 65 in 2018 (third row). Rows four and five compare birthplace with location of residence in 2012 or in 2018, and the analysis is restricted to 15–64 years of age at the time of the survey; 2012 in row four and 2018 in row five.

Source: Authors' calculations based on ELMPS panel data and the ELMPS 2012 and 2018.

While in our analysis we focus on urban/rural or regional level mobility, the importance of peri-urban areas in Egypt needs to be noted. These informal areas are characterized by low service provision and safety threats, and various studies have shown they increase households' vulnerability (Khalil et al, 2018, Sieverding et al. 2019).

Although internal migration rates were low, it is still important to map the mobility among regions over the two recent time periods to better understand the underpinnings of internal migration. Figures 7.4 and 7.5 show similar patterns of mobility between regions in 2012 and 2018 (among movers only), albeit the rates are lower in 2018 than 2012. Although there is a great inward mobility in Greater Cairo from all geographical regions, we notice a large drop between 2012 and 2018. Indeed, the share of individuals moving from other regions into Greater Cairo was larger in 2012 than in 2018, across all geographical regions. There is still evidence of migration from the South (Upper Egypt) to the North (other regions) a pattern that has characterized internal migration in Egypt, as highlighted by Zohry (2009).

The profile of internal migrants also seems to have changed little over the years, as shown in Table 7.2. Recent internal migrants, those who changed the governorate of residence or urban/rural residence with respect to place of birth, were on average similar in terms of educational levels. Internal movers were less likely to be living in Greater Cairo and more likely to be living in other urban areas in 2018 than in 2012. In terms of their current economic activities, internal migrants

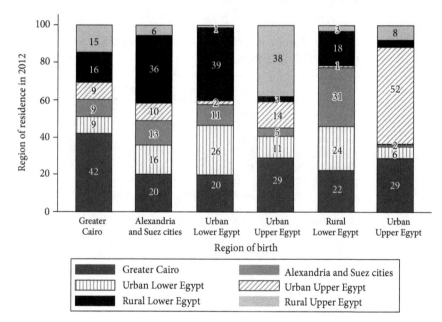

Figure 7.4 Internal mobility between the region of birth and current region of residence, internal migrants in 2012, ages 15–64.

Note: The analysis is restricted to 15–64 years old in 2012. An internal migrant is defined as an individual who changed his or her governorate of residence compared with his or her birth governorate or an individual who was living in an urban area at birth and moved to a rural area (and vice versa).

Source: Authors' calculations based on ELMPS 2012.

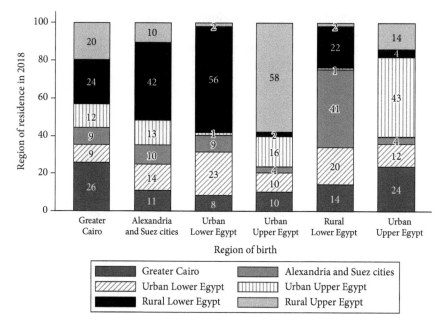

Figure 7.5 Internal mobility between the region of birth and current region of residence, internal migrants in 2018, ages 15–64.

Note: The analysis is restricted to 15–64 years old in 2018. Internal migrants are defined as individuals who changed their governorate of residence compared with their governorate of birth or individuals who were living in an urban area at birth and moved to a rural area (and vice versa).

Source: Authors' calculations based on ELMPS 2018.

in 2018 were also found to be significantly more likely to work in agriculture, education and health and less likely in trade and public administration. This last result is consistent with the findings highlighted in Chapter 2, according to which employment in public sector continued to decrease over the period 2012–18.

We explore in Figure 7.6 the reasons for internal migration in the years 2012 and 2018, by sex. Focusing on individuals aged 15–59 in each survey round, we find important differences in the reasons of migration by gender. In both years, 2012 and 2018, we find that the most important reason for internal mobility among women was to accompany their spouses, while work- and education-related mobility accounted for less than 2 percent. On the other hand, work related mobility accounted for 26 percent and 36 percent for men, in the years 2012 and 2018 respectively. These differences highlight the gendered internal mobility patterns in Egypt.

The low levels of internal migration, presented in Table 7.2, might be partly linked to high rates of commuting. For instance, Assaad and Arntz (2005) showed that there was an increase in men's commuting rates between 1988 and 1998 in order to access non-governmental sector jobs. However, Figure 7.7 shows that

Table 7.2 Characteristics of the 2012 and 2018 internal migrants.

	Internal migrants in 2012	Internal migrants in 2018	
	(1) Mean	(2) Mean	(3) Difference 2012–18
Individual characteristics			
Age	39.9	41.2	−1.4***
Married	82.4	82.8	−0.4
Education			
No education	27.7	26.5	1.2
Primary or preparatory education	17.0	15.7	1.3
Secondary education	31.7	34.7	−3.0**
Above secondary education	23.6	23.1	0.5
Household characteristics			
Household size	4.3	4.2	0.1**
Number of adults	2.9	2.7	0.1***
Number of children	1.4	1.4	0.0
Rural	30.5	30.5	0.0
Current geographical region			
Greater Cairo	40.8	31.8	9.0***
Alexandria and Canal cities	13.0	15.9	−2.9***
Urban Lower Egypt	10.3	12.5	−2.2**
Urban Upper Egypt	7.4	9.7	−2.3***
Rural Lower Egypt	18.0	19.7	−1.7
Rural Upper Egypt	10.6	10.4	0.2
Current job characteristics			
Public sector	37.2	33.2	4.0*
Private sector	62.8	66.8	−4.0*
Job tenure in years	14.2	14.5	−0.3
Current economic activities			
Agriculture	14.9	21.8	−6.9***
Manufacturing	11.6	12.4	−0.8
Trade	16.1	13.1	3.0**
Public administration	10.0	7.3	2.7**
Education and health	16.3	19.3	−3.0*
Other activities	31.1	26.1	5.0**
Observations	2,796	1,974	

Note: *** $p<0.01$, ** $p<0.05$, * $p<0.1$ denote a t-test of whether the difference in means between 2012 and 2018 is statistically significant.

Source: Authors' calculations based on ELMPS 2012 and 2018.

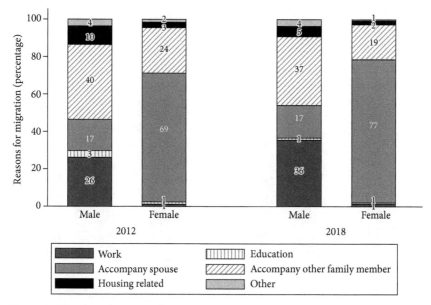

Figure 7.6 Reasons for internal migration (percentage), by sex, ages 15–59, 2012 and 2018.

Note: The figure features the reasons for internal migration, by sex. The analysis is restricted to internal migrants aged 15–59. Internal migrants are those who changed their governorate of residence or urban/rural residence with respect to their place of birth. Other reasons for migration include fleeing violence/persecution, security, health conditions, prison, army, buying land, fear of revenge, and accident/death/family.

Source: Authors' calculations based on ELMPS 2012 and 2018.

there was little to no difference in commuting rates between 2012 and 2018. There was a clear pattern seen in both years: commuting rates were highest for less educated individuals, who were less likely to be able to afford housing in large cities and tended to commute longer distances relative to highly educated individuals.[6]

Our findings highlight that internal migration was low in Egypt. Furthermore, looking at the share of the urban population in Egypt and comparing 1970 with 2018, there was hardly a change in 50 years. The share of the population in urban areas was 43 percent in 2018 compared with 41 percent in 1970, making Egypt the least urbanized North African country. Although Morocco's population was 34 percent urban in 1970 and Tunisia's 43 percent (almost similar to Egypt), Morocco was 62 percent urban in 2018 and Tunisia was 69 percent (UNDP, 2018). Even though Egypt's population tripled during those 50 years from 34.5 million in 1970 to 100 million in 2019, the population did not urbanize, unlike other

---

[6] This result is similar to the findings of Ehab (2018), who found that highly educated males had shorter commuting times.

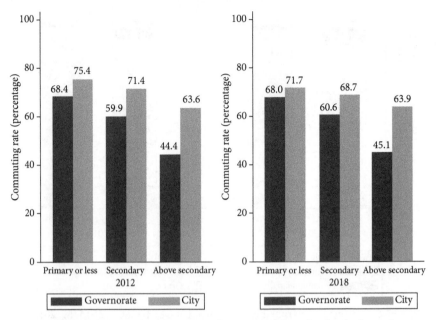

Figure 7.7 Rate of commuting (percentage) among employed individuals aged 15–64, by education, 2012 and 2018.

Note: The figure reports the percentage of workers who commuted at governorate level and the percentage of workers who commuted at city or town level (*qism*). Commuters at governorate (city) level are individuals who worked in a governorate (city) for their primary job that was different from their governorate (city) of residence.

Source: Authors' calculations based on ELMPS 2012 and 2018.

MENA countries.[7] One potential culprit for Egypt's low mobility rates has been the housing market and the severe shortage of affordable housing.[8] We will examine here the extent to which international migration might have reduced internal migration.

7.3.2 Trends and characteristics of international migration

While internal migration is relatively small in the broad picture of mobility in Egypt, international migration, and more particularly return, play an important role. Both the intention to migrate and the reality of international migration are important dimensions to consider.[9] Figure 7.8 examines individuals' intentions to

---

[7] United Nations, Department of Economic and Social Affairs, Population Division (2019).

[8] See Abd El-Hameed, Mansour, and Faggal (2017) on housing problems in Egypt, as well as Assaad and Ramadan (2008) and Assaad, Krafft, and Rolando (2021) on how housing impacts the marriage market in Egypt.

[9] See Pettit and Ruijtenberg (2019) for an analysis of migratory experiences and the impact of migration regimes.

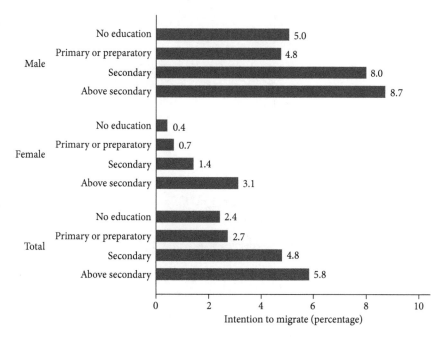

Figure 7.8 Intention to migrate (percentage) by sex and education, ages 15–40, 2018.

Note: This figure presents the percentage of individuals who reported that they intend to travel to any country to work/live/study within the next five years.

Source: Authors' calculations based on ELMPS 2018.

travel to another country for work, to live, or to study in the next five years. Overall, we find only 4 percent of 15–40-year-olds intended to migrate. Migration intentions were much higher among men (5 percent), compared with only 1 percent among women, reflecting how migration is predominantly a male-dominated activity in Egypt. Intentions were even higher among younger men: 7 percent of men aged 15–29 intended to migrate. In Figure 7.8, we show that the intentions to migrate increase with education, for both men and women. These intention rates are lower than other estimates for Egypt and for countries with similar levels of income, where according to the Gallup World Poll survey those rates are over 20 percent; see Migali and Scipioni (2018). Moreover, the 2014 Survey of Young People in Egypt showed that 17 percent of 15–29-year-olds in Egypt aspired to migrate within the next five years (Papoutsaki and Wahba, 2015), though it is not surprising that migration aspirations are higher than migration intentions.

In 2018, current international migrants represented 2 percent of all Egyptian nationals aged 15–59, while returnees represented 7 percent. Almost 9 percent of all individuals aged 15–59 had had an international migration experience and 11 percent of all Egyptian households in 2018 had had a migrant member (Figures 7.9 and 7.10). However, it is worth noting that these rates were slightly

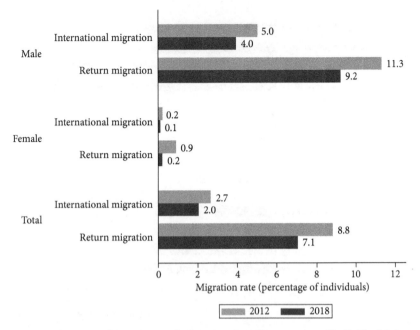

Figure 7.9 Return and international migration rates (percentage of individuals), by sex, ages 15–59, 2012 and 2018.

Note: This figure presents return and international migration rates in the years 2012 and 2018, by sex. For international migration, the figure reports the proportion of international migrants among all Egyptian nationals aged 15–59, by sex. For return migration, the figure reports the proportion of returnees among all individuals aged 15–59, by sex.

Source: Authors' calculations based on ELMPS 2012 and 2018.

lower than in 2012. These rates also clearly show the gendered nature of international migration in Egypt where international migration is an activity dominated by men. This is in contrast to the global trend that has shown growing feminization of international migration (Le Goff, 2016).

Figure 7.11 depicts the share of current and return international migrants by year of migration. Not surprisingly this share is highest for the most recent years, as migration is predominately temporary in nature. Indeed, Figure A7.3 shows the share of returnees by year of return, underscoring the temporary nature of international migration in Egypt.

As Table 7.2 shows, overseas migration is male dominated, with almost 98 percent of current migrants being men in 2018. Hence, focusing on men and looking at their education level, Figure 7.12 shows international migration rates by education levels for 2012 and 2018. We can observe that the decrease in migration rates was mostly among individuals with no education and secondary education or less. This was likely because of the recent political situation in Libya, which was a large destination for less educated individuals (IOM, 2011). The recent decrease

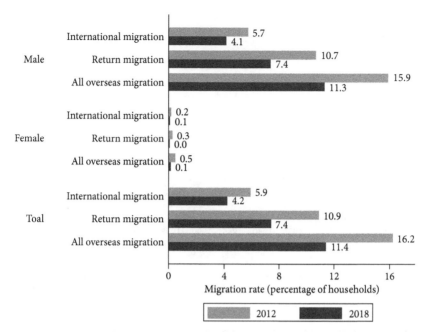

Figure 7.10 Return and international migration rates (percentage of households with an international migrant), 2012 and 2018.

Note: For international migration, the figure reports the percentage of households with a current male or female international migrant. For return migration, the figure reports the percentage of households with a male or female return migrant. For all overseas migrants, the figure reports the proportion of return and international migrant households among all households.

Source: Authors' calculations based on ELMPS 2012 and 2018.

in demand for foreign workers by the Gulf countries and their increasingly selective immigration policies resulted in lowering overall emigration rates and a stable emigration rate of the highly educated, see Fargues and Shah (2018). Altogether, the evidence suggests the important role played by overseas opportunities in directing migration across the Egyptian border.

Table 7.3, comparing current international migrants in 2012 and 2018, confirms that recent international migrants tended to be older and more educated, and thus had a higher probability of being married. They were also significantly more likely to travel alone as opposed to traveling with other family members compared with current migrants in 2012. Potentially reflecting the economic instability that followed the Egyptian uprising as highlighted in Chapter 2, recent migrants were also more often unemployed before they migrated and had more volatile jobs. Among those who were employed before migration, current migrants in 2018 were also significantly more likely to have regular wage work before migration and were less likely to be self-employed than current migrants in 2012.

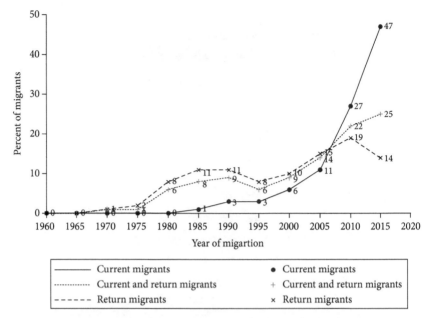

Figure 7.11 Percent of current and return migrants by year of migration, 1960–2018.
Note: The data are categorized into five-year intervals. The 2015 datapoint is not a full five-year interval as it corresponds to the period 2015–18.
Source: Authors' calculations based on ELMPS 2018.

In terms of destinations, it seems that the war in Libya resulted in a switch in migration flows (Figure 7.13), with Kuwait having almost doubled its share of Egyptian migrants: it hosted 15 percent of Egyptian migrants in 2012, while it hosted 29 percent in 2018. Saudi Arabia remains the top destination for Egyptian migrants, a fact highlighted by Wahba (2015). Another noteworthy change is the decrease of migration to EU countries, from around 4 percent in 2012 to 2 percent in 2018.

Concerning returns, the increase in returnees from Saudi Arabia (32 percent in 2018 compared with 24 percent in 2012) might be a sign of the economic downturn in the Gulf countries. The typical profile of the returnee also seems to have changed slightly (Table 7.4): returnees in 2018 were older, as expected, but also less educated and more rural, which was not expected. Their reasons for having migrated also differed from the earlier returnees and reflect economic instability. A higher share declared that they migrated because they were unemployed and looking for higher wages, while a lower percentage declared that they migrated because they had found a better job. Interestingly, most returnees declared that they had returned because of poor working conditions, and this percentage slightly increased in 2018. Reaching the end of a contract or to get married were the other two main reasons for return in both waves. Interestingly, we also find that return migrants in 2018 were more likely to have traveled alone and to have

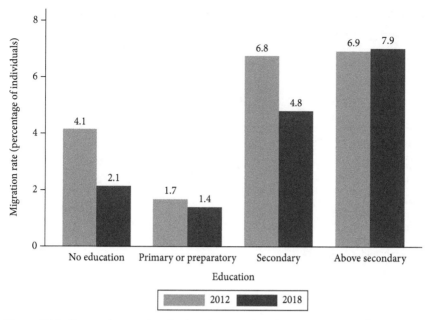

Figure 7.12 Current international migration rates by education, men aged 15–59, 2012 and 2018.

Note: Current international migrants are individuals who are currently working or living abroad. Educational levels include: no education (either illiterate or literate without any diploma), primary or preparatory education, secondary education (general or vocational), and above secondary education (university degree or above).

Source: Authors' calculations based on ELMPS 2012 and 2018.

planned to travel temporarily than return migrants in 2012. Current return migrants were also more likely to be out of the labor force after return than return migrants in 2012, which could be a result of the worsening labor market situation highlighted in Chapter 2.

To sum up, there has been a slight decline in the share of current migrants and returnees in the total population between 2012 and 2018, whether measured at individual or household level. Figure 7.14 shows that there was also a decline in the share of households receiving remittances between 2012 and 2018, from 5.2 to 3.2 percent. It is also important to note that female-headed households have a greater likelihood of receiving remittances than male-headed households. This is because emigration in Egypt is mostly male dominated. Migrating men send remittances back to their households, which are headed by their spouses during their spell abroad. Both immigration and remittances may be playing a smaller role in Egypt's society and economy. However, in the context of the COVID-19 pandemic, this role can still remain important, as various reports suggest a potential surge in return migration, which could reach up to 1 million persons.[10] These

---

[10] See for instance OECD (2020) and Cairo Review (2020).

Table 7.3 Descriptive statistics on current migrants in the years 2012 and 2018.

	Current migrants in 2012	Current migrants in 2018	
	(1) Mean	(2) Mean	(3) Difference 2012–18
Individual characteristics			
Male	96.0	97.5	−1.5
Age	34.6	36.7	−2.1***
Married	76.3	79.8	−3.5*
Education			
No educational degree	16.9	11.5	5.4***
Primary or preparatory education	7.7	7.7	0.0
Secondary education	47.3	45.5	1.8
Above secondary education	28.1	35.4	−7.3***
Relationship to the household head			
Spouse	56.5	66.1	−9.6***
Son or daughter	34.4	30.5	3.9*
Other	9.1	3.4	5.7***
Migration experience			
Traveled alone	88.6	95.7	−7.1***
Traveled with other household members	11.4	4.3	7.1***
Work status before migration			
Working	68.2	65.5	2.7
Unemployed	27.3	29.9	−2.6
Not working and not seeking work	4.5	4.6	−0.1
Employment status before migration			
Regular wage worker	30.1	36.5	−6.4**
Irregular wage worker	48.6	51.4	−2.8
Employer	3.4	1.9	1.6
Self–employed	7.3	2.9	4.4***
Unpaid worker	10.6	7.4	3.2*
Sector of employment and formality status before migration			
Public sector employment	9.2	7.3	1.9
Private sector employment	90.8	92.7	−1.9
Incidence of work contract	29.4	23.9	5.5*
Incidence of social security	18.0	12.0	6.0**
Number of observations	818	810	

Note: *** p<0.01, ** p<0.05, * p<0.1 denote a t-test of whether the difference in means between 2012 and 2018 is statistically significant.

Source: Authors' calculations based on ELMPS 2012 and 2018.

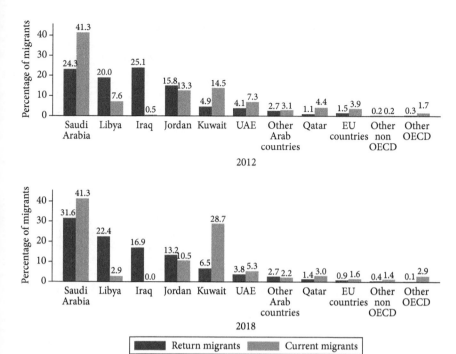

Figure 7.13 Destination countries of return and current migrants, 2012 and 2018 (percentage).

Note: Other Arab states include Algeria, Bahrain, Lebanon, Oman, Sudan, Syria, and Yemen. European Union countries include Cyprus, France, Germany, Greece, Italy, the Netherlands, and the United Kingdom. Other Organisation for Economic Co-operation and Development (OECD) countries include Australia, Bermuda, Canada, Mexico, and the United States. Other non-OECD countries include Argentina, Brazil, Belarus, Colombia, Congo, Hong Kong, Guinea, Russia, Vanuatu, South Africa, Suriname, and Zambia.

Source: Authors' calculations based on ELMPS 2012 and 2018.

returnees would add to the existing challenges in the labor market highlighted in Chapters 1 and 2. Another important effect of the pandemic is the forecasted fall in remittances, up to −9 percent according to Ratha et al. (2020), which could increase households' vulnerability, and also increase gender inequality, as female-headed households are the main recipients of remittances (Figure 7.14).

7.3.3 Internal migration versus international migration

Given low internal migration in Egypt and the resilient trend of international migration, an interesting question is whether the two are linked, and if so, how? In essence, our earlier findings that internal migration rates have been very low and the urban share of the population has hardly increased in 50 years suggest

Table 7.4 Descriptive statistics on return migrants, 2012 and 2018.

	Return migrants in 2012	Return migrants in 2018	
	(1) Mean	(2) Mean	(3) Difference 2012–18
Individual characteristics			
Male	97.5	99.0	−1.5***
Age	43.6	47.8	−4.2***
Married	90.7	91.4	−0.7
No educational degree	27.0	30.9	−3.9**
Primary or preparatory education	15.6	11.9	3.7***
Secondary education	40.6	40.1	0.5
Above secondary education	16.8	17.1	−0.3
Rural	65.6	72.7	−7.1***
Migration spells and experience			
Traveled once abroad for work	79.8	75.8	4.0***
Traveled twice abroad for work	14.3	15.6	−1.3
Traveled more than twice abroad for work	5.9	8.6	−2.6***
Traveled alone	94.2	96.6	−2.4***
Traveled with other household members	5.8	3.4	2.3***
Planned to travel temporarily	85.8	88.2	−2.4*
Planned to travel permanently	14.2	11.8	2.4*
Reasons for migration			
Unemployed and seeking work	19.0	23.8	−4.8***
Found a better job	65.6	49.2	16.4***
Higher wages	5.0	12.6	−7.6***
To help the family financially	3.4	6.7	−3.3***
Other reasons	7.0	7.7	−0.7
Reasons for return			
Poor working conditions	24.4	27.9	−3.5**
Contract ended	21.1	20.2	0.9
To get married	13.8	16.0	−2.2*
Sudden termination by employer	6.6	6.4	0.2
Other reasons	34.1	29.5	4.6***
Current work status			
Employed	91.5	91.1	0.4
Unemployed	3.7	1.8	1.9***
Out of labor force	4.8	7.1	−2.3***
Number of observations	1,381	1,647	

Note: *** p<0.01, ** p<0.05, * p<0.1 denote a t-test of whether the difference in means between 2012 and 2018 is statistically significant.

Source: Authors' calculations based on ELMPS 2012 and 2018.

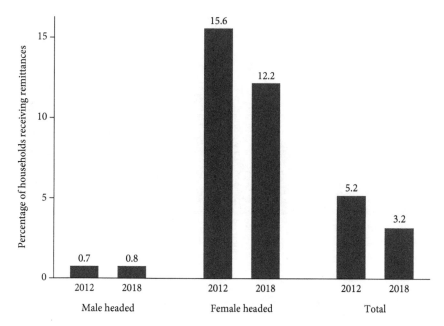

Figure 7.14 Percentage of households receiving remittances, by sex of household head, 2012 and 2018.

Source: Authors' calculations based on ELMPS 2012 and 2018.

that overseas migration might have been a safety valve. Examining migration rates by education levels shows that international migration has not been the sole privilege of the highly educated. While internal migration rates were systematically higher than international migration rates in 2012, internal migration rates decreased substantially in 2018 (Figure 7.15). International migration also fell.

To explore further the relationship between the two types of migration, we examine the extent to which households and individuals engage in both activities. First, we look at the rates of (current and return) international migration and internal migration at household level. The evidence suggests a very small proportion of households engaged in both internal and international migration. More importantly, at the individual level in Figure 7.16, looking at individuals who were returnees and internal migrants we find a very small proportion (less than 1 percent) who engaged in both types of migration. This is also seen when focusing only on men, who tend to have higher international migration rates, in Figure 7.17.

In 2018, among returnees, 6 percent of men were also internal migrants (Figure 7.18). Among internal migrants, 13 percent of men were also return migrants in 2018 (Figure 7.19). Thus, the evidence indicates that the majority of individuals tend not to engage in both types of migration. There is little evidence that internal migration is a steppingstone for international migration.

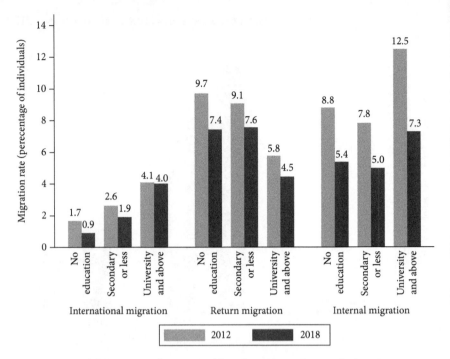

Figure 7.15 Migration rates (percentage) by education and type of migration, men aged 15–59, 2012 and 2018.

Note: Internal migrants are individuals who changed their governorate of residence compared with their governorate of birth or an individual who was living in an urban area at birth and moved to a rural area (and vice versa).

Source: Authors' calculations based on ELMPS 2012 and 2018.

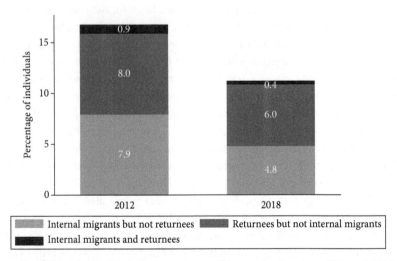

Figure 7.16 The relationship between return and internal migration, 2012 and 2018 (percentage of individuals aged 15–59).

Note: Internal migrants are individuals who changed their place of residence compared with their place of birth.

Source: Authors' calculations based on ELMPS 2012 and 2018.

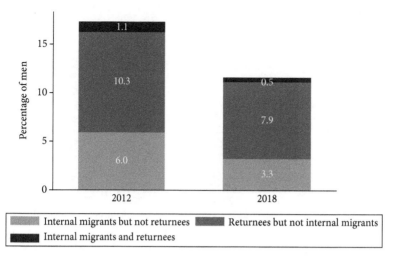

Figure 7.17 The relationship between return and internal migration, men aged 15–59, (percentage), 2012 and 2018.

Note: Internal migrants are individuals who changed their place of residence from their place of birth.
Source: Authors' calculations based on ELMPS 2012 and 2018.

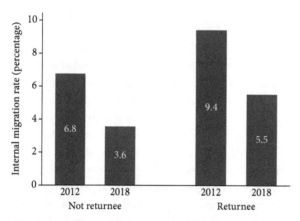

Figure 7.18 Internal migration rates by return migration status (percentage), men aged 15–59, 2012 and 2018.

Note: Internal migrants are individuals who changed their place of residence from their place of birth.
Source: Authors' calculations based on ELMPS 2012 and 2018.

7.4 Conclusion

This chapter has examined the relationship between internal, international, and return migration in Egypt. We have explored the evolution of internal migration and the different patterns of internal migration, focused on mobility between governorates, cities/towns, and villages, as well as internal mobility at the regional level

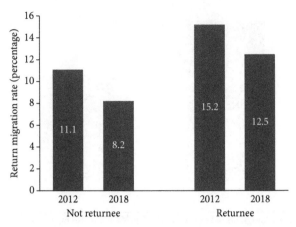

Figure 7.19 Return migration rates by internal migration status (percentage), men aged 15–59, 2012 and 2018.
Note: Internal migrants are individuals who changed their place of residence from their place of birth.
Source: Authors' calculations based on ELMPS 2012 and 2018.

and mobility between urban and rural areas. The findings suggest that internal migration was still low in Egypt, which was consistent with the stagnant share of the urban population that has been around 41–43 percent for the last 50 years, making Egypt the least urbanized North African country (UNDP 2019). This finding is quite remarkable given the size of the population, which has tripled over that period.

Examining the patterns and trends of international and return migration, as well as the characteristics of international and return migrants, the results showed a slight decrease in international migration and return migration rates after a period of increasing international and return migration rates in 2011, see Wahba (2015). However, these muted international migration and return migration trends are also observed in other Arab countries, such as Jordan between 2010 and 2016, see Malaeb and Wahba (2019). Finally, investigating whether individuals engage in both types of migration, we find that people typically engage in one type of migration and very few engage in both types of migration. These findings suggest the need to better understand the barriers to internal migration and their drivers. Moreover, further understanding is needed of the consequences of the low urbanization experienced by Egypt and how this impacts economic development. This might be even more crucial in the upcoming months, as the COVID-19 pandemic will increase the relevance of migration through a surge in return migration and a substantial decrease in remittances.

Acknowledgements

We acknowledge the support of Agence Française de Développement (AFD). We also acknowledge the general support of the World Bank, the International Labour

Organization, AFD, UN Women, and the Arab Fund for Economic and Social Development for the Egypt Labor Market Panel Survey 2018, on which this chapter is based. The authors appreciate the editorial assistance of Barbara Salinas.

Appendix 7.1

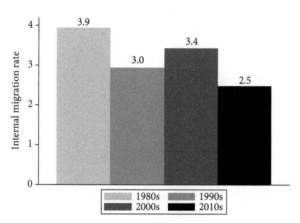

Figure A7.1 Internal migration rates (percentage) by decade of migration, mobility between villages, 1980–2018.

Note: Mobility between villages corresponds to any type of move that involves a change in the village of residence in the years under consideration compared with the previous village of residence.

Source: Authors' calculations based on ELMPS 2018.

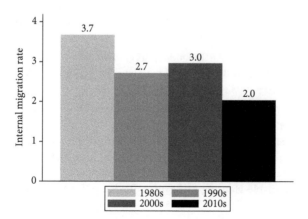

Figure A7.2 Internal migration rates (percentage) by decade of migration, mobility between cities or towns, 1980–2018.

Note: Mobility between cities or towns corresponds to any type of move that involves a change in the city or town of residence in the years under consideration compared to the previous city or town.

Source: Authors' calculations based on ELMPS 2018.

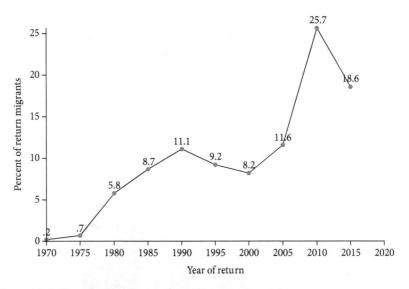

Figure A7.3 Year of return (percentage of return migrants).

Note: This figure presents the share of return migrants as a percentage of total returnees by year of final (most recent) return. The data are calculated over five-year intervals. The 2015 datapoint is not a full five-year interval as it corresponds to the period between 2015 and 2018.

Source: Authors' calculations based on ELMPS 2018.

References

Assaad, R. and M. Arntz (2005) "Constrained Geographical Mobility and Gendered Labor Market Outcomes under Structural Adjustment: Evidence from Egypt," *World Development*, 33 (3): 431–54.

Assaad, R. and M. Ramadan (2008) "Did Housing Policy Reforms Curb the Delay in Marriage Among Young Men in Egypt?" Middle East Youth Initiative Policy Outlook, No. 1. Washington, DC.

Assaad, R., C. Krafft, and D.J. Rolando (2021) "Evaluating the impact of housing market liberalization on the timing of marriage: Evidence from Egypt." *Population Studies*. doi: 10.1080/00324728.2021.1914853.

Abd El-Hameed, Ahmed K., Yasser Mansour, and Ahmed A. Faggal (2017) "Challenges and Issues for Affordable Housing in Egypt: A Review," *Engineering Research Journal*, October. Available at: https://www.researchgate.net/profile/Ahmed-Abd-El-Hameed-4/publication/320183965_Challenges_and_Issues_for_Affordable_Housing_in_Egypt_A_Review/links/59d37aac0f7e9b4fd7ffb0bc/Challenges-and-Issues-for-Affordable-Housing-in-Egypt-A-Review.pdf (Accessed on November 12, 2020)

Cairo Review (2020) "Forced Returns: COVID-19 Puts International Labor Migrants at Risk," *Cairo Review*, July 9. Available at: https://www.thecairoreview.com/midan/forcedreturns-covid-19-puts-international-labor-migrants-at-risk/ (Accessed on November 12, 2020).

Ehab, Maye (2018) "The Commuting Gender Gap and Females' Labor Supply and Earnings in the Egyptian Labor Market." Economic Research Forum Working Paper Series No. 1211. Cairo.

Fargues, Philippe and Nasra M. Shah (eds) (2018) *Migration to the Gulf: Policies in Sending and Receiving Countries.* Jeddah, Geneva, Cambridge: European University Institute, Gulf Research Center.

IOM (International Organization for Migration) (2011) "Egyptian Migration to Libya." Cairo: IOM. Available at: https://reliefweb.int/sites/reliefweb.int/files/resources/99CDE2C6E952C93AC125785D0040635C-Full_Report.pdf. (Accessed on November 12, 2020)

Grogger, J. and Gordon H. Hanson (2011) "Income Maximization and the Selection and Sorting of International Migrants," *Journal of Development Economics,* 95 (1): 42–57.

Herrera, S. and K. Badr (2012) "Internal Migration in Egypt: Levels, Determinants, Wages, and Likelihood of Employment." The World Bank Policy Research Working Paper No. 6166. Washington, DC.

Khalil, D. et al. (2018) "Inclusive Services for Youth in Cairo's Informal Areas." Economic Research Forum Working Paper Series No. 1204. Cairo.

Krafft, C., Ragui Assaad, and Khandker Wahedur Rahman (2021) "Introducing the Egypt Labor Market Panel Survey 2018." *IZA Journal of Development and Migration* (Forthcoming).

Le Goff, M. (2016) "Feminization of Migration and Trends in Remittances." IZA World of Labor. Available at: https://wol.iza.org/uploads/articles/220/pdfs/feminization-of-migration-and-trends-in-remittances.pdf?v=1 (Accessed June 10, 2021).

Malaeb, Bilal and Jackline Wahba (2019) "Migration Dynamics during the Refugee Influx in Jordan," in Caroline Krafft and Ragui Assaad (eds.) *The Jordanian Labor Market Between Fragility and Resilience,* pp. 125-140. Oxford: Oxford University Press.

Migali, S. and M. Scipioni (2018) "A Global Analysis of Intentions to Migrate, European Commission." JRC Technical Report 111207. Available at: https://knowledge4policy.ec.europa.eu/sites/default/files/technical_report_on_gallup_v7_finalpubsy.pdf. (Accessed on November 12, 2020).

OAMDI (Open Access Micro Data Initiative) (2019) Labor Market Panel Surveys. Available at: http://www.erfdataportal.com/. Version 3.0 of Licensed Data Files; ELMPS 2012. Cairo: Economic Research Forum.

OAMDI (2019) Labor Market Panel Surveys (LMPS), http://www.erfdataportal.com/. Version 2.0 of Licensed Data Files; ELMPS 2018. Cairo: Economic Research Forum (ERF).

OECD (Organisation for Economic Co-operation and Development) (2020) "What Is the Impact of the COVID-19 Pandemic on Immigrants and their Children?" *OECD Policy Responses to Coronavirus (COVID-19),* OECD, Paris, October 19, 2020. Available at: http://www.oecd.org/coronavirus/policy-responses/ what-is-the-impact-of-the-covid-19-pandemic-on-immigrants-and-theirchildren-e7cbb7de/. (Accessed on November 12, 2020)

Papoutsaki, Dafni and Jackline Wahba (2015) "The Change in International Migration Aspirations of Egyptian Youth," in Rania Roushdy and Maia Sieverding (eds) *Panel Survey of Young People in Egypt (SYPE) 2014 Generating Evidence for Policy, Programs, and Research*, pp. 69–80. Cairo: Population Council.

Pettit, H. and Ruijtenberg, W. (2019) "Migration as Hope and Depression: Existential Im/Mobilities in and beyond Egypt," *Mobilities*, 14 (5): 730–44.

Ratha, Dilip et al. (2020) "Migration and Development Brief 33: Phase II: COVID-19 Crisis through a Migration Lens." KNOMAD–World Bank, Washington, DC.

Sieverding, Maia et al. (2019) "Perceptions of Service Access in a Context of Marginalization: The Case of Young People in Informal Greater Cairo." Economic Research Forum Working Paper Series No. 1289. Cairo.

Stark, Oded (1991) *The Migration of Labor*. Oxford: Blackwell.

United Nations, Department of Economic and Social Affairs, Population Division (2019) "World Urbanization Prospects: The 2018 Revision." New York: United Nations.

Wahba, Jackline (2009) "An Overview of Internal and International Migration in Egypt," in Ragui Assaad (ed.) *Egypt's Labor Market Revisited*, pp. 157–76. Cairo: The American University in Cairo Press.

Wahba, Jackline (2015) "Through the Keyhole: International Migration in Egypt," in Ragui Assaad and Caroline Krafft (eds) *The Egyptian Labor Market in an Era of Revolution*, pp. 198–217. Oxford: Oxford University Press.

World Bank (2019) "Migration and Remittances Recent Developments and Outlook." World Bank Migration and Development Brief 31. Washington, DC.

Zohry, Ayman (2009) "The Development Impact of Internal Migration: Findings from Egypt." International Union for the Scientific Study of Population.

8

Rural Women in Egypt

Opportunities and Vulnerabilities

Caitlyn Keo, Caroline Krafft, and Luca Fedi

8.1 Introduction

Sixty percent of Egypt's population lives in rural areas (Chapter 1). In a young country overall, Egypt's rural population is even younger than the urban population, making economic and social challenges there of particular importance for the future of Egypt. Young rural women are triply disadvantaged globally, owing to their age, gender, and location; uplifting this group can also be a powerful engine for growth and development (IFAD, 2019). This chapter examines the status of women, their livelihoods, and opportunities, with a particular focus on rural women, and comparisons between urban and rural men and women. The chapter uses the Egypt Labor Market Panel Survey (ELMPS) waves of 1998, 2006, 2012, and 2018 to understand how rural women's lives have evolved over time in Egypt, with a particular focus on their livelihoods.

A number of studies have looked at gender attitudes and the economic empowerment of women in Egypt (Jensen, 1994; Yount, 2005; Drolet, 2010; Henry, 2011; Salem, 2011; Assaad, Nazier, and Ramadan, 2014; Yount, Zureick-Brown, and Salem, 2014; Salemi and Rashed, 2015; Yount et al., 2016; Cheong, Yount, and Crandall, 2017; Miyata and Yamada, 2017; Yount, Crandall, and Cheong, 2018). Qualitative studies have looked at the relationship between microcredit and women's empowerment (Drolet, 2010) and the perception of empowerment from a cultural perspective (Henry, 2011). They show that women's work is often devalued by society unless women hold skilled formal jobs. Quantitative studies look at how factors such as education, marriage, household structure, or domestic violence influence gender preferences and attitudes (Yount, 2005), market and non-market work (Yount, Zureick-Brown, and Salem, 2014; Salem, Cheong, and Yount, 2018), and family decision-making power (Yount, 2005; Cheong, Yount, and Crandall, 2017; Salem, Cheong and Yount, 2018; Yount, Crandall and Cheong, 2018). Household structure and living with marital kin (parents-in-law, brothers-in-law, and the husband) influence women's gendered attitudes. Women living with marital kin are less likely to express equal or favorable interest in female children

Caitlyn Keo, Caroline Krafft, and Luca Fedi, *Rural Women in Egypt: Opportunities and Vulnerabilities* In: *The Egyptian Labor Market: A Focus on Gender and Economic Vulnerability*. Edited by: Caroline Krafft and Ragui Assaad, Oxford University Press.

(Yount, 2005). More educated women, compared to uneducated women without experience in paid work, reported weaker preferences for sons, and greater family power in household decisions and decisions that pertained to children (Yount, 2005).

In rural Egypt, Salem, Cheong, and Yount (2018) looked at three indicators of Egyptian women's agency: economic decision-making, freedom of movement, and attitudes about women's roles and rights. They found that women who participated in subsistence work had similar gender attitudes and equal decision-making power as women who participated in market work. Freedom of movement had positive associations with both subsistence work and market work compared with not working.

Past research emphasizes the complex and contextualized factors that affect rural women's lives. Using data from the ELMPS waves of 1998, 2006, 2012, and 2018, we examine opportunities and vulnerabilities for individuals and households, with a particular emphasis on rural women.[1] We also nuance our understanding of rural women's lives by examining differences in outcomes by education, age group, and marital status. We examine outcomes for rural Egyptian women relative to men and urban women. This chapter investigates rural women's economic engagement, including not only standard measures of employment and labor force participation, but also engagement with farm and non-farm household enterprises and domestic work. We find that adding individuals who worked on a family enterprise or farm to employment leads us to detect substantially more employment specifically among rural women, more than doubling the employment rate by one measure. We also explore family formation, including marriage and fertility, as an important phase of rural women's lives. Women's access to services and the gender role attitudes of their communities shape their opportunities and vulnerabilities and constitute a key focus of this chapter. We conclude with a discussion of the implications of our results for understanding and supporting rural women's lives and livelihoods.

8.2 Economic Engagement of Women

8.2.1 Labor force participation and employment

The labor force participation (LFP) rate, also referred to as the economic activity rate, measures the percentage of the working-age (aged 15–64) population that is working or searching for work. The labor force therefore consists of two key components: the employed and the unemployed. "Standard unemployment"

---

[1] The ELMPS data are publicly available from the Economic Research Forum (ERF) Open Access Microdata Initiative at www.erfdataportal.com. Details on the data are available elsewhere (Assaad and Barsoum, 2000; Barsoum, 2009; Assaad and Krafft, 2013; Krafft, Assaad and Rahman, 2021).

includes individuals who have not worked in the reference period (here, three months), who want to work, are available to start in two weeks, and have actively searched for work in the reference period.[2] As people may become discouraged in their job search, a second definition of unemployment is often used to "relax" the active job search criterion: "broad unemployment" includes non-employed individuals who want to work, are available to work, but are not searching for work (within the past three months).

In terms of employment, the "market definition" of employment only includes those engaged in economic activity for the purposes of market exchange. The "extended definition" of employment also includes subsistence labor that involves the production or processing of primary commodities for own household consumption. Subsistence labor is particularly important to measure for this chapter, as it can help us understand the economic activities that rural women undertake.[3]

8.2.1.1 Labor force participation

Figure 8.1 examines the standard (search required), market definition of LFP. In 2018, half (49 percent) of all working aged people (aged 15–64) participated in

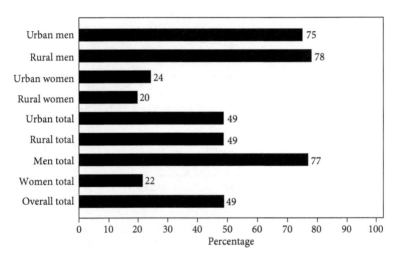

Figure 8.1 Labor force participation rate (percentage) by sex and location, ages 15–64, 2018.

Notes: The market standard (search required) definition of the labor force is based on a three-month reference period.

Source: Authors' calculations based on ELMPS 2018.

---

[2] "Standard unemployment" as is defined by the International Conference of Labour Statisticians (ILO, 2013) and operationalized in our data and chapter. Most national statistical offices, including Egypt's, follow these definitions.
[3] See Chapter 1 for a detailed analysis of labor force participation, employment, and unemployment by these different definitions.

the labor force. This is a low rate by international standards and is largely due to the very low participation of women. Men's participation rates (77 percent) were in line with international rates (including from other Arab and lower-middle-income countries) (ILO, 2019). However, only 22 percent of women were economically active. Women's LFP rate was 14 percentage points lower than the world average for lower-middle income countries, although slightly higher than the average of 19 percent for lower-middle income Arab states. While rural men participated slightly more (78 percent) than urban men (75 percent), the opposite was true for women (20 percent of rural women participated while 24 percent of urban women did so).

8.2.1.2 Employment
A particularly concerning feature of the Egyptian labor market is that rural women's employment rate has fallen over time, even after accounting for the effect of increasing educational attainment. Figure 8.2 shows employment rates comparing the market and the extended definitions of employment over the waves of the

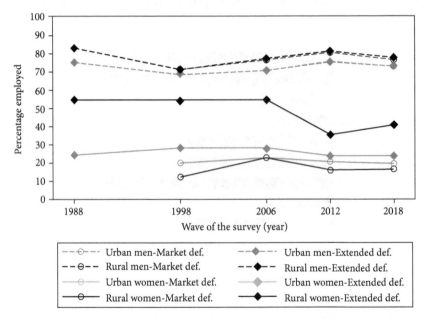

Figure 8.2 Employment rates (percentage) by sex, location, and definition, ages 15–64, 1988–2018.

Note: The market definition only includes those engaged in economic activity for the purposes of market exchange. The extended definition of employment adds those involved in the production or processing of primary commodities for own household consumption (i.e. subsistence labor). Both the market and the extended definition of employment use a three-month reference period.

Source: Authors' calculations based on LFS 1988 and ELMPS 1998–2018.

ELMPS, 1998, 2006, 2012, and 2018, as well as the 1988 special Labor Force Survey (LFS).[4]

Urban women's employment has remained stagnant, at low levels, over 1998–2018, under both the market and extended definitions. Employment rates among both urban and rural men have also remained largely stable across the period. On the other hand, a dramatic decrease in employment rates was observed among rural women under the extended definition, particularly between 2006 and 2012, with only a slight recovery between 2012 and 2018. The substantial increase in rural women's market employment between 1998 and 2006 was largely reversed between 2006 and 2018.

8.2.1.3 Employment statuses

Using the market definition of work, Figure 8.3, focusing on 2018, differentiates among four different employment statuses: waged employee, employer, self-employed, and unpaid family worker. Wage employment was more extensive in urban (83 percent) than rural (73 percent) areas, whereas there were similar rates of self-employment in urban and rural areas (10–11 percent). Among employed rural women, 28 percent were unpaid family workers and 16 percent were

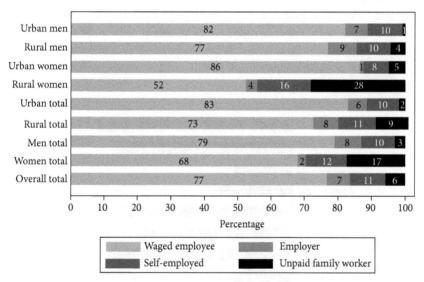

Figure 8.3 Employment status (percentage) by sex and location, ages 15–64 in market employment, 2018.

Note: Market definition of employment with a three-month reference period.

Source: Authors' calculations based on ELMPS 2018.

---

[4] Only the extended definition is available in the LFS.

self-employed. In contrast to 52 percent of rural women, 86 percent of employed urban women were waged employees.

8.2.2 Farm and non-farm enterprises

8.2.2.1 Non-farm enterprises

Entrepreneurship in the form of household enterprises is an important part of Egypt's economy (Chapter 8; Krafft, 2016). ELMPS 2018 captures data on whether households had non-farm enterprises. There were fewer female-headed households with non-farm enterprises compared with male-headed households (Figure 8.4). In rural areas, 7 percent of female-headed households had enterprises compared with 15 percent of male-headed households. Similarly, there were lower rates of non-farm enterprises among female-headed households (5 percent) in urban areas compared with male-headed households (17 percent).

8.2.2.2 Livestock

In rural Egypt, agriculture plays a very important role for many households' livelihoods; 29 percent of rural households owned livestock. Comparatively, only 5 percent of urban households owned livestock. In terms of livestock, there was less of a disparity by the household head's sex than for non-farm enterprises. While 30 percent of rural households with male heads had livestock, 26 percent of rural households with female heads had livestock. Rural women have a key role

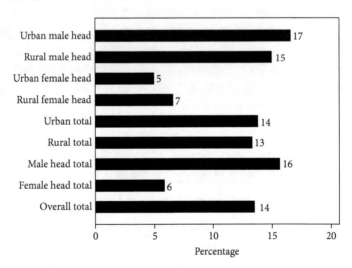

Figure 8.4 Percentage of households with non-farm enterprises by location and sex of head of household, 2018.

Source: Authors' calculations based on ELMPS 2018.

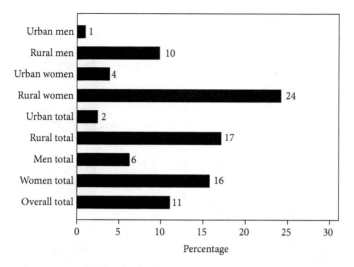

Figure 8.5 Percentage of individuals who were a primary caretaker of livestock, by sex and location, ages 15–64, 2018.

Note: Households with livestock had to report (up to) three primary caretakers for each livestock and these caretakers could be, but did not have to be, household members. Individuals were only considered working with livestock if they were one of the (up to) three primary caretakers for one or more livestock. The livestock included cows, poultry, goats, sheep, camels, donkey/mules, horses, buffaloes, and other animals.

Source: Authors' calculations based on ELMPS 2018.

in livestock care in Egypt, contributing to their families' wellbeing and providing economic opportunities. Figure 8.5 shows that rural women were over twice as likely (24 percent) to be a primary caretaker of livestock than rural men (10 percent). Urban women were also slightly more likely (4 percent) to be the caretakers of livestock, compared with only 1 percent of urban men.

Figure 8.6 shows the percentage of rural women who tended livestock by age group and also by education. Women in older age groups were increasingly likely to tend livestock, up until the age of 49. Among rural women, 11 percent of those aged 15–19 tended livestock, compared with 19 percent of rural women aged 20–29, 28 percent of women aged 30–39, and 33 percent of women aged 40–59. Women in rural Egypt with less education were more likely to tend livestock. Nearly a third (31 percent) of rural women with less than basic education tended livestock (as one of up to three reported primary caretakers). Women with more education worked as caretakers of livestock at lower rates, but still to a substantial extent: 20 percent of rural women with basic education worked with livestock as a primary caretaker, 22 percent of rural women with secondary education, and 15 percent of rural women with higher education. Livestock thus provided an important economic opportunity for older and less educated rural women, but had a role in the lives of younger and more educated women as well.

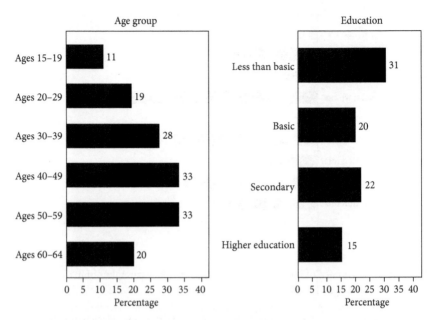

Figure 8.6 Percentage of rural women aged 15–64 who tended livestock by age group and by education, 2018.

Note: Individuals were only considered working with livestock if they were one of the (up to) three primary caretakers for one or more livestock. The livestock included cows, poultry, goats, sheep, camels, donkey/mules, horses, buffaloes, and other animals.

Source: Authors' calculations based on ELMPS 2018.

There were several types of common livestock in rural Egypt. Figure 8.7 shows, among rural households that had livestock, the (potentially multiple) types of livestock they had, by the sex of the household head. Poultry (86 percent) was the most common livestock raised by rural households, followed by cows (29 percent) and donkeys (28 percent). Buffalo (16 percent), goats (9 percent), and sheep (6 percent) were also commonplace. Other animals, such as horses, camels, or anything else, were rare (2 percent). Female-headed households with livestock were much less likely to own more expensive livestock, such as cows or donkeys (17–18 percent versus 31 percent for male-headed households). They were slightly more likely to own poultry (88 percent versus 85 percent for male-headed households). The predominance of poultry, which is likely to produce food for the household but has finite potential as an asset or for market sales, suggests that current livestock rearing patterns were unlikely to act as livestock-based livelihood development strategies or elevate families, particularly female-headed ones, out of poverty.

8.2.2.3 Crops

In addition to owning livestock, working with crops was a substantial part of the agricultural sector in rural Egypt. In rural areas, 14 percent of households

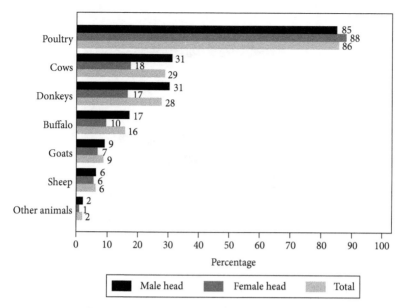

Figure 8.7 Types of livestock owned by rural households (percentage of those households owning livestock) by sex of head of household, 2018.

Note: Adds up to more than 100 percent because households may own multiple types of livestock. Other animals category included the responses horses, camels, and other animals.

Source: Authors' calculations based on ELMPS 2018.

harvested or produced crops in the last year (Figure 8.8). Harvesting and producing crops was very uncommon for urban households (1 percent). Here, as with non-farm enterprises, crops were more common in male-headed households. While 16 percent of rural male-headed households produced crops, only 7 percent of rural female-headed households did so. Whereas women were more likely to work with livestock than men, the opposite was true for crops (not shown). There was a gendered division of labor for working with crops (men) and with livestock (women). In households that harvested crops, 68 percent of rural men and 25 percent of rural women were listed as one of up to three primary caretakers of one or more crops.[5] Among all people who were ranked as the primary worker on a crop, 92 percent were men and only 8 percent were women. However, if we

[5] This percentage might be underestimating the percentage of people who work on crops. At most, households could report three primary caretakers for each crop. The greatest number of crops that any household reported was nine. Furthermore, among all of the reported crops (451 crops were reported by 328 unique households), there were 166 times that three people from a household were listed as a primary worker (and thus there might have been a fourth worker). The question identifying the primary crop worker for each crop asked, "Who from the household worked the most on [this crop] in the past 12 months?" This question, with two additional questions that ask about who worked the "second most" and the "third most" identify the top three people who work on each crop. Finally, the question that identifies who decided the most is "Who from the household decided the most on [this crop] in the past 12 months?"

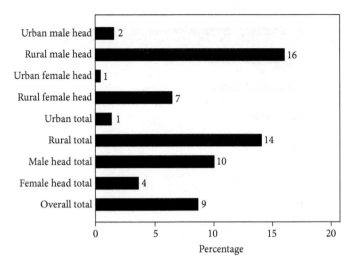

Figure 8.8 Percentage of households that harvested/produced crops in the last year by sex of head of household and location, 2018.
Source: Authors' calculations based on ELMPS 2018.

extend to the top three workers (inclusive of those who were the primary worker) who were reported, 76 percent were men and 24 percent were women. In most instances, the primary worker of the crop was also the person who made the most decisions for the crop. Therefore, the primary decision-makers on crops were predominantly men (93 percent).

Households produced a variety of different crops. Figure 8.9 shows the types of crops that were grown by rural households that reported harvesting/producing crops, by sex of the household head. Households could potentially farm multiple crops. The most common crops that households harvested were wheat (68 percent), clover (55 percent), and corn (51 percent). Rice (21 percent) and vegetables (13 percent) were also fairly common. Less common crops included fruit (4 percent), sugar cane (3 percent), cotton (2 percent), and other crops (3 percent). There were not large differences in crops by the sex of the household head for the most common crops, although female-headed households were less likely to produce rice (13 percent versus 22 percent for male-headed households) and vegetables (7 percent versus 14 percent for male-headed households). The differences may be due to the capital or labor intensity of various crops.

Combining work with livestock and crops together with non-farm enterprises, one can assess the percentage of people who worked on a family enterprise or farm or either. We restrict our definition of work here to those whose crops were sold or whose livestock was sold, to parallel the market definition of employment (we did not restrict thus previously). The share was much higher in rural areas than urban areas (Figure 8.10). About a fifth of rural men (22 percent) and a quarter of rural women (27 percent) worked on a family enterprise or farm. Rural

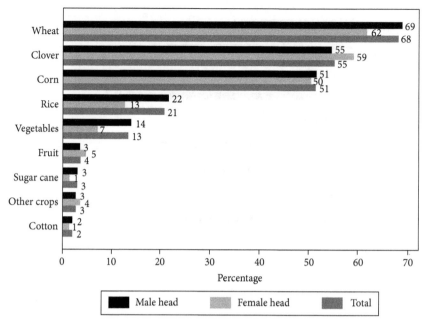

Figure 8.9 Types of crops (percentage of households producing crop), rural households harvesting/producing crops, by sex of household head, 2018.

Note: Adds up to more than 100 percent because households may harvest multiple types of crops. Other crops included parsley, flowers, nuts, sesame, sunflower seed, forage, alfalfa, and pharmaceutical plants.

Source: Authors' calculations based on ELMPS 2018.

women were primarily working in farms (25 percent) rather than enterprises (4 percent), whereas men worked in both farms (14 percent) and enterprises (10 percent).

8.2.3 Measuring rural women's employment

There are concerns in the labor and development literature that those who work in agriculture, especially women, sometimes underreport their employment, an issue that has been identified in Egypt as well (Anker and Anker, 1995; Assaad, 1997; Langsten and Salem, 2008). Figure 8.11 shows employment to population ratios (employment rates) by sex and location for four different definitions of employment. In addition to the market and extended definitions of employment, mentioned previously, we have created two "added" definitions. The added market definition adds to the market definition of employment those individuals who worked on a family enterprise or farmed crops or tended livestock that *were sold*. This allows us to measure whether there was underreporting of market work. Similarly, the added extended definition adds individuals who worked on a family

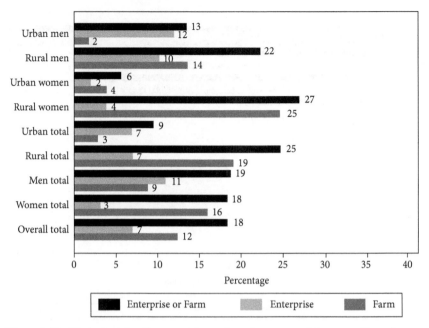

Figure 8.10 Worked on family enterprise or farm (percentage) by sex and location, ages 15–64, 2018.

Note: Individuals were only considered working on a farm if they were one of the (up to) three primary workers for one or more livestock types that were sold or one or more crops that were sold, and to be working on a family enterprise if they were one of the (up to three) primary workers for one or more enterprises.

Source: Authors' calculations based on ELMPS 2018.

enterprise or farmed crops or tended livestock (not conditional that crops or livestock were sold) to the extended definition of employment. This allows us to measure whether there was underreporting of subsistence work. Although the measures have slightly different time frames, they do suggest a new, additional method for detecting employment, particularly among rural women. Employment for rural women more than doubled using the added-market definition of employment (35 percent) compared with the market definition (16 percent). The added-market definition of employment did not affect employment rates for urban women or men very much (at most a 3 percentage point increase). Rural women also experienced small increases in their employment when looking at the added extended definition (43 percent) compared with the extended definition (40 percent).

8.2.4 Market and domestic work

In addition to their underestimated engagement in the market economy, rural women engage in important domestic work. Domestic work includes tasks such

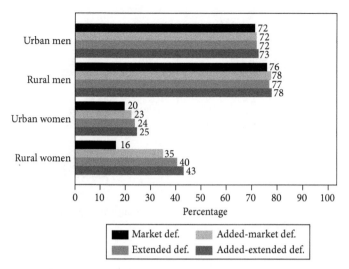

Figure 8.11 Employment to population ratios (percentages) by definition, sex, and location, ages 15–64, 2018.

Note: The added market definition of employment adds individuals who worked on a family enterprise or farm that *sold* crops or livestock they worked with to the market definition of employment. The added extended definition of employment adds individuals who worked on a family enterprise or farm (not conditional on selling crops or livestock) to the extended definition of employment. Individuals were only considered working on a family enterprise or farm if they were one of the (up to) three primary workers for one or more livestock, crop, or non-farm enterprise.

Source: Authors' calculations based on ELMPS 2018.

as raising poultry or livestock, collecting firewood or other fuel or water, cooking, managing or cleaning the household, and taking care of children. It is thus a more expansive definition than subsistence work, which is focused on primary commodities.

Domestic work was overwhelmingly carried out by women (Figure 8.12). For unmarried individuals, rural women spent the most time doing domestic work each week (17 hours), followed by urban women (15 hours). Domestic work increased substantially with marriage for women. For rural women, domestic work was over twice as time consuming for married women (36 hours) than for those who were unmarried (17 hours). Likewise, married urban women spent on average 32 hours per week doing domestic work compared with 15 hours per week for unmarried urban women. Domestic work for men was always low (2–6 hours). The additional time women spent on domestic work was a "second shift" if they engaged in market work. For married women, market work (averaging 35 hours in rural areas and 38 in urban areas) was as time consuming as domestic work (averaging 32 hours in urban areas and 36 in rural areas). While unmarried women worked hours of market work more comparable to unmarried men (40–44 hours for women versus 47–51 for men), married men worked longer hours in market work (50–51) than married women (35–38). Challenges reconciling the "second

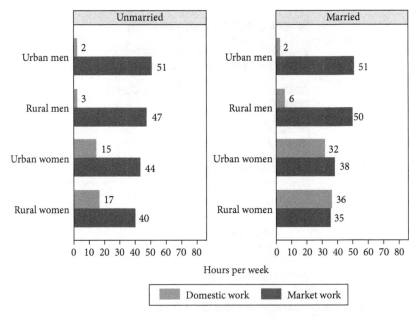

Figure 8.12 Hours spent doing domestic work (all individuals) and market work (employed individuals) per week by sex, location, and marital status, ages 15–64, 2018.

Note: The reference period for both domestic work and market work was the last seven days. Unmarried included never married, contractually married, divorced, and widowed. Domestic work included agricultural activities or raising poultry or livestock; producing ghee, butter, cheese, or non-food goods; collecting firewood or other fuel or water; cooking; washing dishes; doing laundry and ironing; managing the household; cleaning the house; construction/repairs; shopping (food, clothing, etc.); caring for sick or elderly (only); and taking care of children (only).

Source: Authors' calculations based on ELMPS 2018.

shift" of gendered domestic responsibilities, which increase at marriage, with market work may be why women frequently leave market work at marriage (Economic Research Forum and UN Women, 2020; Assaad, Krafft, and Selwaness, 2017; Selwaness and Krafft, 2021).

The amount of time spent doing domestic work increased with age, to a peak for urban women aged 40–49 and a peak for rural women aged 30–39 (Figure 8.13). Rural women aged 30–39 spent on average 39 hours doing domestic work per week and urban women aged 40–49 spent on average 33 hours per week doing domestic work. These peak hours likely represented peak caregiving responsibilities.

With the exception of tending livestock, within marital status there were only subtle differences in the nature of domestic tasks performed by rural or urban women (Figure 8.14). Nearly all married women (85–93 percent) spent time doing each of washing dishes, cooking, doing laundry and ironing, and cleaning the house. Unmarried women also sometimes spent time doing these activities (48–64 percent). Additionally, 61–62 percent of married women spent time

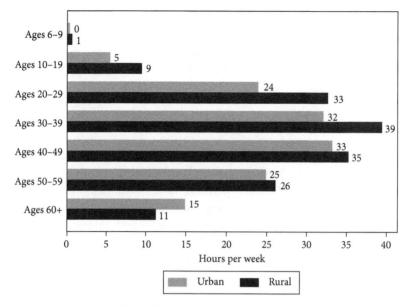

Figure 8.13 Hours spent doing domestic work per week by age group and location, women aged 6+, 2018.

Note: The reference period was the last seven days.

Source: Authors' calculations based on ELMPS 2018.

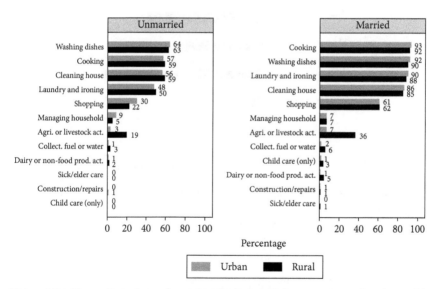

Figure 8.14 Domestic tasks performed in the last week (percentage performing task) by location and current marital status, women aged 15–64, 2018.

Note: Activities were over the last seven-day reference period. Unmarried includes never married, contractually married, divorced, and widowed. Owing to challenges in translation that asked for only "full time," the statistics for child care and sick/elder care were likely incorrect.

Source: Authors' calculations based on ELMPS 2018.

shopping. The ubiquity of these activities for married women, regardless of location, as well as the time they consumed, suggests that labor-saving technologies were not widely available, affordable, or adopted by women; encouraging their spread might help address the "double burden" (Krafft and Assaad, 2015).

8.3 Access to Services

Access to public services such as education and health care has a particularly important effect on the lives of women. Long travel times are one of several potential service access barriers, particularly for households in rural areas. Figure 8.15 shows the average travel time in minutes to basic services for urban and rural households.[6] Travel times were similar for both primary and preparatory schools between urban and rural households (12–14 minutes). Travel to secondary schools in rural areas was five minutes longer (23 minutes) than in urban

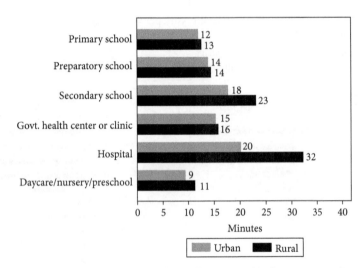

Figure 8.15 Households' average travel time (in minutes) to basic services by location, 2018.
Source: Authors' calculations based on ELMPS 2018.

[6] Households reported commute times in minutes via their most used mode of transportation to each service. For example, while individuals in urban areas might walk 17 minutes to a health clinic, individuals in rural areas might drive 19 minutes to a health clinic, with a two-minute difference in their travel time. The most commonly used modes of transportation to services included walking, public transportation, microbus/private minibus, taxi, toktok, bike/motorcycle, private car, school bus, different modes, and other.

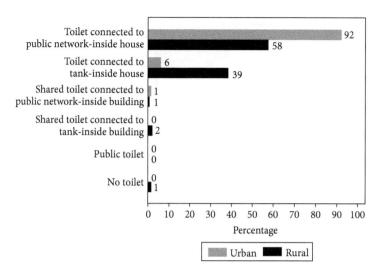

Figure 8.16 Type of sanitation facilities used (percentage) by location, households, 2018.

Source: Authors' calculations based on ELMPS 2018.

areas (18 minutes). Proximity to government health centers or clinics was comparable for rural households and urban households based on travel time. However, travel time to a local hospital was more than 50 percent longer in rural areas; on average, rural households had to travel for 32 minutes to reach the nearest hospital compared with 20 minutes for urban households.

Across Egypt, the vast majority of households had access to modern sanitation; 98 percent of urban households and 97 percent of rural households had toilets inside their house that were either connected to a public network or connected to a tank (Figure 8.16). In urban areas, 92 percent used a toilet that was connected to a public network, and in rural areas 58 percent did. In rural areas, toilets that were connected to tanks (39 percent) were nearly as common as those connected to public networks (58 percent). Although the mode of sanitation and role of public networks varied, overall urban and rural residents had equitable access to modern sanitation.

8.4 Family Formation

8.4.1 Early marriage and age at marriage

Women began family formation and married earlier in rural areas. The median age of marriage was 20 for rural women and 23 for urban women (Figure 8.17).

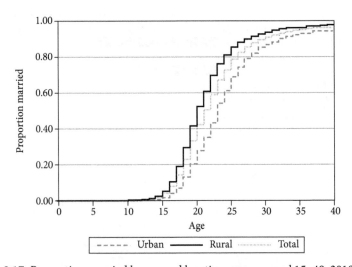

Figure 8.17 Proportion married by age and location, women aged 15–49, 2018.
Note: Showing through age 40 based on sample aged 15–49. Based on Kaplan-Meier failure estimate.
Source: Authors' calculations based on ELMPS 2018.

Early marriage, or child marriage (i.e. marriage before the age of 18), was more common in rural than urban areas of Egypt. In urban areas, 8 percent of women aged 15–49 in 2018 were married before the age of 18, in comparison with 19 percent of women aged 15–49 in rural areas. The gap between the proportion of urban and rural women married at some ages was as large as 0.25. By the age of 30 years old, however, nearly 90 percent of both rural and urban women were married, although rural women slightly more so.

8.4.2 Fertility

Fertility in Egypt, after rising to 3.5 births per woman (total fertility rate (TFR)) in 2012–15, had fallen back to 3.1 births per woman in 2018 (Chapter 1; Ministry of Health and Population, El-Zanaty and Associates, and ICF International, 2015). There were large differences in fertility across rural and urban areas in 2018: births per woman were 2.6 in urban areas and 3.5 in rural areas (Figure 8.18).[7] In urban areas fertility decreased with educational attainment, although not very sharply. The fertility rate for urban women with basic education (2.4) was not very different from that of tertiary graduates (2.2). More counterintuitively, educational attainment was not related to fertility at all in rural areas. Women with no education and women with higher education had essentially the same fertility rate (3.7-3.8), in line with the fertility rates of illiterate urban women.

---

[7] Fertility calculated with the STATA program tfr2 (Schoumaker, 2014).

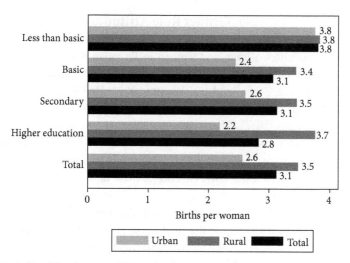

Figure 8.18 Total fertility rates (TFRs, births per woman) by location and education, women aged 15–49, 2018.

Source: Authors' calculations based on ELMPS 2018.

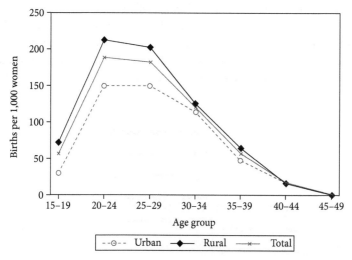

Figure 8.19 Age-specific fertility rates (ASFRs, births per 1,000 women) by location, women aged 15–49, 2018.

Source: Authors' calculations based on ELMPS 2018.

The age-specific fertility rates (ASFRs) for rural women aged 15–39 were higher than for urban women (Figure 8.19). For those aged 15–19, rural women had on average 72 births per every 1,000 women, compared with 30 births per every 1,000 for urban women. Rural women's peak ASFR was in the 20–24 age range, at 213 births per 1,000 women. Urban women's fertility peaked between 20 and 29 years of age, at 150 births per 1,000 women at both ages.

8.5 Gender Role Attitudes

The different activities of men and women in Egyptian society, particularly the disproportionate domestic work of women, are tied to gender role attitudes (Economic Research Forum and UN Women, 2020; Hoodfar, 1997; Salemi and Rashed, 2015; Chamlou, Muzi, and Ahmed, 2016; Sieverding and Hassan, 2016; Miyata and Yamada, 2017). These attitudes shape the beliefs and behaviors of Egyptians on both a societal level and an individual level and are strongly persistent across generations (Sieverding, 2012; Miyata and Yamada, 2017). This section explores attitudes towards domestic violence, the role of women, decision-making, and women's mobility.

The ELMPS 2018 captured attitudes towards domestic violence by asking both men and women if a husband has the right to hit or punish his wife under a variety of circumstances. Responses demonstrated substantial differences in attitudes towards domestic violence by sex and location (Figure 8.20). First, men were more likely to justify domestic violence than women in both rural and urban areas. Second, domestic violence was considered justified more frequently among rural residents than urban residents. In at least one of the given situations (if she burns the food, if she neglects the children, if she argues with him, if she talks to other men, if she wastes his money, or if she refuses to have sex with him), 38 percent of rural men and 25 percent of urban men believed that it was justifiable to hit or punish a wife compared with 29 percent of rural women and 17 percent of urban women. Of the six situations, the single situation in which the

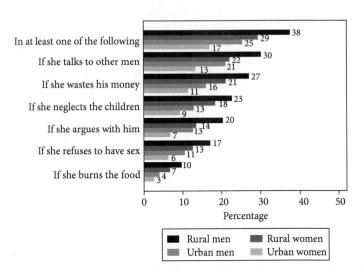

Figure 8.20 Believe that a husband has the right to hit his wife or punish her in the following situations (percentage) by sex and location, ages 15–64, 2018.
Source: Authors' calculations based on ELMPS 2018.

highest percentages of people reported that a husband has a right to hit or punish his wife was if she talks to other men (13-30 percent). Of the six situations, the single situation in which the lowest percentages of people reported that a husband has a right to hit or punish his wife was if she burns the food (3-10 percent).

Figure 8.21 shows gender role attitudes around four issues: household chores; reconciling motherhood and work; access to education; and access to employment opportunities. In Figure 8.12, we saw that urban and rural men do very little domestic work. These low rates of contribution to domestic work contradict the fact that 54 percent of urban men and 48 percent of rural men agreed that husbands should help their wives with household chores. Beliefs around education were overwhelmingly egalitarian. The majority (92–97 percent) of people across sex and location agreed or strongly agreed with the statement that boys and girls should get equal schooling.

A large majority of both urban and rural men (60–61 percent) agreed a woman can be a good mother *and* work outside the household. Overall the finding runs counter to the common argument that women's low economic participation is owing to normative, cultural preferences (World Bank, 2013). Yet a substantial minority of men (18–21 percent) and women (11–14 percent) held the opposite belief.

Negative attitudes towards women working were compounded by the economic context. Only 4–10 percent of individuals disagreed with the proposition

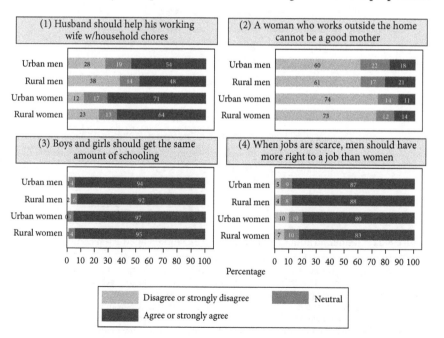

Figure 8.21   Gender attitudes (percentages) by sex and location, ages 15–64, 2018.
Source: Authors' calculations based on ELMPS 2018.

that "when jobs are scarce, men should have more right to a job than women." In times of economic challenges, or in local areas with high unemployment, particularly vulnerable women may be limited in their economic opportunities owing to these attitudes.

Figure 8.22 explores how gender attitudes have shifted over time. For questions that were asked in both 2006 and 2018 (the series was not asked in 2012), we explore the percentage of women agreeing (or strongly agreeing) with various statements. Men were not asked these questions in 2006, so we can only explore shifts in women's attitudes. There was little change over time in attitudes towards women being allowed to work (85–86 percent of women agreed over time). There were some increases in agreeing that the husband should help with children (from 80 percent in 2006 to 89 percent in 2018) and likewise that the husband should help with household chores (from 60 percent in 2006 to 67 percent in 2018). There was a particularly large increase in agreeing that girls should go to school to prepare for jobs (from 55 to 76 percent) and that women should have earnings (from 57 to 66 percent). There were slight decreases in the share agreeing that a working woman cannot be a good mother (from 15 to 13 percent) and that work interferes with marriage (from 19 to 18 percent). The same share

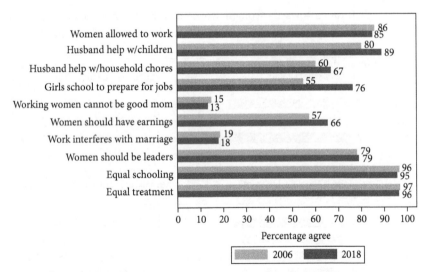

Figure 8.22 Gender attitudes (percentage agree), women aged 15–64, 2006 and 2018.

Note: Full statements were: (1) "A woman's place is not only in the household, but she should also be allowed to work." (2) "The husband should help his working wife raise their children." (3) "Husband should help his working wife with household chores." (4) "Girls should go to school to prepare for jobs, not just to make them good mothers and house-wives." (5) "A woman who works outside the home cannot be a good mother." (6) "For a woman's financial autonomy, she must work and have earnings." (7) "A woman's work interferes with her ability to keep a good relationship with her husband." (8) "Women should continue to obtain leadership positions in society." (9) "Boys and girls should get the same amount of schooling." (10) "Boys and girls should be treated equally."

Source: Authors' calculations based on ELMPS 2018.

continued to agree women should be leaders (79 percent) for equal schooling (95 to 96 percent) and for equal treatment (96 to 97 percent) over time. Gender role attitudes were relatively slow to change over more than a decade. Some attitudes appeared particularly entrenched, while others shifted towards greater gender equity. Overall, there was slow progression towards gender equity.

Decision-making power within their household is an important element of the economic agency of women (Kabeer, 1999; Assaad, Nazier, and Ramadan, 2014; Glennerster, Walsh, and Diaz-Martin, 2018; Friedrich, Engelhardt, and Schulz, 2020). Women aged 15–64 were asked who in the household had the final say about household decisions such as purchasing a major household item, making household purchases for daily needs, visits to family or friends, or cooking for the family. Figure 8.23 shows the distribution of who has the final say in each situation. The deciders could be you alone; spouse; parents; you and spouse jointly; or other combinations. For women who were not married, it was most common that their parents made the household decisions (39–59 percent). It was slightly more common that parents of rural unmarried women (46–59 percent) had the final say than for urban unmarried women (39–54 percent).

The final decider in common household decisions for married women had more variation across decisions. When it came to purchasing major household items, 24 percent (urban) and 35 percent (rural) said that their spouse had the

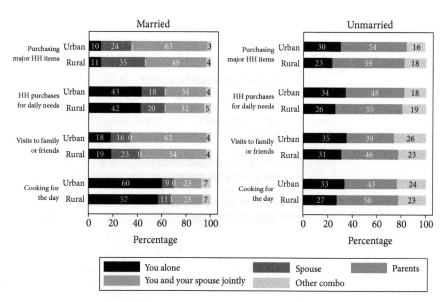

Figure 8.23 Who has the final say in common household decisions (percentage) by location and marital status, women aged 15–64, 2018.

Note: Other combo includes the responses parents; in-laws; relatives; you, your spouse, with parents or in-laws; you and your parents; and others.

Source: Authors' calculations based on ELMPS 2018.

final say, and 63 percent (urban) versus 49 percent (rural) said that they and their spouse made the decision jointly. Visits to family or friends were often made jointly by women and their spouses (62 percent urban, 54 percent rural). Yet a substantial percentage (16 percent urban, 23 percent rural) of women said that their spouse had the final say about visits to family and friends. However, in decisions about cooking for the day, 57 percent of married women in rural households said that they alone were able to make the decision, as well as 60 percent of married women in urban households. Household purchases for daily needs were often (42–43 percent) women's own decisions as well. While major decisions appear to be a joint or spouse decision, daily decisions were more likely to be women's own decisions—or their own responsibility, in that they were largely responsible for tasks such as cooking.

Focusing only on responses from married women aged 15–64, Figure 8.24 first shows the distribution of who had the final say in personal decisions such as going to the doctor or buying personal clothes. For each situation, it was most common that women either had the final say in the decisions or participated in the final decision-making jointly with their spouses. For instance, most women (51-54 percent) made the decision about going to the doctor jointly with their spouses and many made the decision alone (22-34 percent). However, a substantial percentage of married women did not get to participate in the final say for

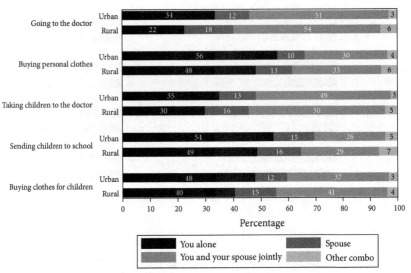

Figure 8.24 Who in the household has the final say in decisions about self and children (percentage) by location, married women aged 15–64, 2018.

Note: Other combo includes responses: parents; parents, in-laws, relatives; you, your spouse, with parents or in-laws; you and your parents; and others.

Source: Authors' calculations based on ELMPS 2018.

these personal decisions. Spouses alone had the final say in decisions about going to the doctor for 12–18 percent of married women.

Figure 8.24 also shows who had the final say in decisions for children such as taking children to the doctor, sending children to school, or buying clothes for children. Decisions about children were often made solely by married women or by married women jointly with their spouses. In rural areas, nearly half (49 percent) of women had the final say about sending children to school and 29 percent of women made the decision jointly with their spouses. Comparatively, 54 percent of married urban women made the decision alone and 26 percent of married women in urban areas made the decision jointly with their spouses. However, 15–16 percent of women did not get to participate in deciding whether to send children to school because this decision was made solely by their spouse. Similarly, it was most common that married women had the final say about buying clothes for their children (40–48 percent), followed by women who make the decision jointly with their spouses (37–41 percent). Women had the most solo decision-making power in buying their own clothes (48 percent rural, 56 percent urban) and the least in going to the doctor (22 percent rural, 34 percent urban), with most of the rest of decisions made jointly, yet some still made solely by spouses. Comparing the results in 2018 with the patterns in previous waves of the ELMPS (Assaad, Nazier, and Ramadan, 2014), women have experienced increases in decision-making power over time, including an increase in both solo and joint decisions.

Another important element of a woman's economic agency is measured in her freedom of movement (Assaad, Nazier, and Ramadan, 2014; Glennerster, Walsh, and Diaz-Martin, 2018; Friedrich, Engelhardt, and Schulz, 2020). Figure 8.25 shows whether permission was needed and the type of permission needed for women aged 15–64 to visit common destinations such as the local market, the doctor (for self or children), or relatives, friends, and neighbors. Very low percentages of rural (6–12 percent) and urban (8–13 percent) women went to any of the destinations alone without permission, but a sizeable share of urban (30–41 percent) and rural (25–34 percent) women went after informing family. Across destinations, 28–46 percent of rural and urban women went alone with permission. Finally, some women reported that they could not go alone to these destinations. A slightly higher percentage of rural women could not go alone in comparison with urban women. Going to the doctor for treatment has the highest percentages of rural (40 percent) and urban (33 percent) of women saying that they could not go alone.

8.6 Discussion and Conclusions

Egypt's rural population is a substantial share of its economy and society—a particularly young population, whose future will drive the direction of Egypt. This chapter illustrated the underestimated yet important role that Egyptian

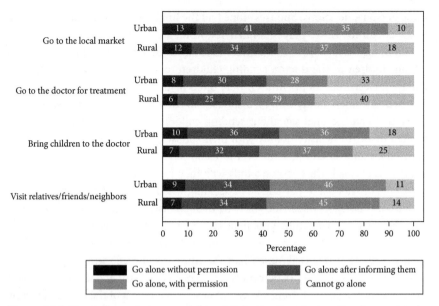

Figure 8.25 Type of permission needed to visit destinations by location (percentage), women aged 15–64, 2018.

Source: Authors' calculations based on ELMPS 2018.

women, especially rural women, play in the economy and society. Women make critical, and often unmeasured, contributions to the agricultural and care economies in particular, a pattern noted around the world in the women in development and gender and development literatures (Boserup, 1970; Beneria, Berik, and Floro, 2016). Women's opportunities and vulnerabilities are shaped not only by their economic context, but also by social norms and government policies, generating important interlinkages across a variety of domains.

Globally, increases in education tend to translate into decreases in fertility (Osili and Long, 2008; Kim, 2010; Cygan-Rehm and Maeder, 2013). While historically the education–fertility relationship held in Egypt (Ali and Gurmu, 2018; Krafft, 2020), as of 2018 this relationship held only in urban areas. In rural areas, women with no education and women with higher education had essentially the same fertility rate (3.7–3.8), in line with the fertility rates of illiterate urban women. The breakdown of the education-fertility relationship merits further research, especially since rural areas are also where most of the population growth occurs.

While rural Egyptian women do have some important vulnerabilities, in comparison with men and their urban counterparts, they also have a number of unique opportunities and strengths. While less likely to be wage workers than urban women, rural women were much more likely to engage in subsistence work or market work in a farm or non-farm enterprise. Women were particularly engaged in livestock, such that policies and programs that support livestock opportunities could disproportionately benefit women (IFAD Independent Office of Evaluation, 2017).

Women, and especially rural women, face challenges owing to gender role attitudes and high domestic workloads. Almost everyone agreed that girls and boys should receive equal education, an egalitarian attitude that is increasingly realized in terms of educational attainment (Krafft, 2012; Chapter 1; Elbadawy, 2015). While most men and women agreed that working did not prevent a woman from being a "good" mother, a substantial minority disagreed. Moreover, the vast majority of Egyptians agreed that men should have employment priority when jobs were scarce. These attitudes may contribute to women's low rates of economic activity, and in particular marginalize women in areas with limited employment opportunities.

Only 24 percent of urban and 20 percent of rural women were "economically active" according to the international definition. A particularly important finding was how, despite using the best practices in design including keyword detection questions, we showed that standard measures were severely underestimating rural women's participation in market work. Half of women who engaged in a non-farm enterprise or producing a crop or livestock for market (in the past year) did not report market work in the past three months. While some of this difference may be due to different time frames, further research on seasonality and the applicability of this approach—capturing different economic activities, if they involved market transactions, and who participated in them—is merited.

An important factor limiting women's participation in the market economy was their substantial "second shift" domestic workloads, 32–36 hours per week for married women, compared with 2–6 hours for men. In the long term, for women to increase their participation in the labor force, they will need to be able to reduce their second shift. This can be done through an increase in men's participation in domestic work, possibly incentivized with paternity leave, as well as through access to services such as child and elder care and labor-saving devices (Economic Research Forum and UN Women, 2020; Krafft and Assaad, 2015; World Bank, 2018). Work that is more reconcilable with women's domestic responsibilities, such as part-time work or work from home, may also help. Stagnant, segmented, and even falling (female) labor demand has contributed to women's low participation (World Bank, 2018; Assaad et al., 2019, 2020; Assaad, Krafft, and Yassin, 2020). Stronger (female) labor demand, coupled with reductions in the second shift of domestic work, will be an important part of any future increase in women's participation in market work.

The COVID-19 pandemic and its health, social, and economic implications have created additional challenges for rural women. While our data predate the start of the crisis, they have important implications for understanding the gendered vulnerability of rural women in the face of the crisis. Increases in domestic violence are a concerning consequence of the crisis (OECD, 2020b, 2020a), and our results show that rural women were already at greater risk. The attitude, which is strong nationally but stronger in rural areas, that men should have priority for jobs when employment is scarce may further limit women's market employment (OECD, 2020a). Policy responses in the labor market have focused primarily on irregular wage workers (OECD, 2020c), who, although disproportionately vulnerable to the crisis, are also disproportionately men (Chapter 2).

At the same time, the closure of schools and nurseries has further increased women's domestic work (CARE, 2020). Our analyses demonstrated that hours of domestic work were already higher for rural women pre-crisis. In response to these challenges, the Egyptian government has targeted important COVID-19 social protection efforts towards rural women, for instance by increasing payments to women community leaders in rural areas and expanding the Takaful and Karama programs that primarily benefit rural women (Chapter 9; OECD, 2020c). While these targeted efforts are important and promising, a critical area for future research will be assessing and ameliorating any disproportionate impact of the crisis on rural women.

Acknowledgments

We acknowledge the support of the International Labour Organization (ILO) and the International Fund for Agricultural Development (IFAD) through the "Strengthening gender monitoring and evaluation in rural employment in the Near East and North Africa" project. We also acknowledge the general support of the World Bank, the ILO, Agence Française de Développement, UN Women, and the Arab Fund for Economic and Social Development for the Egypt Labor Market Panel Survey 2018, on which this chapter is based. We appreciate the comments of participants in the 2019 "The Egyptian Labor Market: A Focus on Gender and Economic Vulnerability" workshop, especially those of our discussant Maria Laura Sanchez Puerta.

References

Ali, F.R.M. and S. Gurmu (2018) "The Impact of Female Education on Fertility: A Natural Experiment from Egypt," *Review of Economics of the Household*, 16 (3): 681–712. doi: 10.1007/s11150-016-9357-6.

Anker, R. and M. Anker (1995) "Measuring Female Labour Force with Emphasis on Egypt," in N.F. Khoury and V.M. Moghadam (eds) *Gender and Development in the Arab World: Women's Economic Participation: Patterns and Policies*, pp. 148–76. Tokyo: United Nations University Press.

Assaad, R. (1997) "The Employment Crisis in Egypt: Current Trends and Future Prospects," *Research in Middle East Economics*, 2 (1): 39–66.

Assaad, R. and G. Barsoum (2000) *Egypt Labor Market Survey, 1998: Report on the Data Collection and Preparation*. Cairo. Available at: http://www.erfdataportal.com/index.php/catalog/28/download/260 (Accessed August 29, 2021).

Assaad, R. and C. Krafft (2013) "The Egypt Labor Market Panel Survey: Introducing the 2012 Round," *IZA Journal of Labor & Development*, 2 (8): 1–30.

Assaad, R., C. Krafft, and I. Selwaness (2017) "The Impact of Marriage on Women's Employment in the Middle East and North Africa." Economic Research Forum Working Paper Series No. 1086. Cairo.

Assaad, R., C. Krafft, and S. Yassin (2020) "Job Creation or Labor Absorption? An Analysis of Private Sector Job Growth in Egypt," *Middle East Development Journal*, 12 (2): 177–207. doi: 10.1080/17938120.2020.1753978.

Assaad, R., H. Nazier, and R. Ramadan (2014) "Individual and Households Determinants of Women Empowerment: Application to the Case of Egypt." Economic Research Forum Working Paper Series No. 867. Cairo.

Assaad, R. et al. (2019) "Job Creation in Egypt: A Sectoral and Geographical Analysis Focusing on Private Establishments, 1996–2017." Economic Research Forum Policy Research Report. Cairo.

Assaad, R. et al. (2020) "Explaining the MENA Paradox: Rising Educational Attainment, Yet Stagnant Female Labor Force Participation," *Demographic Research*, 43 (28): 817–50.

Barsoum, G. (2009) "Methodological Appendix 1: The Egypt Labor Market Panel Survey 2006: Documentation of the Data Collection Process," in R. Assaad (ed.) *The Egyptian Labor Market Revisited*, pp. 259–84. Cairo: American University in Cairo Press.

Beneria, L., G. Berik, and M.S. Floro (2016) *Gender, Development, and Globalization: Economics as if All People Mattered*. Second edition. New York: Routledge.

Boserup, E. (1970) *Women's Role in Economic Development*. New York: St. Martin's Press.

CARE (2020) *CARE MENA COVID-19 Response: Rapid Gender Analysis – COVID-19 Middle East and North Africa Region*. CARE.

Chamlou, N., S. Muzi, and H. Ahmed (2016) "The Determinants of Female Labor Force Participation in the Middle East and North Africa Region: The Role of Education and Social Norms in Amman, Cairo, and Sana'a," in N. Chamlou and M. Karshenas (eds) *Women, Work, and Welfare in the Middle East and North Africa: The Role of Socio-Demographics, Entrepreneurship and Public Policies*, pp. 323–50. London: Imperial College Press.

Cheong, Y.F., K.M. Yount, and A.A. Crandall (2017) "Longitudinal Measurement Invariance of the Women's Agency Scale," *Bulletin de Methodologie Sociologique*, 134: 24–36. doi: 10.1177/0759106317693787.

Cygan-Rehm, K. and M. Maeder (2013) "The Effect of Education on Fertility: Evidence from a Compulsory Schooling Reform," *Labour Economics*, 25: 35–48. doi: 10.1016/j.labeco.2013.04.015.

Drolet, J. (2010) "Women, Micro Credit and Empowerment in Cairo, Egypt," *International Social Work*, 54 (5): 629–45. doi: 10.1177/0020872810382681.

Economic Research Forum and UN Women (2020) *Progress of Women in the Arab States 2020: The Role of the Care Economy in Promoting Gender Equality*. Cairo: UN Women.

Elbadawy, A. (2015) "Education in Egypt: Improvements in Attainment, Problems with Quality and Inequality," in R. Assaad and C. Krafft (eds) *The Egyptian Labor Market in an Era of Revolution*, pp. 127–46. Oxford: Oxford University Press.

Friedrich, C., H. Engelhardt, and F. Schulz (2020) "Women's Agency in Egypt, Jordan, and Tunisia: The Role of Parenthood and Education," *Population Research and Policy Review*: 1–34. doi: 10.1007/s11113-020-09622-7.

Glennerster, R., C. Walsh, and L. Diaz-Martin (2018) *A Practical Guide to Measuring Women's and Girls' Empowerment in Impact Evaluations*. JPAL.

Henry, H.M. (2011) "Egyptian Women and Empowerment: A Cultural Perspective," *Women's Studies International Forum*, 34 (3): 251–59. doi: 10.1016/j.wsif.2011.03.001.

Hoodfar, H. (1997) *Between Marriage and the Market: Intimate Politics and Survival in Cairo*. Berkeley: University of California Press.

IFAD (International Fund for Agricultural Development) (2019) *Creating Opportunities for Rural Youth: 2019 Rural Development Report*. Rome: IFAD.

IFAD Independent Office of Evaluation (2017) *Arab Republic of Egypt: Country Strategy and Programme Evaluation*. Rome: IFAD.

ILO (International Labour Organization) (2013) "Resolution Concerning Statistics of Work, Employment, and Labour Underutilization Adopted by the Nineteenth International Conference of Labour Statisticians." October.

ILO (2019) "Labour Force Participation Rate by Sex and Age—ILO modelled estimates, July 2018 (%)." Available at: www.ilo.org/ilostat (accessed August 21, 2019).

Jensen, K. (1994) "Who Carries the Load? Who Carries the Cash? Work and Status among Egyptian Farm Women," *Frontiers: A Journal of Women Studies*, 15 (2): 133–54. doi: 10.2307/3346779.

Kabeer, N. (1999) "Resources, Agency, Achievements: Reflections on the Measurement of Women's Empowerment," *Development and Change*, 30: 435–65.

Kim, J. (2010) "Women's Education and Fertility: An Analysis of the Relationship between Education and Birth Spacing in Indonesia," *Economic Development and Cultural Change*, 58 (4): 739–74. doi: 10.1086/649638.

Krafft, C. (2012) *Challenges Facing the Egyptian Education System: Access, Quality, and Inequality*, SYPE Policy Brief 2. New York: Population Council.

Krafft, C. (2016) "Understanding the Dynamics of Household Enterprises in Egypt: Birth, Death, Growth, and Transformation." Economic Research Forum Working Paper Series No. 983. Cairo.

Krafft, C. (2020) "Why is Fertility on the Rise in Egypt? The Role of Women's Employment Opportunities," *Journal of Population Economics*, 33 (4): 1173–1218. doi: 10.1007/s00148-020-00770-w.

Krafft, C. and R. Assaad (2015) "Promoting Successful Transitions to Employment for Egyptian Youth." Economic Research Forum Policy Perspective 15. Cairo.

Krafft, C., R. Assaad, and K.W. Rahman (2021) "Introducing the Egypt Labor Market Panel Survey 2018." *IZA Journal of Development and Migration* (Forthcoming).

Langsten, R. and R. Salem (2008) "Two Approaches to Measuring Women's Work in Developing Countries: A Comparison of Survey Data from Egypt," *Population and Development Review*, 34 (2): 283–305.

Ministry of Health and Population, El-Zanaty and Associates, and ICF International (2015) *Egypt Demographic and Health Survey*. Cairo: Ministry of Health and Population and ICF International.

Miyata, S. and H. Yamada (2017) "Do Female Gender Role Attitudes Affect Labour Market Participation in Egypt?" *The Journal of Development Studies*, 52 (6): 876–94. doi: 10.1080/00220388.2015.1113262.

OECD (Organisation for Economic Co-operation and Development) (2020a) *COVID-19 Crisis in the MENA Region: Impact on Gender Equality and Policy Responses, Tackling Coronavirus (COVID-19): Contributing to a Global Effort.* Paris: OECD.

OECD (2020b) *COVID-19 Crisis Response in MENA Countries, Tackling Coronavirus (COVID-19): Contributing to a Global Effort.* Paris: OECD.

OECD (2020c) *The COVID-19 Crisis in Egypt, Tackling Coronavirus (COVID-19): Contributing to a Global Effort.* Paris: OECD.

Osili, U.O. and B.T. Long (2008) "Does Female Schooling Reduce Fertility? Evidence from Nigeria," *Journal of Development Economics*, 87 (1): 57–75. doi: 10.1016/j.jdeveco.2007.10.003.

Salem, R. (2011) "Women's Economic Resources and Bargaining in Marriage: Does Egyptian Women's Status Depend on Earnings or Marriage Payments?" Gender and Work in the MENA Region Working Paper Series No. 18: Poverty, Job Quality, and Labor Market Dynamics. Cairo.

Salem, R., Y.F. Cheong, and K.M. Yount (2018) "Is Women's Work a Pathway to their Agency in Rural Minya, Egypt?" *Social Indicators Research*, 136: 807–31.

Salemi, C. and A. Rashed (2015) "Gender Attitudes among Egyptian Youth: An Analysis of the 2014 SYPE Outcomes," in R. Roushdy and M. Sieverding (eds) *Panel Survey of Young People in Egypt (SYPE) 2014: Generating Evidence for Policy and Programs*, pp. 242–74. Cairo: Population Council.

Schoumaker, B. (2014) *TFR2: Stata Module to Compute Age-Specific Fertility Rates (ASFRs), Total Fertility Rates (TFRs), Fertility Trends and Rate Ratios from Birth Histories*, Statistical Software Components S457766, Boston College Department of Economics.

Selwaness, I. and C. Krafft (2021) "The Dynamics of Family Formation and Women's Work: What Facilitates and Hinders Female Employment in the Middle East and North Africa?" *Population Research and Policy Review*, 40(3): 533–587.

Sieverding, M. (2012) *Gender and Generational Change in Egypt*. University of California, Berkeley.

Sieverding, M. and R. Hassan (2016) *"Her Future is Marriage": Young People's Attitudes towards Gender Roles and the Gender Gap in Egypt.* Cairo: Population Council.

World Bank (2013) *Opening Doors: Gender Equality and Development in the Middle East and North Africa.* Washington, DC: World Bank.

World Bank (2018) *Women Economic Empowerment Study.* Washington, DC: World Bank.

Yount, K.M. (2005) "Women's Family Power and Gender Preference in Minya, Egypt," *Journal of Marriage and Family,* 67 (2): 410–28.

Yount, K.M., A.A. Crandall, and Y.F. Cheong (2018) "Women's Age at First Marriage and Long-Term Economic Empowerment in Egypt," *World Development,* 102: 124–34. doi: 10.1016/j.worlddev.2017.09.013.

Yount, K.M., S. Zureick-Brown, and R. Salem (2014) "Intimate Partner Violence and Women's Economic and Non-Economic Activities in Minya, Egypt," *Demography,* 51 (3): 1069–99.

Yount, K.M. et al. (2016) "Measurement of Women's Agency in Egypt: A National Validation Study," *Social Indicators Research,* 18 (3): 386–92. doi: 10.1007/s11205-015-1074-7.

9

Social Protection and Vulnerability in Egypt

A Gendered Analysis

Irene Selwaness and Maye Ehab

9.1 Introduction

This chapter evaluates the state of social protection coverage in Egypt, examining contributory and non-contributory schemes. Over 20 years, poverty rates in Egypt experienced continuous and sharp increases from 16.7 percent in 1999 to 32.5 percent in 2018. There is a transformation into a new "unsocial" contract (El-Haddad, 2020), where an increasing proportion of the population is left behind. There is an immediate need to assess and further develop social protection systems in a sustainable way over the life course, in order to maintain living standards and to help attenuate increased vulnerabilities due to these poverty hikes (ILO, 2017; Selwaness and Messkoub, 2019).

The chapter examines three timely areas of social protection on the social policy agenda in Egypt that experienced noticeable changes in the past two decades. The first is contributory social insurance coverage among workers, and the time to acquire such coverage on the labor market. This is to assess who the most vulnerable workers are in terms of lack of social insurance coverage, and how persistent is such vulnerability. The second relates to the patterns of receipt of social protection benefits at the household level and the extent of effective social protection coverage at the national level. These benefits include retirement pensions, transfers from faith-based organizations, and non-contributory social assistance benefits that we refer to as "social pensions." The social pensions include the new conditional cash transfer (CCT) programs Takaful (Solidarity) and Karama (Dignity). It is important to note that non-contributory benefits are tax-financed ones that aim to provide a minimum income and often involve targeting. On the other hand, benefits based on contributory schemes are based on workers' contributions/payments to a social insurance scheme, in order to guarantee consumption smoothing in retirement periods or in times of shocks (Kidd, 2016).

We also show the effective social protection coverage, at the household level, following the methodology of the International Labour Organization (ILO, 2017),

Irene Selwaness and Maye Ehab, *Social Protection and Vulnerability in Egypt: A Gendered Analysis* In: *The Egyptian Labor Market: A Focus on Gender and Economic Vulnerability*. Edited by: Caroline Krafft and Ragui Assaad, Oxford University Press. © Economic Research Forum 2022. DOI: 10.1093/oso/9780192847911.003.0010 which is the proportion of households that either receive at least one type of social protection benefits or have a working member contributing to social security.[1] This is a new piece of information that was not previously explored in Egypt. Moreover, given the important changes that were introduced in the smart food ration card system since 2014, the chapter explores the patterns of having these cards in 2018. Finally, the third topic is the evolution of health insurance coverage to identify who are the most vulnerable groups.[2]

9.1.1 Background

The labor market has been characterized by a continuing decline in the share of public sector jobs (Chapter 2, Chapter 5, this volume). In 2006, such a decline was associated with an equivalent rise in informal (socially uninsured) private wage employment (Assaad, 2009). In 2012, the situation worsened and irregular wage work expanded, rather than informal but regular private wage employment (Assaad and Krafft, 2015). In 2018, irregularity declined, but there was an unprecedented and high share of informal private sector wage employment, especially such employment outside a fixed establishment (Chapter 2, this volume). High rates of informal wage employment may be related to relatively high social insurance contributions rates, which are jointly paid by the employee (14 percent), the employer (25 percent), and the government (1 percent) (Helmy, 2008; Loewe, 2014; Roushdy and Selwaness, 2019). The law mandates employers to enroll their workers in the social insurance scheme. Yet, in a context of weak enforcement of law, employers often do not enroll their workers to avoid formalization costs (social insurance contributions, paying full wages during paid/sick leave, and during maternity leave in case of women), or tend to underreport the insurable wage to the social insurance scheme (Roushdy and Selwaness, 2019). In 2019, the government introduced a reform in the social insurance scheme (Law 148/2019) in which contribution rates will be reduced to 11 percent by employees and 18.75 percent by private sector employers. This will bring total contribution rate to 29.75 percent for private sector workers, instead of around 40 percent under the old law (Official Gazette, 2019). The impact of this law and whether it would lead to higher social insurance coverage needs further research, as there has been a reform in wage taxation at the same time, and in 2020 an additional 1 percent tax on all salaries to raise more funds after the COVID-19 shock (Enterprise, 2020).

---

[1] This is the methodology proposed to calculate SDG indicator 1.3.1 on "the percentage of the total population covered by at least one type of social protection benefit" (ILO, 2017: 123). It is noteworthy that the ILO's social protection coverage rates are computed at the individual level. Thus, any difference between our estimates of coverage rates and theirs is likely because our calculation is based on the household level, rather than the individual level.

[2] See Krafft, Assaad, and Rahman (2021) for more details on ELMPS 2018. Data are publicly available from www.erfdataportal.com.

On the non-contributory schemes front, there have been important changes and reforms. In 2015, Egypt introduced Takaful (Solidarity) and Karama (Dignity), two CCT programs (World Bank, 2015). Their objective was reducing poverty and vulnerability among the poorest households. Takaful targets poor households who have children under 18 years old, conditional on their schooling enrollment and health care follow-up. Karama provides cash income to disabled people and the poor elderly who are not able to work. To be able to target the right families and individuals, eligibility to participate is determined using a proxy means test (Breisinger et al., 2018; Selwaness and Messkoub, 2019). Breisinger et al. (2018) examined program satisfaction drawing on a sample of Takaful beneficiaries and the program's impact on consumption, education, and health outcomes. In addition, the latest report of World Social Protection (ILO, 2017) highlighted that Egypt was ranked second (37 percent) in terms of effective (as opposed to legal) coverage rates, after South Africa (48 percent). Around 37 percent of the Egyptian population were covered by at least one social protection scheme, whether by receiving contributory or non-contributory benefits,[3] or by having at least one working family member who was actively contributing to the social insurance system.

The food ration card system has also been reformed. The government had been suffering from increased expenditure on food subsidies, weak targeting, and high leakage to the non-poor. In 2000, the Egyptian government tried to improve targeting through the use of self-targeting, in which products of lower quality were offered to discourage rich people from buying them. However, the government spending on food subsidies was still high and required restructuring (Ghoneim, 2013). In 2006, the smart food ration card system was introduced to improve both the targeting and the efficiency of the food subsidy system. In 2010, regulations governing the smart ration cards were revised. Until 2014, the number of beneficiaries on the smart food ration cards was restricted to a maximum of four individuals per household. In 2014, this number of individuals per family restriction was removed in accordance with Ministerial Decree No. 215 for 2014. Afterwards, the beneficiaries used their savings from the Balady bread consumption subsidy to purchase goods under the ration cards. Thus, not only did the number of individuals become unrestricted, but also the two subsidy systems were merged into one (Abdalla and Al-Shawarby, 2017).

Finally, Egypt embarked upon health insurance program reform in July 2018 to expand coverage and enhance the quality of this program. The low quality of medical services and care in the government facilities shift individuals, even if insured through the government's Health Insurance Organization, to use private

---

[3] Non-contributory benefits are tax-financed benefits that aim to provide a minimum income, often known as social assistance pensions, especially when they involve targeting. On the other hand, benefits based on contributory schemes are based on workers' contributions/payments to a social insurance scheme, in order to guarantee consumption smoothing in retirement periods or in times of shocks (Kidd, 2016).

sector services that are associated with a substantial amount of out-of-pocket expenditures (World Bank, 2018). In this context, the poor and the most vulnerable segments of the population are not only likely to be excluded from public health insurance, but they also face greater challenges in accessibility and affordability to private clinics and hospitals. They are thus more exposed to worse health outcomes than average.

Our findings show that vulnerability has deepened in many forms. In the labor market, social insurance coverage has substantially declined, leaving an important share of workers without any protection against injuries, sickness, disability, unemployment, and death. This will translate into fewer elderly receiving employment-related pensions, hence more old-age fragility; these pensions represent a key social protection benefit that households rely on. Household receipt of social assistance has slightly increased over time, with the introduction of Takaful and Karama. With the increase in poverty rate during the last decade, the fast increases in prices, and the COVID-19 shock that led to many job/income losses, this implies that more households are prone to fall into poverty. Health insurance coverage is limited to privileged segments in society. The vast majority lack any form of health insurance, in particular rural women and young people aged 20–29, which may have consequences for their health and wellbeing (Chapter 11, this volume).

This chapter is organized into six sections. Following this introduction, Section 9.2 introduces the ELMPS data used in the analysis. Section 9.3 investigates the pattern of contributory social insurance at work and its evolution over time. The effective social protection coverage of households and the different sources of contributory and non-contributory benefits are examined in Section 9.4, with a special focus on recipients of social assistance non-contributory pensions as well as Takaful and Karama beneficiaries. Section 9.5 examines the evolution of health insurance coverage along with the different types of insurance over time. Section 9.6 provides conclusions and policy implications.

9.2 Data Sources

The 1998 to 2018 ELMPS waves were used to analyze access to social insurance coverage over time, and how it varies by worker- and firm-level characteristics. For the analysis of social insurance coverage, our sample consists of workers aged 18–59 years, as this is the age bracket where individuals are legally eligible to enroll in the social insurance scheme, with a minimum age of 18 and a mandatory retirement age set at 60.[4] Our analysis focuses on the market definition of work.

---

[4] Public sector workers are eligible to enroll by age 16, and non-wage workers are legally entitled to retirement by age 65. Yet, we checked coverage rates for workers aged 15–64 and found similar patterns as our chosen sample of ages 18–59.

The analysis of the receipt of social protection benefits was based on the 2006, 2012, and 2018 waves that include questions on non-labor income sources. We harmonized these to be comparable over time. The 2006 and 2012 waves had information on whether the household received, during the last year, Sadat or Mubarak pensions, which were forms of non-contributory social assistance benefit, also known as the comprehensive scheme (Ma'ash al-daman); other types of social assistance from the Ministry of Social Solidarity; retirement pensions, which are employment-related pensions based on contributory schemes;[5] transfers from faith-based organizations; and other sources of non-labor income such as interest or rent on buildings/lands. The 2018 questionnaire included information on the receipt of the newly introduced CCTs—Takaful and Karama—other types of social assistance benefits,[6] transfers from faith-based organizations, and other sources of non-labor income. The 2018 wave also provided information on whether households had smart food ration cards, a piece of information that was not available in 2006 or 2012. For health insurance coverage, we used the 2012 and 2018 waves that have comparable questions on the coverage and the different types of health insurance for individuals aged 15 and above (2012) or those aged six years and above (2018).

9.3 The Evolution of Social Insurance Coverage at Work

9.3.1 Coverage gap by type of employment

The percentage of workers covered by social insurance (the incidence of social insurance coverage) has substantially declined over time. In 2018, coverage reached around 30 percent of overall employment for men and 43 percent for women (Figure 9.1). This was the lowest coverage rate over this 20-year period among male workers, decreasing from 50 percent in 1998, to 43 percent in 2006, and 39 percent in 2012. As for female workers, coverage in 2018 was almost at the same level as it was in 2006 (41 percent), down from 61 percent in 1998.[7]

Among men, the most vulnerable type of wage work in terms of access to social insurance was private sector wage work outside a fixed establishment, where only

---

[5] Retirement pensions can also be received by persons who never worked or were never socially insured during their career, if they were eligible to inherit the pension, including widows, dependent sons/brothers younger than 21, disabled dependent sons/brothers of any age, and unmarried daughters and sisters (ISSA, 2017). This type of retirement pension is called a survivor pension.

[6] The questionnaire did not specify this "other type of social assistance benefits." Thus we assume that it can be a continuity of Sadat/Mubarak benefits, as well as the "other type of pensions" category that was indicated in 2006 and 2012.

[7] Note that the increase in coverage rates among female workers in 2012 relative to 2006, reaching 54 percent, was probably an artifact of a selection effect. There was a sharp decline in female labor force participation between 2006 and 2012, which led the good jobs to be overrepresented (Roushdy and Selwaness, 2015).

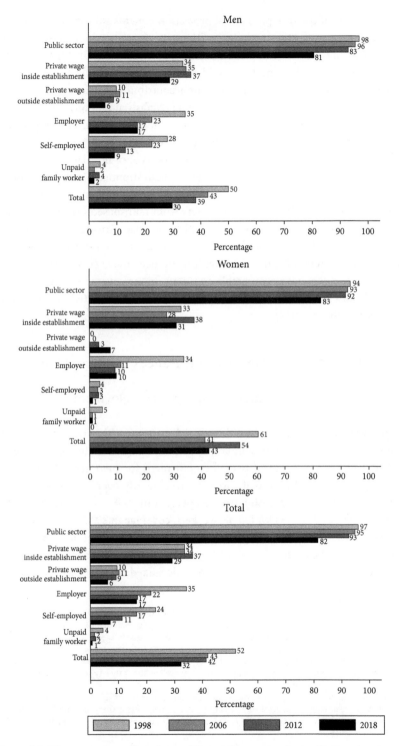

Figure 9.1 The percentage of workers with social insurance by institutional sector, sex, and wave, employed individuals aged 18–59, 1998–2018.

Source: Authors' calculations based on data from ELMPS 1998–2018.

6 percent of wage workers were covered in 2018, down from around 9 percent to 11 percent during 1998–2012. This is alarming since the share of private sector wage work outside a fixed establishment in overall employment increased substantially in 2018 (see Chapter 2), reaching almost a third of male employment (31 percent), representing by far the largest type of employment in Egypt for men.

Private sector wage work inside an establishment, the second largest type of work in relative terms (28 percent), also experienced important declines in social insurance coverage rates from 37 percent in 2012 to 29 percent in 2018 (Figure 9.1). The same pattern was observed for women who were employed in private sector wage work inside establishments, but to a lesser extent than men.

There is an important gender gap in terms of social insurance coverage among non-wage workers. Only 10 percent of female employers were covered in 2018, compared with an average of 17 percent among men. Moreover, coverage among self-employed women was barely at 1 percent in 2018, down from 3–4 percent in earlier years, compared with 9 percent for men. This is problematic, because almost a third of employed women (31 percent) were concentrated in non-wage market work in 2018. This implies that an important share of employed women was unprotected against unforeseen events and had no access to job-related benefits such as maternity or paid leaves.

Surprisingly, there also exists a widening coverage gap in the public sector, which is almost similar for men and women. The percentage of socially insured workers in the public sector declined substantially to 82 percent in 2018, down from 93–5 percent in 2006–12.

With this declining trend in social insurance coverage in various types of employment, the labor market is becoming more vulnerable, with important shares of workers outside the purview of social security. By 2018, of all employed men, almost half worked in informal (i.e. without social insurance coverage) private sector wage work (29 percent outside establishments and 20 percent inside establishments); this had almost doubled since 1998, whereas the share of men in formal private sector wage work in total employment was almost stalling over time (8–12 percent).[8] As for women, while the largest employer remained the public sector, followed by non-wage work that was almost uncovered, women also became more likely to engage in informal private sector wage work.

9.3.2 Coverage gap by wage level

The patterns of social insurance coverage by monthly wage quintiles reveal that the incidence of social insurance coverage is positively associated with the monthly wage level (Figure 9.2). The lowest paid were generally the most

[8] See Table A9.1 and Figure A9.2 in Selwaness and Ehab (2019).

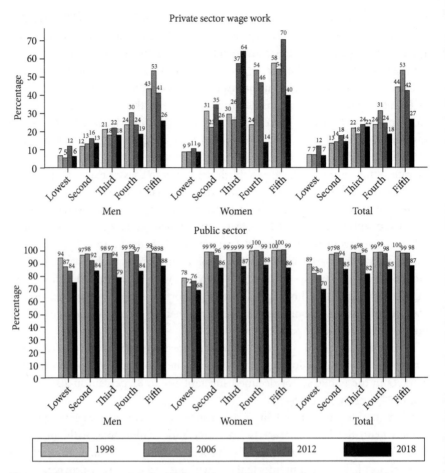

Figure 9.2 The percentage of workers with social insurance by sector, monthly wage quintile, sex, and wave, wage workers aged 18–59, 1998–2018.
Source: Authors' calculations based on data from ELMPS 1998–2018.

vulnerable workers in terms of lack of coverage. For example, in the private sector, male wage workers in the bottom 20 percent of the wage distribution, those whose monthly wage earnings were in the lowest quintile, had the lowest proportion of covered workers (6–12 percent during 1998–2018), whereas those whose monthly wage earnings were situated in the fifth quintile had the highest incidence of social insurance coverage over time (26–53 percent during 1998–2018). This is consistent with the fact that the working poor might not be able to afford contributing to social insurance and have high discount rates (Palacios and Robalino, 2009). The high discount rates are also reflected in the consistent preference among unemployed individuals for a higher minimum pay to accept a formal job (a job that is subject to taxation and social insurance contributions) than the minimum pay for an informal job (Chapter 5, this volume). While this holds for both the public and the private sector, low-paid wage workers in the public sector were almost ten times more likely to be socially insured (average of 70 percent in 2018) than their peers in the private sector (7 percent overall in 2018). Over time, coverage rates have deteriorated for all wage quintiles. Yet the decline was accentuated for the higher wage quintiles, although they still had the highest coverage rate across all quintiles (27 percent in the private sector). This can suggest that the deterioration in job quality has even affected high-wage earners.

9.3.3   Coverage gap in private sector wage work

Because an important share of the Egyptian workforce is engaged in uncovered private sector wage work, both inside and outside establishments, it is therefore necessary to examine who is more prone to work without social insurance in the private wage sector, in terms of firm size, economic activity, and individual characteristics such as age, education, and marital status. The share of uncovered private sector workers in total employment has been expanding to constitute 49 percent among men, 19 percent among women, and 43 percent overall in 2018.[9]

In terms of firm size, Figure 9.3 shows that coverage rates were positively associated with larger firm size/work inside establishments. Yet all firm size categories witnessed a decline in coverage rates. Male workers outside establishments or in micro-firms were, on average, the least likely to be socially insured over the 20-year period. The coverage rates in outside establishment jobs were already low, ranging between 10–11 percent in 1998–2006, and declined to 6 percent in 2018. Although male workers in small firms had better coverage rates than those in micro-firms or those outside establishments, they also experienced an important decline of 17 percentage points (p.p.) between 2006 (29 percent) and 2018 (12 percent).

Thus, between 2012 and 2018, the widened coverage gap in private sector wage employment was primarily due to the rapid employment growth, in 2018, in outside establishment jobs where 94 percent of workers lacked social insurance, and small firms with 5 to 24 workers, where 88 percent of workers lacked social insurance (Chapter 2, this volume; Assaad et al., 2019).

As for medium firms, slightly more than half of workers were covered in 1998 and 2006 (56–55 percent). In 2018 this proportion of covered workers decreased by 13 p.p. (to 42 percent). While it is true that large firms' male workers remained the most likely to be covered, when compared with other firm size categories, their coverage rates also declined from around 70 percent in 1998, 2006, and 2012, to 59 percent in 2018 (an 11 p.p. decline).

---

[9] See Table A9.1 and Figure A9.2 in Selwaness and Ehab (2019).

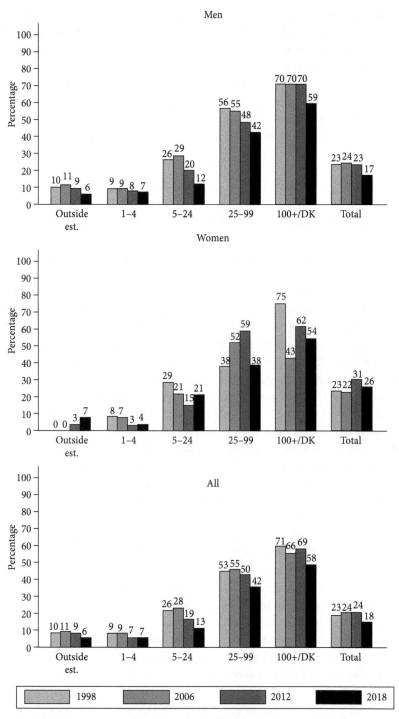

Figure 9.3 The percentage of workers with social insurance by firm size, sex, and wave, private sector wage workers aged 18–59, 1998–2018.

Source: Authors' calculations based on data from ELMPS 1998–, 2006, 2012, and 2018.

Women in the private sector became on average less likely to be socially insured in 2018 (26 percent) than in 2012 (31 percent). But unlike men, the decline in social insurance coverage rates was not cross-cutting for all firm size categories. As shown in Figure 9.3, employed women in small firms were more likely to be socially insured in 2018. The proportion of women covered in small firms followed a U-shape, declining between 2006 and 2012, then increasing in 2018 to reach the same level as 2006. This could be good news for the dynamics of women's employment and its quality, if policies to promote small firms' expansion, and to alleviate their tax burden, were adopted.

Like men, women who worked in both medium (25-99 workers) and large (100 or more/DK) firms were overall much more likely to be socially insured than their peers in smaller firms or outside establishments. Yet the coverage gap in these firms became larger between 2012 and 2018, as coverage dropped from 59 percent to 38 percent in medium firms and from 62 percent to 54 percent in large firms. Although coverage rates increased among the growing forms of employment for women, namely small firms, such an increase was not high enough to counteract sharp declines in coverage rates in medium and large firms, thus resulting in an overall widening of the coverage gap among women.

We now turn to coverage rates by economic activity (ISIC 1-digt level),[10] shown in Figure 9.4. For men, broad manufacturing and utilities was the sector that

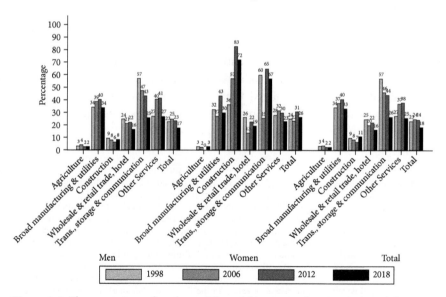

Figure 9.4 The percentage of workers with social insurance by economic activity, sex, and wave, private sector wage workers aged 18–59, 1998–2018.

Source: Authors' calculations based on data from ELMPS 1998–2018.

[10] In order to ensure adequate cell sizes, we grouped the economic activity sectors, based on the International Standard Industrial Classification (ISIC) at the one-digit level, in six categories. The first was agriculture, forestry and fishing; the second was broad manufacturing and utilities, which includes

provided most social insurance coverage (34 percent in 2018, down from 39 percent in 1998). Transportation, storage, and communications, as well as the "other services" sector, both had around a quarter of their workers covered in 2018, yet they had the fastest decline in coverage rates since 2012. As expected, and because the majority of their jobs were outside establishments, agriculture (2 percent in 2018) and construction (8 percent in 2018) maintained the lowest coverage rates over time. For women, the two sectors with the highest coverage rates were broad manufacturing and utilities (30 percent in 2018), as well as "other services" (23 percent in 2018). It is worth noting that the latter sector, including education, and human health and social work activities, usually recruited the highest share of women.[11] Both sectors had some of the largest declines in terms of social insurance coverage since 2012, with a 13 p.p. decline for the broad manufacturing sector, and a 7 p.p. decline for the "other services" sector.

As for occupation (Figure 9.5),[12] among male private sector workers, the white-collar high skilled were the most likely to have social insurance coverage in their jobs (48 percent in 2018), followed by blue-collar low skilled (23 percent in 2018). The blue-collar high-skilled group had the lowest coverage rates (5 percent in 2018), because by definition of their occupations, they were likely working in outside establishment jobs. These rankings in coverage rates were the same over time, yet between 2012 and 2018, coverage rates declined the most for workers in blue-collar low-skilled jobs (16 p.p.).

The coverage gap also varies by individual characteristics. According to Figure 9.6, there is a strong and positive association between coverage and education level, where those with university education were the most likely to be socially insured in their jobs for both men and women (36 percent in 2018). Over time, all education levels suffered from a widening coverage gap. The largest decline in coverage rates was among workers with university education (a 12 p.p. decline for both men and women over the period 2012–18).

---

manufacturing, mining and quarrying, electricity and gas, steam and air conditioning supply, and water supply, and sewage and waste management. Construction is the third category. Wholesale and retail trade, and repair of motor vehicles and motorcycles were combined with accommodation and food service activities to form the fourth category. The fifth category was composed of transportation and storage, and information and communication. Finally, "other services" was the sixth category, including the remaining economic activities such as financial and insurance activities, real estate activities, professional, scientific, and technical activities, administrative and support service activities, education, human health and social work activities, arts, entertainment and recreation, etc.

[11] For further details on the evolution of the employment structure in the Egyptian labor market, see Chapter 2 (this volume) and recent research on the Egyptian labor market (Assaad et al., 2019; Assaad et al., 2020).

[12] We grouped the nine occupations based on the ISCO 88 one-digit level in four categories. Managers, professionals, technicians, and associate professionals constituted the white collar high skilled; Clerks and service and sales workers represented the white collar low-skilled category. The blue-collar high-skilled category is composed of skilled agricultural, forestry and fishery workers, and craft and trade workers. Finally, the fourth category, which is the blue-collar low skilled, includes plant and machine operators as well as those engaged in elementary occupations.

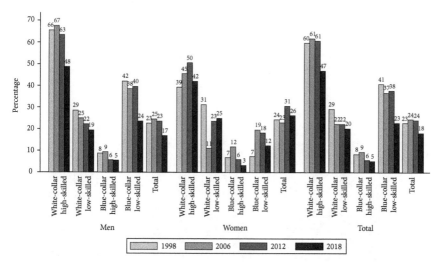

Figure 9.5 The percentage of workers with social insurance by occupation, sex, and wave, private sector wage workers aged 18–59, 1998–2018.

Source: Authors' calculations based on data from ELMPS 1998–2018.

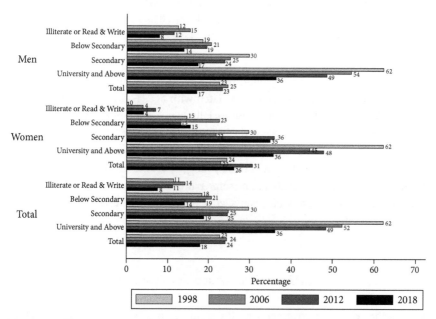

Figure 9.6 The percentage of workers with social insurance by education level, sex, and wave, private sector wage workers aged 18–59, 1998–2018.

Source: Authors' calculations based on data from ELMPS 1998–2018.

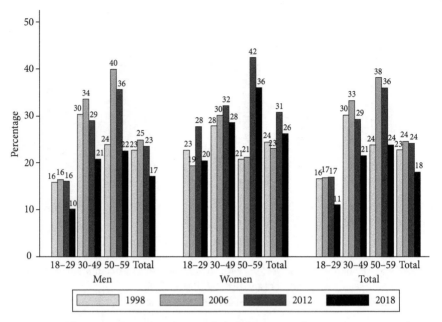

Figure 9.7 The percentage of workers with social insurance by age group, sex, and wave, private sector wage workers aged 18–59, 1998–2018.
Source: Authors' calculations based on data from ELMPS 1998–2018.

Finally, we see that, among men in private sector wage employment, social insurance coverage was positively associated with age (Figure 9.7). Young workers (18–29) were the least likely to be socially insured (16 percent between 1998 and 2012) and experienced a 6 p.p. decline in their coverage rates in 2018 to reach 10 percent. Although coverage rates for prime age workers (30–49) and older workers (50–59) were higher than their younger peers, they experienced sharper declines between 2012 and 2018. The same pattern was observed for women who were employed in private sector wage work inside establishments, but to a lesser extent than men.

9.3.4 Dynamics of access to coverage

Besides the widening coverage gap, the duration of time spent working before gaining social insurance became longer for specific types of first jobs, indicating the existence of an informality trap. To show this, we use survival analysis to calculate the proportion of workers covered by years of work since first job (Kaplan-Meier failure curves), excluding spells of non-employment between jobs (if the individual experienced any).[13] Not only were new entrants increasingly engaged in informal jobs in the recent years (Chapter 4, this volume) or in uncovered wage work,[14] but also the duration to gain social insurance became longer for specific types of first jobs, indicating a sort of an informality trap.

Figure 9.8 shows the proportion of workers who acquired social insurance coverage with each year of work, distinguishing between the different types of first jobs (public sector, private sector wage work inside a fixed establishment, private sector regular wage work outside a fixed establishment, and non-wage work including employers, self-employed, and unpaid family workers). Entrants starting in the public sector were the most likely to acquire social insurance coverage immediately upon getting hired (71 percent of men and 74 percent of women). In

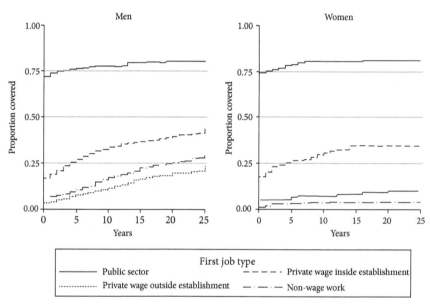

Figure 9.8 Proportion of workers with social insurance by years since the start of first job, by the type of first job in the labor market and by sex, ages 15–64, 2018.

Note: Kaplan-Meier failure curves.

Source: Authors' calculations based on data from ELMPS 2018.

---

[13] The duration to acquire social insurance coverage on the labor market is computed as the number of years an individual had to wait before acquiring it, even if he/she moved between jobs. If he/she never had social insurance in any of his/her jobs, then our duration variable is censored (this includes those who left the labor force and never had social insurance, whose variable is censored at the year they moved to inactivity). If the individual got social insurance before going out of the labor force, the variable has a value (which is the numbers of years it took him/her to get social insurance). If he/she experienced episodes of non-employment, whether unemployment and inactivity, and is still working until the survey year, we only count the years of work until acquiring social insurance coverage, if ever.

[14] See Appendix Figure 3 in Selwaness and Ehab (2019) for more details.

contrast, only 16 percent of male and 17 percent of female workers who started as a wage worker inside a fixed establishment in the private sector got social insurance coverage upon hire. They had somewhat increasing chances of acquiring social insurance coverage on the labor market over time, whether remaining at this same type of first job or by moving to other jobs. In spite of this, their coverage rates remained considerably lower than that of their peers who started in public sector jobs (e.g. after ten years, 32 percent for men and 28 percent for women). This is why there is a continued strong preference for the public sector, especially for women (Chapter 5, this volume).

As for men whose first job was in private sector wage work outside a fixed establishment, they were four times less likely to get covered immediately upon hire (4 percent), compared with their peers who initially engaged in inside establishment private sector wage work. Although the proportion covered among wage workers who started outside establishments more than doubled in ten years of employment, their chances of coverage over time remained the lowest and did not even exceed 18 percent in 20 years of work. This indicates that the coverage gap is likely to be persistent over time for those whose first jobs were outside establishment private sector wage work. Male new entrants in non-wage market work not only were slightly more likely to be covered upon starting their first job (17 percent) than those who started in outside establishment private sector wage work, but also gained faster access to coverage.

Thus, the most disadvantaged group of workers in terms of social insurance coverage were those who started as private sector wage workers outside establishments, followed by those starting in non-wage work. Furthermore, even the new entrants who started in private sector wage work inside establishments, while they face higher coverage rates at the start of their jobs and might have shorter time until coverage, have coverage rates that were far from being universal.

The firm characteristics of the first job, in terms of formality status and size categories, substantially matter for the dynamics of access to social insurance coverage. On the left panel of Figure 9.9, we show the proportion covered, among men, by formality status of the first job firm combined with the type of this first job, distinguishing between starting inside establishments in informal private sector firms, outside establishments in informal private sector firms, private sector wage work in formal firms (whether inside or outside), and public sector work.[15] As for the right panel, we show the proportion covered among male workers by

---

[15] Formal firms are defined as those with at least one worker who is formally hired, while informal firms as those with no formal workers. We construct the formality status of the firm based on the question on whether other workers were covered or had legal contracts, in case the interviewed worker does not have any of them. Thus, the firm is formal if the interviewed worker holds a contract and/or is covered (i.e. formally hired), or if he/she reported that other workers have contracts or are covered in case he/she is informally hired. The firm is considered informal if the individual is informal and if he/she reported that the other workers were informal too.

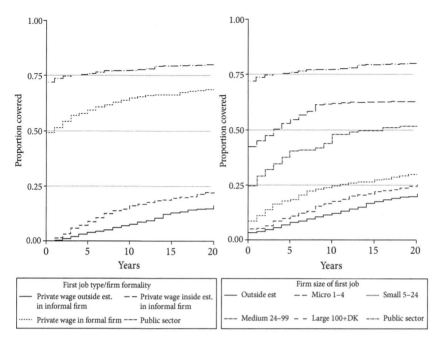

Figure 9.9 Proportion of workers with social insurance by years since the start of first job, by firm formality status and firm size category of first job, men aged 18–59, 2018.

Notes: Kaplan-Meier failure curves. Restricted to those entering since 1981.

Source: Authors' calculations based on data from ELMPS 2018.

size categories of the first job firm (outside establishment, micro-, small/medium, large, or public sector establishment).

Around 49 percent of male workers who started their first jobs in private sector formal firms were covered at the start of their jobs with a median duration of one year for acquiring coverage. The proportion covered among this group of workers starting in formal firms reached 65 percent after ten years of work. On the other hand, after ten years of work, men who started in informal private sector firms, whether outside or inside establishments, reached a coverage rate of 16 percent (for those starting inside establishments) and 8 percent (for those starting outside establishments).

In terms of firm size, the second lowest coverage rates upon hire and over time, after outside establishment private sector wage work, were for first jobs in micro-firms. The proportion covered at the start of their jobs was only 5 percent and increased to 17 percent in ten years of employment. This is a similar proportion to those who started in informal firms inside establishments. Starting in small firms was associated with slightly higher chances of social insurance coverage upon getting hired (9 percent) or in ten years of work (25 percent). Male new entrants who started in medium firms were substantially better off than those who started in micro- or small firms, since their coverage rates at the start of their jobs were about 25 percent and increased to 48 percent after ten years of employment. The shortest duration to coverage in the private sector was observed for first jobs located in large firms, where 43 percent of workers were covered at the start of their jobs and 62 percent became so in ten years of work, with a median time of three years to social insurance coverage. This pattern for large firms was quite similar to the pattern of access to social insurance among workers who started in formal private sector firms.

A similar pattern of time to social insurance is observed for women (Figure 9.10), except for two differences. First, if they started in formal private sector firms (on the left panel), although their median time was the same as for men, the proportion of female workers covered upon starting (43 percent) were a little lower than that for their male peers (47 percent). Second, compared with men (43 percent), they were less likely to acquire social insurance upon starting their first jobs in large firms (36 percent). They acquired it slower than men as coverage rates reached around 45 percent after ten years of employment. This suggests that employers may wait a little longer to formalize their newly hired women, given that the potential higher costs related to their formal hiring (such as paying full maternity leave, or establishing a nursery in case the hired number of women exceeded 99 workers).

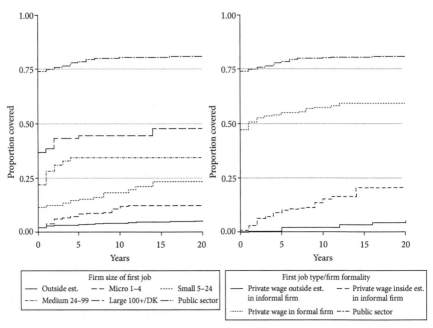

Figure 9.10 Proportion of workers with social insurance by years since the start of first job, by firm formality status and firm size category of first job, women aged 18–59, 2018.
Note: Kaplan-Meier failures curves. Restricted to those entering since 1981.
Source: Authors' calculations based on data from ELMPS 2018.

9.4 Social Protection Benefits and Effective Coverage

This section discusses the evolution in coverage and targeting of social protection benefits in Egypt. The extent of coverage is reflected in the percentage of households that received at least one type of social protection benefit, whether contributory or not. As for the degree of targeting efficiency, by analyzing the characteristics of the beneficiary households, we show the percentage of beneficiary households who are most vulnerable or can be identified as poor.

9.4.1 Social protection coverage over time

Figure 9.11 shows the percentage of households covered with at least one social protection benefit as described in the introduction. In terms of overall social protection coverage, around 57 percent of households in 2018 either received non-contributory or contributory benefit entitlements, or had at least one actively contributing member. This coverage rate fell from 62 percent in 2012 and 68 percent in 2006. This decline in the overall social protection coverage was mainly driven by the decline in the percentage of households with at least one actively contributing member. The proportion of households with at least one working member who actively contributed to the social insurance scheme declined in

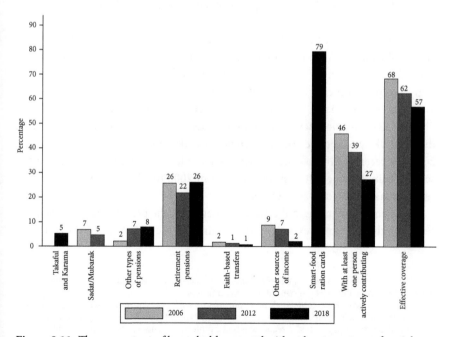

Figure 9.11 The percentage of households covered with at least one type of social protection scheme/benefit, 2006–18.

Source: Authors' calculations based on ELMPS 2006–18.

2018, to 27 percent, compared with 39 percent in 2012 and 46 percent in 2006. This indicates that the decrease in social insurance coverage rates among workers also led many households, not only individuals, to fall outside the social insurance scheme umbrella.

Employment-related retirement pensions represent the most common type of benefit that households receive. Around 26 percent of Egyptian households received retirement pensions in 2006 and 2018. As for social assistance benefits, in 2006 around 7 percent and in 2012 around 5 percent of households received either Sadat or Mubarak pensions. In 2018, a similar percentage (5 percent) received Takaful or Karama. There was an important rise in the percentage of households receiving other types of social assistance transfers from 2 percent in 2006 to 7 percent in 2012, and a slight increase to 8 percent in 2018. If we combine the different types of social assistance transfers disbursed by the state (Sadat/Mubarak pensions, Takaful and/or Karama, and other types of social assistance), then the overall percentage of households covered by any of these social assistance transfers increased from 9 percent of households in 2006 to 13 percent in 2018. Faith-based transfers were received by 1–2 percent of households over the period 2006–18. As for in-kind transfers, smart food ration cards were the largest source of protection. The share of households who had food ration cards was 79 percent in 2018.

9.4.2 Receipt of social pensions and retirement pensions

This section examines the characteristics of households receiving social benefits,[16] and employment-related retirement pensions, in terms of wealth quintiles, region of residence, and gender of the head of household.[17]

By wealth quintiles,[18] the percentage of households who benefited from social assistance was inversely related to the household wealth quintile (left panel of Figure 9.12). The good news is that households in the lowest wealth quintile were the most likely to receive social assistance benefits over time. Between 2006 and 2018, the receipt of these benefits increased for all wealth quintiles, except for the second quintile, where it first increased from 2006 to 2012 (from 12 to 16 percent), then decreased in 2018 (13 percent).

As for employment-related retirement pensions, the percentage of households receiving these benefits experienced a decline between 2006 and 2012 across all

---

[16] We use terms such as social benefits/pensions or social assistance pensions interchangeably to designate non-contributory tax-financed pensions/transfers.

[17] For this analysis, we combined all non-contributory social assistance transfers (Sadat/Mubarak pensions in 2006-12, Takaful/Karama in 2018, and other types of social assistance pensions) into one measure. The more disaggregated categories of social protection transfers are depicted in Figure 9.11.

[18] We only show association, not causation, between wealth quintiles and the incidence of receiving specific types of benefits.

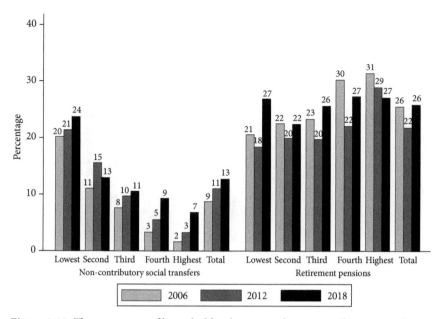

Figure 9.12 The percentage of households who received non-contributory social pensions or contributory retirement pensions by household wealth quintiles, 2006–18.
Source: Authors' calculations based on ELMPS 2006–18.

wealth quintiles. However, there was a reversal in 2018, except for the highest wealth quintile that was the most likely to benefit from retirement pensions in previous years (right panel of Figure 9.12). On the other hand, it is remarkable that the proportion of lowest wealth quintile households who received retirement pensions increased from 21 percent in 2006 to 27 percent in 2018, thus reaching similar levels to households in the fourth and fifth wealth quintiles. The lowest percentage of households benefiting from retirement pensions became the second wealth quintile households (22 percent), who also experienced a decline in social assistance pensions receipt. With the falling proportion of households with at least one actively contributing member, it is likely that, in the future, the proportion of households receiving retirement pensions will drop too.

The gender of the head of household is a strong predictor for the receipt of social assistance and retirement pensions. Overall, female-headed households were three times more likely than male-headed households to receive social assistance benefits (left panel of Figure 9.13) or employment-related retirement pensions (right panel of Figure 9.13). Yet the proportion of female-headed households who benefited from social assistance substantially declined from 22–25 percent in 2006–12 to 18 percent in 2018. On the other hand, the percentage of male-headed households who received social assistance increased from 7–8 percent in 2006–12 to 12 percent in 2018, likely owing to the introduction of Takaful/Karama.

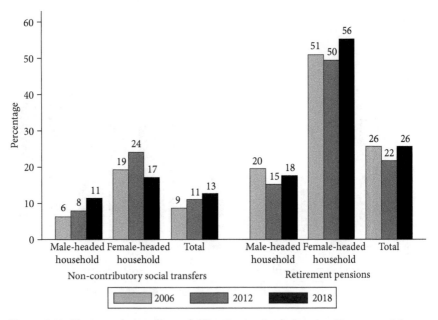

Figure 9.13 The percentage of households who received non-contributory social pensions or contributory retirement pensions by household head sex, 2006–18.
Source: Authors' calculations based on ELMPS 2006–18.

As for households who received employment-related retirement pensions, around 50–51 percent of all female-headed households received retirement pensions between 2006 and 2012, which further increased to 56 percent in 2018. This is in comparison with only 18 percent among male-headed households. These patterns are likely because female heads were more likely to be widowed (67 percent) than male heads (3 percent), and to be above 65 years old (31 percent) relative to male heads (12 percent), thus being more dependent on survivorship/retirement pensions.

The receipt of social assistance or retirement pensions also had important differences at the regional level. In 2006 and 2012, households in rural Upper Egypt were the most likely to receive social assistance, as opposed to Greater Cairo and Alexandria and the Suez Canal cities, where the proportion of such households was the lowest (Figure 9.14). In 2018, the patterns of receipt of social assistance had changed. It rose in Greater Cairo to reach around 20 percent of households, at almost similar rates to rural Upper Egypt. Households in rural Upper Egypt also became more likely to receive social assistance in 2018 (22 percent) than in 2006 or 2012 (16–17 percent). As for Lower Egypt, the receipt of social assistance in both urban and rural areas dropped.

The regional pattern of retirement pension receipt is opposite to that of social assistance receipt (right panel of Figure 9.14). Between 2006 and 2012, Greater Cairo and Alexandria and the Suez Canal cities had the highest receipt rates of retirement pensions, reaching around a third of households in these areas. Rural

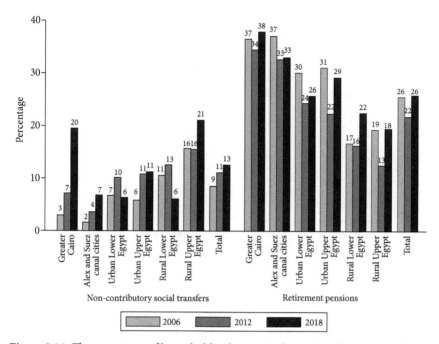

Figure 9.14 The percentage of households who received non-contributory social pensions or contributory retirement pensions by region of residence, 2006–18.
Source: Authors' calculations based on ELMPS 2006–18.

areas in Lower and Upper Egypt were associated with the lowest percentage of households receiving contributory pensions. This pattern is largely due to differences in access to formal jobs and social insurance coverage across regions.

9.4.3 Characteristics of households receiving social pensions

Moving to the targeting efficiency of social assistance non-contributory benefits, Table 9.1 shows the characteristics of households covered with these benefits. As expected, the majority of these households belong to the lowest and second wealth quintiles (64–72 percent over 2006–18). However, by 2018, they became less concentrated in these quintiles and more concentrated in the fourth (12 percent) and fifth (8 percent) wealth quintiles, hence suggesting increased leakage to the non-poor. The share of female-headed households receiving social pensions sharply dropped to 24 percent in 2018 (also reflected in their falling receipt rates in Figure 9.13), highlighting that female-headed households were increasingly exposed to vulnerability. Additionally, the regional distribution of receiving social assistance had changed by 2018, with relatively more beneficiary households in rural Upper Egypt (47 percent), fewer in rural Lower Egypt (17 percent), and more concentration in Greater Cairo (20 percent). This is in line with the changes in the percentage of households receiving social pensions, shown in Figure 9.14.

Table 9.1 Characteristics of households and heads of households receiving non-contributory social pensions (percentage), 2006–18.

	2006	2012	2018
Household wealth quintile			
Lowest	48	40	41
Second	24	28	23
Third	17	18	16
Fourth	8	9	12
Highest	3	5	8
Gender of head of household			
Male-headed household	58	60	76
Female-headed household	42	40	24
Region of residence			
Greater Cairo	6	12	20
Alex and Suez Canal cities	2	3	4
Urban Lower Egypt	9	10	5
Urban Upper Egypt	9	7	7
Rural Lower Egypt	37	36	17
Rural Upper Egypt	38	33	47
Household size			
1–4 individuals	47	58	51
5–8 individuals	42	37	47
More than 8	11	6	2
Education of head of household			
Illiterate or read and write	79	71	55
Below secondary	9	12	14
Secondary	9	14	26
University and above	2	4	6
Work status of head of household			
Public	9	8	8
Private wage work	14	17	41
Non-wage	37	23	21
No job	40	52	30
Total (%)	100	100	100
N (receiving households)	650	1,185	1,479
Percentage receiving	10	12	13
N (all households)	8,351	12,060	15,720

Source: Authors' calculations based on ELMPS 2012 and 2018.

9.4.4 Takaful and Karama coverage and targeting

Table 9.2 shows both the rate of receiving Takaful and/or Karama at the household level in 2018 by household and head of household characteristics, as well as the characteristics of beneficiary households. On average, 5 percent of households received these benefits (Figure 9.11). The rate of receipt of these cash transfers

Table 9.2 The percentage of households receiving Takaful and/or Karama (rate of receipt) and the distribution (percentage) of recipients by household and head of household characteristics, 2018.

	Rate of receipt		Distribution of recipients (percent)
	(percent)	N	
Household wealth quintile			
Lowest	13	3,491	51
Second	7	3,383	27
Third	3	3,028	13
Fourth	2	3,034	6
Highest	1	2,808	2
Gender of head of household			
Male-headed household	6	12,729	87
Female-headed household	3	3,017	13
Region of residence			
Greater Cairo	1	1,316	3
Alex and Suez Canal cities	2	1,009	4
Urban Lower Egypt	1	1,717	2
Urban Upper Egypt	6	2,000	9
Rural Lower Egypt	2	4,562	14
Rural Upper Egypt	14	5,142	68
Household size			
1–4 individuals	3	10,057	36
5–8 individuals	9	5,517	62
More than 8	13	172	3
Education of head of household			
Illiterate or read and write	8	5,718	55
Below secondary	5	1,991	13
Secondary	5	5,522	30
University and above	1	2,371	2
Missing	2	144	0
Work status of head of household			
Public sector	1	2,598	2
Private wage work	8	5,527	53
Non-wage	7	3,252	25
No Job	3	4,369	20
Age group of head of household			
15–24	1	519	1
25–29	5	1,567	7
30–64	6	11,320	84
65+	3	2,322	9
Percentage receiving	5		100
All		15,746	958

Source: Authors' calculations based on data from ELMPS 2018.

was inversely associated with wealth quintiles (Table 9.2).[19] The poorest house-holds, in the lowest wealth quintile, were the most likely to be receiving such cash transfers (13 percent). This is a little below the targeted program coverage, which was initially 20 percent of the poor in Egypt (World Bank, 2015). Moreover, households living in Upper Egypt were more likely than average to receive these benefits (14 percent in rural and 6 percent in urban areas). The lowest coverage rate was among households residing in Greater Cairo and urban Lower Egypt, where only 1 percent of households were enrolled.

Looking at the characteristics of beneficiary households (Table 9.2), around half of recipient households were among the poorest households who belong to the first quintile (51 percent). This share is not too far from the projected target-ing efficiency (60 percent), that is the share of recipient households who were under the poverty line. Rural areas included more than 80 percent of all Takaful and/or Karama recipient households, in particular rural Upper Egypt, where more than two-thirds (68 percent) of beneficiary households resided.

As for the characteristics of individuals, rather than households, who received Takaful and/or Karama in beneficiary households (Table 9.3), the majority of individual direct recipients were women (80 percent), illiterate or could read and write (62 percent), had no job (56 percent), and were aged 30–64 (61 percent).[20] A comparison reveals interesting differences between the characteristics of recip-ients at household level and those at individual level. While male-headed house-holds represented around 87 percent of recipient households, women constituted 80 percent of individual beneficiaries, showing that women were actually the direct recipient of these transfers in male-headed households.

9.4.5   Food ration card coverage

Despite the efforts made for improving the targeting of the food subsidy, three-quarters of the richest households had these cards in 2018, 77 percent of house-holds in the fourth and 70 percent in the fifth wealth quintile (Table 9.4, column one). Food ration card possession was highest in rural Upper Egypt (86 percent of households). Receipt of these smart cards was slightly higher for female-headed

---

[19] To mitigate the risk of reverse causality, we extracted the 2012 wealth quintiles for these benefi-ciary households from the panel data for the households who were tracked between 2012 and 2018. In doing so, the sample size of households for this variable became 11,992 (down from 15,742 house-holds in 2018. Yet when we compared the lagged wealth quintile and the 2018 wealth quintiles, the incidence rates of receiving those transfers and distribution of beneficiary households remained almost unchanged with quite similar associations in terms of magnitude and direction. Thus, we opted to keep the full sample of 2018 and use the 2018 wealth quintiles.
[20] For households receiving any type of benefit entitlement, the questionnaire included informa-tion on to whom these benefits accrued.

Table 9.3 The characteristics of individuals receiving Takaful and/or Karama in beneficiary households (percentage), 2018.

	Distribution of recipients (percent)
Sex	
Men	20
Women	80
Education	
Illiterate or read and write	62
Below secondary	16
Secondary	19
University and above	1
Missing	2
Work status	
Public sector	0
Private wage work	9
Non-wage	34
No Job	56
Age group	
0–14	12
15–24	7
25–29	13
30–64	61
65+	7
N	977

Source: Authors' calculations based on data from ELMPS 2018.

households (82 percent) than in male-headed households (78 percent). Possession of cards was inversely related to education level, where 85 percent of households whose head had no education had them, compared with 70 percent of those with university-educated heads.

We also examined the possession of food ration cards among those households that were not covered by any other type of the aforementioned benefits and with no actively contributing members. We found that the chance of having food ration cards was slightly lower (70 percent) among the households that fell out of any other type of coverage, relative to the average rate of receipt (79 percent) computed for all households. Female headed-households with no other safety net became less likely (67 percent) to have food ration cards than male-headed households (71 percent), contrary to the pattern observed including all households. Households with no other benefits in Greater Cairo (49 percent) and Alexandria and Suez Canal (31 percent) had much lower rates of food ration cards than average (70 percent) and compared with other regions.

Table 9.4 Percentage of households with smart food ration cards by household and head of household characteristics, 2018.

	Households with food ration cards		Households with food ration cards among those with no other benefits/coverage	
	Percent (1)	N (2)	Percent (3)	N (4)
Household wealth quintile				
Lowest	84	3,491	75	1,514
Second	84	3,383	76	1,781
Third	82	3,028	73	1,470
Fourth	77	3,034	67	1,411
Highest	69	2,808	57	980
Gender of head of household				
Male-headed household	79	12,729	71	6,268
Female-headed household	82	3,017	67	890
Region of residence				
Greater Cairo	68	1,316	49	351
Alexandria and Suez Canal	56	1,009	31	359
Urban Lower Egypt	83	1,717	75	814
Urban Upper Egypt	84	2,000	76	772
Rural Lower Egypt	84	4,562	77	2,379
Rural Upper Egypt	86	5,142	78	2,483
Household size				
1–4 individuals	75	10,057	64	4,714
5–8 individuals	86	5,517	81	2,381
More than 8	87	172	74	63
Education of head of household				
Illiterate or read and write	85	5,718	75	2,429
Below secondary	80	1,991	71	1,002
Secondary	79	5522	72	2,837
University and above	70	2,371	58	776
Missing	46	144	37	114
Work status of head of household				
Public sector	84	2,598	75	378
Private wage work	73	5,527	69	3,659
Non-wage	85	3,252	81	1,874
No job	80	4,369	59	1,247
Percentage receiving	**79**	**15,746**	**70**	**7,158**

Source: Authors' calculations based on data from ELMPS 2018.

9.5 Health Insurance Coverage

There are different modalities of health insurance coverage that we grouped into five categories: coverage through the general agency for health insurance,[21] coverage by syndicates, coverage through school if the individual is still in schooling,[22] coverage through employer or privately purchased insurance,[23] and no health insurance coverage. Figure 9.15 shows how individuals aged 15 years and above were distributed along these different categories of health insurance coverage and evolution over time. Almost three-quarters of the population (72 percent) reported not being covered by any type of health insurance in 2018, up from 68 percent in 2012. Such a decline in health insurance coverage was associated with a commensurate decline in the share of those who reported being covered by health insurance through the general agency for health insurance, which declined to 15 percent

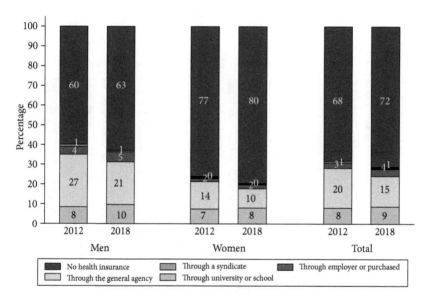

Figure 9.15 Health insurance coverage (percentage) by sex and wave, individuals aged 15+, 2012 and 2018.

Note: The category by employer/purchased includes private health insurance purchased through the employer of another family member, or health insurance through the armed forces. Health insurance through the general agency includes treatment at state's expense.

Source: Authors' calculations based on data from ELMPS 2012 and 2018.

[21] This category includes treatment at the state's expense.
[22] Through school or university. This type represents the students' general health insurance system available in Egypt.
[23] This category includes health insurance through armed forces, private health insurance through own employer or employer of a family working member, or if individuals purchased their own insurance.

in 2018, down from 20 percent in 2012. This shows not only limited health insurance coverage among the population but also a slight decline in the coverage rate over time, just like the evolution of the social insurance coverage rate.

There are important gender differences in the health insurance coverage rates. As expected, owing to the low levels of women's labor force participation, they were much more likely than men to fall out of health insurance coverage (80 percent in 2018). Women are therefore the most vulnerable to the absence of universal health insurance.

Looking at the patterns of health insurance coverage rates by location, while there was an increasing percentage of uninsured individuals in urban areas, for both men and women, the coverage in urban areas substantially exceeded that in rural areas (Figure 9.16). Also, while women in general were more likely to lack health insurance coverage, rural women specifically were the most vulnerable in terms of health insurance coverage. This adds to the multiple aspects of vulnerability that these women face (Chapter 8, this volume).

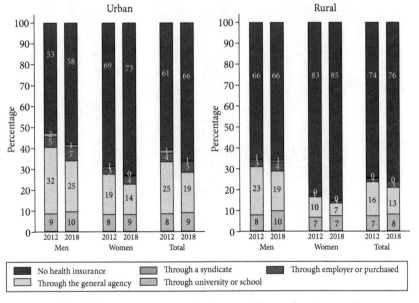

Figure 9.16 Health insurance coverage (percentage) by sex, location, and wave, individuals aged 15+, 2012 and 2018.

Note: The category by employer/purchased includes private health insurance purchased through the employer of another family member, or health insurance through the armed forces. Health insurance through the general agency includes treatment at the state's expense.

Source: Authors' calculations based on data from ELMPS 2012 and 2018.

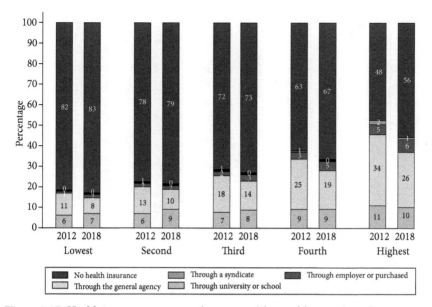

Figure 9.17 Health insurance coverage (percentage) by wealth quintile and wave, individuals aged 15+, 2012 and 2018.

Note: The category by employer/purchased includes private health insurance purchased through the employer of another family member, or health insurance through the armed forces. Health insurance through the general agency includes treatment at the state's expense.

Source: Authors' calculations based on data from ELMPS 2012 and 2018.

Commensurate with the growing lack of social insurance, there was a rise in the percentage of uninsured individuals in all wealth quintiles between 2012 and 2018. Nevertheless, there was a positive association between health insurance and wealth. Individuals in the lowest wealth quintiles were the most likely to lack health insurance coverage (84 percent in 2018), compared with 56 percent of the highest quintile. This indicates that the less fortunate were worse off in terms of health insurance coverage and access to health services, raising issues of vulnerability and coping with shocks as well as social justice. Moreover, previous studies also found that their out-of-pocket expenditure represented a higher share of their total expenditure than in richer households (World Bank, 2018). The poor also have worse health outcomes than the non-poor (Chapter 11, this volume).

Furthermore, examining health insurance coverage by age groups reveals the highest coverage was among those aged 19 or younger (Figure 9.18). This is because they were largely insured by the schools' health insurance system. The coverage gap was highest among those aged 20–24 (only 18 percent insured in 2018) and 25–29 (only 10 percent insured in 2018).

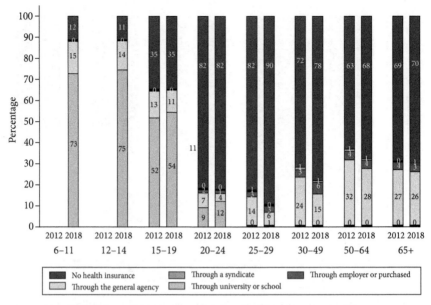

Figure 9.18 Health insurance coverage (percentage) by age group and wave, individuals aged 6+, 2012 and 2018.

Note: The category by employer/purchased includes private health insurance purchased through the employer of another family member, or health insurance through the armed forces. Health insurance through the general agency includes treatment at the state's expense. Because no information was available on health insurance for ages 6–14 in 2012, we only show it for 2018.

Source: Authors' calculations based on data from ELMPS 2012 and 2018.

9.6 Discussion and Conclusion

This chapter presents a comprehensive review of the state of social protection in Egypt, focusing on three components: social insurance schemes, benefit entitlements whether based on contributory (employed-related) or non-contributory (social assistance) schemes, and health insurance.

In 2018, the social insurance coverage rate declined. The percentage of workers who had social insurance coverage was only 30 percent. This development was mostly associated with the expansion of private sector wage employment outside establishments and the expansion of employment in small firms between 2006 and 2017 (Assaad et al., 2019). Moreover, non-wage workers witnessed important drops in their social insurance coverage. These findings, holding for both men and women, were alarming since they reflect a heightened sense of vulnerability among Egyptian workers. In particular, with the shrinking role of the public sector, this is not good news for women who do not have an alternative except non-wage work and precarious types of private wage work.

The lack of social security was highest and persistent among the most volatile jobs, namely the rapidly growing segments of outside establishments and small firms. Workers who were most likely to work in these jobs such as blue-collar high-skilled/low-skilled workers, the less educated, and the young were the most likely to bear the brunt of this drop in social security coverage. The real problem is that these groups of workers will likely suffer from low chances of social security coverage throughout their career. Consistent with the literature, the poorest workers had the lowest coverage reflecting their strong preference for liquidity and high discount rates (Palacios and Robalino, 2009), and also their higher propensity to work in precarious employment.

In terms of receiving social protection benefits, households covered with at least one type of social protection benefit or that had an actively contributing member to social insurance schemes declined to 57 percent of households in 2018, down from 68 percent in 2006. This was because of the falling trend in social insurance coverage among workers, which led to relatively fewer households with at least one socially covered working member (27 percent in 2018). A key source of cash benefits for households was employment-related retirement pensions (26 percent), followed by non-contributory social assistance (13 percent). If the social insurance coverage gap continues to widen, social protection coverage. will be strongly affected both through a decline in the proportion of households who would receive retirement pensions in the future, and through a decline in the proportion of households with at least one working member who is actively contributing to social insurance schemes.

Efforts are still needed to expand the coverage of social assistance among the households in the lowest quintiles, as the receipt rate is still lower than the initially targeted rate, and even declining in particular for the second wealth quintile. Finally, despite the efforts made for improving the targeting of the food subsidy, close to three-quarters of households in the two highest quintiles hold these cards. Moreover, the majority of individuals (aged 15 and above) fall out of the health insurance system. Women in general and rural women in particular, as well as youth aged 20–29 were the most vulnerable groups in terms of health insurance coverage. Unfortunately, households in the lowest quintile were more likely to fall out of health insurance coverage, which is associated with worse health outcomes among the poor. This shows the importance of a universal health insurance coverage of good quality that would particularly benefit women, youth, and the poor.

With the COVID-19 shock, it is expected that poverty rates will further increase. This in part due to reduced income and job losses associated with the precautionary measures and the struggle of sectors that were most hit such as tourism, accommodation and food services, and education. Since of the emergence of COVID-19, 62 percent of workers' employment status changed as of May 2020 and 55 percent as of September 2020 (CAPMAS, 2020a; CAPMAS, 2020b). Among these workers, 26 percent became unemployed (CAPMAS,

2020a). The crisis has thus pointed to the critical need of Egypt to develop a reliable unemployment insurance scheme. Three-quarters (74 percent) of workers experienced a drop in their income, owing to precautionary measures or unemployment (CAPMAS, 2020a). Consequently, around 33 percent of households stated that their income was not sufficient to meet their needs in May 2020 (CAPMAS, 2020a), which improved in September 2020 to 23 percent of households (CAPMAS, 2020b). This may lead to rising working poverty and increased chances of working in unprotected employment, with no social insurance coverage. The government has taken several emergency measures to target the most vulnerable households and workers. An additional 100,000 households, living in poorest governorates or in areas that have been strongly hit with the crisis, were enrolled to Takaful and Karama (El-Laithy, 2020; Zeitoun, 2020). The proxy-means-tested cutoff was also revised to allow the eligibility of more beneficiaries who were on the edge of falling in poverty (El-Laithy, 2020; Zeitoun, 2020). A transfer of EGP 500 was provided for between 1.6-2 million irregular workers for multiple months (Krafft, Assaad, and Marouani, 2021; Zeitoun, 2020). Yet, there is a strong need to further expand coverage and assistance to households who fall outside the receipt of any social safety net and those who are most prone to becoming vulnerable. Moreover, the shift in the employment mix towards more unstable and unprotected forms of jobs, such as outside establishments, calls for immediate actions around measures of social protection and adequate schemes for this growing segment of workers.

Appendix 9.1

Table A9.1 The percentage of private sector wage workers covered by social insurance, by job and individual characteristics, sex and wave, ages 18–59, 1998–2018.

	Men								Women					
	Percent				N				Percent			N		
	1998	2006	2012	2018	1998	2006	2012	2018	2006	2012	2018	2006	2012	2018
Socially insured in private sector	23	25	23	17	1,714	3,315	5,423	7,304	23	31	26	409	416	658
Private wage outside establishment	10	11	9	6	739	1,381	2,803	4,138	0	3	7	53	84	184
Private wage inside establishment	34	35	37	29	975	1,934	2,620	3166	28	38	31	356	332	474
Economic activity (ISIC, 1st digit)														
Agriculture	3	4	2	2	279	441	921	1,437	2	0	3	32	45	112
Broad manufacturing and utilities	34	39	40	34	459	789	1,087	1,120	27	43	30	106	83	99
Construction	9	8	6	8	321	655	1,276	1,860						
Wholesale and retail trade, hotels and accommodation	25	21	22	16	290	758	1,081	1,399	13	22	19	93	73	104
Transport, storage, and communication	57	47	43	25	172	439	638	856						
Other services	27	40	41	27	193	232	420	627	32	30	23	149	195	309
Occupation														
White collar, high skilled	66	67	63	48	184	411	578	692	45	50	42	138	171	194

Continued

Table A9.1 Continued

	Men								Women					
	Percent				N				Percent			N		
	1998	2006	2012	2018	1998	2006	2012	2018	2006	2012	2018	2006	2012	2018
White collar, low skilled	29	25	22	19	315	679	881	1,403	11	23	25	146	87	216
Blue collar, high skilled	8	9	6	5	933	1,594	2,735	3,749	12	6	3	69	57	144
Blue collar, low skilled	42	38	40	23	282	630	1,229	1,402	19	18	12	56	101	99
Firm Size														
Outside establishments	10	11	9	6	738	1,381	2,803	4,134	0	3	7	53	84	184
1–4 workers	9	9	8	7	331	737	851	909	7	3	4	111	85	126
5–24 workers	26	29	20	12	311	492	643	1,014	21	15	21	98	79	154
25–99 workers	56	55	48	42	122	268	310	355	52	59	38	62	67	62
More than 100/DK	70	70	70	59	197	416	816	892	43	62	54	77	101	132
Age group														
18–29	16	16	16	10	841	1,797	2,660	2,821	19	28	20	256	202	263
30–49	30	34	29	21	738	1,330	2,436	3,959	30	32	28	135	189	337
50–59	24	40	36	22	128	181	307	496			36			54
Education														
Illiterate or read and write	12	15	12	8	638	915	1,258	1,837	4	7	4	80	95	180
Below secondary	19	20	19	14	414	665	1,087	1,195	23	13	15	40	47	74
Secondary	30	25	24	17	499	1,328	2,362	3,363	22	36	35	181	133	214
University and above	63	54	49	36	157	406	713	907	44	48	36	108	139	190
Head of household														
Head	17	17	15	10	907	1,617	2,001	2,056	24	34	22	383	371	592
Otherwise	29	33	29	20	807	1,698	3,422	5,248		7	48		45	66
Marital status														
Never married	16	16	14	11	789	1,336	1,652	1,866	20	34	25	242	173	188
Ever married	27	32	28	19	925	1,979	3,771	5,426	28	28	27	167	243	469

Note: Women's sample sizes were quite small in 1998. This is why we carry out and show the analysis for women for only 2006, 2012, and 2018.

References

Abdalla, M. and S. Al-Shawarby (2017) "The Tamween Food Subsidy System in Egypt: Evolution and Recent Implementation Reforms," in H. Alderman, U. Gentilini, and R. Yemtsov (eds) *The 1.5 Billion People Question: Food, Vouchers, or Cash Transfers?*, pp. 107–50). Washington, DC: The World Bank.

Assaad, R. (2009) "Labor Supply, Employment and Unemployment in the Egyptian Economy, 1988–2006," in R. Assaad (ed.), *The Egyptian Labor Market Revisited*, pp. 1–52. Cairo: American University in Cairo Press.

Assaad, R. and C. Krafft (2015) "The Structure and Evolution of Employment in Egypt," in R. Assaad and C. Krafft (eds.), *The Egyptian Labor Market in an Era of Revolution*, pp. 27–51. Oxford: Oxford University Press.

Assaad, R., C. Krafft, and S. Yassin (2020) "Job creation or labor absorption? An analysis of private sector job growth in Egypt." *Middle East Development Journal*, 12(2), 177–207.

Assaad, R. et al. (2019) *Job Creation in Egypt: A Sectoral and Geographical Analysis Focusing on Private Establishments, 1996–2017*. Cairo: Economic Research Forum.

Breisinger, C. et al. (2018) "Impact Evaluation Study for Egypt's Takaful and Karama Cash Transfer Program: Part 1: Quantitative Report" (October). MENA RP Working Paper 14. Washington, DC and Cairo, Egypt: International Food Policy Research Institute (IFPRI).

CAPMAS (Central Agency for Public Mobilization and Statistics) (2020a) "The Impact of Corona Virus on Egyptian Households till May 2020." CAPMAS Bulletin Series, June. https://www.capmas.gov.eg/Pages/StaticPages.aspx?page_id=7233 [last accessed July 6th 2021].

CAPMAS (Central Agency for Public Mobilization and Statistics) (2020b) "The Impact of Corona Virus on Egyptian Households till September 2020." CAPMAS Bulletin Series, June. https://www.capmas.gov.eg/Pages/StaticPages.aspx?page_id= 7233 [last accessed July 6th 2021].

El-Haddad, A. (2020) "Redefining the Social Contract in the Wake of the Arab Spring: The Experiences of Egypt, Morocco and Tunisia," *World Development*, *127*: 104774.

El-Laithy, H. (2020) "Impact of Covid on Poverty." Presentation at IFPRI Egypt Seminar Covid-19 and Social Protection: From Effective Crisis Protection to Self-Reliance, September 22.

Enterprise (2020) "Egypt to Introduce 1% Tax on All Salaries to Fund Covid-19 Fight." *Entreprise*. Available at: https://enterprise.press/stories/2020/05/21/egypt-to-introduce-1-tax-on-all-salaries-to-fund-covid-19-fight-16282/ (Accessed: December 2, 2020).

Ghoneim, H. (2013) "Ration Cards in Egypt: Targeting, Leakage, and Costs." Working papers 36, The German University in Cairo, Faculty of Management Technology

Helmy, O. (2008) "Toward a More Efficient and Equitable Pension System in Egypt," in H. Kheir-El-Din (ed.) *The Egyptian Economy: Current Challenges and Future Prospects*, pp. 201–20. Cairo: American University in Cairo Press.

ILO (International Labour Organization) (2017) *World Social Protection Report 2017-19: Universal Social Protection to Achieve the Sustainable Development Goals.* Geneva: ILO.

ISSA (International Social Security Association) (2017) "Egypt," in *Social Security Programs Throughout the World: Africa, 2017*, pp. 97–104. Geneva: International Social Security Association No. 13-11804.

Kidd, S. (2016) "Contributory and Non-Contributory Social Security." Webinar Presentation: Fiscal Space for Social Protection: Harmonization of Contributory and Non-Contributory Programs (September 8).

Krafft, C., R. Assaad, and M. A. Marouani (2021) "The Impact of COVID-19 on Middle Eastern and North African Labor Markets: Glimmers of Progress but Persistent Problems for Vulnerable Workers a Year into the Pandemic", Economic Research Forum Policy Brief No. 57.

Krafft, C., R. Assaad, and K.W. Rahman (2021) "Introducing the Egypt Labor Market Panel Survey 2018." *IZA Journal of Development and Migration* (Forthcoming).

Loewe, M. (2014) "Pension Schemes and Pension Reforms in the Middle East and North Africa," in K. Hujo (ed.), *Reforming Pensions in Developing and Transition Countries*, pp. 69–101. Basingstoke: Palgrave Macmillan.

Official Gazette (2019) "Law No. 148 for 2019 for Social Insurance and Pensions." Available at http://www.mof.gov.eg/Arabic/_Layouts/MOF/ExternalPages/Laws/pdf/2076.pdf (Accessed: December 2, 2020).

Palacios, R. and Robalino, D. A. (2009) "Matching Defined Contributions: A Way to Increase Pension Coverage," in R. Holzmann, D.A. Robalino, and N. Takayama (eds), *Closing the Coverage Gap: The Role of Social Pensions and Other Retirement Income Transfers*, pp. 187–202. Washington, DC: World Bank.

Roushdy, R. and I. Selwaness (2015) "Duration to Coverage: Dynamics of Access to Social Security in the Egyptian Labor Market in the 1998–2012 Period," in R. Assaad and C. Krafft (eds) *The Egyptian Labor Market in an Era of Revolution*, pp. 241–58. Oxford: Oxford University Press.

Roushdy, R. and I. Selwaness (2019) "Who Is Covered and Who Under-Reports: An Empirical Analysis of Access to Social Insurance in Egypt," *Journal of International Development* 31(8), 720–751.

Selwaness, I. and M. Ehab (2019) "Social Protection and Vulnerability in Egypt: A Gendered Analysis." Economic Research Forum Working Paper Series No. 1363. Cairo.

Selwaness, I. and M. Messkoub (2019) "Social Policy in the Middle East and North Africa," in R. Jawad, N. Jones, and M. Messkoub (eds), *Social Policy in the Middle East and North Africa Region and the New Social Protection Paradigm: From Social Assistance to Universalism?*, pp. 84–115. Cheltenham: Edward Elgar Publishing.

World Bank (2015) "Strengthening Social Safety Net Project." Report No. PAD611. Washington, DC: World Bank.

World Bank (2018) "Transforming The Egyptian Healthcare System." Project Appraisal Document Report No. PAD2850. Washington, DC: World Bank.

Zeitoun, N. (2020) "Covid-19 Outbreak: Social Safety Net Policy Response." Presentation in IFPRI Egypt Seminar: Covid-19 and Social Protection: From Effective Crisis Protection to Self-Reliance, September 22.

10
Household Vulnerability and Resilience to Shocks in Egypt

Imane Helmy and Rania Roushdy

10.1 Introduction

Rural and urban households face different risks that could lead to adverse shocks. Managing risks and reducing vulnerability to shocks enhances the wellbeing of households and encourages investment in human capital (Holzmann and Jorgensen, 1999; Heitzmann, Canagarajah, and Siegel, 2002; World Bank, 2011, 2020). Poverty and vulnerability to shocks are interlinked given the limited opportunities of poor households to use assets or diversify income. Social safety nets may be useful for protecting against shocks or mitigating their effects, but their impact could be limited (Dercon, 2002; Skoufias, 2003; ESCWA, 2020; World Bank, 2020). Consequently, exploring the nature of shocks and identifying the characteristics of households who are more vulnerable to shocks and their different coping strategies are vital to ultimately reducing vulnerability. Understanding these issues can inform the design of interventions that prevent households from falling into poverty or using stressful strategies that may harm their human capital.

This chapter describes the different shocks experienced by Egyptian households and the coping mechanisms that they adopted to respond to shocks using the 2018 round of the Egypt Labor Market Panel Survey (ELMPS). Studying household exposure to shocks in Egypt extends the empirical literature on developing countries. The existing literature on shocks and coping in such countries focuses mostly on theoretical discussions (Knight et al., 2015). Following the January revolution in 2011, the political turmoil in Egypt adversely affected the economy. In 2014, the government started economic reform measures, including removal of subsidies and currency devaluation, which led to a very high level of inflation (International Monetary Fund, 2014, 2015). These economic challenges are expected to affect the vulnerability of Egyptian households to shocks, which further motivates research on the case of Egypt. We discuss the theoretical framework for understanding shocks in Section 10.2 and describe the data and research methods in Section 10.3. Section 10.4 presents the results of the study, and Section 10.5 concludes.

Imane Helmy and Rania Roushdy, *Household Vulnerability and Resilience to Shocks in Egypt* In: *The Egyptian Labor Market: A Focus on Gender and Economic Vulnerability*. Edited by: Caroline Krafft and Ragui Assaad, Oxford University Press.
© Economic Research Forum 2022. DOI: 10.1093/oso/9780192847911.003.0011

10.2 Background and Theoretical Framework

Figure 10.1 shows a conceptual framework that links shocks and vulnerability. Exposure to macro- (covariate) or micro- (idiosyncratic) shocks pushes households to employ diverse coping measures that could be classified into behavior-based, asset-based, or assistance-based measures. The coping measures undertaken will affect the community and the wellbeing of households through different channels including schooling, nutrition, and asset depletion. Consequently, household resilience and vulnerability are affected by shocks (Heltberg et al., 2012).

Mitigating risks to decrease the probability of shocks or reducing the impact of shocks after their occurrence requires an in-depth understanding of different types of shocks (Table 10.1). Shocks are idiosyncratic, micro-shocks when they affect specific individuals or households, while covariant shocks include meso-shocks that affect communities or villages and macro-shocks that affect the whole nation. Another dimension of classification is the nature of the shock (natural, economic, political, or social) (Holzmann and Jorgensen, 1999; World Bank, 2001; Heitzmann, Canagarajah, and Siegel, 2002).

Empirical evidence from developing countries shows that households are exposed to both idiosyncratic and covariant shocks. Although idiosyncratic shocks explain a large percentage of income variation in some contexts, in other contexts, idiosyncratic shocks have little effect on real consumption expenditure. These contrasts highlight the importance of understanding context-specific shocks and coping (Dercon, 2002; Ajefu, 2017).

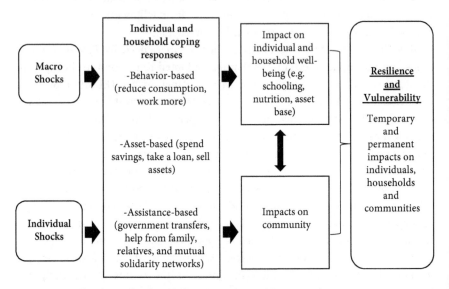

Figure 10.1 Shocks and vulnerability: A conceptual framework.
Source: Compiled by authors based on Heltberg et al. (2012).

Table 10.1 Main sources of shocks.

Type of shock	Micro (Idiosyncratic)	Macro (Covariant)	
	Affecting individual or household	Affecting groups of households or communities (meso)	Affecting regions or nations (macro)
Environmental		Rainfall	Earthquake/Flood
			Drought/High winds
Health	Illness/Injury	Epidemic	
	Disability/Old age	Pollution/Deforestation	
	Death		
Social	Crime	Terrorism	Civil war
	Domestic violence	Gang activity	Social upheaval
Economic	Job loss	Unemployment	Changes in food prices
		Resettlement	Hyperinflation
		Harvest failure	Financial crisis
			Technology shock
			Transition costs of economic reforms
Political		Riots	Coup d'état

Source: Compiled by authors based on World Bank (2001); Heitzmann, Canagarajah, and Siegel (2002).

The mechanisms for managing risks can be broadly classified into three categories: risk reduction; risk mitigation (*ex ante*) to reduce the probability of shocks; and coping measures (*ex post*) to relieve the impact of shocks after occurrence (World Bank, 2001). These measures can be taken at individual, household, group, or national levels as indicated in Table 10.2 (Holzmann and Jorgensen, 1999). Formal credit and insurance mechanisms as well as social safety nets play a crucial role in managing risks (Dercon, 2002; Okamoto, 2011).

Nevertheless, financial market failures and weak social protection drive informal risk-sharing between households who rely on family, friends, and neighbors in times of trouble. There is a large body of literature discussing the role of social capital in coping with shocks. Mutual assistance between households could take multiple forms, such as providing gifts or loans, labor pooling, child fostering, exchanging information on job opportunities, or starting a business (Dercon, 2002; Fafchamps and Lund, 2003; Fafchamps and Gubert, 2007; Fafchamps, 2011). On the other hand, some studies found that households do not heavily rely on gifts and transfers, which highlights the need for formal protection systems (Okamoto, 2011; Yilma et al., 2014).

A number of studies found that household characteristics strongly affect the availability and choice of coping mechanisms (Lokshin and Yemtsov, 2004; Okamoto, 2011; Santos et al., 2011). Moreover, the frequency of shocks affects coping ability and the capacity of households to absorb subsequent shocks. Households are able to cope with low-frequency shocks, even if their long-term effect is severe, while consumption smoothing is more difficult among households that face high-frequency shocks (Dercon, 2002).

The literature on shocks has also established an interlinkage with food insecurity that could be associated with vulnerability to external shocks, especially economic and environmental shocks. Previous studies have mostly differentiated between two dimensions of food insecurity: duration and severity. The duration dimension indicates whether food insecurity is a long-term persistent food deficit (chronic) or a temporary decline in food access (transitory). Moreover, the severity dimension reflects the intensity and the magnitude of food insecurity (mild, moderate, or severe) (Staatz, D'Agostino, and Sundberg, 1990; Altman, Hart, and Jacobs, 2009; Akramov and Shreedhar, 2012).

10.3 Data and Methods

This chapter used data from ELMPS 2018 (OAMDI, 2018). The survey included 15,746 households (61,231 individuals). ELMPS 2018 collected information on a variety of individual and household characteristics, including housing information, transfers, health, education, employment, job characteristics, marriage, and fertility. Moreover, for the first time, the survey included a module to explore

Table 10.2 Risk management mechanisms.

Objective	Informal mechanisms		Formal mechanisms	
	Individual and household	Group based	Market based	Publicly provided
Reducing/preventing risk	Preventive health measures Migration	Collective action for infrastructure		Sound macroeconomic practices for infrastructure, policy Environmental policy Education and training policy Public health policy Infrastructure (dams, roads) Active labor market policies Liberalized trade Protection of property
Mitigating risk (compensating against expected loss) Diversification	Crop diversification Income source diversification Investment in physical and human capital	Rotating savings and credit associations	Savings accounts in financial institutions Microfinance	
Insurance	Marriage and extended family Buffer stocks	Investment in social capital networks, association, rituals, gift giving	Old age annuities Accident, disability, and insurance	Pension systems Insurance for unemployment, illness, disability

Continued

Table 10.2 Continued

	Informal mechanisms		Formal mechanisms	
Objective	Individual and household	Group based	Market based	Publicly provided
Coping with shocks	Sale of assets Loans from moneylenders Child labor Reduced food consumption Seasonal or temporary migration	Transfers from networks of mutual support	Sale of financial assets Loans from financial institutions	Social assistance Subsidies Social funds Cash transfers

Source: Compiled by authors based on Holzmann and Jorgensen (1999); World Bank (2001); Heitzmann, Canagarajah, and Siegel (2002).

exposure to shocks during the year preceding the survey (Krafft, Assaad, and Rahman, 2021).

The shocks module started by asking questions regarding food insecurity and its severity with a recall period of four weeks. The three domains of food insecurity that were covered by seven questions were: perception of food insecurity (anxiety and uncertainty about household food supply); experiencing insufficient quality (variety and preferences of the type of food); and experiencing insufficient food intake (smaller or fewer meals). Each question was followed by frequency of occurrence questions to assess how often the condition took place during the preceding month. This frequency of occurrence was used to develop a food insecurity access scale score (Coates, Swindale, and Bilinsky, 2007).

The second part of the module addressed exposure to shocks during the past year. Different shocks include health-related events (illness, death, accident), environmental events (flood, drought, etc.), economic events (loss of employment, reduced income), social shocks (crime, conflict, or theft). In addition, the survey enquired about various formal and informal coping mechanisms. Descriptive analysis is used to analyze the data in this chapter (see Appendix 10.1 for the description of key variables used in the analysis).

10.4 Results

This section investigates the incidence of food insecurity and shocks that Egyptian households faced during the year prior to the ELMPS 2018 interview. Based on the ELMPS 2018 data, 16 percent of the Egyptian households were exposed to at least one type of shock during the year preceding the ELMPS interview, and 25 percent experienced food insecurity during the month preceding the survey interview. About 15 percent of households experienced food insecurity solely, while about 10 percent experienced both food insecurity and at least one type of shock simultaneously.

In the following, we separately analyze exposure to shocks and exposure to food insecurity given their distinct nature. As we have discussed, food insecurity may often be of a chronic nature rather than transitory, which is generally not the case for an environmental, health, economic, or social shock. Our analysis is limited by the questions included in the ELMPS, and hence we cannot determine from the data whether a reported food insecurity episode is chronic or transitory. Moreover, we can identify associations between food insecurity and shocks, but we cannot identify their sequence or causal relationship. Accordingly, we chose not to combine them. The following section starts by examining the occurrence of shocks, the characteristics of the households that were exposed to shocks, and their coping strategies. Afterwards, we explore food insecurity and coping mechanisms.

10.4.1 Shocks

Shocks are grouped in this chapter into four categories: environmental, economic, social, and health (see Figure A10.1). As Figure 10.2 shows, an economic shock was the type of shock most frequently reported by Egyptian households during the year preceding the survey. About 14 percent of the households were exposed to an economic shock, 5 percent to a health shock, 2 percent to an environmental shock, and 1 percent to a social shock. Reduced income (12 percent) followed by loss of employment (7 percent) were the most prevalent types of economic shocks. Health shocks varied slightly between human disease (3 percent), accident (2 percent), and death (2 percent).

Among the group of households who were exposed to a shock, 73 percent experienced only one type of shock (58 percent experienced only an economic shock, 11 percent experienced only a health shock, 3 percent experienced only an environmental shock, and 1 percent experienced only a social shock) (Figure 10.3). Around 22 percent were exposed to two types of shocks simultaneously, and 5 percent were exposed to three or more. More specifically, Figure 10.3 shows that almost 15 percent of the households experienced both health and economic shocks, 5 percent experienced economic and environmental shocks, and 3 percent experienced these three types of shocks together.

Furthermore, some households had simultaneously experienced several different shocks within the same type of shock. For instance, Figure 10.4 shows that around 50 percent of the households that had an economic shock experienced at least two different economic shocks. By the same token, about 21 percent of those who experienced health shocks were exposed to two or more different health shocks.

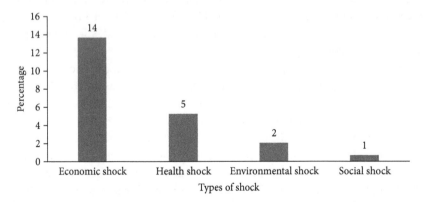

Figure 10.2 Percentage of households who were exposed to shocks during the past year by type of shock, 2018.

Note: Multiple shocks are possible (N=15,746).

Source: Authors' calculation based on ELMPS 2018.

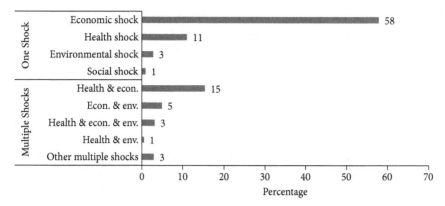

Figure 10.3 Percentage of households who were exposed to shocks experiencing single or multiple shocks during the past year, by type of shocks, 2018.
Note: N=2,546.
Source: Authors' calculation based on ELMPS 2018.

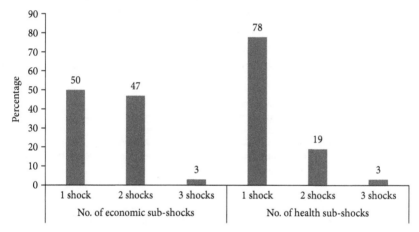

Figure 10.4 Percentage of households experiencing one, two, or three economic or health shocks during the past year, 2018.
Note: N=2,145 for economic shocks and N=832 for health shocks.
Source: Authors' calculation based on ELMPS 2018.

10.4.1.1 Which households are more vulnerable to shocks?

We turn in this section to investigating which households were more vulnerable to shocks during the study year, in terms of place of residence, living standard, the characteristics of the head of the household and household members, and potential coverage by social protection schemes.[1]

---

[1] A detailed analysis of the coverage of social protection schemes in Egypt is in Chapter 9 in this volume.

Figure 10.5 shows that exposure to shocks was highest in rural Upper Egypt (21 percent) and rural Lower Egypt (20 percent), followed by the Alexandria and Suez Canal region (19 percent). Surprisingly, and contrary to the pattern of food insecurity discussed in this section, rural households residing in the poorest 1,000 villages reported lower rates of exposure to shocks (15 percent) than rural households residing in the remaining villages (20 percent).

Exposure to shocks varied slightly by household size. About 17 percent of households with large families (more than four members) were exposed to shocks as compared with 15 percent among households consisting of four or fewer members (Figure 10.5). Households belonging to the poorest wealth quintile (23 percent) were more than twice as likely to be exposed to a shock during the preceding year as compared with those falling in the fourth (12 percent) and fifth (9 percent) wealth quintiles. Nevertheless, one should be careful about the potential endogeneity of household wealth status and exposure to shocks, because it is not only that poor households were more likely to get exposed to a shock, but also that exposure to shock may have caused a household to become poorer.[2]

Accordingly, in Figure 10.6, we investigate other measures of household living standards. Previous research has shown that there are strong intergenerational transfers of education levels and social welfare in Egypt. For instance, young people of highly educated parents are more likely to have access to better

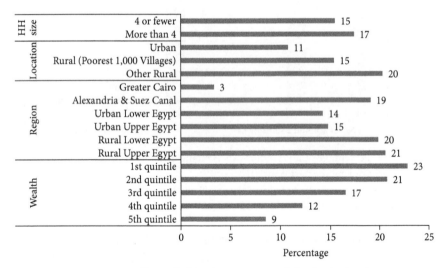

Figure 10.5 Percentage of households who experienced shocks during the past year by household characteristics, 2018.

Note: N=15,746.

Source: Authors' calculation based on ELMPS 2018.

---

[2] This also holds true for households' access to social protection schemes.

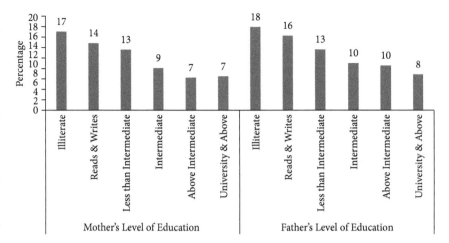

Figure 10.6 Percentage of households who experienced shocks during the past year by parental education of the head of household, 2018.

Note: N=15,611 for mother's education and 15,625 for father's education.

Source: Authors' calculation based on ELMPS 2018.

education, good quality jobs, and in turn higher wealth status than those of low educated parents (Assaad and Krafft, 2014, 2015; Krafft 2015). Hence, Figure 10.6 shows household exposure to shocks by the household head's parents' educational attainment as a proxy for natal household poverty status. As expected, exposure to shocks substantially decreased with both parents' education levels.

Similarly, a household's exposure to shocks was lower if its own household head was more educated (Figure 10.7). Exposure to shocks was highest among households headed by illiterate individuals (20 percent) or those who could read and write with no formal schooling completed (18 percent). Moreover, households of heads with less than an intermediate education (19 percent) were more than twice as likely to be exposed to a shock than households of university or above educated heads (7 percent). In addition, exposure to shocks was slightly higher among households of young adult and adult heads. Surprisingly, household vulnerability to shocks varied only slightly by the sex of the household head, with male heads appearing to be 1 percentage point more likely to be exposed to shocks than their female counterparts. Household members' characteristics also affected the household's vulnerability to shocks. Exposure to shocks decreased as the number of educated members of the household increased (Figure 10.8).

Furthermore, the employment status of the household head, in terms of formality and sector, seems to play a vital role in the household's vulnerability to shocks. Figure 10.9 shows that exposure to shocks was highest among household heads working outside establishments (either in non-wage work or informal private sector wage work) (24 percent). Exposure to shocks was almost double among

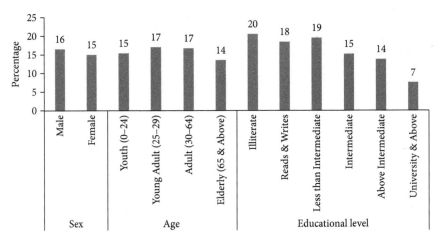

Figure 10.7 Percentage of households who experienced shocks during the past year by characteristics of the household head, 2018.

Note: N=15,746.

Source: Authors' calculation based on ELMPS 2018.

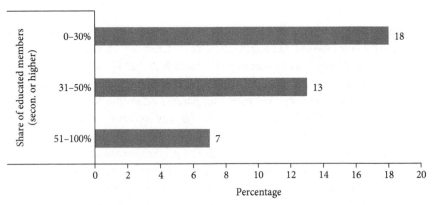

Figure 10.8 Percentage of households who experienced shocks during the past year by share of household members aged 18 and above with secondary or higher education, 2018.

Note: (N=15,667).

Source: Authors' calculation based on ELMPS 2018.

households with heads working in the informal private sector outside establishments as compared with households with heads working in the formal private or public sectors (10–11 percent). It is also important to note here how if at least one member of the household was working in the public sector or in the formal private sector, the rate of exposure to shocks decreased by almost 7 percentage points.

Likewise, exposure to shocks varied by the economic activity of the head of household. We followed Chapter 2 in this volume in categorizing the economic activities included in ELMPS 2018. The results show that vulnerability to shocks was substantially higher among households with heads working in the agriculture sector, and lowest among households of heads working in the professional, financial, and information services, and education sectors (Figure 10.10).

Figure 10.11 may provide evidence that social protection schemes have been well targeted towards more vulnerable households; however, despite receiving such schemes, their exposure to shocks was still relatively higher than households that did not receive or were not eligible for such benefits (see Chapter 9 or World Bank

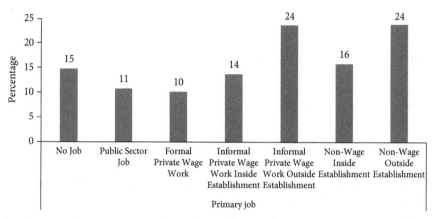

Figure 10.9 Percentage of households who experienced shocks during the past year by sector of employment of the head of household, 2018.

Note: Primary job (3 months) (N=15,740).

Source: Authors' calculation based on ELMPS 2018.

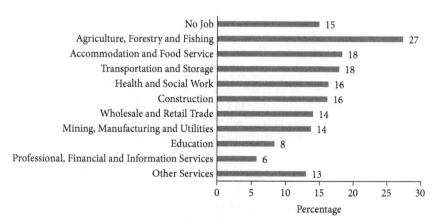

Figure 10.10 Percentage of households who experienced shocks during the past year by economic activity of the head of household, 2018.

Note: Primary job (3 months) (N=15,746).

Source: Authors' calculation based on ELMPS 2018.

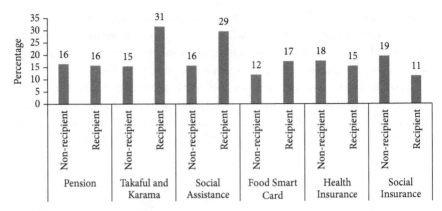

Figure 10.11 Percentage of households who experienced shocks during the past year by social protection coverage, 2018.

Note: At least one member has access. N=15,694 for health insurance and 12,371 for social insurance. *Source*: Authors' calculation based on ELMPS 2018.

(2015) for the details of Takaful and Karama programs). For instance, 31 percent of households that received Takaful or Karama conditional and unconditional cash transfers were exposed to shocks in the preceding year, compared with 15 percent among those households that did not get such transfers. Similar results are observed for the social assistance and food smart cards. In contrast, households that had regular health insurance (15 percent versus 18 percent among non-receivers) or social insurance benefits (11 percent versus 19 percent among non-receivers) were less likely to get exposed to a shock during the study period.

10.4.1.2 Households' coping mechanisms

This section explores how households respond to shocks and how their response varies by household characteristics. Figure 10.12 shows the households' most frequently used coping mechanisms and their combinations in response to a shock. Consumption rationing (55 percent) following by borrowing (43 percent) were the two most frequently reported coping mechanisms. Social capital was also an important safety net for Egyptian households, as almost a third (29 percent) of households reported seeking assistance from relatives and friends in response to a shock.

Furthermore, the majority of the households that reported borrowing as a coping strategy purchased goods on credit or used their social capital as the source of credit. About 28 percent of the households borrowed money from their relatives or friends, compared with only 5 percent that borrowed from a bank or a money lender. Consumption rationing as a coping strategy primarily consisted of reducing spending on health (36 percent), eating less food (35 percent), and reducing spending on education (22 percent). All these strategies are likely to have adverse

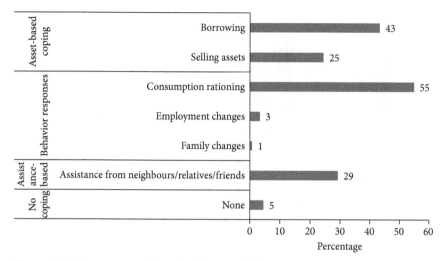

Figure 10.12 Percentage of households using different coping mechanisms, households with shocks during the past year, 2018.

Note: Multiple strategies are possible (N=2,723).

Source: Authors' calculation based on ELMPS 2018.

effects on the household's human capital, and hence render the household even more vulnerable to shocks.

Figure 10.13 plots the most frequently reported coping strategy by type of shock experienced by the household. The pattern of coping strategies did not vary much across the four types of shocks. Consumption rationing followed by borrowing/purchasing on credit were the two most commonly used strategies regardless of the type of shock. Over a third of the households also reported using assistance from their social network when exposed to any of the four types of shocks.

Figure 10.14 shows the pattern of coping strategies by household's place of residence. Over half of the households residing in the poorest 1,000 villages used borrowing (57 percent) as a coping mechanism when exposed to a shock, as compared with 47 percent among those residing in other rural villages and 35 percent among urban households. Consumption rationing was more commonly used as a coping strategy in other rural areas (56 percent) than in the poorest 1,000 villages (52 percent) and in urban areas (53 percent).

As for the region of residence, consumption rationing was most frequently reported by households residing in the Alexandria and Suez Canal region (64 percent), while borrowing was most commonly reported in rural Upper Egypt (52 percent). Contrary to expectations, assistance from neighbors, relatives or friends as a coping strategy was most prevalent in Greater Cairo (56 percent) rather than in rural areas, where using social capital as a safety net was expected

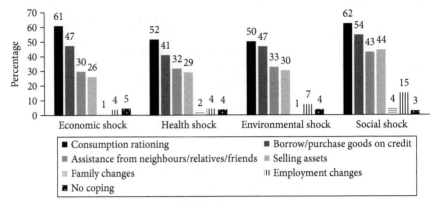

Figure 10.13 Percentage of households using different coping mechanisms by type of shock, households who experienced shocks during the past year, 2018.

Note: Multiple shocks and strategies are possible. N=2,145 for economic shock; 823 for health shock; 106 for environmental shock and 200 for social shock.

Source: Authors' calculation based on ELMPS 2018.

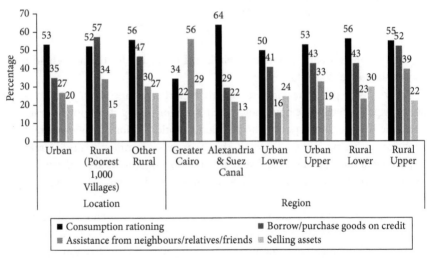

Figure 10.14 Percentage of households using different coping mechanisms by location and region, households who experienced shocks during the past year, 2018.

Note: Multiple strategies are possible (N=2,723). Showing most common strategies only.

Source: Authors' calculation based on ELMPS 2018.

to be stronger. This may be because people living in Greater Cairo may have relatively more rich neighbors, friends, and relatives, who can afford to provide assistance without expecting it back, when compared with those residing in rural areas.

Moreover, as the education level of the household head increased, the household tended to use the different types of coping strategies more evenly (Figure 10.15).

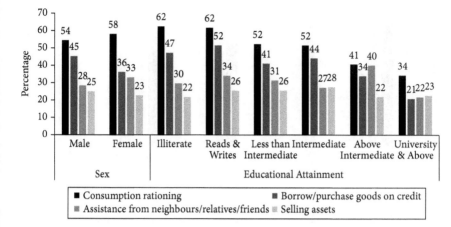

Figure 10.15 Percentage of households using different coping mechanisms by characteristics of household head, households with shocks during the past year, 2018.
Note: Multiple strategies are possible (N=2,723). Showing most common strategies only.
Source: Authors' calculation based on ELMPS 2018.

Borrowing and purchasing on credit were more prevalent as coping strategies among male-headed households (45 percent) than female-headed households (36 percent). In contrast, assistance from neighbors, relatives, and friends was more frequently reported by female-headed households (33 percent) than by male-headed households (28 percent). This confirms the existing evidence regarding the hardship position of women in Egypt in terms of access to formal credit as compared with their male peers (see Roushdy and Selwaness, 2015; and World Bank, 2018).

A similar pattern of coping strategies is observed among rich households when compared with their poorer counterparts (Figure 10.16). The pattern does not vary much by household head job formality and sector of activity (Figure 10.17). Consumption rationing, followed by borrowing and assistance, remain the most commonly used strategies regardless of type of social assistance received (Figure 10.18).

10.4.2 Food insecurity

In this section, we turn to investigate food insecurity and the characteristics of households who experienced food insecurity. As stated earlier, around 25 percent experienced some form of food insecurity during the month preceding the survey interview. Figure 10.19 shows the percentage of households who experienced food insecurity during the month that preceded the survey interview by food insecurity domain (See Appendix 10.1 for details). About 15 percent of Egyptian

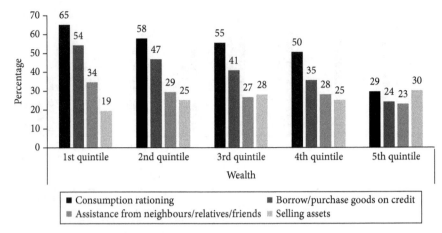

Figure 10.16 Percentage of households using different coping mechanisms by wealth quintile, households with shocks during the past year, 2018.
Note: Multiple strategies are possible (N=2,723). Showing most common strategies only.
Source: Authors' calculation based on ELMPS 2018.

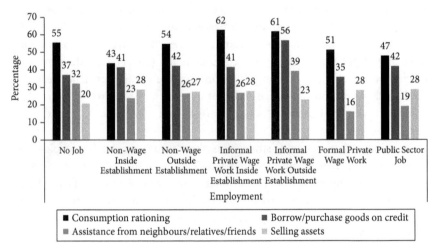

Figure 10.17 Percentage of households using different coping mechanisms by sector of employment of head of household, households with shocks during the past year, 2018.
Note: Multiple strategies are possible (N=2,723). Showing most common strategies only.
Source: Authors' calculation based on ELMPS 2018.

households experienced anxiety or uncertainty about food supply, 24 percent had insufficient quality of food, and 13 percent had insufficient food intake.

Moreover, households' perception of the severity of food insecurity varied substantially across households. Figure 10.20 indicates that among households that reported food insecurity, 28 percent reported a mild level of food insecurity,

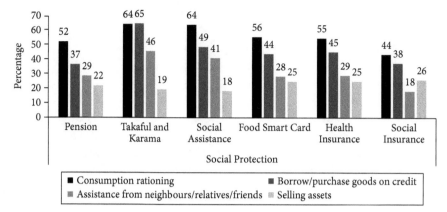

Figure 10.18 Percentage of households using different coping strategies by type of social protection, households with shocks during the past year, 2018.

Note: Multiple strategies are possible. N=682 for pension; 264 for Takaful and Karma; 209 for social assistance; 2,309 for food ration cards; 1,648 for health insurance; 535 for social insurance. Showing most common strategies only.

Source: Authors' calculation based on ELMPS 2018.

38 percent reported a moderate level, while 34 percent reported a severe food insecurity (See details in Appendix 10.1). Around 48 percent of the households that were exposed to severe food insecurity in the past month were exposed to an economic shock in the past year, compared with 34 percent among households that experienced a moderate degree, 23 percent among those that experienced a mild degree of food insecurity, and 6 percent among households that were food secure (Figure 10.20).

10.4.2.1 Which households were food insecure?

Figure 10.21 shows food insecurity by household head characteristics. Male-headed households were more likely to be food insecure (26 percent), compared with female-headed households (22 percent). Food insecurity was highest among households with adult and young adult heads. Food insecurity substantially decreased with the household head's educational attainment as well as his/her parents' education level (Figure 10.21 and Figure 10.22). Moreover, exposure to food insecurity was lower if more members of the household held a secondary or higher education degree (Figure 10.23) or enjoyed the stability of a public or a formal private job.

Household head job security and place of work were closely related to the household's vulnerability to food insecurity. More than a third of the households whose heads had an informal private sector job or non-wage job outside establishments suffered from food insecurity, as opposed to 20 percent if the head was working in the public or the formal private sectors (Figure 10.24).

Households were more vulnerable to food insecurity if the head was working in the accommodation and food service sector (33 percent) or in the agriculture sector (31 percent) (Figure 10.25).

Panel A:

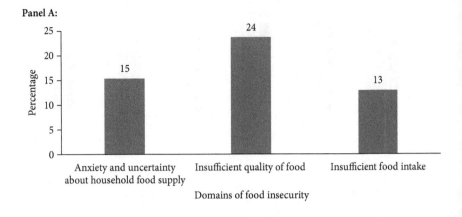

Panel B:

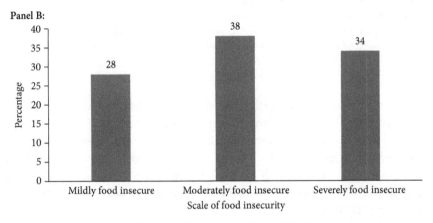

Figure 10.19 Percentage of households who experienced food insecurity in the past month by domain and degree, 2018.

Note: Multiple domains are possible for Panel A, N=15,746 for Panel A and N= 3,840 for Panel B.

Source: Authors' calculation based on ELMPS 2018.

Similar to exposure to shocks, experiencing food insecurity substantially decreased with household wealth status. About 39 percent of the poorest quintile of households were food insecure, compared with only 11 percent among the richest quintile of households. Large households of more than four members were more food insecure (30 percent) than smaller households (22 percent) (Figure 10.26).

Additionally, Figure 10.33 indicates that food insecurity was highest in the 1,000 poorest villages (31 percent), followed by other rural areas (28 percent), compared with 21 percent among urban households. Nevertheless, the severity of the exposure only slightly varied among both groups of rural areas. The two regions that had the highest rates of food insecurity were rural Upper Egypt (32 percent)

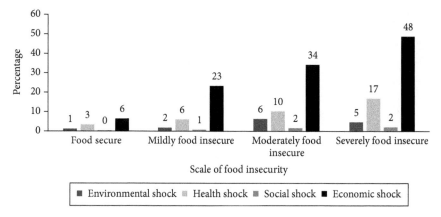

Figure 10.20 Percentage of households who experienced shocks by degree of food insecurity, 2018.

Note: (N=15,584).

Source: Authors' calculation based on ELMPS 2018.

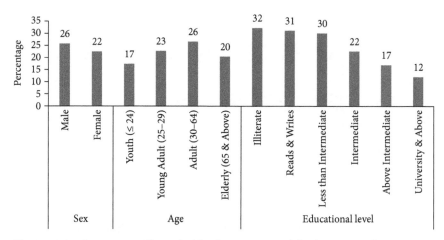

Figure 10.21 Percentage of households who experienced food insecurity by characteristics of head of household, 2018.

Note: N=15,746.

Source: Authors' calculation based on ELMPS 2018.

and Alexandria and Suez Canal (31 percent). Around 10–11 percent of the households residing in urban and rural Upper Egypt, and in rural Lower Egypt were exposed to severe food insecurity, compared with less than 2 percent among Greater Cairo households (Figure 10.27).

Similar results are also observed for the relationship between social protection schemes and food insecurity as with exposure to shocks (Figure 10.28). The highest rate of food insecurity was observed among Takaful and Karama beneficiaries

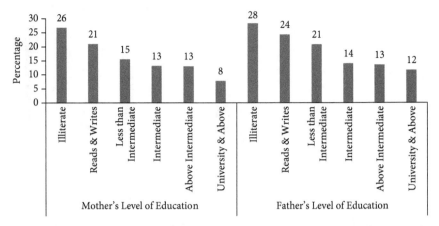

Figure 10.22 Percentage of households who experienced food insecurity by parental education of head of household, 2018.

Note: N=15,611 for mother's education and N=15,625 for father's education.

Source: Authors' calculation based on ELMPS 2018.

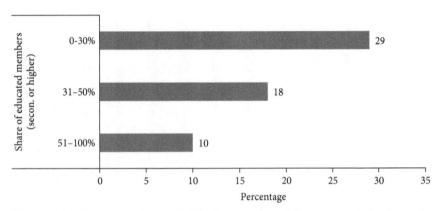

Figure 10.23 Percentage of households who experienced food insecurity by share of household members aged 18 and above with secondary or higher education, 2018.

Note: N=15,667.

Source: Authors' calculation based on ELMPS 2018.

(53 percent) and those receiving social assistance (45 percent), while the lowest rates were observed among households that had access to social insurance (21 percent), pensions (23 percent), or health insurance benefits (25 percent).

It is also worth mentioning that over a quarter of the households who received food smart cards suffered from food insecurity over the previous month. Furthermore, the degree of the food insecurity was highest among households receiving social assistance or Takaful and Karama conditional cash transfers. Less than 9 percent of the households receiving pensions or insurance benefits reported severe food insecurity, compared with 18 percent of the households

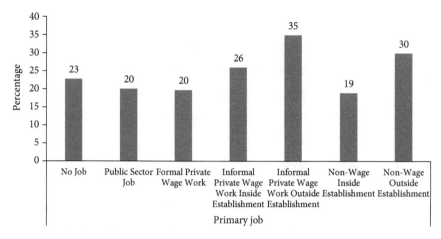

Figure 10.24 Percentage of households who experienced food insecurity by sector of employment of head of household, 2018.

Note: Primary job (3 months) (N=15,740).

Source: Authors' calculation based on ELMPS 2018.

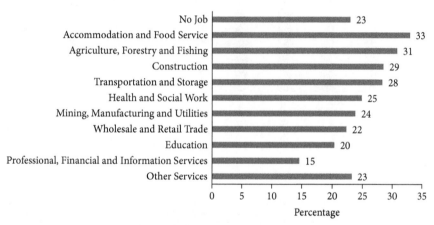

Figure 10.25 Percentage of households who experienced food insecurity by economic activity of the head of household, 2018.

Note: Primary job (three month reference period) (N=15,746).

Source: Authors' calculation based on ELMPS 2018.

receiving social assistance and 15 percent of the Takaful and Karama beneficiaries (Figure 10.28).

10.4.2.2 Households' strategies to cope with food insecurity

Contrary to exposure to shocks, where only 5 percent of the households reported doing nothing to cope with the shock (Figure 10.12), over 54 percent of the households did not adopt any coping mechanism when experiencing food insecurity. This provides evidence that food insecurity is probably mostly chronic

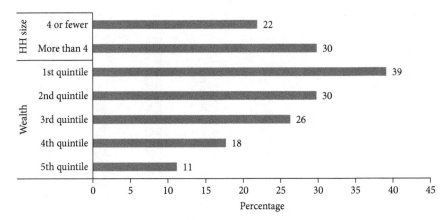

Figure 10.26 Percentage of households who experienced food insecurity by characteristics of the household, 2018.

Note: N=15,746.

Source: Authors' calculation based on ELMPS 2018.

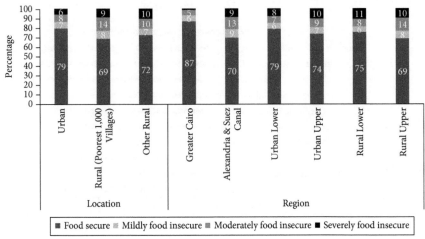

Figure 10.27 Percentage of households who experienced different degrees of food insecurity, by location and region, 2018.

Note: (N= 15,746).

Source: Authors' calculation based on ELMPS 2018.

rather than a sudden episode or a temporary shock. On the other hand, 34 percent of the households who experienced food insecurity borrowed or purchased food on credit, 19 percent received assistance from neighbors, relatives, and friends to cope with the food insecurity.[3] Other coping strategies were very minimally reported by households (Figure 10.29).

---

[3] The analysis of this section focuses on households who experienced food insecurity alone without other types of shocks to ensure that the adapted coping strategies were used to cope with food insecurity exclusively.

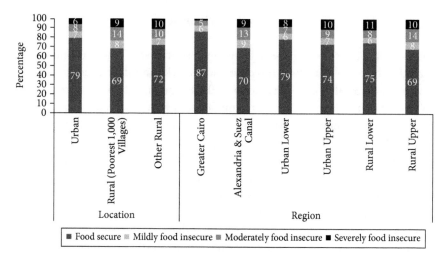

Figure 10.28 Percentage of households who experienced different degrees of food insecurity by social protection coverage, 2018.

Note: Coverage for at least one member. N=4,031 for pension; 777 for Takaful and Karama; 658 for social assistance; 12,385 for food ration cards; 9,924 for health insurance; 4,410 for social insurance.

Source: Authors' calculation based on ELMPS 2018.

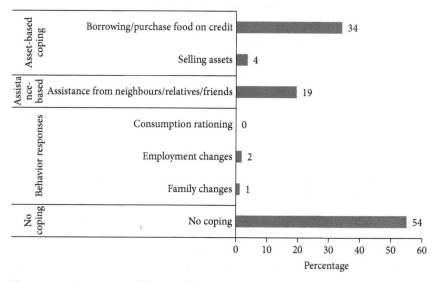

Figure 10.29 Percentage of households using different coping strategies, households with food insecurity, 2018.

Note: Multiple coping strategies are possible (N=2,608).

Source: Authors' calculation based on ELMPS 2018.

10.5 Conclusion

This chapter aims to provide a better understanding of the vulnerability of Egyptian households to food insecurity and shocks and their coping strategies. The results show that almost a quarter of the Egyptian households were exposed to food insecurity either solely or in combination with shocks. Economic shocks were the most common distress (14 percent), mostly in the form of reduced income or loss of employment, followed by health shocks (5 percent).

Households residing in rural areas, particularly in Upper Egypt, or large in size were more vulnerable to shocks and food insecurity during the study period. Food insecurity, but not shocks, was slightly more prevalent among the 1,000 poorest villages of Egypt than their other rural counterparts. Yet overall, poor households were almost four times as likely to have experienced food insecurity and more than twice as likely to have experienced shocks than their rich household peers. The characteristics of both the head and all members of the household were closely related to their vulnerability and resilience. Households with heads who had less than intermediate education, worked in the informal private sector, were self-employed, or outside an establishment, or in the agriculture sector were more likely to have experienced food insecurity and shocks.

Similarly, the higher the share of household members with secondary education or above or having at least one member of the household with a formal job (whether in the public or private sector) substantially decreased the household's vulnerability. Male-headed households appeared to be slightly more vulnerable, particularly to food insecurity, than female-headed households. This could be a question of gender differences in household resource allocation. A large body of research argues that household resources controlled by women are often associated with better child welfare in terms of educational and nutritional outcomes (Namoro and Roushdy, 2010; Roushdy, 2004, and Quisumbing and Maluccio, 2000). It may also be owing to the existence of social protection schemes that particularly target female headed households, or the effect of the gender and culture norms where people generally feel that single mothers or female breadwinners need more support than men.

Household coping mechanisms were primarily consumption rationing and borrowing or receiving assistance from neighbors, relatives, and friends. Over 50 percent of the households who experienced shocks used consumption rationing in the form of reduced spending on health, food, or education. All of these have the potential to harm the human capital of the households and its vulnerability to shocks and severe food insecurity. On the other hand, over a third of the households depended on informal borrowing and assistance, which provides evidence of how social capital plays a vital role in households' resilience to turbulent events, more than formal sources of loans and use of assets. The results also highlight some gender difference in coping mechanisms, where male household heads were more likely to use borrowing while female household heads were more likely to receive assistance. This is consistent with our potential explanation regarding receiving assistance and culture norms. It may also confirm previous evidence on the weaker position of women in Egypt in accessing not only formal credit but also informal borrowing.

In 2020, Egyptian households were hit by the economic slowdown and health shocks caused by the COVID-19 pandemic. Similar to the coping mechanisms reported in this chapter, most households whose income was affected during the crisis relied on stressful strategies such as consumption rationing: reducing consumption of meat, poultry, and fish (90 percent), reducing the amount of food (36 percent), or reducing the number of meals (20 percent). Additionally, around half of these households reported borrowing from friends and relatives (CAPMAS, 2020).

The results of this chapter call for several interlinked policy measures to increase the resilience of Egyptian households to shocks and prevent them from using stressful strategies that may harm their human capital and render them more vulnerable to shocks. First, it is important to note how, despite the fact that formal credit and insurance mechanisms play a crucial role in managing risks worldwide (Dercon, 2002; Okamoto, 2011), this does not seem to be the case in Egypt. Poor Egyptian households did not access formal loans, which left them with only the option of informal borrowing, which may be costly. It is crucial to develop policies that aim to increase the access of households owning few assets to low-cost loans. Special attention should be given here to female-headed households, which generally experience low access to formal credit in Egypt. This measure would not only provide such under-privileged households with a more effective way to cope with shocks, but also has the potential to decrease their vulnerability to future shocks and chronic food insecurity.

Second, it is also vital to provide poor households with formal social safety nets that are flexible enough to help poor households that are already covered by social protection schemes through adjusting their cash transfers as needed and new households that may suddenly fall under the poverty line during shocks. Third, expanding the types of cash transfer programs that deliberately target women, such as the Takaful program, is vital given the evidence on how household vulnerability and child welfare is related to the gender of who controls the resources of the household.

Fourth, the coping strategies adapted by Egyptian households in response to shocks, which were mostly in the form of consumption rationing, were not effective enough in protecting them but rather had clear and irreversible consequences on the nutritional and educational status of future generations. Accordingly, the government's top priority should be towards developing *ex ante* risk reduction programs beside *ex post* poverty alleviation and coping programs, in order to prevent deterioration in the nutritional health and educational status of children.

Fifth, labor market reforms are urgently needed to help poor household members to find a formal job that provides social insurance coverage and other non-monetary benefits. Special efforts should be directed towards inaugurating a better investment climate combined with a well-functioning private sector, in order to boost the creation of new long-term, formal, good-quality jobs. Such interventions have proved successful in preventing the adverse effects of major crisis in several developing countries (see Skoufias, 2003). The results show access to formal, inside establishment jobs and to social security benefits were associated with considerably lower exposure to shocks and food insecurity in Egypt.

Appendix 10.1

Table A10.1 Description of key variables.

Variable	Description
Food insecurity	Experienced anxiety and uncertainty about household food supply, insufficient quality, insufficient food intake during the past four weeks
Food insecurity access scale score	Degree of food insecurity
Food secure	Household did not experience any food insecurity condition during the past four weeks or experienced worry but rarely
Mildly food insecure	Experienced worries about not having enough food sometimes or often, inability to eat preferred foods, rarely eating less variety of meals than desired, rarely eating undesirable meals
Moderately food insecure	Experienced lack of food quality by eating less variety of meals or undesirable food-sometimes or often, reducing the size of meals or number of meals rarely or sometimes
Severely food insecure	Experienced reduced size or number of meals often, running out of food even if rarely
Shocks	
Environmental shock	Experienced drought, flood, erosion, crop pest, or livestock disease during the past 12 months
Economic shock	Experienced high cost of agricultural input, loss of employment, or reduced income during the past 12 months
Health shock	Experienced human disease, accident, death of working member, or death of a household member during the past 12 months
Social shock	Experienced theft, conflict, violence, or a fire during the past 12 months
Coping Strategies	
A. Behavior-based coping strategies	
1. No coping	No coping strategy used

Table A10.1 Continued

Variable	Description
2. Consumption rationing	Coped by reducing consumption, eating less food, reducing spending on health, reducing spending on education
3. Employment changes	Coped by working, migrating, working for food
4. Family changes	Coped by sending members to beg, sending a family member to live with other relatives
B. Assistance-based coping strategies	Coped by receiving cash or in-kind assistance from neighbors/ relatives
C. Asset-based coping strategies	
1. Borrowing	Coped by formal or informal borrowing (cash or in kind) as well as purchasing food/goods on credit
2. Use of assets	Coped by selling assets or spent savings or consuming seed stock/ livestock
Household characteristics	
Age group-head of household	Youth (≤24), young adult (25–29), adult (30–64) and elderly (65+)
Education of household members	Share of household members with secondary or higher education (age 18 and above)
Wealth	Categorical variable that uses household wealth score to assign each household to five income quintiles

Source: Authors' compilation.

References

Ajefu, J.B. (2017) "Income Shocks, Informal Insurance Mechanisms, and Household Consumption Expenditure Micro-Evidence from Nigeria," *International Journal of Social Economics*, 44 (12): 1818–32.

Akramov, K.T. and G. Shreedhar (2012) "Economic Development, External Shocks, and Food Security in Tajikistan," International Food Policy Research Institute, Discussion Paper 01163.

Altman, M., T.G.B. Hart, and P.T. Jacobs (2009) "Household Food Security Status in South Africa," *Agrekon: Agricultural Economics Research, Policy and Practice in Southern Africa*, 48 (4): 345–61.

Assaad, R. and C. Krafft (2014) "Youth Transitions in Egypt: School, Work, and Family Formation in an Era of Changing Opportunities." Silatech, Working Paper. doi: 10.1017/CBO9781107415324.004.

Assaad, R. and C. Krafft (2015) "Is Free Basic Education in Egypt a Reality or a Myth?" *International Journal of Educational Development*, 45: 16–30. doi: 10.1016/j.ijedudev.2015.09.001.

CAPMAS (Central Agency for Public Mobilization and Statistics) (2020) *The Impact of Coronavirus on Egyptian Households*. Cairo: CAPMAS.

Coates, J., A. Swindale, and P. Bilinsky (2007) *Household Food Insecurity Access Scale (HFIAS) for Measurement of Household Food Access: Indicator Guide (v. 3)*. Washington, DC. Food and Nutrition Technical Assistance Project, Academy for Educational Development.

Dercon, S. (2002) "Income Risk, Coping Strategies, and Safety Nets," *The World Bank Research Observer*, 17 (2): 141–66.

ESCWA (United Nations Economic and Social Commission for West Asia) (2020) *Mitigating the Impact of COVID-19: Poverty and Food Insecurity in the Arab Region*. Beirut: ESCWA.

Fafchamps, M. (2011) "Risk Sharing between Households," in J. Benhabib, A. Bisin, and M.O. Jackson (eds) *Handbook of Social Economics*, pp. 1255–79. San Diego, CA and Amsterdam: North-Holland.

Fafchamps, M. and F. Gubert (2007) "The Formation of Risk Sharing Networks," *Journal of Development Economics*, 83 (2): 326–50.

Fafchamps, M. and S. Lund (2003) "Risk-Sharing Networks in Rural Philippines," *Journal of Development Economics*, 71 (2): 261–87.

Heitzmann, K., S. Canagarajah, and P. Siegel (2002) "Guidelines for Assessing the Sources of Risk and Vulnerability." Social Protection Discussion Paper Series. Washington, DC.

Heltberg, R. et al. (2012) "Anatomy of Coping: Evidence from People Living through the Crises of 2008–11." World Bank, Policy Research Working Paper No. WPS 5957.

Holzmann, R. and S. Jorgensen (1999) "Social Protection as Social Risk Management: Conceptual Underpinnings for the Social Protection Sector Strategy Paper." Washington, DC: World Bank.

International Monetary Fund (2014) *Arab Republic Of Egypt: First Review Under The Extended Arrangement*. Washington, DC: International Monetary Fund.

International Monetary Fund (2015) *Arab Republic of Egypt: 2014 Article IV Consultation-Staff Report*. Washington, DC: International Monetary Fund.

Knight, L. et al. (2015) "Household Shocks and Coping Strategies in Rural and Peri-Urban South Africa: Baseline Data from the Size Study in Kwazulu-Natal, South Africa," *Journal of International Development*, 27: 213–33.

Krafft, C., R. Assaad, and K. Rahman (2021) "Introducing the Egypt Labor Market Panel Survey 2018." *IZA Journal of Development and Migration* (Forthcoming).

Lokshin, M.M. and R. Yemtsov, R. (2004) "Household Strategies of Coping with Shocks in Post-Crisis Russia," *Review of Development Economics*, 8 (1): 15–32.

Namoro, S.D. and R. Roushdy, R. (2010) "Intrahousehold Resource Allocation in Egypt: Women Empowerment and Investment in Children," *Middle East Development Journal*, 1 (1): 105–21.

OAMDI (Open Access Micro Data Initiative) (2018) "Labor Market Panel Surveys (LMPS), http://erf.org.eg/data-portal/. Version [2.0] of Licensed Data Files; ELMPS 2018." Egypt: Economic Research Forum (ERF).

Okamoto, I. (2011) "How Do Poor Rural Households in Myanmar Cope with Shocks? Coping Strategies in a Fishing and Farming Village in Rakhine State," *Developing Economies*, 49 (1): 89–112.

Quisumbing, A. and J.A. Maluccio (2000) "Intrahousehold Allocation and Gender Relations: New Empirical Evidence from Four Developing Countries." Discussion Paper No 84 - Food Consumption and Nutrition Division, International Food Policy Research Institute. Washington, DC.

Roushdy, R. (2004) "Intrahousehold Resource Allocation in Egypt: Does Women's Empowerment Lead to Greater Investments in Children?" Economic Research Forum Working Paper Series No. 410. Cairo.

Roushdy, R. and I. Selwaness (2015) "Young People's Labor Market Outcomes during a Period of Transition," in R. Rania and M. Sieverding (eds) *Panel Survey of Young People in Egypt (SYPE) 2014: Generating Evidence for Policy, Programs, and Research.* Cairo: The Population Council.

Santos, I. et al. (2011) "How Do the Poor Cope with Shocks in Bangladesh? Evidence from Survey Data." World Bank Policy Research Working Paper No. 5810 (September).

Skoufias, E. (2003) "Economic Crises and Natural Disasters: Coping Strategies and Policy Implications," *World Development*, 31 (7): 1087–1102.

Staatz, J.M., V.C. D'Agostino, and S. Sundberg (1990) "Measuring Food Security in Africa: Conceptual, Empirical, and Policy Issues," *American Journal of Agricultural Economics*, 72 (5): 1311–17.

World Bank (2001) *World Development Report 2000/2001: Attacking Poverty.* New York: Oxford University Press.

World Bank (2011) *No Small Matter: The Impact of Poverty, Shocks and Human Capital Investments in Early Childhood Development*, edited by Harold Alderman. Washington, DC: World Bank.

World Bank (2015) *International Bank For Reconstruction And Development Project Appraisal Document On A Proposed Loan In The Amount Of USD400 Million To The Arab Republic Of Egypt For A Strengthening Social Safety Net Project.* Washington, DC: World Bank.

World Bank (2018) *The Global Findex Database 2017.* Available at: https://globalfindex.worldbank.org/. Accessed 20 August 2020.

World Bank (2020) *Poverty and Shared Prosperity: Reversals of Fortune, Nature.* doi: 10.1038/302765a0. Washington, DC: World Bank.

Yilma, Z. et al. (2014) "Coping with Shocks in Rural Ethiopia," *Journal of Development Studies*, 50 (7): 1009–24.

11

Associations between Economic Vulnerability and Health and Wellbeing in Egypt

Maia Sieverding and Rasha Hassan

The link between health and people's social and economic circumstances was clearly established in the 1948 Constitution of the World Health Organization (WHO), which defined health as "a state of complete physical, mental and social wellbeing and not merely the absence of disease or infirmity" (WHO, 1995). Since that time, there has been a burgeoning field of study on the social determinants of health, or the aspects of our social and economic conditions that affect health, and particularly inequalities in health. Numerous aspects of economic vulnerability, including poverty, income inequality, and employment conditions, are recognized as social determinants of health that impact the distribution of health outcomes across populations (Marmot et al., 2008). The relationship between human wellbeing and economic, social, and environmental vulnerabilities has also received renewed attention through the 2030 Sustainable Development Goals (SDGs). The intersectoral nature of the SDGs emphasizes how good health and wellbeing (the focus of Goal Three) are closely related to goals that address economic vulnerability, including reducing poverty (Goal One) and promoting full employment and decent work for all (Goal Eight).

Although there is a well-established relationship between economic vulnerability and a wide range of health outcomes, the study of this relationship is complicated by reverse causality. Poor economic outcomes contribute to poor health, and poor health can also lead to worse economic outcomes, as well as greater vulnerability to the effects of negative economic shocks (UNDP, 2014). Health is thus a critical aspect of multidimensional poverty in Egypt and elsewhere in the region (ESCWA, 2017). Health and access to healthcare are also important dimensions of inequality. Compared with those who are poor or vulnerable to poverty in Egypt, the middle class spends more on health and is more likely to benefit from health insurance (World Bank, 2019). There are also disparities in access to health-promoting services such as skilled birth attendance, as well as child health outcomes, including infant mortality and nutrition, by wealth and urbanity (ESCWA and ERF, 2019).

Maia Sieverding and Rasha Hassan, *Associations between Economic Vulnerability and Health and Wellbeing in Egypt* In: *The Egyptian Labor Market: A Focus on Gender and Economic Vulnerability.* Edited by: Caroline Krafft and Ragui Assaad, Oxford University Press. © Economic Research Forum 2022. DOI: 10.1093/oso/9780192847911.003.0012

The relationships between health and economic outcomes are also nuanced and may depend on other sociodemographic factors, such as education or gender. For example, in Egypt unemployment is only a risk factor for poor mental health among young men, and not among young women (Liu, Modrek, and Sieverding, 2017). Working conditions also have impacts on health outcomes among the employed. For instance, while being employed is generally associated with better mental health (van der Noordt et al., 2014), precarious and temporary work is associated with poor mental health globally (Marmot et al., 2008) and among youth in Egypt in particular (Rashad and Sharaf, 2018). Hazardous working conditions, high job stress, and low control over working conditions can all lead to negative physical and mental health outcomes (Marmot et al., 2008).

Although there is an extensive body of research on economic and especially labor market dynamics in Egypt (e.g. Assaad, 2009; Assaad and Krafft, 2015; Chapter 1), very little of this research has addressed the associations between economic vulnerability, employment, and health outcomes. These relationships are consequently poorly understood in Egypt, reflecting the broader scarcity of studies in the Middle East and North Africa (MENA) region that have addressed the social determinants of health. The main objectives of this chapter are thus to provide a descriptive analysis of the sociodemographic correlates of health and wellbeing in Egypt and to examine how different measures of economic vulnerability are associated with health outcomes.

11.1 Methods

11.1.1 Measures of health and wellbeing

The Egypt Labor Market Panel Survey (ELMPS) 2018 (see Krafft, Assaad, and Rahman, 2021 for details on the ELMPS) includes several new health measures that allow us for the first time to conduct a detailed examination of the associations between economic vulnerability and different health outcomes in the Egyptian population. We focus on three measures of health and wellbeing: disability, self-rated health, and subjective wellbeing. Together, these outcomes capture dimensions of both physical and psychological health, which is central to the WHO definition of health as a state of overall wellbeing.

As with most censuses and household surveys, prior to 2018 the ELMPS collected information on disability through a single question "do you have any kind of mental or physical disability?" This question formulation has been shown to lead to considerable underestimation of disability rates owing to the widespread stigmatization of disability, including in the MENA region (El-Saadani and

Metwally, 2019). The definition of disability adopted by the WHO and others has also shifted toward a focus on disability as an interaction between an individual's functional status and her environment; with more accessible physical and social environments, functional limitations may not affect individuals' participation in society (UN-WG, 2009). To capture this conceptualization of disability, the UN-Washington Group on Disability Statistics (UN-WG, 2009) developed a new measurement tool for disability that captures different levels of difficulty in six functional domains: seeing, hearing, walking, cognition, self-care, and communication. For each domain, the response options are "no difficulty," "some difficulty," "a lot of difficulty," and "cannot do it at all" (see Table A11.1).

In addition to presenting the detailed prevalence of different forms of functional limitation in the Egyptian population, we construct three measures of disability following the UN-WG guidance (UN-WG, 2009). The "broad" definition of disability categorizes as disabled any individual with at least some difficulty in performing tasks in at least one of the six domains. The "narrow" definition categorizes as disabled only individuals who cannot do tasks in at least one of the six domains at all. In between these two definitions, the "medium" definition of disability categorizes as disabled those who responded that they have a lot of difficulty performing or cannot do tasks at all in any of the six domains.

We also analyze self-rated health, the only one of our measures that was also captured in the ELMPS 2012 using the same question format. Self-rated health is one of the most widely used measures of general health status in social science and health literature, and has been shown to predict mortality when adjusted for age (Jylhä, 2009). The self-rated health measure in the ELMPS asks respondents "how is your health in general?" with response categories of "very good or excellent," "good," "fair," "bad," or "very bad". Owing to the small sample size of respondents who gave answers of "bad" or "very bad," we aggregate these two categories with "fair."

Finally, the ELMPS 2018 included the World Health Organization Wellbeing Index (WHO-5), a simple and widely used measure of general subjective wellbeing that has also been validated as a screening tool for depression (Topp et al., 2015). The WHO-5 consists of a set of five positively phrased statements about the respondent's life over the past two weeks for which the response choices range from five (all the time) to zero (none of the time). The full WHO-5 scale is shown in Table A11.2. The total raw score for the index ranges from 0 to 25, and is then multiplied by four to convert to a more easily interpretable scale ranging from zero (minimal wellbeing) to 100 (maximal wellbeing) (Topp et al., 2015). A cutoff point of 50 is commonly used to indicate low wellbeing (Harsha et al., 2016; Topp et al., 2015), and we follow this convention, presenting in most of our analyses the percentage of individuals who suffered from low subjective wellbeing.

11.1.2 Operationalization of economic vulnerability

Vulnerability is conceptualized as the "prospect of eroding people's capabilities and choices" (UNDP, 2014). While all people may experience unexpected events that lead to greater vulnerability (shocks), the capabilities conceptualization of vulnerability recognizes that certain categories of people tend to be structurally vulnerable and thus face long-term barriers to improving their circumstances (UNDP, 2014). People can thus be vulnerable *to* different types of negative outcomes and experiences that can be social or environmental as well as economic. In focusing on economic vulnerability, we are emphasizing factors that are associated with poorer economic outcomes or the risk of experiencing poor economic outcomes, factors that can be operationalized in many ways. Our analysis is not focused on what causes economic vulnerability, but rather on how economic vulnerability may lead to other forms of vulnerability, namely poor health and wellbeing. For instance, poverty is both an indicator of economic vulnerability and a factor that makes people vulnerable to negative health outcomes. Disability and sex are examples of structural factors that contribute to vulnerability to poor health both directly as well as through their association with economic vulnerability.

To examine the relationship between economic vulnerability and vulnerability to poor health and wellbeing, we analyze our three health outcomes according to indicators that capture several different dimensions of economic vulnerability. The first dimension is **sociodemographic characteristics** that may be associated with structural vulnerability, both in terms of economic and health outcomes. These factors include sex, age, and education, as well as marital status. Marital status is included because women who are divorced or widowed may face stigma and weakened structures of economic support that make them more vulnerable (Sieverding and Hassan, 2016).[1] We also look at several geographic indicators given the uneven development levels within Egypt, namely region of residence (Greater Cairo, Alexandria and the Suez Canal Cities, Urban Lower, Urban Upper, Rural Lower, and Rural Upper), and rural versus urban residence. Lastly, we examine the broad measure of disability and a yes/no indicator of whether the individual reports having a chronic illness, both of which are important indicators of structural vulnerability, as correlates of self-rated health and subjective wellbeing.

We then look at several measures related to **poverty.** Our main measure in this category is wealth quintiles derived from the ELMPS asset index (Krafft, Assaad, and Rahman, 2021). We also construct a measure that examines poverty by urban

---

[1] Divorce rates have also increased in Egypt from 0.9 percent in 2006 to 2.2 percent in 2018 (CAPMAS, 2018), making this a growing category of potentially vulnerable women.

versus rural residence. Although rural areas in Egypt are disadvantaged according to many economic and social indicators (Chapter 8), urban areas—and informal and poor urban neighborhoods in particular—also suffer from social and economic marginalization (Khalil et al., 2018; Sieverding et al., 2019), which may impact health outcomes. Our measure thus consists of four categories: urban residents in wealth quintiles one and two (urban poor), urban residents in quintiles three through five (urban non-poor), rural residents in quintiles one and two (rural poor), and rural residents in quintiles three through five (rural non-poor). We also construct a variable that compares the poor in Greater Cairo to the non-poor in Greater Cairo in order to explore health outcomes in Egypt's capital megacity. In addition to these measures of poverty, we look at the association between health indicators and household food security, which is closely correlated with poverty (Coates, Swindale, and Bilinsky, 2007). We use the Household Food Insecurity Access Scale (HFIAS) included in the ELMPS to categorize households as food secure, mildly food insecure, moderately food insecure, and severely food insecure following Coates, Swindale, and Bilinksy (2007).[2]

We also examine a group of indicators related to **employment vulnerability**. The first of these is labor force status, which is categorized as employed, unemployed, or out of the labor force.[3] For those who are employed, we then look at a measure of sector of employment that takes into consideration whether employment is formal (with a contract or social insurance coverage) and/or regular. We follow Chapter 2 in using the categorization of public sector employment (almost all of which is formal and regular), formal regular private wage work, informal regular private wage work, irregular wage work, self-employment, employers, and unpaid family workers. Irregular wage work is a particularly vulnerable category in Egypt (Chapter 2).

For the employed, our indicators of workplace conditions that may be associated with economic and health vulnerability are whether the respondent experienced a workplace-related injury or health issue in the past 12 months (yes/no),[4] and the number of hazards the respondent reported being exposed to in her/his workplace, categorized as no hazards, one hazard, two to three hazards, and four

---

[2] Two items in the original HFIAS scale were not included in the ELMPS; these items only affect the measurement of the severely food insecure category, which may therefore be underestimated in our data. According to the HFIAS categorization, a food secure household may experience some worry about food access, but rarely, and does not experience food access restrictions. A mildly food insecure household worries about food access sometimes or often, and/or is unable to eat preferred foods or a diversity of foods, but rarely. A moderately food insecure household experiences these conditions of non-preferred or monotonous diets more regularly and/or has started to cut back on food quantity. A severely food insecure household in the ELMPS data is one that cuts back on food quantity often and/or has no food to eat at times, even if rarely (Coates, Swindale, and Bilinsky, 2007).

[3] This measure is based on the market definition of labor force, with search required for unemployment and a one-week reference period.

[4] In the 2012 ELMPS questionnaire the reference period for workplace injury was "ever" rather than "in the past 12 months."

or more hazards.[5] Finally we look at job satisfaction, which may reflect a combination of physical and psychological conditions in the workplace, as well as respondents' aspirations or expectations for employment. Job satisfaction is maintained as in the original question in the ELMPS, with the options of "fully satisfied," "rather satisfied," "neither satisfied nor dissatisfied," "rather dissatisfied," and "fully dissatisfied."

We examine an additional two sets of measures of economic vulnerability only in relation to subjective wellbeing. The first of these is household exposure to **shocks**, or unexpected events, in the 12 months prior to the survey. Whereas poverty is a form of structural vulnerability, shocks of different kinds can affect all households and may lead to direct or indirect health consequences. To operationalize household experience of shocks, we follow Chapter 10 in categorizing shocks as natural, economic, health, or social.[6]

Finally, we include a set of gender-specific measures related to **women's autonomy**, which is associated with positive reproductive and maternal health outcomes for women and their children (Ewerling et al., 2017). The relationship between women's autonomy and their mental health or subjective wellbeing has been less studied. Our measures of women's autonomy include several single-question indicators in the ELMPS that capture women's direct access to financial resources or ability to access financial and social support. These gender-specific dimensions of economic vulnerability are particularly important in a context where the majority of women are not in the labor force (Chapter 1) and thus do not have personal wage income, but may have access to financial resources that can reduce vulnerability to negative outcomes. Importantly, some of these measures also capture women's economic vulnerability *within* the household, for example if they are dependent on their husbands for financial support. The measures of access to financial and social support are all binary indicators coded one if a woman has access to money in her hand; personally owns property or another asset; has a family member close enough that she can visit and return home in the same day; has a family member with whom she could spend the night if she had a problem; and has a family member who could help her financially if she had a problem.[7] We also include a measure of decision-making, which

---

[5] The hazards that respondents were asked about were dust and flames, fire or fuel, loud noise and vibrations, extreme high or low heat, high-risk equipment, working underground, working in a sea/river, working in a dark place, insufficient ventilation, chemicals/pesticides, explosives, bending for a long time, and no toilet. This measure is not available in ELMPS 2012.

[6] Natural shocks were drought, flood, erosion, crop pest, and a high level of livestock disease. Economic shocks were if the household experienced unusually high costs of agricultural inputs, loss of employment, or reduced income. Health shocks were the death of a family member, unusually high rate of illness, or an accident. Social shocks were fire, theft, and exposure to conflict or violence (Chapter 10). The shocks section of the questionnaire was new in the ELMPS 2018, so these measures cannot be constructed for 2012.

[7] The answer choice "don't know" was coded to "no" for the latter two items.

is commonly used in the literature as an indicator of women's autonomy (Salem, VanderEnde, and Yount, 2015; Samari and Pebley, 2018). The decision-making variable is constructed from a nine-item sequence about who in the household has primary say over decisions related to daily activities, purchases, and children. Since the answer choices are different for married and unmarried women, we restrict this analysis to married women only, with the categories of joint decision-making; mostly joint, then husband; mostly joint, then wife; primarily husband; and primarily wife.[8]

11.1.3 Analysis

Our analysis is descriptive and examines associations between the measures of economic vulnerability laid out here and health outcomes. The results should thus be interpreted with the reverse causality between poor economic outcomes and poor health in mind. Many of the economic vulnerabilities we examine are also overlapping, such that individuals may be vulnerable by multiple measures (e.g. having both low education and insecure or hazardous employment).

In keeping with our focus on economic vulnerability, we conduct most of our analyses for the working age population aged 15–64. Although health and wellbeing among older adults and children are important topics, the determinants of health among these populations are likely different than those for general adult population and are thus outside the scope of the chapter. An important exception is that we present disability rates for the entire population aged five and above to be able to compare with the 2017 Egyptian Census, which also used the UN-WG measure (CAPMAS, 2019). For self-rated health, we descriptively compare patterns for the working age population between ELMPS 2012 and 2018.

Owing to the inherently subjective nature of the WHO-5 and self-rated health questions, individuals for whom responses were given by proxy were removed from the analyses for these questions.[9] All analyses are divided by sex both because of our focus on women's economic vulnerability and because the burden of poor health among men and women differs substantially in the region (Mokdad et al., 2014). Disaggregating by sex is also particularly important for a focus on economic vulnerability in a context where there is a strong gendered division of

---

[8] To construct the aggregated measure all nine decision-making items were first coded into whether the decision was primarily made by the wife, husband, jointly, or by someone else. If seven or more decisions were made jointly, this was coded as joint decision-making. If three to six decisions were taken jointly and the husband made more of the remaining decisions than the wife, this was coded as "mostly joint, then husband." The converse was coded as "mostly joint, then wife." If two or fewer decisions were made jointly and the husband made more decisions alone than the wife, this was coded as "primarily husband" and conversely for "primarily wife."

[9] The corresponding sample sizes were N=5,260 (10.3 percent) total, N=2,833 (7.2 percent) for those aged 15 and above, and N=2,663 (7.4 percent) for the working age population 15–64.

labor within the household (El-Feki, Barker, and Heilmen, 2017) and women who participate in the labor market tend to hold different types of jobs than men (Chapter 2). Men and women are thus exposed to different risk factors for poor health and may be affected differently by the same risk factors owing to differences in social and economic structures.

11.2 Results

11.2.1 Disability

11.2.1.1 Prevalence of disability

Whereas the single-question measure of disability in the ELMPS 2012 produced a disability rate of 2.8 percent for the Egyptian population aged five and above (3.8 percent for men and 1.8 percent for women), the expanded UN-WG measure used in ELMPS 2018 produced rates of 16.6 percent using the broad definition, 4.6 percent using the medium definition, and 0.9 percent using the narrow definition. Interestingly, the disability rates found in the ELMPS 2018 were considerably higher than those found in the 2017 Egyptian Census, which also used the UN-WG instrument. The Census found rates of 10.5 percent, 2.5 percent and 0.5 percent for the broad, medium, and narrow definitions respectively (CAPMAS, 2019). Figure 11.1 compares the rates found in the Census and ELMPS by sex and definition of disability. The Census estimates were consistently lower than the ELMPS estimates across definition and sex. Yet whereas the Census found very slightly higher rates of disability for men than women under the broad and medium definitions, the ELMPS found higher rates for women under both definitions. Nevertheless, both results confirm those of previous studies that the single question measure of disability is a severe underestimate for disability when defined as any level of functional limitation (El-Saadani and Metwally, 2019), and appears to have underestimated the disability rate more for women. The single question measure of disability appears to produce a disability rate most comparable with the medium definition using the UN-WG measure.

Figure 11.2 shows the prevalence of any level of limitation (some difficulty or greater; broad definition) or considerable limitation (a lot of difficulty or cannot do at all; medium definition) for each of the six domains captured in the UN-WG instrument, by sex, comparing the Census 2017 and ELMPS 2018. The comparison reveals that the difference in overall disability rates between the two datasets stemmed primarily from two functional domains. The ELMPS found higher rates of disability in the domains of vision and mobility for both men and women. Mobility was the most common form of disability (by any definition) for both sexes in both datasets, at 4.7 percent for men in the Census and 7.9 percent for men in ELMPS, and 6.3 percent (Census) and 11.4 percent (ELMPS) for women.

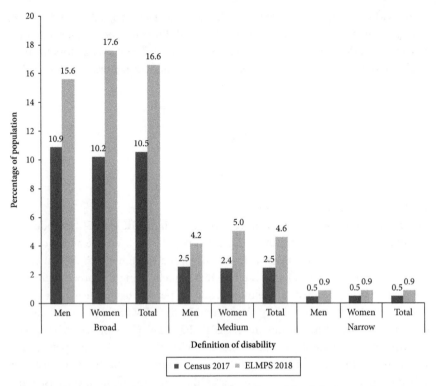

Figure 11.1 Rates of disability (percentage of population) by definition and sex, population aged 5+, Census 2017 and ELMPS 2018.

Source: Census results are authors' calculations from data in CAPMAS (2019, Table 29). ELMPS results are authors' calculations from the ELMPS 2018.

The ELMPS also found a higher rate of disability among women in the domain of remembering (6.1 percent any limitation) as compared to the Census (3.6 percent). Differences between the Census and ELMPS in other domains were less than one percentage point, and functional limitations in self-care and communication were the least prevalent in both datasets. Why the two datasets found different rates for vision and mobility in particular is unclear.

As expected, across all domains rates of disability increased considerably with age and were highest for the age group 65 and above (see detailed Table A11.3 in Appendix 11.1). Among the youngest age groups, disabilities in the domains of seeing and remembering or concentrating were the most common, but less than 3 percent of the age group in all cases. The increasing prevalence of disability with age is an important concern for overall population health and service provision in the context of aging populations such as that of Egypt. Figures 11.3 and 11.4 illustrate the increase in different levels of functional limitation, by age, for men and women aged 45 and older, using mobility and remembering or concentrating as

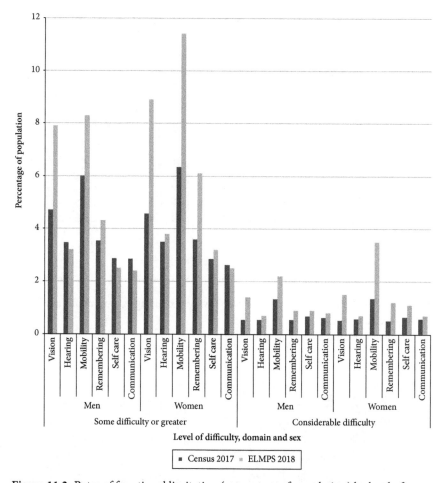

Figure 11.2 Rates of functional limitation (percentage of population) by level of limitation, domain and sex, population aged 5+, Census 2017 and ELMPS 2018.

Source: Census results are authors' calculations from data in CAPMAS (2019, Table 29). ELMPS results are authors' calculations from the ELMPS 2018.

examples. By the 60–64 age group about a quarter of men and nearly 40 percent of women had at least some difficulty walking or climbing stairs (Figure 11.3). Rates of mobility limitation rose rapidly for each age group after age 60, reaching around two-thirds of women and 60 percent of men by the 75 and above age group. In the oldest age group, 8 percent of women and 3 percent of men said they could not walk or climb stairs at all.

Figure 11.4 shows the results for remembering or concentrating, which was one of the domains with the widest gender gap in disability rates. Although the disability rate in this domain was lower than with mobility, just over 30 percent of men and nearly half of women experienced at least some difficulty remembering

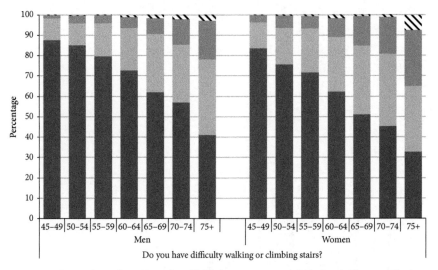

Figure 11.3 Functional limitations in mobility by sex and age group, adults aged 45+, 2018 (percentage).

Source: Authors' calculations from the ELMPS 2018.

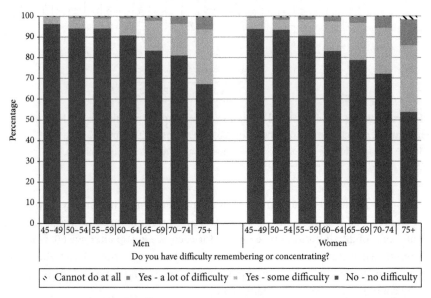

Figure 11.4 Functional limitations in remembering or concentrating by sex and age group, adults aged 45+, 2018 (percentage).

Source: Authors' calculations from the ELMPS 2018.

or concentrating by age 75 and above. The consistently higher rates of disability among older women as compared with men may be due in part to differential mortality, which means that, particularly in the oldest age groups, there will be more women at the higher end of the age group than men. However, the differential rates of disability appear to begin as early as the 40s and 50s for some domains, so this may also be related to factors such as physical activity, overall physical health, or differences in risk factors for disability onset.

11.2.1.2 Disability rates by sociodemographic characteristics and poverty indicators

Figure 11.5 shows the broad disability rate among the working age population by sociodemographic characteristics (medium and narrow definition rates by these characteristics can be found in Appendix 11.1 Table A11.4). The total broad disability rate for the working age population was 15.6 percent, much higher than the 2.3 percent obtained in the ELMPS 2012 using the single question measure. The much higher rate of disability among the working age population detected using the UN-WG measure has wide-ranging economic implications, from the need for medical devices or services, to accommodations that individuals should be granted in education and workplaces, to potential impacts on labor force participation.

The prevalence of any form of disability was considerably higher for the least educated, particularly the illiterate and those who could only read and write. This is likely in part because of the strong barriers that children and youth face in accessing schooling when they have a disability at a young age (El-Saadani and Metwally, 2019), as well as the fact that older individuals are overrepresented among the lowest education categories. It is also possible that low-educated individuals were more exposed to the risk of becoming disabled, for example through engagement in hazardous work, but since we do not know when individuals acquired a disability this is not possible to determine. Turning to marital status, disability was most common among the widowed, which is expected as this population is generally older, and lowest among the never married who are likely to be younger than the married. Disability rates were also higher in urban areas than rural ones, which is likely owing to the older age profile of urban populations (Chapter 1). However, when looking at the results by region, it becomes clear that the higher rate of disability in urban areas is driven by Greater Cairo and Alexandria and the Suez Canal cities. Disability rates in urban Lower and Upper Egypt were not higher than in the rural areas of these regions.

In Figure 11.6 we examine the prevalence of disability, using the broad definition, by our set of poverty indicators. The disability rate was higher among the poorest wealth quintile (18 percent) than in wealth quintiles two through five, for which disability rates ranged from 14 to 16 percent and did not decrease

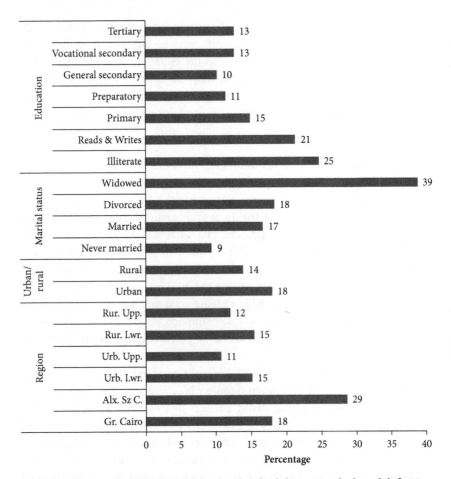

Figure 11.5 Percentage of the population with a disability, using the broad definition, by sociodemographic characteristics, working aged population 15–64, 2018.
Source: Authors' calculations from the ELMPS 2018.

consistently by quintile. The high rates of disability in the poorest quintile may reflect the disadvantage that disabled individuals face in terms of earning a livelihood.

By urban/rural and poverty status, disability rates were highest among the urban poor and lowest among the rural non-poor. This reflects a combination of the older profile of urban residents and the association of disability with poverty. Disability rates were high in Greater Cairo overall, at 18 percent among the non-poor and 19 percent among the poor. Finally, disability rates increased progressively with greater levels of food insecurity. This is expected given the association of poverty with both disability and food security, but is greatly concerning in terms of the double burden of poorer health and food insecurity among those

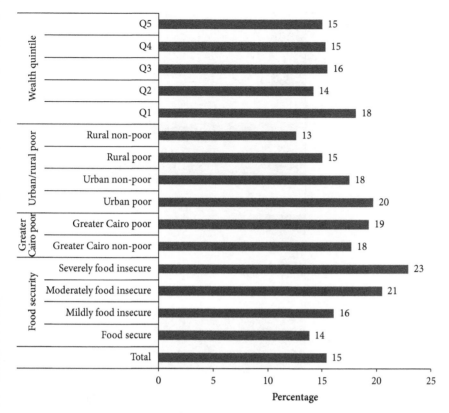

Figure 11.6 Percentage of the population with a disability, using the broad definition, by poverty indicators, working aged population 15–64, 2018.
Source: Authors' calculations from the ELMPS 2018.

who were disabled. Patterns for men and women were similar across all of the indicators (data not shown), but one notable difference was that disability rates among women in Cairo were higher for both the non-poor (19 percent compared with 16 percent for men) and the poor (21 percent compared with 18 percent for men).

11.2.1.3 Disability and employment

In this section, we turn to the association between disability and our employment-related measures of economic vulnerability. It is important to remember in this analysis that disability can affect individuals' employment opportunities, and that hazardous forms of employment could lead to increased disability rates, for example owing to workplace injuries. Beginning with labor force participation, Figure 11.7 shows different patterns by sex. Whereas employed men were somewhat less likely to have a disability, by either the broad or medium definitions,

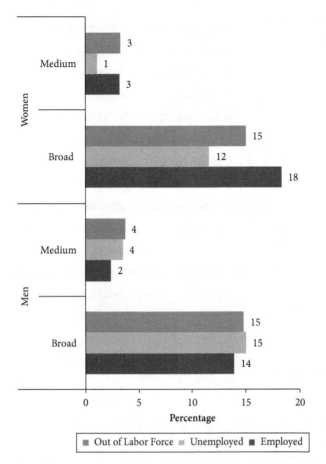

Figure 11.7 Disability rates (broad and medium definitions) by labor force status and sex (percentage), working aged population 15–64, 2018.
Source: Authors' calculations from the ELMPS 2018.

than those who are unemployed or out of the labor force, for women the opposite was true. The higher rates of disability among women who were employed may be because employed women are older than those who are out of the labor force or unemployed (Chapter 1). Unemployed women in particular tend to be younger (Chapter 1), likely explaining the low rates of disability, although the number of unemployed women with a disability using the medium definition is small, and the result should be interpreted with caution.

For men, in contrast, who tend to work across the age distribution (Chapter 1), having a disability of some form may lead to a disadvantage in finding employment. This interpretation is supported by looking at the results a different way, in terms of the composition of men who do and do not have a disability by labor force status. Whereas a similar percentage of men with and without disability by the broad definition were employed (71 percent with and 73 percent without disability), unemployed (5 percent with and 4 percent without disability), and out of the labor force (24 percent with and 23 percent without a disability,) this was not the case when we used the medium definition of disability. Using this definition, employment rates for men with a disability (63 percent) were considerably lower than for those without a disability (73 percent), and they were more likely to be out of the labor force (31 percent, compared with 23 percent among men who did not have a disability). This suggests that men with higher levels of functional limitation may face barriers to employment.

Other results indicate that exposure to work hazards is associated with the prevalence of disability. The percentage of men with a disability increased from 11 percent among those who were exposed to no hazards at work, to 14 percent among those exposed to one hazard or two or three hazards, and 19 percent among those exposed to four or more hazards. For women, the corresponding disability rates increased from 15 percent to 19 percent, 22 percent, and 28 percent respectively. Exposure to hazards was more common in more vulnerable forms of work, and particularly irregular wage and unpaid family work (data not shown), yet the disability rate in these categories was lower. This indicates that disentangling the relationship between disability and employment type requires multivariate analysis that takes into account the age profiles of the different categories of employment.

11.2.2 Self-rated health

11.2.2.1 Self-rated health by demographic characteristics
As with disability, self-rated health is strongly associated with age. The percentage of people who rated their health as very good was highest in 2018 among the youngest age group (15–24) at 56 percent for men and women (Figures 11.8A and 11.8B, respectively). By the oldest age group of those aged 65 and above, these percentages decreased to 9 percent for men and 6 percent for women. A similar pattern by age was observed in 2012, but comparing the ELMPS 2012 and ELMPS 2018 data, Figures 11.8A and 11.8B show that the percentage of people who rated their health fair, bad, or very bad declined substantially in 2018 (14 percent in 2018 versus 21 percent in 2012 for men, and 16 percent in 2018 versus 23 percent in 2012 for women). Correspondingly, the percentage of both men and women who rated their health as very good increased from 2012 to 2018. Increases in self-rated health were seen across the age distribution but particularly among the youngest aged 15–24. Women had somewhat lower levels of self-rated health than men in both years.

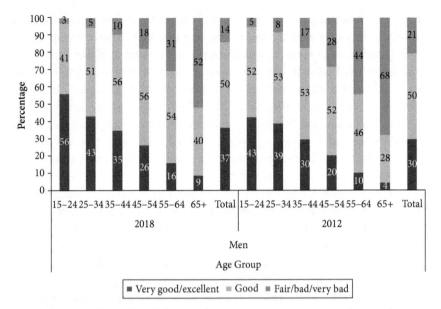

Figure 11.8A Self-rated health by age group, men aged 15+, 2012 and 2018 (percentage).

Source: Authors' calculations from the ELMPS 2012 and 2018.

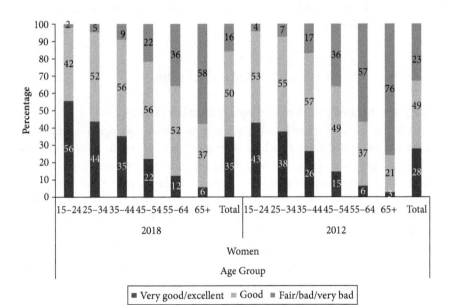

Figure 11.8B Self-rated health by age group, women aged 15+, 2012 and 2018 (percentage).

Source: Authors' calculations from the ELMPS 2012 and 2018.

As the patterns of self-rated health were generally similar across 2012 and 2018, apart from the higher overall levels of self-rated health in 2018, for the remainder of this section we focus on the results for 2018. Marital status was associated with self-rated health in a manner that is consistent with the age gradient in self-rated health. Widowed men (22 percent) and women (33 percent), who were likely to be older, were most likely to report poor health, whereas among the never married, who were likely to be younger, few men (4 percent) or women (3 percent) reported poor health. Among both married and divorced men, about 13 percent reported poor health. For women, in contrast, 10 percent of married women reported poor health whereas 21 percent of divorced women reported poor health.

There was also substantial regional variation in self-rated health. Overall, rural residents had an advantage in self-rated health as compared with urban residents, with 45 percent of rural men reporting very good or excellent health compared with 32 percent of urban men. Among women, the corresponding shares were 43 percent among rural residents and 31 percent among urban residents. This urban disadvantage in self-rated health was likely due in part to the older age structure of urban areas, but is a pattern we see repeated in subjective wellbeing (see Section 11.2.3.1) and may also be due to factors related to living conditions in urban areas. As seen in Figure 11.9, the urban disadvantage in self-rated health seems to be driven by major urban areas, and particularly Greater Cairo, where only 18 percent of men and women reported that their health was very good or excellent. The gap in self-rated health between Urban and Rural Lower Egypt was smaller, and self-rated health in Urban Upper Egypt was somewhat better than in Rural Upper Egypt for both men and women.

Finally, as expected, both self-rated chronic illness and disability were highly correlated with self-rated health. Only 8 percent of working-age men with a chronic illness reported that they had very good or excellent health, compared with 44 percent of those without a chronic illness. Among women, the comparable figures were 9 percent for those with a chronic illness and 44 percent for those without a chronic illness. The percentage of people reporting very good health was also lower for those with a disability by the narrow definition (12 percent of men and 6 percent of women) as compared with those with a disability by the broad definition (15 percent of men and women; see Appendix 11.1 Table A11.5 for full data).

11.2.2.2 Self-rated health by economic vulnerability

There was not a strong gradient in self-rated health by wealth quintile for either men or women. For men, 36–40 percent consistently reported themselves as having very good or excellent health across wealth quintiles, and for women 37–41 percent. The main difference in self-rated health by wealth was that somewhat

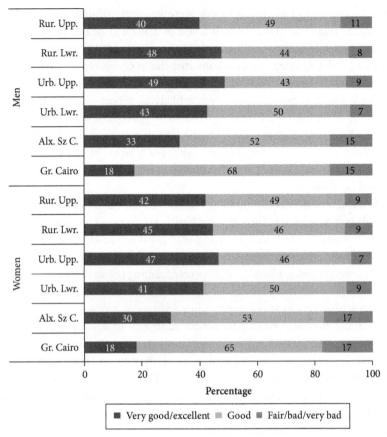

Figure 11.9 Self-rated health by region and sex, working age population 15–64, 2018 (percentage).
Source: Authors' calculations from the ELMPS 2018.

higher percentages of men (15 percent) and women (14 percent) in the poorest wealth quintile reported themselves as having poor health as compared with the other quintiles.

A stronger gradient was seen when examining the overlap of urbanity with poverty (Figure 11.10). Among men, the percentage with very good health was nearly the same for the urban poor and non-poor, but poor urban men suffered higher rates of poor health (16 percent versus 11 percent). Non-poor rural men had a small advantage in self-rated health over poor rural men, but both had higher levels of very good health than urban men. Among women, a consistent gradient in self-rated health can be seen in which the urban poor were the least healthy and the rural non-poor the healthiest according to their own assessments.

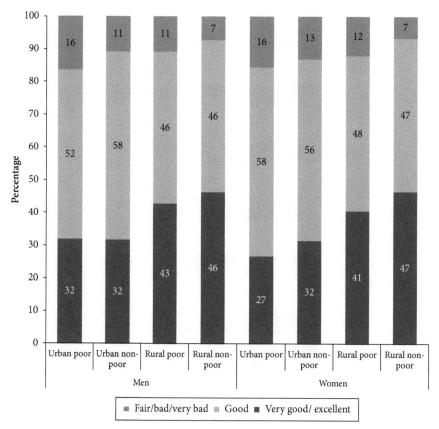

Figure 11.10 Self-rated health by urban/rural poverty and sex, working age population 15–64, 2018 (percentage).
Source: Authors' calculations from the ELMPS 2018.

Turning to employment indicators, Figure 11.11 shows that there were differences by sex in the associations between self-rated health and labor force status. Among men, those who were out of the labor force were most likely to rate their health as very good (48 percent), followed by the unemployed (41 percent), and then the employed (37 percent). The unemployed, however, were more likely to rate their health as poor (13 percent) than men in the other two categories. Among women, the pattern was quite different, with the unemployed most likely to rate their health as very good (45 percent), which may be owing to the young age profile of this relatively small group. As with men, women who were employed were least likely to rate their health as very good (33 percent), and those who were out of the labor force lay in the middle (39 percent).

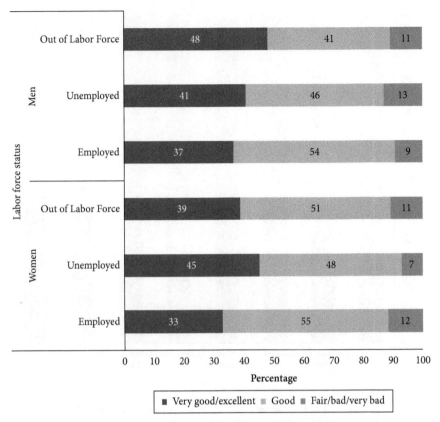

Figure 11.11 Self-rated health by labor force status and sex, working age population 15–64, 2018 (percentage).
Source: Authors' calculations from the ELMPS 2018.

11.2.3 Subjective wellbeing

11.2.3.1 Subjective wellbeing by sociodemographic characteristics

The mean WHO-5 score for the 36,321 individuals aged 15 and above in the ELMPS 2018 who completed the WHO-5 scale was 52.6, with no difference in the mean score for men (52.8) versus women (52.4). Using the cutoff score of less than 50 for low wellbeing, 44.5 percent of men and 45.2 percent of women suffered from low wellbeing. This is higher than the population rate of 33.8 percent found in Palestine (sex-disaggregated data was not reported; mean WHO-5 score for the population was 58.0) (Harsha et al., 2016). This is the only other national-level data on the WHO-5 that we are aware of in the region, so it is unclear how Egypt compares with other countries in the MENA region on subjective wellbeing.

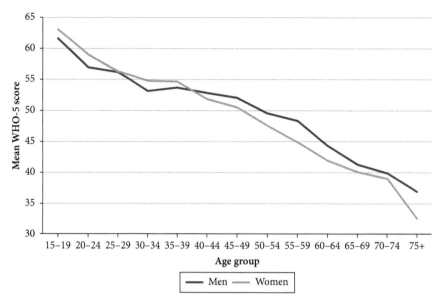

Figure 11.12 Mean WHO-5 score by age group and sex, ages 15+, 2018.
Source: Authors' calculations from the ELMPS 2018.

Figure 11.12 shows that there was a strong age gradient in wellbeing for both men and women. Whereas the mean WHO-5 scores for the youngest age group (15–19) were above 60 for both sexes, among those aged 70 and above the mean scores declined to below 40. Whereas women had a slight advantage in wellbeing scores at younger ages, this reversed around age 40 to a slight disadvantage.

Marital status again showed a clear relationship with low wellbeing (Figure 11.13). Low wellbeing was most prevalent among divorced women, with 64 percent experiencing low wellbeing compared with 51 percent of divorced men. Likewise, widowed women had high rates of experiencing low wellbeing (59 percent) compared with widowed men (49 percent). In contrast, unmarried women were the least likely to experience low wellbeing (32 percent) along with unmarried men (38 percent). The gender gap in wellbeing for those who were married or never married was much smaller than for the divorced and widowed.

In terms of residence, the percentage of people suffering from low wellbeing was higher among those living in urban areas than those living in rural areas (48 percent in urban areas and 39 percent in rural areas). Corresponding to this division, the data shows that the low wellbeing was considerably more prevalent in Greater Cairo (59 percent) than in other regions in the country (37–41 percent; data not shown).

In Figure 11.14 we examine the correlation between subjective wellbeing and other measures of health, using chronic illness and the broad and narrow definitions of disability. Low wellbeing was highest among people with a disability

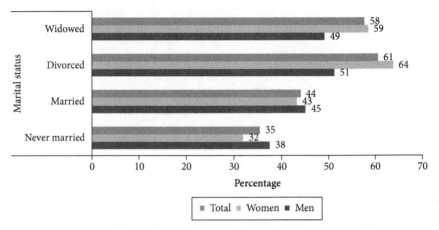

Figure 11.13 Low wellbeing by marital status and sex, working age population 15–64, 2018 (percentage).

Source: Authors' calculations from the ELMPS 2018.

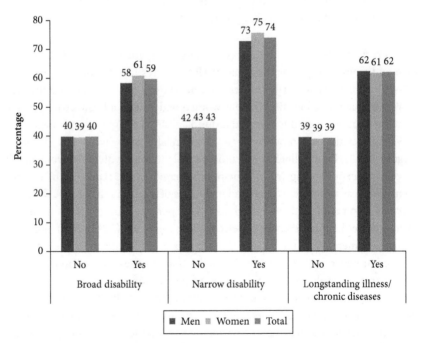

Figure 11.14 Low wellbeing (percentage) by disability and health status and sex, working age population 15–64, 2018.

Source: Authors' calculations from the ELMPS 2018.

according to the narrow definition (74 percent), whereas the percentage was lower among people with a disability according to the broad definition (59 percent). There was also a strong correlation between low wellbeing and long-standing illness and chronic diseases. These correlations, while expected, emphasize the relationship between physical and mental health.

11.2.3.2 Subjective wellbeing by poverty indicators and exposure to shocks

Turning to our measures of poverty and exposure to shocks, those in the poorest wealth quintile were the most likely to experience low wellbeing (47 percent), followed by those in quintile three (45 percent), quintile two (42 percent), quintile four (41 percent), and quintile five (39 percent; data not shown). The higher level of low wellbeing among quintile three was driven by men, whereas among women the percentage with low wellbeing declined across quintiles, but not by large amounts.

Figure 11.15 shows the association between low wellbeing and our other measures of poverty. Poor women in urban areas were the most likely to experience low wellbeing (51 percent), compared with poor urban men (46 percent) and men and women in other areas. As with self-rated health, there was a gradient by wealth and residency in which the urban poor experienced the worst subjective wellbeing and the rural non-poor the best. The 'urban penalty' was very clear among poor women in Greater Cairo, among whom 76 percent reported low wellbeing, compared with 59 percent of men and 57 percent of non-poor women in Cairo. In addition, people whose households were food secure—which is likely to be correlated with wealth—were considerably less likely to suffer from low wellbeing than people whose households suffered from even mild food insecurity.

The results also indicate that household exposure to most types of shocks was associated with low wellbeing. Figure 11.16 demonstrates that both men and women whose households experienced social shocks were the most likely to experience low wellbeing (60 percent and 63 percent), followed by people whose households experienced health shocks (53 percent among men and 56 percent among women). Among those whose households experienced natural shocks, in contrast, the percentage of men and women experiencing low wellbeing was similar to that of the population overall.[10]

11.2.3.3 Subjective wellbeing and employment

In this section, we turn to the relationships between labor force participation, employment, and wellbeing. Figure 11.17 again shows that patterns differ by sex; whereas unemployed men were the most likely to experience low wellbeing (48 percent), compared with men who were employed (43 percent) or out of the labor force (38 percent), among women there was no relationship between labor force

---

[10] The categories of shocks are not mutually exclusive, and some households may have experienced multiple shocks.

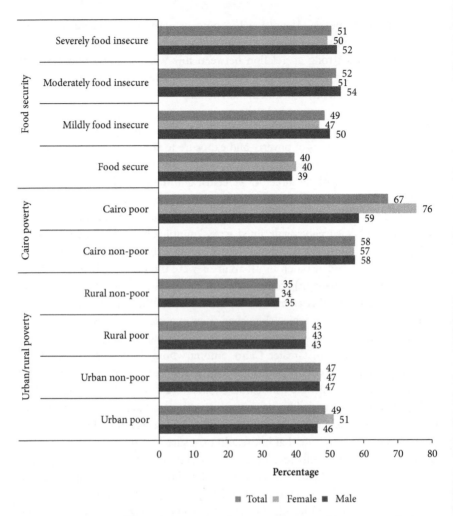

Figure 11.15 Low wellbeing by poverty indicators and sex, working age population 15–64, 2018 (percentage).
Source: Authors' calculations from the ELMPS 2018.

status and wellbeing. This is consistent with other studies showing that employment is associated with mental health among men in Egypt but not women (Liu, Modrek, and Sieverding, 2017).

Working conditions were also strongly associated with low wellbeing (Figure 11.18). Low wellbeing was more prevalent among those who had been injured at work (54 percent among men and 55 percent among women), compared with those who had not experienced a work injury in the previous 12 months (43 percent among men and 42 percent among women). Among women,

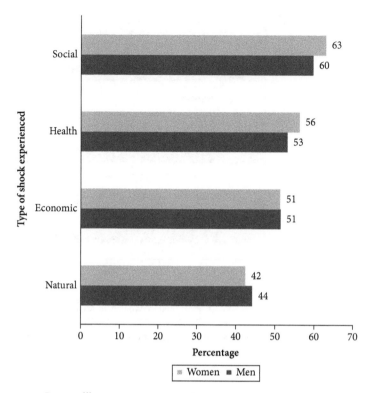

Figure 11.16 Low wellbeing among respondents whose households experienced a shock in the twelve months prior to the survey by type of shock and sex, working age population 15–64, 2018 (percentage).
Source: Authors' calculations from the ELMPS 2018.

very few had experienced a workplace injury, so the result should be interpreted with caution. In addition, people who were exposed to four or more hazards at work had the highest rates of experiencing low wellbeing and those who were not exposed to any hazards at work the lowest rates of low wellbeing. This result may be driven by hazards leading to health problems or injuries that affect wellbeing or by the association of hazards with job satisfaction. As also shown in Figure 11.18, those who were fully dissatisfied with their jobs, as well as men who were rather dissatisfied, were considerably more likely to report low wellbeing than those who expressed neutral or positive job satisfaction.

11.2.3.4 Low wellbeing and women's agency
In this section we examine the correlation between different indicators of women's agency and their subjective wellbeing. Given the importance of women's household structure for the theoretical linkages between agency and wellbeing,

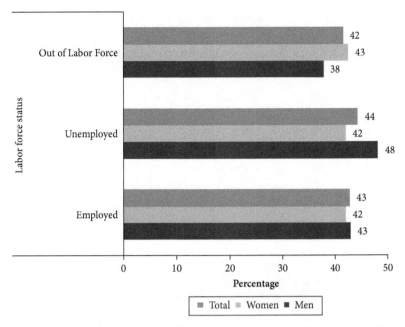

Figure 11.17 Low wellbeing by labor force status and sex, working age population 15–64, 2018 (percentage).
Source: Authors' calculations from the ELMPS 2018.

we divide this analysis by marital status. However, divorced and widowed women are combined into one category owing to sample size. Figure 11.19 illustrates the results for three of our indicators, not all of which support classic hypotheses about the role of financial independence for women. Regardless of marital status, the results show that women who did have direct access to household money had somewhat higher rates of low wellbeing than those who did not have direct access to money. The ELMPS data also do not show a consistent relationship between personal property or savings and wellbeing. Whereas unmarried women with personal property or savings had higher wellbeing, among the married and divorced or widowed the opposite was true.

The one indicator where we consistently found the expected relationship between financial autonomy and higher wellbeing was whether women had a family member who could help them financially if needed. Across marital statuses, women who said they had a family member they could turn to had somewhat lower rates of poor wellbeing. We did not find a consistent association between the other measures of family support and low wellbeing (data not shown). The lack of association between these factors and subjective wellbeing may be related to the simplicity of the single-item measures, or may be driven by other factors, such as poverty or employment, that affect both agency and wellbeing.

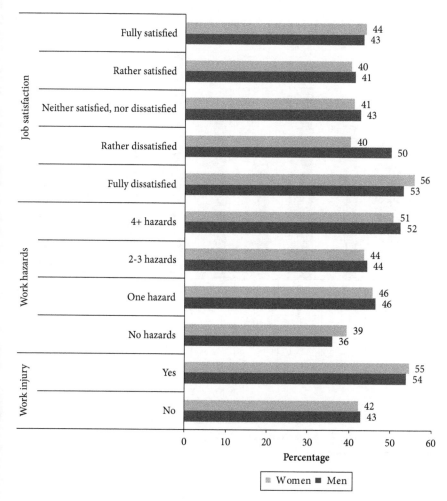

Figure 11.18 Low wellbeing by employment characteristics, working age population 15–64, 2018 (percentage).
Source: Authors' calculations from the ELMPS 2018.

Finally, turning to household decision-making (Figure 11.20), which we examine for married women only, we find that women who reported that they were the primary decision maker were most likely to experience low wellbeing (60 percent), whereas women who reported that they made decisions jointly with their husbands had the lowest rates of low wellbeing (41 percent). These results need to be examined in a multivariate context, as decision-making within the household may be correlated with sociodemographic characteristics. However, this calls into question whether women's independent decision-making—which is often used as an indicator of agency—is better for their wellbeing more broadly speaking.

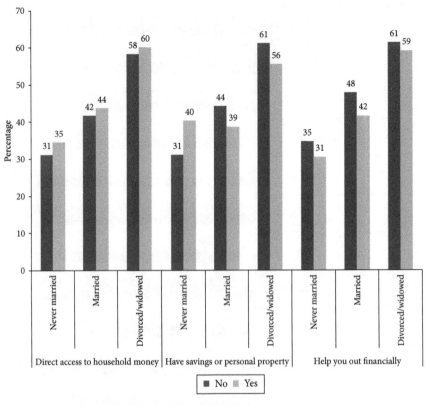

Figure 11.19 Low wellbeing by access to financial resources and marital status, women aged 15–64, 2018 (percentage).
Source: Authors' calculations from the ELMPS 2018.

11.3 Conclusion

Using the new measures available in the ELMPS 2018, our results demonstrate the relationship between different indicators of economic vulnerability and poor health in Egypt, as well as the substantial burden of poor health among the working age population that may in turn affect economic indicators. According to the ELMPS data, around one in six working-age individuals in Egypt has some level of disability in one of the six UN-WG domains. This is higher than the rate found in the 2017 Census and should be further explored. The implications of these figures for accommodations and environmental changes that are needed to help people with disabilities integrate into and remain in the labor market, as well as gain equal access to schooling among the young (see also El-Saadani and Metwally, 2019) are of critical importance at the social, economic, and personal levels. The fact that disability was strongly associated with low levels of subjective

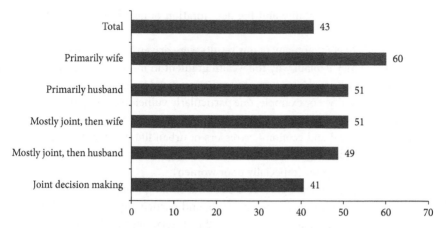

Figure 11.20 Low wellbeing by household decision-making, married women aged 15–64, 2018 (percentage).
Source: Authors' calculations from the ELMPS 2018.

wellbeing may be one indication of the degree to which such conducive environments do not currently exist.

Our results also found a high rate of low subjective wellbeing in the Egyptian population. The only available national comparator in the MENA region is Palestine, where the percentage of the population suffering from low wellbeing on the WHO-5 scale was around 10 percentage points lower (Harsha et al., 2016) than we find in Egypt with the ELMPS. To the best of our knowledge, there is no validated cutoff point for the WHO-5 scale to be used as an indicator for clinical depression in Egypt. Given the simplicity of the scale and its clear sensitivity to different socioeconomic characteristics of the population, this would be a useful area for future research into vulnerability and health, particularly mental health, in the country.

Across our health measures, there were several groups that appear to be particularly vulnerable to poor outcomes. Key among these were divorced and, to a somewhat lesser degree, widowed women. The burden of poor health among divorced women is likely related to the social stigma attached to divorce in Egypt, as well as greater economic vulnerability among this group. The poor health indicators among widowed women are likely due to poorer health among the elderly population in general, across measures of disability, self-rated health, and subjective wellbeing. Poor health and economic vulnerability among the elderly may also be self-reinforcing, particularly if they do not have social and/ or health insurance coverage. With the aging of the Egyptian population and populations in the MENA region in general (Angeli and Novelli, 2017; Hussein and Ismail, 2017), the elderly are thus a key population for whom further research is needed on mechanisms of economic support and means to address both economic vulnerability and the deterioration of health indicators after the age of 60.

Finally, it is likely that many of our results were driven by overlapping vulnerabilities. These may explain why the wealth gradient in most of our health indicators is not as stark as when we examine more nuanced indicators of employment, poverty, or urbanity. For example, one particularly vulnerable group that emerges from our analysis is the urban poor, and particularly poor urban women. The nature of the social and economic stressors of urban life in Egypt that appear to be negatively impacting health deserve further exploration, as well as how these stressors act on the poor (especially poor women).

Another important example is related to our finding that poorer working conditions were associated with poorer health, and particularly low subjective wellbeing. These results may be driven by direct relationships between working environments and health, as well as accumulated forms of disadvantage. For instance, the least educated are more likely to be engaged in less secure forms of employment that may also expose them to greater hazards at work. Similarly, the effect of women's agency on subjective wellbeing may be conditional on age, education, or household structure.

It is particularly important that future studies aim to better understand these overlapping vulnerabilities to poor health given the ongoing global COVID-19 pandemic. The widespread social distancing and lockdown measures that have been put in place across countries, including in Egypt, are uneven in their impacts on different population groups. Essential workers, those who do not have the option to work remotely owing to the nature of their jobs, and those who do not have the option to follow distancing measures owing to the economic necessity of working—in other words, many of those who are already vulnerable workers—may be more likely to be exposed to the virus. The pandemic is also likely to have impacts on mental health and wellbeing owing to factors including fear of infection, social isolation, job losses, and the added stresses of caregiving when services are closed (United Nations, 2020). For these reasons, further multivariate studies are needed in order to disentangle the relationships between health and economic vulnerability in Egypt, not only to explore the potential effects of the pandemic, but also to determine where interventions to improve health may be most successful in general.

Acknowledgments

We acknowledge the general support of the World Bank, the International Labour Organization, Agence Française de Développement, UN Women, and the Arab Fund for Economic and Social Development for the Egypt Labor Market Panel Survey 2018, on which this chapter is based. The authors appreciate the editorial assistance of Mattie Claire Albrecht.

Appendix 11.1

Table A11.1 UN-Washington Group on Disability Statistics Instrument.

Do you have difficulty seeing, even if wearing glasses?	1. No—no difficulty
Do you have difficulty hearing, even if using a hearing aid?	2. Yes—some difficulty
Do you have difficulty walking or climbing stairs?	3. Yes—a lot of difficulty
	4. Cannot do at all
Do you have difficulty remembering or concentrating?	
Do you have difficulty (with self-care such as) washing all over or dressing?	
Using your usual (customary) language, do you have difficulty communicating, for example understanding or being understood?	

Source: UN-Washington Group on Disability Statistics (2009)

Table A11.2 WHO-5 Wellbeing Scale

Over the past two weeks....						
..I have felt cheerful and in good spirits	All of the time (5)	Most of the time (4)	More than half the time (3)	Less than half the time (2)	Some of the time (1)	None of the time (0)
..I have felt calm and relaxed						
..I have felt active and vigorous						
..I woke up feeling fresh and rested						
..my daily life has been filled with things that interest me						

Table A11.3 Detailed disability rates by age group (percentage) using the UN-WG instrument, 2018.

	Age Group							
	5–14	15–24	25–34	35–44	45–54	55–64	65+	Total
Do you have difficulty seeing, even if wearing glasses?								
No—no difficulty	97.7	96.9	96.4	93.1	86.1	79.7	63.2	91.6
Yes—some difficulty	2.0	2.8	2.9	6.2	12.0	17.5	27.4	7.0
Yes—a lot of difficulty	0.3	0.3	0.5	0.6	1.7	2.5	8.3	1.2
Cannot do at all	0.0	0.0	0.1	0.1	0.2	0.2	1.1	0.2
Do you have difficulty hearing, even if using a hearing aid?								
No—no difficulty	99.1	99.1	98.8	98.5	96.6	92.0	75.0	96.5
Yes—some difficulty	0.6	0.6	0.8	1.3	2.9	6.7	20.4	2.9
Yes—a lot of difficulty	0.1	0.1	0.2	0.1	0.2	1.1	4.1	0.5
Cannot do at all	0.1	0.2	0.2	0.1	0.3	0.1	0.6	0.2
Do you have difficulty walking or climbing stairs?								
No—no difficulty	99.0	98.3	96.1	92.5	83.1	71.6	48.6	90.1
Yes—some difficulty	0.7	1.1	3.0	5.9	12.9	21.4	32.5	7.1
Yes—a lot of difficulty	0.1	0.5	0.7	1.3	3.6	6.1	16.3	2.4
Cannot do at all	0.1	0.2	0.1	0.2	0.3	0.9	2.6	0.4
Do you have difficulty remembering or concentrating?								
No—no difficulty	97.8	97.8	97.2	96.4	94.6	89.6	73.1	94.8
Yes—some difficulty	1.7	1.6	2.3	3.0	4.5	8.7	21.1	4.2
Yes—a lot of difficulty	0.3	0.4	0.4	0.4	0.7	1.5	5.2	0.8
Cannot do at all	0.2	0.2	0.2	0.3	0.2	0.1	0.6	0.2

Age Group								
	5–14	15–24	25–34	35–44	45–54	55–64	65+	Total
Do you have difficulty (with self-care such as) washing or dressing?								
No—no difficulty	98.5	99.0	99.2	98.6	97.5	94.8	81.9	97.2
Yes—some difficulty	1.1	0.5	0.5	0.8	1.8	3.7	11.6	1.9
Yes—a lot of difficulty	0.2	0.3	0.2	0.3	0.6	1.1	4.3	0.6
Cannot do at all	0.2	0.2	0.1	0.3	0.2	0.4	2.2	0.3
Using your usual (customary) language, do you have difficulty communicating?								
No—no difficulty	98.2	98.7	98.7	98.5	97.3	96.7	88.6	97.5
Yes—some difficulty	1.3	0.7	0.9	0.9	1.7	2.7	8.5	1.7
Yes—a lot of difficulty	0.3	0.4	0.2	0.3	0.6	0.4	2.4	0.5
Cannot do at all	0.2	0.2	0.2	0.3	0.4	0.2	0.6	0.2
Total	100.0	100.0	100.0	100.0	100.0	100.0	100.0	100.0
N	11,505	9,857	10,457	7,152	4,646	3,744	3,273	50,634

Source: Authors' calculations from the ELMPS 2018.

Table A11.4 Percentage of population with a disability using broad, medium, and narrow definitions, by sociodemographic characteristics, working aged population 15–64, 2018.

| | Definition | | |
	Broad	Medium	Narrow
Education			
Illiterate	24.6	7.5	1.9
Reads and writes	21.3	4.2	0.4
Primary	14.9	3.3	0.7
Preparatory	11.4	2.7	0.5
General secondary	10.2	2.2	0.5
Vocational secondary	12.7	2.2	0.2
Tertiary	12.7	2.4	0.3
Marital status			
Never married	9.4	3.1	1.2
Married	16.7	3.4	0.4
Divorced	18.3	3.4	0.6
Widowed	38.8	11.3	1.3
Region			
Gr. Cairo	17.9	4.5	0.8
Alx. Sz C.	28.6	6.3	0.5
Urb. Lwr.	15.1	3.4	0.8
Urb. Upp.	10.7	2.2	0.7
Rur. Lwr.	15.4	3.6	0.7
Rur. Upp.	12.0	2.9	0.6
Urban/Rural			
Urban	18.0	4.2	0.7
Rural	13.9	3.3	0.7
Total	15.6	3.7	0.7

Source: Authors' calculations from the ELMPS 2018.

Table A11.5 Self-rated health by sex, disability, and chronic illness status, working aged population 15–64, 2018.

			Very good/ excellent	Good	Fair/bad/ very bad	Total
Women	Broad disability	No	42	52	6	100
		Yes	15	46	40	100
	Narrow disability	No	38	51	11	100
		Yes	6	16	78	100
	Chronic illness	No	44	52	4	100
		Yes	9	48	43	100
Men	Broad disability	No	43	51	6	100
		Yes	15	48	37	100
	Narrow disability	No	39	51	10	100
		Yes	12	23	65	100
	Chronic illness	No	44	51	5	100
		Yes	8	46	46	100

Source: Authors' calculations from the ELMPS 2018.

References

Angeli, Aurora and Marco Novelli (2017) "Transitions in Late-Life Living Arrangements and Socio-Economic Conditions of the Elderly in Egypt, Jordan, and Tunisia." Economic Research Forum Working Paper Series No. 1083. Cairo.

Assaad, Ragui (ed.) (2009) *The Egyptian Labor Market Revisited*. Cairo: American University in Cairo Press.

Assaad, Ragui and Caroline Krafft (eds) (2015) *The Egyptian Labor Market in an Era of Revolution*. Oxford: Oxford University Press.

CAPMAS (Central Agency for Public Mobilization and Statistics) (2018) "Number of Divorce Cases [in Arabic]." Available at: https://www.capmas.gov.eg/Pages/IndicatorsPage.aspx?Ind_id=1089. Accessed September 8, 2019.

CAPMAS (2019) *Final Results of the Population and Housing Census of Year 2017 (Long Form)* [in Arabic]. Cairo: CAPMAS.

Coates, Jennifer, Anne Swindale, and Paula Bilinsky (2007) "Household Food Insecurity Access Scale (HFIAS) for Measurement of Food Access: Indicator Guide (Version 3)." Food and Nutrition Technical Assistance Project, Academy for Educational Development, Washington, DC.

El Feki, Shereen, Gary Barker, and Brian Heilmen (eds) (2017) "Understanding Masculinities: Results from the International Men and Gender Equality Survey (IMAGES) – Middle East and North Africa." UN Women and Promundo-US, Cairo and Washington, DC.

El-Saadani, Somaya, and Soha Metwally (2019) "Inequality of Opportunity Linked to Disability in School Enrollment among Youth: Evidence from Egypt," *International Journal of Educational Development*, 67 (May): 73–84.

ESCWA (United Nations Economic and Social Commission for West Asia) (2017) "Arab Multidimensional Poverty Report." ESCWA, Beirut.

ESCWA and ERF (Economic Research Forum) (2019) "Rethinking Inequality in Arab Countries." ESCWA, Beirut.

Ewerling, Fernanda, et al. (2017) "The SWPER Index for Women's Empowerment in Africa: Development and Validation of an Index Based on Survey Data," *The Lancet Global Health*, 5 (9): e916–23.

Harsha, Nouh, et al. (2016) "Wellbeing and Associated Factors among Adults in the Occupied Palestinian Territory (oPt)," *Health and Quality of Life Outcomes*, 14 (122).

Hussein, Shereen, and Mohamed Ismail (2017) "Ageing and Elderly Care in the Arab Region: Policy Challenges and Opportunities," *Ageing International*, 42 (3): 274–89.

Jylhä, Marja (2009) "What Is Self-Rated Health and Why Does it Predict Mortality? Towards a Unified Conceptual Model," *Social Science & Medicine*, 69 (3): 307–16.

Khalil, Deena, et al. (2018) "Inclusive Services for Youth in Cairo's Informal Areas." Economic Research Forum Working Paper Series No. 1204. Cairo.

Krafft, Caroline, Ragui Assaad, and Khandker Wahedur Rahman (2021) "Introducing the Egypt Labor Market Panel Survey 2018." *IZA Journal of Development and Migration* (Forthcoming).

Liu, Jenny, Sepideh Modrek, and Maia Sieverding (2017) "The Mental Health of Youth and Young Adults during the Transition to Adulthood in Egypt," *Demographic Research*, 36 (56): 1721–58.

Marmot, Michael, et al. (2008) "Closing the Gap in a Generation: Health Equity through Action on the Social Determinants of Health," *The Lancet*, 372 (9650): 1661–9.

Mokdad, Ali H, et al. (2014) "The State of Health in the Arab World, 1990–2010: An Analysis of the Burden of Diseases, Injuries, and Risk Factors," *The Lancet*, 383 (9914): 309–20.

Noordt, Maaike van der, et al. (2014) "Health Effects of Employment: A Systematic Review of Prospective Studies," *Occupational and Environmental Medicine*, 71 (10): 730–6.

Rashad, Ahmed Shoukry and Mesbah Fathy Sharaf (2018) "Does Precarious Employment Damage Youth Mental Health, Wellbeing and Marriage? Evidence from Egypt Using Longitudinal Data." Economic Research Forum Working Paper Series No. 1200. Cairo.

Salem, Rania, Kristin VanderEnde, and Kathryn Yount (2015) "Is Women's Work a Pathway to Their Agency in Rural Egypt?" Economic Research Forum Working Paper Series No. 922. Cairo.

Samari, Goleen and Anne R. Pebley (2018) "Longitudinal Determinants of Married Women's Autonomy in Egypt," *Gender, Place & Culture*, 25 (6): 799–820.

Sieverding, Maia and Rasha Hassan 2016. "'Her Future Is Marriage': Young People's Attitudes towards Gender Roles and the Gender Gap in Egypt." Population Council, Cairo.

Sieverding, Maia et al. (2019) "Perceptions of Service Access in a Context of Marginalization: The Case of Young People in Informal Greater Cairo." Economic Research Forum Working Paper Series No. 1289. Cairo.

Topp, Christian Winther et al. (2015) "The WHO-5 Wellbeing Index: A Systematic Review of the Literature," *Psychotherapy and Psychosomatics*, 84 (3): 167–76.

UNDP (United Nations Development Programme) (2014) "Human Development Report 2014: Sustaining Human Progress: Reducing Vulnerabilities and Building Resilience." New York.

United Nations (2020) "Policy Brief: COVID-19 and the Need for Action on Mental Health." New York: United Nations. Available at: https://www.un.org/sites/un2.un.org/files/un_policy_brief-covid_and_mental_health_final.pdf. Accessed July 1, 2020.

UN-WG (UN-Washington Group on Disability Statistics) 2009. "Understanding and Interpreting Disability as Measured Using the WG Short Set of Questions." Washington

Group on Disability Statistics. 2009. Available at: http://www.washingtongroup-disability.com/washington-group-question-sets/short-set-of-disability-questions/.

WHO (World Health Organization) (1995) "Constitution of the World Health Organization." World Health Organization. Available at: https://apps.who.int/iris/handle/10665/121457. Accessed August 15, 2019.

World Bank (2019) *Understanding Poverty and Inequality in Egypt.* Washington, DC: The World Bank.

Epilogue

Events since 2012 have presented both new opportunities and new challenges for the Egyptian labor market. The chapters of this book have leveraged the new Egypt Labor Market Panel Survey (ELMPS) 2018 data to explore a variety of important labor market issues ranging from migration to entrepreneurship. Key themes about gender and vulnerability in the labor market are illustrated in terms of the overall labor market situation, lack of good jobs, particularly vulnerable groups, unique and developing challenges, and how Egyptians are coping with challenges.

The overall employment situation has deteriorated between 2012 and 2018. Economic growth eventually recovered after the downturn induced by the global financial crisis and the disruptions following the January 25, 2011 revolution, but growth was relatively jobless (Chapter 2). Employment growth was in fact slower than the growth of the working age population. Women's labor force participation continued to decline, a long-standing trend despite their rising education (Chapter 1). A more recent development, however, was the reduction in men's labor force participation between 2012 and 2018, a pattern that particularly affects youth (Chapter 4). The declines in labor force participation and employment rates are particularly troubling as they were occurring in a period of recovering economic growth and declining labor supply pressures. COVID-19 and the major economic challenges accompanying it in 2020 and 2021 are worsening short-term labor market prospects. The long-term outlook is also concerning. While 2012–2018 had low labor supply pressures that will continue for another five to ten years owing to the slow growth in the youth and young adult populations, the "echo" of the youth bulge will come of age within a decade and will result in a major increase in labor supply (Chapter 1; Krafft and Assaad, 2014a; Assaad, 2020).

Not only was job creation anemic over 2012 to 2018, new jobs were also of low-quality, characterized by informality and vulnerability to economic shocks. As public sector employment continued to shrink, formal private sector employment growth was anemic, and much of job creation was made up of informal employment, primarily outside fixed establishments, a particularly vulnerable form of employment (Chapter 2, Chapter 4, Chapter 5). Job creation was strongest in sectors such as retail, construction, and transport. These sectors rarely create formal jobs, and aside from retail create jobs that are largely outside establishments. These forms of vulnerable and precarious employment are not only highly susceptible to economic downturns, but are also associated with exposure to hazardous

Caroline Krafft and Ragui Assaad, *Epilogue* In: *The Egyptian Labor Market: A Focus on Gender and Economic Vulnerability.*
Edited by: Caroline Krafft and Ragui Assaad, Oxford University Press. © Economic Research Forum 2022.
DOI: 10.1093/oso/9780192847911.003.0013

working conditions (Chapter 2, Chapter 11). Whereas between 2006 and 2012, vulnerability manifested itself in the rise of irregular wage work (Assaad and Krafft, 2015b), in the 2012–18 period it was associated with the expansion of informal work outside establishments. This work had become more regular owing to improved economic conditions, but remained highly vulnerable to economic downturns such as the one brought about by the COVID-19 pandemic (Chapter 2). Besides the challenge of creating good jobs in terms of social protection, resilience to shocks, and working conditions, Egypt has struggled to create well-paid jobs. Real wages declined from 2012 to 2018 (Chapter 3). The decline in real wages has a number of potential causes, including the spike in inflation following the 2017 floating of the Egyptian pound (EGP), but an important long-term issue is that job creation in growing sectors tends to be in jobs with relatively low productivity (Krafft and Assaad, 2018; Assaad et al., 2019; Assaad, Krafft, and Yassin, 2020; World Bank, 2020b).

The book has highlighted a number of groups that were particularly vulnerable in the labor market. Although the focus on gender and vulnerability was planned prior to ELMPS 2018 data collection and was incorporated in the survey design (Krafft, Assaad, and Rahman, 2021), this focus was particularly timely in that it helps us to understand the groups vulnerable to economic shocks, such as the COVID-19 crisis. Women had already experienced declining employment rates as the public sector shrank and private sector jobs were irreconcilable with the "second shift" of married life (Assaad, Krafft, and Selwaness, 2017; World Bank, 2018; Assaad et al., 2020; Economic Research Forum and UN Women, 2020; Selwaness and Krafft, 2020). COVID-19, creating sudden and additional caregiving responsibilities as schools and nurseries closed, may accelerate women's exit from the labor force as their "second shift" becomes much more onerous. The continued contraction of public sector employment has been especially challenging for women with intermediate (secondary) levels of education, who have increasingly withdrawn from the labor force in light of limited labor market opportunities. Access to formal jobs in the private sector increasingly depends on socioeconomic status (World Bank, 2018; Assaad, Krafft, and Salemi, 2019; Assaad and Krafft, 2021). While rural women make important and underappreciated contributions to the economy (Chapter 8), they also face a number of vulnerabilities and constraints. Women's potential to be entrepreneurs remains untapped; women have low rates of entrepreneurship; and they tend towards survival self-employment (Chapter 6).

Food insecurity remains a challenge in Egypt (Chapter 10); one with negative associations with wellbeing (Chapter 11). This situation is despite the food ration card system and bread subsidies, which are broadly available but may not be well targeted (Chapter 9). Egyptians, particularly poor urban women, struggle with low levels of wellbeing (Chapter 11). Reductions in the reach of social protection, particularly social insurance (Chapter 9), created increased vulnerability in advance of the pandemic, although the new Takaful and Karama cash transfer programs, targeting vulnerable rural women, were an important part of the social safety net that expanded in response to the pandemic (OECD, 2020).

Even prior to the COVID-19 crisis, Egyptian households frequently experienced regular economic and health shocks (Chapter 10). Coping strategies centered around consumption reduction (especially of education and health services) are particularly concerning in light of the pandemic. Although internal migration and urbanization rates were low (Chapter 7), temporary international migration served as an important economic opportunity for men to cope with limited job prospects in Egypt. This option may be closing with the onset of the pandemic, the associated declines in oil prices, and their effects on labor demand in the main destination countries for Egyptian migrant workers (World Bank, 2020a). These developments are creating further labor market challenges that emphasize the importance of developing a robust social protection system that covers a variety of vulnerable workers.

The COVID-19 pandemic and ensuing economic and social upheavals present enormous new challenges for Egypt's economy. As of the start of July 2021, Egypt had more than 280,000 cases and more than 16,000 COVID-related deaths (WHO, 2021). Reduced global demand generally, the collapse of oil prices and labor demand in the Gulf, and especially reductions in key industries of manufacturing and tourism have led to a decline in gross domestic product growth from an annual rate of 5.6 percent in fiscal year (FY) 2018/19 to 3.6 percent in FY 2019/20 (including a 1.7 percent year-on-year contraction during April to June 2020) (World Bank, 2020b).

Although government and formal workers were, to a degree, protected from the COVID-19 economic shock, informal workers were not. Informal workers (those not registered in the social insurance system), and, in particular, those who worked on a daily or intermittent basis, were especially vulnerable (Krafft, Assaad, and Marouani, 2021). They were targeted by a new cash assistance program providing assistance of EGP 500 per month, which was recently extended to March 2021 (Krafft, Assaad, and Marouani, 2021). The monthly payments from this cash transfer are equivalent to approximately a quarter of private sector informal median monthly wages (Ismail, Laessing, and Mourad, 2020; OECD, 2020). Since informal workers were not registered with any ministry, targeting beneficiaries remains an issue. While 1.5 million informal workers have registered for payments through an online registration system and been found eligible (Ismail, Laessing, and Mourad, 2020), this is only a fraction of Egypt's more than 26 million workers, the majority of whom are informal (Chapter 2). Tax and credit measures may help formal firms weather the crisis (OECD, 2020). However, informal enterprises, which are primarily micro and small but constitute an important share of the economy, may particularly suffer during the downturn (Krafft, 2016; Krafft et al., 2020).

Youth are particularly vulnerable to both short-term loss of employment and earnings (CAPMAS, 2020c). Furthermore, youth who were seeking work before the pandemic or graduated during the pandemic now face very limited labor market opportunities and may experience permanently poorer labor market outcomes (Cockx, 2016). While the unemployment rate rose from 7.7 percent in the first quarter of 2020 to 9.6 percent in the second quarter (CAPMAS, 2020a, 2020b) those who can afford to be openly unemployed are typically not the most vulnerable to the economic harms of the virus (Krafft and Assaad, 2014b). In fact, unemployment rates fell among women, as they left the labor force in large numbers in response to the pandemic, resulting in steep declines in participation rates from the first to the second quarter of 2020 (Chapter 1).

Expanding the social protection system to support all informal workers, as well as informal firms, will be critically important to cushioning the economic shock of the pandemic and precluding negative coping strategies. Extra policy attention will be needed to support women's ability to persist in or return to the labor force, as well as to ensure young people's labor market trajectories are not permanently scarred by exiting school into an economic crisis. Although this book has illustrated vulnerability in Egypt's labor market and society prior to COVID-19, future research needs to further examine which groups and workers have disproportionately suffered and their particular challenges, to design better policy responses to ameliorate the crisis and its potentially lasting effects. Understanding the impact on formal and informal workers and firms, as well as on youth and women, will be an important area for future research. Health, human capital, and wealth may also be impacted by the pandemic and perceptions of risk and preferences for job security shifted, but impacts must be determined by future research.

The COVID-19 pandemic and ensuing economic crisis have underscored the importance of addressing some of Egypt's long-standing structural labor market issues. Labor demand is derived demand, based in part on workers' productivity and the dynamics of product markets. That economic and employment growth have been concentrated in low-productivity sectors remains a key barrier to creating more and better jobs (Krafft and Assaad, 2018; Assaad et al., 2019; Assaad, Krafft, and Yassin, 2020; World Bank, 2020b). The growing sectors also have even lower-than-average employment of women, creating further labor demand constraints on women's employment (Assaad et al., 2019). Increasing competition among firms in Egypt's economy and improvements in the business environment are particularly important to productivity-enhancing reallocations and job creation (Diwan, Keefer, and Schiffbauer, 2014; Krafft and Assaad, 2015, 2018).

The chapters in this book illustrate critical issues in the Egyptian labor market, but are barely scratching the surface of what it is possible to analyze using the ELMPS data. Past research has built on the ELMPS data and on the book series in Egypt (Assaad, 2002, 2009; Assaad and Krafft, 2015a) as well as data and books from Jordan (Assaad, 2014; Krafft and Assaad, 2019) and Tunisia (Assaad and

Boughzala, 2018). A future research agenda includes a better understanding of, and attempts to intervene in, long-standing challenges around women's employment, creating good jobs, persistent inequality, and social protection coverage. New developments, such as the decline of men's labor force participation, the drop in real wages, and the impending arrival of labor supply pressures from the echo of the youth bulge generation merit pressing attention to ameliorate. New data, particularly around shocks and coping, social protection, health, and vulnerability open up new avenues for research. The ELMPS data have always been particularly valuable for the richness of topics that allow researchers to link the labor market to other important issues in society, from health to social protection. This book and the ELMPS data are only the initial foundation upon which we hope to see a rich body of additional research built.

Caroline Krafft and Ragui Assaad

July 2021

References

Assaad, R. (ed.) (2002) *The Egyptian Labor Market in an Era of Reform*. Cairo: American University in Cairo Press.

Assaad, R. (ed.) (2009) *The Egyptian Labor Market Revisited*. Cairo: American University in Cairo Press.

Assaad, R. (ed.) (2014) *The Jordanian Labour Market in the New Millennium*. Oxford: Oxford University Press.

Assaad, R. (2020) "Prospects for Egypt's Population and Labor Force: 2000 to 2050." Economic Research Forum Working Paper Series No. 1398. Cairo.

Assaad, R. and M. Boughzala (eds) (2018) *The Tunisian Labor Market in an Era of Transition*. Oxford: Oxford University Press.

Assaad, R. and C. Krafft (eds) (2015a) *The Egyptian Labor Market in an Era of Revolution*. Oxford: Oxford University Press.

Assaad, R. and C. Krafft (2015b) "The Structure and Evolution of Employment in Egypt: 1998–2012," in R. Assaad and C. Krafft (eds) *The Egyptian Labor Market in an Era of Revolution*, pp. 27–51. Oxford: Oxford University Press.

Assaad, R. and C. Krafft (2021) "Excluded Generation: The Growing Challenges of Labor Market Insertion for Egyptian Youth," *Journal of Youth Studies*, 24 (2): 186–212. doi: 10.1080/13676261.2020.1714565.

Assaad, R., C. Krafft, and C. Salemi (2019) "Socioeconomic Status and the Changing Nature of the School-to-Work Transition in Egypt, Jordan, and Tunisia." Economic Research Forum Working Paper Series No. 1287. Cairo.

Assaad, R., C. Krafft, and I. Selwaness (2017) "The Impact of Marriage on Women's Employment in the Middle East and North Africa." Economic Research Forum Working Paper Series No. 1086. Cairo.

Assaad, R., C. Krafft, and S. Yassin (2020) "Job Creation or Labor Absorption? An Analysis of Private Sector Job Growth in Egypt," *Middle East Development Journal*, 12 (2): 177–207. doi: 10.1080/17938120.2020.1753978.

Assaad, R. et al. (2019) "Job Creation in Egypt: A Sectoral and Geographical Analysis Focusing on Private Establishments, 1996–2017." Economic Research Forum Policy Research Report. Cairo.

Assaad, R. et al. (2020) "Explaining the MENA Paradox: Rising Educational Attainment, Yet Stagnant Female Labor Force Participation," *Demographic Research*, 43 (28): 817–50.

CAPMAS (Central Agency for Public Mobilization and Statistics) (2020a) *Quarterly Bulletin of the Labor Force Survey, First Quarter, Jan/Feb/Mar 2020*. Cairo: CAPMAS.

CAPMAS (2020b) *Quarterly Bulletin of the Labor Force Survey, Second Quarter, Apr/ May/Jun 2020*. Cairo: CAPMAS.

CAPMAS (2020c) *The Effect of the Coronavirus on Egyptian Households (Arabic)*. Cairo: CAPMAS.

Cockx, B. (2016) "Do Youths Graduating in a Recession Incur Permanent Losses?" *IZA World of Labor*, 281: 1–11. doi: 10.15185/izawol.281.

Diwan, I., P. Keefer, and M. Schiffbauer (2014) *On Top of the Pyramids: Cronyism and Private Sector Growth in Egypt*. Mimeo. Washington, DC: World Bank.

Economic Research Forum and UN Women (2020) Progress of Women in the Arab States 2020: The Role of the Care Economy in Promoting Gender Equality. Cairo: UN Women.

Ismail, A., U. Laessing, and M. Mourad (2020) "Coronavirus Crisis Spells Trouble for many Egyptian Breadwinners," *Reuters*, April 7. Available at: https://www.reuters.com/article/us-health-coronavirus-egypt-economy-idUSKBN21P1OD (Accessed November 17, 2020).

Krafft, C. (2016) "Understanding the Dynamics of Household Enterprises in Egypt: Birth, Death, Growth, and Transformation." Economic Research Forum Working Paper Series No. 983. Cairo.

Krafft, C. and R. Assaad (2014a) "Beware of the Echo: The Impending Return of Demographic Pressures in Egypt." Economic Research Forum Policy Perspective 12. Cairo.

Krafft, C. and R. Assaad (2014b) "Why the Unemployment Rate is a Misleading Indicator of Labor Market Health in Egypt." Economic Research Forum Policy Perspective 14. Cairo.

Krafft, C. and R. Assaad (2015) "Promoting Successful Transitions to Employment for Egyptian Youth." Economic Research Forum Policy Perspective 15. Cairo: Economic Research Forum.

Krafft, C. and R. Assaad (2018) "Do More Productive Firms Pay Workers More? Evidence from Egypt." Economic Research Forum Working Paper Series No. 1222. Cairo.

Krafft, C. and R. Assaad (eds) (2019) *The Jordanian Labor Market between Fragility and Resilience*. Oxford: Oxford University Press.

Krafft, C., R. Assaad, and M. A. Marouani (2021) "The Impact of COVID-19 on Middle Eastern and North African Labor Markets: Glimmers of Progress but Persistent Problems for Vulnerable Workers a Year into the Pandemic." Economic Research Forum Policy Brief 57. Cairo: Economic Research Forum.

Krafft, C., R. Assaad, and K.W. Rahman (2021) "Introducing the Egypt Labor Market Panel Survey 2018." *IZA Journal of Development and Migration* (Forthcoming).

Krafft, C. et al. (2020) "How Do Small Formal and Informal Firms in the Arab Republic of Egypt Compare?" World Bank Policy Research Working Paper Series No. 9423. Washington, DC.

OECD (Organisation for Economic Co-operation and Development) (2020) The COVID-19 Crisis in Egypt, Tackling Coronavirus (COVID-19): Contributing to a Global Effort. Paris: OECD.

Selwaness, I. and C. Krafft (2021) "The Dynamics of Family Formation and Women's Work: What Facilitates and Hinders Female Employment in the Middle East and North Africa?" *Population Research and Policy Review*, 40(3): 533–587.

World Bank (2018) *Women Economic Empowerment Study*. Washington, DC: World Bank.

World Bank (2020a) COVID-19 Crisis Through a Migration Lens, Migration and Development Brief. 32. Washington, DC: World Bank.

World Bank (2020b) Egypt Economic Monitor: From Crisis to Economic Transformation: Unlocking Egypt's Productivity and Job-Creation Potential. Washington, DC: World Bank.

WHO (World Health Organization) (2021) *Egypt Situation, WHO Health Emergency Dashboard WHO (COVID-19) Homepage*. Available at: https://covid19.who.int/region/emro/country/eg (Accessed: July 2, 2021).

Index